BLACK POWER MUSIC!

Black Power Music! Protest Songs, Message Music, and the Black Power Movement critically explores the soundtracks of the Black Power Movement as forms of "movement music." That is to say, much of classic Motown, soul, and funk music often mirrored and served as mouthpieces for the views and values, as well as the aspirations and frustrations, of the Black Power Movement. *Black Power Music!* is also about the intense interconnections between Black popular culture and Black political culture, both before and after the Black Power Movement, and the ways in which the Black Power Movement in many senses symbolizes the culmination of centuries of African American politics creatively combined with, and ingeniously conveyed through, African American music. Consequently, the term "Black Power music" can be seen as a code word for *African American protest songs and message music* between 1965 and 1975. "Black Power music" is a new concept that captures and conveys the fact that the majority of the messages in Black popular music between 1965 and 1975 seem to have been missed by most people who were not actively involved in, or in some significant way associated with, the Black Power Movement.

Reiland Rabaka is Professor of African, African American, and Caribbean Studies in the Department of Ethnic Studies and the Founder and Director of the Center for African & African American Studies at the University of Colorado Boulder. He is also a Research Fellow in the College of Human Sciences at the University of South Africa (UNISA). Rabaka has published 17 books and more than 85 scholarly articles, book chapters, and essays. His books include *Civil Rights Music, Hip Hop's Inheritance, Hip Hop's Amnesia, The Hip Hop Movement, Africana Critical Theory, Against Epistemic Apartheid: W.E.B. Du Bois and the Disciplinary Decadence of Sociology, Forms of Fanonism: Frantz Fanon's Critical Theory and the Dialectics of Decolonization, Concepts of Cabralism: Amilcar Cabral and Africana Critical Theory, The Negritude Movement, The Routledge Handbook of Pan-Africanism,* and *Du Bois: A Critical Introduction*. His cultural criticism, social commentary, and political analysis have been featured in print, radio, television, and online media venues such as NPR, PBS, BBC, CNN, ABC, NBC, CBS, MTV, BET, VH1, *The Guardian,* and *USA Today,* among others.

"*Black Power Music!* is a boldly conceived, brilliantly executed, and surpassingly timely volume that eloquently explains how Black Power music was able to reconstitute African American culture in the decade 1965–1975. Professor Rabaka's originality in using ideas from disciplines traditionally kept apart enables him to find the consilience that binds these disciplines together vis-à-vis Black Power music, to succeed where others have not. The volume's ambitious thesis is as compelling as it is clear, and the discussion of the cultural and intellectual politics of sex and gender in Chapters 4 and 5 ought to be required reading in many disciplines."

John Michael Cooper, *Southwestern University, USA*

"*Black Power Music!* is a cogent study of the connections between the Black Power Movement and Black popular music of the 1960s and 1970s. Taking a cue from Black Power and Black Arts participants themselves, it successfully argues that much of that music was an integral part of Black Power. While that argument has been made previously, never before have the material links between Black Power and Black popular music been studied in such detail."

James Smethurst, *W.E.B. Du Bois Department of Afro-American Studies, University of Massachusetts Amherst, USA*

BLACK POWER MUSIC!

Protest Songs, Message Music, and the Black Power Movement

Reiland Rabaka

Routledge
Taylor & Francis Group

LONDON AND NEW YORK

Cover image: © Getty Images

First published 2022
by Routledge
4 Park Square, Milton Park, Abingdon, Oxon OX14 4RN

and by Routledge
605 Third Avenue, New York, NY 10158

Routledge is an imprint of the Taylor & Francis Group, an informa business

British Library Cataloguing-in-Publication Data
A catalogue record for this book is available from the British Library

Library of Congress Cataloging-in-Publication Data
Names: Rabaka, Reiland, 1972– author.
Title: Black power music! : protest songs, message music, and the black
    power movement / Reiland Rabaka.
Description: [01.] | Abingdon, Oxon ; New York : Routledge, 2022. |
    Includes bibliographical references and index.
Identifiers: LCCN 2022001142 (print) | LCCN 2022001143 (ebook) |
    ISBN 9781032184326 (hardcover) | ISBN 9781032184319 (paperback) |
    ISBN 9781003254492 (ebook)
Subjects: LCSH: African Americans—Music—History and criticism. |
    Music—Political aspects—United States—History. | Black power—
    United States.
Classification: LCC ML3479 .R27 2022 (print) | LCC ML3479 (ebook) |
    DDC 780.89/96073—dc23
LC record available at https://lccn.loc.gov/2022001142
LC ebook record available at https://lccn.loc.gov/2022001143

ISBN: 978-1-032-18432-6 (hbk)
ISBN: 978-1-032-18431-9 (pbk)
ISBN: 978-1-003-25449-2 (ebk)

DOI: 10.4324/9781003254492

Typeset in Bembo
by Apex CoVantage, LLC

*For my grandmother and grand aunt, Rita and Arcressia,
and for the musicians of the Black Power Movement and
their many musical heirs*

CONTENTS

ACKNOWLEDGEMENTS

In this book I have attempted to guide readers through the protest songs and message music of the Black Power Movement in a way that is clear, accurate, and critical. Although the focus of the book is on the music of the Black Power Movement, the historical and cultural context in which the music emerged and evolved has not been neglected. *Black Power Music! Protest Songs, Message Music, and the Black Power Movement* is not an exhaustive overview of each and every genre of "Black Power music." Instead, it is an introduction to the "Black Power music" concept and its most distinctive features through a focus on two of the most popular soundtracks of the Black Power Movement: soul and funk.

I am grateful to many musicians and musicologists throughout the years who have contributed to the research, writing, and revision of this book. Also, I would be remiss if I did not offer my sincere gratitude to the editorial team at Routledge, especially Heidi Bishop and Kaushikee Sharma. Lastly, I thank my friends and family for their support during the many years it took me to research, write, and revise this book.

Reiland Rabaka
Center for African and African American Studies
University of Colorado Boulder
September 2021

INTRODUCTION

Protest songs, message music, and the Black Power Movement

Movement music: the Black Power Movement and the African American movement music tradition

Blackness. Power. Music. These concepts are at the core of this book. Over the last four decades or so since its end, there has been a great deal of discussion concerning the Black Power Movement and the ways in which it deconstructed and reconstructed American culture, politics, and society. Indeed, there have been a number of scholarly studies of the movement's politics, as well as several books centered around the social justice agenda and economic impact of the movement.[1] Additionally, there have been studies that have examined the ways in which the movement represented a revitalization of post-Civil Rights Movement African American culture, and other studies that have explored the regional and local cultures, politics, and tactics of the movement.[2] In spite of these very often innovative studies, most work within the world of "Black Power studies" seems to only superficially treat its soundtracks and the wider historical, cultural, social, political, economic, and aesthetic contexts from which "Black Power music" emerged and evolved.[3]

Even in light of all of its sonic and aesthetic innovations, it is important to point to Black Power music's extra-musical aspects. Too often African American music is treated as though it exists outside of African American musical and other artistic traditions. This is not only unfortunate but also extremely disingenuous, because it makes it appear as though each new form of Black popular music is some sort of free-floating, "postmodern" sonic signifier and not, as is most often the case, deeply connected to, and undeniably indicative of, the origins and evolution of African American musical history and culture, as well as African American social history and political culture. Therefore, to really and truly understand Black Power music much must be understood about the history, culture, and ongoing struggles

DOI: 10.4324/9781003254492-1

of its primary producers: Black ghetto youth in particular and African Americans in general.

In often unrecognized ways, the origins and evolution of Black Power music have actually come to be treated or, rather, ill-treated much like African Americans – especially Black ghetto youth – in mainstream American history, culture, and society. To return to the theme of one of my previous volumes of African American musicology, *Hip Hop's Amnesia*, there seems to be a serious *amnesia* surrounding the origins and evolution of Black Power music and the broader Black Power Movement that the music reflected. Conceptually *amnesia*, which according to *Merriam-Webster's Dictionary* means "a partial or total loss of memory," offers us an interesting angle to revisit and re-evaluate the origins and evolution of Black Power music and the Black Power Movement.

At this point it can be said with little or no fanfare that most work in Black Power studies only anecdotally explores the origins and evolution of Black Power music and Black Power popular culture more generally. Consequently, Black Power studies stands in need of serious scholarly works that transcend the anecdotal and critically engage not only Black Power music's musical history but also its spiritual, intellectual, cultural, social, and political history. If, as most Black Power studies scholars would more than likely concede, Black Power music reflects more than merely the "young folk's foolishness" and naïveté of Black Power Movement Black ghetto youth, then a study that treats Black Power music as a reflection of post-war Black youth's politics and social justice agenda between 1965 and 1975 is sorely needed. *Black Power Music!* was researched and written specifically with this dire need in mind.

It is generally accepted that Black popular music and Black popular culture frequently reflect the conservatism *and* radicalism, the moderatism *and* militantism of the major African American movements of the milieu in which they initially emerged.[4] Bearing this in mind, *Black Power Music!* critically explores how the soundtracks of the Black Power Movement were *movement musics* – which is to say, much of classic Motown, soul, and funk often literally mirrored and served as mouthpieces for the views and values, as well as the aspirations and frustrations, of the Black Power Movement.

There is, indeed, a serious need for more music-focused historically rooted, culturally relevant, and politically radical research within the world of Black Power studies. Too often fans and critics listen to, speak of, and write about Black Power music and Black Power popular culture as though contemporary Black popular music and contemporary Black popular culture are not in any way connected to a historical and cultural continuum that can be easily traced back to the Black popular music and Black popular culture of the Black Power Movement. Building on the history of music, sociology of music, and politics of music-centered studies published by Michael Awkward, Tony Bolden, Robert Bowman, Aaron Cohen, Peter Guralnick, Michael Haralambos, Claudrena Harold, Gerri Hirshey, John Jackson, Rochelle Larkin, Emily Lordi, Maureen Mahon, Portia Maultsby, Mitchell Morris, Robert Pruter, Rickey Vincent, Brian Ward, and Craig Werner, *Black*

Power Music! is a study about music *and* socio-political movements, aesthetics *and* politics, as well as the ways in which African Americans' unique history, culture, and struggles have consistently led them to create musics that have served as the soundtracks for their socio-political aspirations and frustrations, their socio-political organizations and movements.[5]

Obviously at this point many of my readers may be asking themselves a couple questions: "But does classic Motown, soul, and funk music really reflect the ideals of the Black Power Movement?" "If there is really and truly such a thing as 'Black Power music,' how come I haven't heard of it before?" And "Can music be popular, but yet politically progressive and convey a serious social justice message?"

These questions lie at the heart of this book, and indeed, they are questions that have burned and bothered me longer than I care to remember. It should be stated openly and outright: These are very valid questions. In fact, they are critical questions that I am sincerely seeking to ask *and* answer throughout the following pages of this book. In a nutshell, what I have come to call "Black Power music" actually does not remotely resemble any previous African American musicological concept. But by the time my readers get to the fifth and final chapter of this book they will see that, yet and still, "Black Power music" historically has been, and currently continues to be, a musical and political reality. As will be revealed in the chapters to follow, the origins and early evolution of Black popular music, especially Black Power musics such as classic Motown, soul, and funk, are very varied. Rapid and radical changes in "mainstream" American history, culture, politics, economics, and society have made it such that there are great and often grave differences between the origins and early evolution of each form of Black popular music, just as there are great and often grave differences between the origins of each Black popular movement.

Black Power Music! argues that many of these "great and often grave differences" are easily observed in the history of Black popular music and Black popular culture and that, even more, Black popular music and Black popular culture are often incomprehensible without some sort of serious working knowledge of historic African American social and political movements. Taking this line of logic even further, *Black Power Music!* contends that neither Black Power Movement aesthetics nor Black Power Movement politics can be adequately comprehended without some sort of serious working knowledge of historic African American social and political movements. Ultimately, then, this book is about "partial or total loss of memory" or, rather, *what has been forgotten but should be remembered* about the origins and early evolution of Black popular music in direct relationship to the Black Power Movement.

However, *Black Power Music!* is not simply about the historical, cultural, and musical "amnesia" surrounding Black Power music and the Black Power Movement. It is also about the intense interconnections between Black popular culture and Black political culture, both before and after the Black Power Movement, and the ways in which the Black Power Movement in many senses symbolizes the culmination of centuries of African American politics creatively combined with, and ingeniously conveyed through, African American music. Even the term "Black Power music" can be seen as a code word for *African American message music* between 1965 and 1975, and this even though most of the messages in the music seem to have been missed by many, if not most, people who were not actively involved in, or in some significant way associated with, the Black Power Movement.[6]

The main aim of this introduction is to offer an analysis of the unique role of Black popular music in Black popular movements in an effort to ultimately develop *a musicology of the Black Power Movement*. Prior to our protracted exploration of Black Power music, it will be important to place the soundtracks of the Black Power Movement within *the African American movement music tradition*. If, indeed, "music is more than merely music" for many, if not most, African Americans (especially those actively involved in social, political, and cultural movements), *when, where, why*, and *how* the unique relationship between Black popular music and Black popular movements developed are key questions. Beginning with a brief discussion of the broader historical, cultural, social, and political contexts of the Black Power Movement, next the introduction gives way to a discussion of the often-overlooked popular culture of the Black Power Movement – what I call "Black Power popular culture." The introduction will conclude with an examination of Black popular music as a form of cultural expression *and* cultural action, in a sense setting up the subsequent chapters by providing the reader with an overview of *the African American movement music tradition* that Black Power music arose out of.

The Black Power Movement: a creative combination of Black political culture and Black popular culture

Although there is much nostalgia surrounding the Black Power Movement today, we should note that not every aspect of it and its popular culture was progressive or even morally commendable. As a matter of fact, during the Black Power Movement longstanding African American traditions were mobilized by movement leaders, intellectuals, artists, and rank and filers in the interest of a wide range of social visions and political agendas, some of which were obviously sexist, heterosexist, Eurocentric, and very often bourgeois, even though the African American masses of the era were, as they remain up to the present moment, primarily working-class and underclass. When engaged objectively, we must concede that the Black Power Movement harbored evident regressive, if not outright reactionary, elements. Obviously, it was not the squeaky clean and ethically irreproachable movement that the Civil Rights Movement is often portrayed as today.[7]

However, whether deemed progressive or regressive, it is virtually impossible to deny that the Black Power Movement actually reconstituted African American cultural resources in the immediate post-Civil Rights Movement period. This reconstitution of African American cultural resources during the movement ultimately translated into myriad creative works of artistic experimentation and critical, extraordinarily reflective works of evaluation. Through its songs, dance, theater, literature, and visual art, over forty years after its end the Black Power Movement has retained a presence in our collective cultural memory and social imagination in the absence of many of the particular social and political conditions that initially brought it into being. Bearing this in mind, it is easy to see why I argue that even if only through the memory of its political praxes, cultural contributions, and innovative evaluative criteria, the Black Power Movement has a living legacy in the twenty-first century. But its legacy is often shrouded in mystery and misinterpretation because most of its cultural contributions have been coopted, depoliticized and deradicalized, and often reduced to either the most controversial or the most commercial and mainstream America-friendly aspects of the movement.[8]

The popular culture, including the popular music, of the Black Power Movement has rarely been examined in a serious and systematic way, either by academics, activists, or general observers. In fact, many movement members have great difficulty distinguishing the political from the cultural in the Black Power Movement. And, partly as a consequence of this dichotomy, the Black Power Movement is typically discussed and interpreted in purely political terms: organizations, issues, ideologies, campaigns, marches, demonstrations, protests, boycotts, strategies, and tactics. The dominant interpretive and discursive frameworks usually paint a picture of the Black Power Movement's famous political figures and how these extraordinary individuals channeled the human, material, and organizational resources of the era into the overarching political struggle. What is of greatest interest is the effectiveness with which the Black Power Movement was able to achieve many, if not most, of its political goals. However, where most Black Power studies scholars have long overlooked it, here I am most interested in the deeper and longer-lasting impact that the Black Power Movement had on cultural transformation and specifically cultural expression through the Black popular music emerging out of the movement. While "movement cultures" have been taken more seriously in recent years, there still has been little or no real attempt to come to terms with the ways in which the Black popular culture and Black popular music of the Black Power Movement often arose out of, and in turn influenced, the internal culture and external cultural work of the movement.

While there are innumerable works by historians of art, music, and literature on the cultural activities and cultural expressions of political movements, for the most part political scientists, sociologists, and musicologists have curiously left the cultural activities and cultural expressions of political movements, especially African American political movements, woefully under-analyzed. Frequently, the historians of art, music, and literature produce accounts of the cultural activities and cultural expressions of political movements that fall squarely in the idioms of cultural or literary history, where almost invariably aesthetic work takes precedence over social and political work. Although there have been biographies and scholarship about selected artists of the Black Power Movement, for the most part, this work has not significantly contributed to our understanding of the overarching movement because of the understandably narrow, *autobiocentric* nature of the focus of most of these studies.

For my purposes here, when taken collectively these studies open up a rich field for critical interdisciplinary analysis. On the one hand, these studies point to the crucial importance of political commitment in Black cultural expression and artistic production during the Black Power Movement. As is now well known, many of the leading artists, writers, and musicians of the Black Power Movement era were involved, at arguably the most formative phase of their lives, in the movement. I would be the first to admit that this does not mean that the monumental artistic achievements of, for example, James Brown, Sonia Sanchez, Amiri Baraka, Nikki Giovanni, Curtis Mayfield, Nina Simone, Haki Madhubuti, Maya Angelou, Marvin Gaye, Donny Hathaway, Aretha Franklin, Archie Shepp, Larry Neal, and Pharoah Sanders, among many others, can be reduced to their political commitments to the Black Power Movement. However, it does seem to suggest that without having taken an active role in the Black Power Movement they probably would have produced distinctly different work. Additionally, it is important to observe that in most instances movement involvement was a defining moment and remained, however furtively, central to their artistry even after the Black Power Movement ended.[9]

These artists' activism was objectified in their art and, as a consequence, to a certain extent the movement came to be embodied in them. When the Black Power Movement ended, the ideals and ethos of the movement lived on in their iconic art. In many instances, their "movement art" helped to inspire post-Black Power Movement popular movements (albeit not merely *Black* popular movements) by serving to keep the Black Power Movement and its distinct aesthetic alive in the American social imagination and collective cultural memory long after 1975.

On the other hand, studies focused on the relationship between the Black aesthetic and Black Power politics provided me with ideal examples and sources of inspiration for my conception of *music as a form of, and force for, cultural transformation during the Black Power Movement*. What I previously proclaimed as the distinctive soundtracks of African American social movements and "movement musicians" can now be comprehended, with the intellectual assistance of this scholarship, as a kind of cultural production and cultural praxis that harbors deep historical, political, sociological, legal, educational, economic, and religious implications for the critical study of the Black Power Movement. Here the Black Power Movement is seen as a breeding ground for qualitatively new kinds of politicized, radicalized, and ritualized thought and practices, as well as for new artistic, literary, and, most especially, musical innovation and experimentation.[10]

Bearing all of this in mind, I openly acknowledge how profoundly my work here has been influenced by several important studies that have focused on how the artist-activists of the Black Power Movement politicized and mobilized the music of the movement in the interest of the movement's social and political goals. I would be remiss if I did not make special mention of Amiri Baraka's *Black Music* (1967), Phyl Garland's *The Sound of Soul* (1969), Frank Kofsky's *Black Nationalism and the Revolution in Music* (1970), Rickey Vincent's *Funk: The Music, the People, and the Rhythm of the One* (1996), Robert Bowman's *Soulsville, U.S.A.: The Story of Stax Records* (1997), Mark Anthony Neal's *What the Music Said: Black Popular Music and Black Public Culture* (1998), Brian Ward's *Just My Soul Responding: Rhythm & Blues, Black Consciousness, and Race Relations* (1998), Scott Saul's *Freedom Is, Freedom Ain't: Jazz and the Making of the Sixties* (2003), George Lewis' *A Power Stronger Than Itself: The AACM and American Experimental Music* (2008), Patrick Thomas' *Listen, Whitey!: The Sounds of Black Power, 1965–1975* (2012), Rickey Vincent's *Party Music: The Inside Story of the Black Panthers' Band and How Black Power Transformed Soul Music* (2013), Shana Redmond's *Anthem: Social Movements and the Sound of Solidarity in the African Diaspora* (2014), Andrew Darlington's *"Don't Call Me Nigger, Whitey": Sly Stone & Black Power* (2014), Robert Gordon's *Respect Yourself: Stax Records and the Soul Explosion* (2015), Gayle Wald's *It's Been Beautiful: Soul! and Black Power Television* (2015), Stephen Rush, *Free Jazz, Harmolodics, and Ornette Coleman* (2016), Philippe Carles and Jean-Louis Comolli's *Free Jazz/Black Power* (2016), Aaron Cohen's *Move On Up: Chicago Soul Music and Black Cultural Power* (2019), Tony Bolden's *Groove Theory: The Blues Foundation of Funk* (2020), Maureen Mahon's *Black Diamond Queens: African American Women and Rock & Roll* (2020), and Claudrena Harold's *When Sunday Comes: Gospel Music in the Soul and Hip Hop Eras* (2020).[11] These studies, along with the myriad others to be discussed in the subsequent chapters, not only enriched my conception of music as a form of, and force for, cultural transformation during the Black Power Movement, but they also deftly demonstrate that Black Power music had a significant impact on subsequent popular music and popular culture both nationally and internationally.

Several cultural historians, as well as historians of art, music, and literature, have begun to look more closely at the social and political contexts within which culture is created and disseminated. Consequently, we now have a body of literature on specific cultural "movements" and artistic "worlds," ranging from the "slave narratives" of the Abolitionist Movement to the radical writers of the Harlem Renaissance and extending through to the evolution of classic jazz into "bebop" during the Bebop Movement. In the bulk of this work there is a concerted effort to socialize the subject, to contextualize the individual artist as not simply expressing their personal views and values, but instead to comprehend, for instance, Nina Simone, Curtis Mayfield, Aretha Franklin, James Brown, Martha Reeves, Marvin Gaye, Sly & the Family Stone, and Parliament/Funkadelic, to name some of the musicians who will appear later in this book, as representative figures who captured and communicated the ideals and ethos of the Black Power Movement.

As much as I intellectually admire and greatly appreciate the above-mentioned work, I must admit that it has had virtually little or no influence on the sociopolitical history of social movements – one of my chief areas of concern here. This is primarily due to a discursive difference in focus: for most social movement theorists and other social historians, culture is something that forms or "frames" social movements and other distinctly "social" activities as a set of (external) conditioning factors, while for cultural theorists it is social movements and cultural history that provide the external contexts or conditions that shape the primary objects of analysis: art, literature, music, and their creators. Where the social theorists highlight the social background that the artist and their artistry is embedded in, or that has shaped and shaded the artist and their artistry, the cultural theorists emphasize "movement culture" or a cultural frame for movement campaigns and activities. One might surmise that the real difference has to do with what is influencing what and the discursive direction of the context and conditioning. Even more important, however, seems to be a fundamental difference in discursive devices, language, methods, and interpretive orientation. Indeed, sociologists, political scientists, and humanists are subjected to different processes of academic acculturation and are very rarely given an opportunity to learn about, let alone really critically engage, each other's work.

My approach here seeks to synthesize history, sociology, politics, economics, and African American studies in an effort to develop an alternative history and musicology of the Black Power Movement by exploring the texts and contexts of Black popular music as a form of, and force for, cultural transformation between 1965 and 1975. As Houston Baker observed in *Modernism and the Harlem Renaissance*, African American life, culture, and struggle have distinct, signature "soundings" and "resoundings," and it is an " 'alien' *sound*" that "gives birth to notions of the indigenous – say, Africans, or Afro-Americans – as *deformed*."[12] But, Baker boldly asserted, African Americans' "indigenous *sound* appears monstrous and deformed *only* to the intruder" and, I would add, to the enslaver, to the colonizer, and to the oppressor.[13] African Americans' unique "soundings" and "resoundings," therefore, have been a core component of Black popular movements going all the way back to the spirituals and the Abolitionist Movement. And, according to Baker, African American musical traditions are recreated and given new life as they either arise out of, or intensely interact with, Black popular movements. However, the inverse is also true: Black popular movements often express their meaning and frequently gain coherence and sustenance through the powerful medium of Black popular music.

Arguably, nowhere has the role of Black popular music in a Black popular movement been more pronounced than in the Black Power Movement. From the Abolitionist Movement to the Black Power Movement, Black popular music helped to shape the mission, message, and cultural memory of African American social and political movements. As a matter of fact, a case could be made concerning the ways in which it has been chiefly through Black popular music that most Black popular movements, especially the Black Power Movement, have exerted their enormous influence and long-lasting legacy on American culture, as well as on the wider world.

By focusing on Black popular music as a form of, and force for, cultural transformation during the Black Power Movement, I hope to reveal a significant but neglected element of the movement that was central to its success and certainly deserves just as much scholarly attention as its more renowned social and political strategies and tactics. Even though the Black Power Movement will serve as our primary point of departure throughout this book, it is hoped that its politicization, radicalization, and mobilization of various African American traditions – spiritual, intellectual, cultural, social, political, and musical – will inspire a new politicization, radicalization, and mobilization of various African American traditions in the present, where many of the issues the Black Power Movement sought to eradicate have sadly been recycled and returned with a vengeance.[14]

By selectively and very critically recreating Black Power cultural traditions and cultural expressions, we can reinvent a new Black Power Movement (or something of the sort) aimed at the most pressing problems of the twenty-first century. Moreover, as was the case during the Black Power Movement in the 1960s and 1970s, Black popular music will more than likely provide us with one of the key mediums through which to capture and convey the emancipatory ideals and ethos of the much-needed new movement.[15] As a result, the analysis in the chapters to follow should be interpreted as part alternative history and musicology of the Black Power Movement of the twentieth century, and part intense invocation and sacred summoning of a new Black Power Movement in the twenty-first century. The struggle, as they say, continues. *A luta continua, vitória é certa.*

Blackness, power, and music . . .

Black Power Music! seeks to set afoot a new version of Black Power studies that is grounded in Black popular music, Black popular culture, and Black popular movement-based "popular knowledges" that break through the borders and boundaries of ahistorical, apolitical, and mostly male-centered famous-figure interpretations of the Black Power Movement. It aims to articulate a new, Black Power Movement-inspired "popular knowledge," a knowledge that emerges out of Black lives and struggles. It is through the re-emergence of these new, Black Power Movement-inspired "popular knowledges," these equally Black music-informed popular knowledges, that *Black Power Music!* ultimately advances an alternative history and musicology of the Black Power Movement.

When Black popular music and Black popular culture are engaged as historical and cultural artifacts with incredible explanatory power, then it is possible to perceive the ways that they historically have, and currently continue to, indelibly influence and inform race relations, gender identity, sexuality, spirituality, religiosity, class struggles, cultural conventions, social views, and broader political values. Revealingly, Black popular music and Black popular culture are often relegated to the realm of "low culture" (as opposed to "high culture"), which means they are frequently overlooked and, accordingly, under-scrutinized as "serious" sites of historical, cultural, social, and political study. This lame line of logic also overlooks the fact that Black popular music and Black popular culture, in their own sometimes warped and sometimes wicked ways, represent distinct sites of ideological and counter-ideological production, articulation, and contestation. Consequently, the chapters to follow aim to critically engage the ideological and counter-ideological currents and undercurrents deeply embedded in the Black Power Movement, its popular culture, and, most especially, its popular music.

The first chapter, "The Black Power Movement, the Black Arts Movement, and the Black Aesthetic," will provide a broad overview of the Black Power Movement and its cultural arts offshoot, the Black Arts Movement. Without critically under-standing the Black Power Movement and Black Arts Movement, as well as the ways in which the Black aesthetic virtually influenced everything brought into and emerging out of the Black Power Movement, it is almost impossible to fully grasp Black Power music. Soul music was the unsanctioned sound of primarily Black ghetto youth expressing not only their adolescent love (à la Motown-styled rhythm & blues), but also their discontent with both American democracy and the increasingly placid moderatism of the Civil Rights Movement. Serving as a major mouthpiece for the rhetoric, politics, and aesthetics of the Black Power Movement, classic soul music sought to decolonize and re-politicize Black popular music, if not Black people more generally. Essentially mirroring the Black Power Move-ment's efforts to radicalize African American politics in the aftermath of the mixed results and mostly disappointing outcomes of the Civil Rights Movement, soul represented a radicalization and, truth be told, a *re-African Americanization* of Black popular music in the 1960s and 1970s. Because of the often overtly political nature of a lot of soul music, and considering the ways in which all post-soul Black popu-lar music drew from classic soul aesthetics and Black Power politics, it is incredibly important to understand the larger social, political, and cultural landscape in which soul music emerged. Consequently, this chapter will provide snapshot histories of the Black Power Movement, Black Arts Movement, and Black aesthetic to histori-cally and culturally ground readers in the ideals and ethos of the era in which Black Power music emerged.

Chapter 2, "Motown and the Emergence of Message Music," critically engages a longstanding tendency among African American music scholars when and where they historicize and analyze Black popular music during the 1960s and 1970s and either outright erase or ignore Motown music and any other music deemed "pop-R&B," "sell-out" soul, or superficial funk. The real rub here lies in the simple fact that Motown's music was among the most audible and omnipresent popular music at the core of Black popular culture, if not American popular culture, during the later years of the Civil Rights Movement and most certainly throughout the Black Power Movement era. This chapter provides a study of classic Motown that emphasizes that along with its obsession with landing hit singles on the pop charts, it also represented an emerging Black consciousness that musically matured during the Black Power Movement era, roughly between 1965 and 1975. For instance, and going against those critics who disavow Motown as "sell-out" soul music, between 1965 and 1975 the storied record company released dozens of "message" soul and funk songs, from Marvin Gaye's immortal "What's Going On?" and Eddie Kendricks' "My People . . . Hold On" to Stevie Wonder's "Living for the City" and the Temptations' "Message from a Black Man." Likewise, Motown soul sisters also released several "message" songs, for example, Martha Reeves & the Vandellas issued "I Should Be Proud," Gladys Knight & the Pips offered "Friendship Train," and Syreeta put out "Black Maybe." Although often overlooked, it is important to point out that even the iconic Diana Ross & the Supremes sang "message" songs, such as "I'm Livin' in Shame," "The Young Folks," and "Shadows of Society," among others. As a result, there is a real need to reevaluate Motown in relationship to the Black Power Movement and other forms of Black Power music.

The third chapter, "Soul Men, Musical Machismo, and the Black Power Movement," examines the cultural, gender, and sexual politics of male soul music during the peak years of the movement. The work of major male soul icons such as Otis Redding, Wilson Pickett, and the Temptations will be engaged with an eye on the ways in which their music frequently reflected the cultural and sexual politics of the Black Power Movement. Ultimately the chapter emphasizes that at its core soul was a sound that captured and frequently conveyed not merely the ideals and ethos of the Black Power Movement, but also the complex and often contradictory spiritual, sexual, and cultural thought that emerged in the immediate aftermath of the Civil Rights Movement. The Black Power Movement was characterized by the simultaneous dense and tense interplay of Black insurgency and Black apathy, Black empowerment and Black disenfranchisement, Black pragmatism and Black dogmatism, all of which was coupled with a distinct post-Civil Rights Movement Black cultural consciousness that was one of the hallmarks and lasting legacies of the movement. On the one hand, the Black Power Movement allowed African Americans to collectively articulate some of the most penetrating critiques of American racism and set into motion some of the most inspirational, progressive, and creative efforts to economically, socially, politically, culturally, and intellectually empower African Americans since the New Negro Movement and its artistic off-shoot, the Harlem Renaissance (circa 1895–1945). On the other hand, the Black Power Movement also gave rise to some of the most ignominious, pessimistic, exploitative, misogynist, homophobic, and outright reactionary impulses passing themselves off as Black Power politics. Consequently, at both its best and its worst, soul music seemed to express this tangle of paradoxes, enabling African Americans to intensify and radicalize the "we can implicitly sing what we cannot explicitly say" aesthetic carried over from the soundtracks of the Civil Rights Movement. Indeed, this *lyrically deeper* and *sonically darker* music gave voice to both the progressive and retrogressive ethos of the Black Power Movement.

Chapter 4, "Soul Sisters, Musical Feminism, and the Black Women's Liberation Movement," analyzes female soul singers of the classic soul period between the mid-1960s and mid-1970s and argues that legends like Aretha Franklin, Nina Simone, and Laura Lee created a distinct kind of cultural, social, and political expression that was ideologically situated somewhere between the Black Power Movement and the Women's Liberation Movement. For the most part, soul women's work was centered around many of the same topics as their soul brother counterparts, but, most importantly, they engaged these topics from African American women's point of view. As male soul and funk music resuscitated Black machismo and embraced the *Moynihan Report*'s myth of Black matriarchy in the late 1960s, female soul and funk music registered the complicated and frequently conflicted responses of African American women to the changing tenor of Black protest. African American women obviously took note of the resurgence of Black male militancy during the Black Power Movement. As African American men's exasperation with the system increased and often transformed itself into various kinds of compensatory machismo and misogyny, African American women largely ended up in the unpleasant position of having to choose between supporting the Black Power Movement, which was now largely defined and led by Black men, or supporting the Women's Liberation Movement, which had increasingly come to be defined and led by White women. Many African American women, understandably, found very little common ground with the essentially White women-centered, middle-class, college-educated, and career-oriented overarching agenda of the Women's Liberation Movement, and ultimately decided to create their own distinct movement that combined the struggle for racial justice emerging from the Black Power Movement with the struggle for gender justice emerging from the Women's Liberation Movement. Consequently, this chapter initially offers a brief history of the Black Women's Liberation Movement, and then explores several of its musical icons and anthems.

The concluding chapter, "Funk, Musical Militancy, and the Black Power Movement," explores the ways in which funk music frequently captured and conveyed distinct aspects of the militancy of the Black Power Movement. Primarily utilizing the work of James Brown, Sly & the Family Stone, and George Clinton and Parliament/Funkadelic, the chapter emphasizes how funk was emblematic of some of the ways Black popular music reflected key changes taking place during the final phase of the Black Power Movement. Classic funk continued the hard and heavy, driving rhythms that characterized classic soul at its inception but, by the mid-1970s, were regularly being reduced to the soft-sounding middle-of-the-road (MOR) music primed for the commercial radio format. Funk was a deeper and darker "underground" sound that initially found few White fans in its "pure" and "uncut" form (to paraphrase funkmaster George Clinton in "P-Funk [Wants To Get Funked Up]"). With its references to pimps, players, prostitutes, drugs, drinking, other worlds, extraterrestrials, spaceships, parties, poverty, and Black cultural politics, at its inception funk captured the experiences of economically impoverished and politically pessimistic African Americans in the aftermath of the Civil Rights Movement in ways that no other form of Black popular music did during the 1970s. Therefore, the book ends much like it began, by emphasizing the unique centrality of music during the Black Power Movement and the ways in which Black Power music offers us an alternative interpretive angle to critically introduce and explore the movement – indeed, the movement's *Blackness, power,* and *music.*

Notes

1 For examples of noteworthy works on the Black Power Movement's politics, economics, and social justice agenda, see Devin Fergus, *Liberalism, Black Power, and the Making of American Politics, 1965–1980* (Athens: University of Georgia Press, 2009); Karen Ferguson, *Top Down: The Ford Foundation, Black Power, and the Reinvention of Racial Liberalism* (Philadelphia: University of Pennsylvania Press, 2013); Cedric Johnson, *Revolutionaries to Race Leaders: Black Power and the Making of African American Politics* (Minneapolis:

University of Minnesota Press, 2007); Jeffrey Ogbar, *Black Power: Radical Politics and African American Identity* (Baltimore: Johns Hopkins University Press, 2004); Junius Williams, *Unfinished Agenda: Urban Politics in the Era of Black Power* (Berkeley: North Atlantic Books, 2014).

2 For examples of noteworthy works that engage the ways in which the Black Power Movement helped to revitalize African American culture roughly between 1965 to 1975 in general, and regional and local cultures in particular, see Lucas N. N. Burke and Judson L. Jeffries, *The Portland Black Panthers: Empowering Albina and Remaking a City* (Seattle: University of Washington Press, 2016); Christina Greene, *Our Separate Ways: Women and the Black Freedom Movement in Durham, North Carolina* (Chapel Hill: University of North Carolina Press, 2005); Hasan Kwame Jeffries, *Bloody Lowndes: Civil Rights and Black Power in Alabama's Black Belt* (New York: New York University Press, 2009); Judson L. Jeffries, ed., *The Black Panther Party in a City Near You* (Athens: University of Georgia Press, 2018); Judson L. Jeffries, ed., *Black Power in the Belly of the Beast* (Urbana: University of Illinois Press, 2006); Judson L. Jeffries, ed., *Comrades: A Local History of the Black Panther Party* (Bloomington: Indiana University Press, 2007); Judson L. Jeffries, ed., *On the Ground: The Black Panther Party in Communities across America* (Jackson: University Press of Mississippi, 2010); Peniel E. Joseph, *Neighborhood Rebels: Black Power at the Local Level* (New York: Palgrave Macmillan, 2010); Tiyi Makeda Morris, *Womanpower Unlimited and the Black Freedom Struggle in Mississippi* (Athens: University of Georgia Press, 2015); Donna Jean Murch, *Living for the City: Migration, Education, and the Rise of the Black Panther Party in Oakland, California* (Chapel Hill: University of North Carolina Press, 2010); Jeanne Theoharis and Komozi Woodard, eds., *Freedom North: Black Freedom Struggles Outside the South, 1940–1980* (New York: Palgrave Macmillan, 2003); Jeanne Theoharis and Komozi Woodard, eds., *Groundwork: Local Black Freedom Movements in America* (New York: New York University Press, 2005); Yohuru R. Williams, *Black Politics/White Power: Civil Rights, Black Power and the Black Panthers in New Haven* (St. James, NY: Brandywine Press, 2000); Yohuru R. Williams and Jama Lazerow, eds., *Liberated Territory: Untold Local Perspectives on the Black Panther Party* (Durham: Duke University Press, 2009).

3 In *The Black Power Movement*, Peniel Joseph offered an insightful conceptualization of "Black Power studies," contending: "'Black Power studies' highlights connections between two historical periods, characterizing the Civil Rights and Black Power era as a complex mosaic rather than mutually exclusive and antagonistic movements. While the individual subject matter, organizations, and approach of these recent works vary, they converge in at least four important ways." First, "this new scholarship reperiodizes the Civil Rights-Black Power era by pushing the chronology of Black radicalism back to the 1950s and forward into the 1970s." Second, Black Power studies "place[s] early Black Power activists at the center of Cold War intrigues." Third, "this new scholarship documents both the iconic and unglamorous." And, lastly, "new works on the Black Power era contribute to, and expand the scope of, a larger contemporary discussion about the legacy of Civil Rights; a debate that, more often than not, ignores or demonizes the Black Power era." Peniel E. Joseph, ed., *The Black Power Movement: Rethinking the Civil Rights-Black Power Era* (New York: Routledge, 2006), 8–9.

4 For further discussion of the contention that Black popular music and Black popular culture frequently reflect the conservatism *and* radicalism, the moderatism *and* militantism of the major African American movement of the milieu in which they initially emerged, see Iain Anderson, *This Is Our Music: Free Jazz, the Sixties, and American Culture* (Philadelphia: University of Pennsylvania Press, 2007); Ruth Feldstein, *How It Feels to Be Free: Black Women Entertainers and the Civil Rights Movement* (New York: Oxford University Press, 2013); Waldo E. Martin, *No Coward Soldiers: Black Cultural Politics in Postwar America* (Cambridge: Harvard University Press, 2005); Mark Anthony Neal, *What the Music Said: Black Popular Music and Black Public Culture* (New York: Routledge, 1998); Burton W. Peretti, *Lift Every Voice: The History of African American Music* (Lanham, MD: Rowman & Littlefield, 2009); Shana L. Redmond, *Anthem: Social Movements and*

the Sound of Solidarity in the African Diaspora (New York: New York University Press, 2014); Lawrence Schenbeck, *Racial Uplift and American Music, 1878–1943* (Jackson: University Press of Mississippi, 2012); Wyatt Tee Walker, *"Somebody's Calling My Name": Black Sacred Music and Social Change* (Valley Forge, PA: Judson Press, 1979); Brian Ward, *Radio and the Struggle for Civil Rights in the South* (Gainesville: University Press of Florida, 2004); Craig H. Werner, *Change Is Gonna Come: Music, Race & the Soul of America* (Ann Arbor: University of Michigan Press, 2006).

5 For some of the history of music, sociology of music, and politics of music-centered studies this book builds on, see Michael Awkward, *Soul Covers: Rhythm & Blues Remakes and the Struggle for Artistic Identity (Aretha Franklin, Al Green, Phoebe Snow)* (Durham: Duke University Press, 2007); Tony Bolden, *Groove Theory: The Blues Foundation of Funk* (Jackson: University Press of Mississippi, 2020); Robert M. J. Bowman, *Soulsville, U.S.A.: The Story of Stax Records* (New York: Schirmer Books, 1997); Aaron Cohen, *Move On Up: Chicago Soul Music and Black Cultural Power* (Chicago: University of Chicago Press, 2019); Peter Guralnick, *Sweet Soul Music: Rhythm & Blues and the Southern Dream of Freedom* (New York: Harper & Row, 1986); Michael Haralambos, *Soul Music: The Birth of a Sound in Black America* (New York: Da Capo, 1975); Claudrena N. Harold, *When Sunday Comes: Gospel Music in the Soul and Hip Hop Eras* (Champaign: University of Illinois Press, 2020); Gerri Hirshey, *Nowhere to Run: The Story of Soul Music* (New York: Times Books, 1984); John A. Jackson, *A House on Fire: The Rise and Fall of Philadelphia Soul* (New York: Oxford University Press, 2004); Rochelle Larkin, *Soul Music: The Sound, the Stars, the Story* (New York: Lancer Books, 1970); Emily J. Lordi, *The Meaning of Soul: Black Music and Resilience since the 1960s* (Durham: Duke University Press, 2020); Maureen Mahon, *Black Diamond Queens: African American Women and Rock & Roll* (Durham: Duke University Press, 2020); Portia K. Maultsby, "Soul Music: Its Sociological and Political Significance in American Popular Culture," *Journal of Popular Culture* 17, no. 2 (1983): 51–60; Portia K. Maultsby, "Funk Music: An Expression of Black Life in Dayton, Ohio and the American Metropolis," in *The American Metropolis: Image and Inspiration*, eds. Hans Krabbendam, Marja Roholl and Tity De Vries (Amsterdam: Vu University Press, 2001), 197–213; Mitchell Morris, *The Persistence of Sentiment: Display and Feeling in Popular Music of the 1970s* (Berkeley: University of California Press, 2013); Robert Pruter, *Chicago Soul* (Urbana: University of Illinois Press, 1991); Rickey Vincent, *Party Music: The Inside Story of the Black Panthers' Band and How Black Power Transformed Soul Music* (Chicago: Lawrence Hill Books, 2013); Brian Ward, *Just My Soul Responding: Rhythm & Blues, Black Consciousness, and Race Relations* (Berkeley: University of California Press, 1998); Craig Werner, *Higher Ground: Stevie Wonder, Aretha Franklin, Curtis Mayfield, and the Rise and Fall of American Soul* (New York: Crown Publishers, 2004); Werner, *Change Is Gonna Come*.

6 For further discussion of African American "message music" and for the works that factored into my interpretation here, see R. A. Lawson, *Jim Crow's Counterculture: The Blues and Black Southerners, 1890–1945* (Baton Rouge: Louisiana State University Press, 2013); Burton W. Peretti, "Signifying Freedom: Protest in Nineteenth Century African American Music," in *The Routledge History of Social Protest in Popular Music*, ed. Jonathan C. Friedman (New York: Routledge, 2013), 3–18; James Smethurst, "A Soul Message: R&B, Soul, and the Black Freedom Struggle," in *The Routledge History of Social Protest in Popular Music*, 108–20; Diane D. Turner, ed., *Feeding the Soul: Black Music, Black Thought* (Chicago: Third World Press, 2011); Katherine L. Turner, "Sonic Opposition: Protesting Racial Violence before Civil Rights," in *The Routledge History of Social Protest in Popular Music*, 44–56; Werner, *Change Is Gonna Come*.

7 For further discussion of the Black Power Movement's regressive, if not outright reactionary, elements and for the works which influenced my interpretation here, see Ashley D. Farmer, *Remaking Black Power: How Black Women Transformed an Era* (Chapel Hill: University of North Carolina Press, 2017), 50–92; Fergus, *Liberalism, Black Power, and the Making of American Politics*, 166–95; Phillip Brian Harper, *Are We Not Men?: Masculine*

Anxiety and the Problem of African American Identity (New York: Oxford University Press, 1996), 39–53; Peniel E. Joseph, *Waiting 'Til the Midnight Hour: A Narrative History of Black Power in America* (New York: Henry Holt, 2006), 241–75; Ogbar, *Black Power,* 100–6, 144–45; Robyn C. Spencer, *The Revolution Has Come: Black Power, Gender, and the Black Panther Party in Oakland* (Durham: Duke University Press, 2016); William L. Van Deburg, *New Day in Babylon: The Black Power Movement and American Culture, 1965–1975* (Chicago: University of Chicago Press, 1992), 260–72.

8 My emphasis on the Black Power Movement in the American social imagination and American cultural memory has been influenced by a number of noteworthy works, including Dan Berger, "Rescuing Civil Rights from Black Power: Collective Memory and Saving the State in Twenty-First-Century Prosecutions of 1960s-Era Cases," *Journal for the Study of Radicalism* 3, no. 1 (2009): 1–27; Carol Bunch Davis, *Prefiguring Post-Blackness: Cultural Memory, Drama, and the African American Freedom Struggle of the 1960s* (Jackson: University Press of Mississippi, 2015); Tom Adam Davies, *Mainstreaming Black Power* (Berkeley: University of California Press, 2017); Sylviane A. Diouf and Komozi Woodward, eds., *Black Power 50* (New York: New Press, 2016); Monique Guillory and Richard C. Green, eds., *Soul: Black Power, Politics, and Pleasure* (New York: New York University Press, 1998); Russell Rickford, *We Are an African People: Independent Education, Black Power, and the Radical Imagination* (New York: Oxford University Press, 2016); James B. Stewart, "Neutering the Black Power Movement: The Hijacking of Protest Symbolism," in *Soul Thieves: The Appropriation and Misrepresentation of African American Popular Culture,* eds. Tamara L. Brown and Baruti N. Kopano (New York: Palgrave Macmillan, 2014), 91–108; Pat Thomas, *Listen, Whitey!: The Sights and Sounds of Black Power, 1965–1975* (New York: Norton, 2012).

9 For further discussion of the impact of the Black Power Movement on Black cultural expression and artistic production between the mid-1960s and mid-1970s, see James L. Conyers, ed., *Engines of the Black Power Movement: Essays on the Influence of Civil Rights Actions, Arts, and Islam* (Jefferson, NC: McFarland & Co., 2007); Guillory and Green, *Soul;* Tanisha C. Ford, *Liberated Threads: Black Women, Style, and the Global Politics of Soul* (Chapel Hill: University of North Carolina Press, 2017); James C. Hall, *Mercy, Mercy Me: African American Culture and the American Sixties* (New York: Oxford University Press, 2001); Errol A. Henderson, *The Revolution Will Not Be Theorized: Cultural Revolution in the Black Power Era* (Albany: State University of New York Press, 2016); Scott Saul, *Freedom Is, Freedom Ain't: Jazz and the Making of the Sixties* (Cambridge: Harvard University Press, 2003); James Edward Smethurst, *The Black Arts Movement: Literary Nationalism in the 1960s and 1970s* (Chapel Hill: University of North Carolina Press, 2005); William L. Van Deburg, *Black Camelot: African American Culture Heroes in Their Times, 1960–1980* (Chicago: University of Chicago Press, 1997); Daniel Widener, *Black Arts West: Culture and Struggle in Post-War Los Angeles* (Durham: Duke University Press, 2010).

10 My emphasis here on the Black Power Movement as a breeding ground for qualitatively new kinds of politicized, radicalized, and ritualized thought and practices, as well as for new artistic, literary, and, most especially, musical innovation and experimentation, has been deeply influenced by Van Deburg, *New Day in Babylon,* 192–247.

11 Amiri Baraka, *Black Music* (New York: Quill, 1967); Phyl Garland, *The Sound of Soul* (Chicago: H. Regnery Book Co, 1969); Frank Kofsky, *Black Nationalism and the Revolution in Music* (New York: Pathfinder, 1991; orig. pub. 1970); Rickey Vincent, *Funk: The Music, the People, and the Rhythm of the One* (New York: St. Martin's Griffin, 1996); Bowman, *Soulsville, U.S.A.: The Story of Stax Records;* Neal, *What the Music Said;* Ward, *Just My Soul Responding;* Saul, *Freedom Is, Freedom Ain't;* George Lewis, *A Power Stronger Than Itself: The AACM and American Experimental Music* (Chicago: University of Chicago Press, 2008); Thomas, *Listen, Whitey!;* Vincent, *Party Music;* Redmond, *Anthem;* Andrew Darlington, *"Don't Call Me Nigger, Whitey": Sly Stone & Black Power* (New York: Leaky Boot Press, 2014); Robert Gordon, *Respect Yourself: Stax Records and the Soul Explosion* (New York: Bloomsbury, 2015); Gayle Wald, *It's Been Beautiful: Soul!*

and Black Power Television (Durham: Duke University Press, 2015); Stephen Rush, *Free Jazz, Harmolodics, and Ornette Coleman* (New York: Routledge, 2016); Philippe Carles and Jean-Louis Comolli, *Free Jazz/Black Power* (Jackson: University Press of Mississippi, 2016); Cohen, *Move On Up*; Bolden, *Groove Theory*; Mahon, *Black Diamond Queens*; Harold, *When Sunday Comes*.

12 Houston A. Baker, *Modernism and the Harlem Renaissance* (Chicago: University of Chicago Press, 1987), 51, all emphasis in original.

13 Ibid., 52, all emphasis in original.

14 See, for instance, Michelle Alexander, *The New Jim Crow: Mass Incarceration in the Age of Colorblindness* (New York: New Press, 2012); Alicia Garza, *The Purpose of Power: How We Come Together When We Fall Apart* (New York: One World, 2020); Laurie Collier Hillstrom, *Black Lives Matter: From a Moment to a Movement* (Santa Barbara: Greenwood, 2018); Patrisse Khan-Cullors, *When They Call You a Terrorist: A Black Lives Matter Memoir*, ed. Asha Bandele (New York: St. Martin's Press, 2018); Barbara Ransby, *Making All Black Lives Matter: Reimagining Freedom in the Twenty-First Century* (Berkeley: University of California Press, 2018); Keeanga-Yamahtta Taylor, *From #BlackLivesMatter to Black Liberation* (Chicago: Haymarket Books, 2016).

15 Fernando Orejuela and Stephanie Shonekan, eds., *Black Lives Matter and Music: Protest, Intervention, Reflection* (Bloomington: Indiana University Press, 2018).

1

THE BLACK POWER MOVEMENT, THE BLACK ARTS MOVEMENT, AND THE BLACK AESTHETIC

"Black is beautiful!": introduction to Black power studies

The Black Power Movement is arguably one of the most important, yet most misunderstood, episodes in African American history. Something similar could be said – indeed, *should be said* – about the various musics that emerged out of the movement. Logically, a misunderstood and underappreciated movement is liable to leave a number of misunderstood and underappreciated social, political, and cultural artifacts and expressions. It is possible that a major reason the movement has been misconstrued may have much to do with many Whites and, truth be told, even some African Americans' misapprehensions surrounding the "Black Power" slogan. From the very first time Stokely Carmichael passionately shouted the provocative phrase on the night of June 16, 1966, in the midst of the March Against Fear in Greenwood, Mississippi, through to the present moment, "Black Power," both as a concept and as a movement, has been mostly misunderstood.[1] Consequently, the music that conveyed the ideals and captured the ethos of the movement has, for the most part, been grossly misinterpreted or marginalized.

Whether we turn to William Van Deburg's *New Day in Babylon: The Black Power Movement and American Culture, 1965–1975*, Jeffrey Ogbar's *Black Power: Radical Politics and African American Identity*, Ashley Farmer's *Remaking Black Power: How Black Women Transformed an Era*, Judson Jeffries' *Black Power in the Belly of the Beast*, Rhonda Williams' *Concrete Demands: The Search for Black Power in the 20th Century*, or, of course, Peniel Joseph's magisterial *Waiting' Til the Midnight Hour: A Narrative History of Black Power in America*, it is evident that in the minds of many Americans, both Black and White, the Black Power Movement is synonymous with violence, "reverse racism," or, even worse, "Black supremacy."[2] How most Americans came to their conclusions about the Black Power Movement is something of a mystery, considering the fact that comprehensive studies of the movement have been few

DOI: 10.4324/9781003254492-2

and far between. As we have witnessed with the recent news coverage of the Black Lives Matter Movement, the media is neither an adequate nor an objective interpreter of Black life, Black love, and Black quests for liberation. As the first major Black popular movement to emerge in the aftermath of the Civil Rights Movement, the Black Power Movement is most often juxtaposed with the Civil Rights Movement and rarely engaged on its own terms. However, as this chapter seeks to demonstrate, the Black Power Movement was as dissimilar from, as it was similar to, the Civil Rights Movement. For instance, one of the most distinctive features of the Black Power Movement was its cultural arts offshoot movement, the Black Arts Movement. The core concept of the Black Arts Movement was *the Black aesthetic*, and this *set of principles and criteria for creating Black art*, both visual and performing art, influenced everything brought into, and emerging out of, the Black Power Movement.

Because most White Americans consider the 1963 March on Washington, the Civil Rights Act of 1964, and the Voting Rights Act of 1965 as the crowning achievements and concrete accomplishments of the Civil Rights Movement, few have understood that for many African Americans by the mid-1960s the Civil Rights Movement was understood to be in its last stages as a viable vehicle for social, political, and economic change. Even though a great many folks hold the view that the Civil Rights Movement and the Black Power Movement are distinctly different movements, influenced by Jacquelyn Dowd Hall's "The Long Civil Rights Movement and the Political Uses of the Past," I believe that the latter movement is actually a logical extension of the former.[3] In other words, the Black Power Movement undeniably built on the foundation laid by the Civil Rights Movement. In fact, it is possible to conceive of the Black Power Movement as the radical, more militant phase of the "long Civil Rights Movement." Where Civil Rights moderates, especially Martin Luther King, frequently invoked the "founding fathers" of the United States, among other White intellectual authorities, Black Power militants drew inspiration and insights from a Pan-African pantheon that included Toussaint L'Ouverture, David Walker, Nat Turner, Henry Highland Garnet, W.E.B. Du Bois, Marcus Garvey, Ida B. Wells, Malcolm X, Robert F. Williams, Kwame Nkrumah, Sékou Touré, Frantz Fanon, and Amilcar Cabral, among others.[4]

In the American social imagination of the twenty-first century the Civil Rights Movement is understood to have been squarely situated in the South. Which is to say, most folk think of the movement as a Southern movement. Even though many believe that most of the "action" and major episodes of the Civil Rights Movement took place in the South, it is important to come to terms with the fact that what we now think of as the Civil Rights Movement has been heavily manufactured. The actual movement was as Northeastern, Midwestern, and Western as it was Southern, and each region developed distinct programs and practices to challenge racial segregation and bring about integration.[5] As Hall reminds us, "remembrance is always a form of forgetting, and the dominant narrative of the Civil Rights Movement – distilled from history and memory, twisted by ideology and political contestation, and embedded in heritage tours, museums, public rituals, textbooks, and various artifacts of mass culture – distorts and suppresses as much as it reveals."[6] The roots of what could be called the "master narrative" of the Civil Rights Movement can be found in the back-and-forth between the movement's members and the alleged objectivity of journalists and historians. In dramatic protest after protest, in rousing march after march, in sensational sit-in after sit-in, movement members articulated their demands employing Christian universalism and the discourse of democratic rights; demonstrated their awe-inspiring courage and commitment to freedom; and countered hate speech, fists, billy clubs, and guns with various forms of nonviolence, passive resistance, and civil disobedience.

Unfolding with more thrilling twists and turns than an Alfred Hitchcock, M. Night Shyamalan, or Jordan Peele film, key scenes of the Civil Rights Movement played themselves out in courtrooms and classrooms, churches and mosques, city streets and country roads, and the accumulation of each of these events eventually brought down America's system of de jure segregation and disfranchisement. Undoubtedly, the mass media of the movement era made the marches and protests of the Civil Rights Movement among the most noted news stories of the 1950s and 1960s, but, bearing in mind the simple fact that the media is not objective, they only selectively reported on movement activities. Contingent on activists' ability to offer up colorful, larger-than-life personalities and telegenic showdowns, typically ones where White wrongdoers unleashed racist violence on nonviolent Black protesters dressed in the finest fashions their meager money could buy, most journalists' interest in the Civil Rights Movement waxed and waned. The Civil Rights Movement and the new medium of television emerged and evolved along parallel paths, and for one of the first times in American history White citizens could bear witness to the ways in which, even after more than 350 years of enslavement, African Americans continued to be mistreated. In many White Americans' minds these images of racist violence seemed to arise from the ether, to come out of the blue, essentially to have no historical precedent. Sadly, this situation, this distortion of historical fact and favoring of historical fiction, was compounded when the national media's mostly favorable, even if most often misleading, coverage of the Black Freedom Movement abruptly ended in the mid-1960s as the moderatism of the Civil Rights Movement gave way to the militantism of the Black Power Movement.[7]

Unambiguously turning a hostile eye toward the radicalization of the Civil Rights Movement and the emergence of the Black Power Movement, national news networks' cameras quickly turned away from the South and in so doing ignored the ways in which the Southern movement continued to evolve after 1965 and set more radical social and political goals in line with many of the goals of the Black Power Movement. Frequently by over-relying on the national press' coverage of both the end of the Civil Rights Movement and the beginning of the Black Power Movement, not only were the evolving objectives of the "long Civil Rights Movement" disregarded, but the continuities and similarities, the actual overlapping interregional agendas of the Civil Rights Movement and the Black

Power Movement, have been obfuscated. This has, obviously, created a narrative breach, a rupture in the historical narrative between, on the one side, what people conceive of as the Civil Rights Movement and, on the other side, the historically documented ways in which the Civil Rights Movement morphed into the Black Power Movement.[8] In agreement with Hasan Kwame Jeffries, I firmly believe that it is important for us to challenge and replace "earlier arguments positing that the Civil Rights Movement ended in 1965 or 1968" with "the idea that Civil Rights struggles continued into the Black Power era."[9] In fact, Jeffries continued:

> Rather than viewing Civil Rights and Black Power as unconnected, scholars have begun to see the latter as an extension of the former. Merging Civil Rights and Black Power struggles has required scholars to go beyond simplistic understandings of the era. The Civil Rights Movement, for example, was more than what [Martin Luther] King and [the Southern Christian Leadership Conference] SCLC did. Similarly, the Black Power Movement was more than what Stokely Carmichael said and the Black Panther Party did. . . . The literature on the Civil Rights Movement has matured substantially over the last quarter-century. Scholars have transcended narrow understandings of the movement's chronology, extending its temporal boundaries both forward and backward in time. They have complicated Civil Rights leadership, broadening definitions of leaders to incorporate women and the grassroots. No longer is the prototypical Civil Rights leader the Black Baptist minister. They have also placed ordinary Black folk, local people, at the center of study, recognizing not only their agency as historical actors, but also their desire and capacity to make the decisions that shape their lives.[10]

Interestingly, I have found both White folk and a great many Black folk who are willing to concede that rhythm & blues laid the foundation for, and eventually morphed into, soul music but who adamantly refuse to even entertain the idea that the Black Power Movement may have actually been nothing more than the final, more militant phase of the Civil Rights Movement. Here the music of the Black Power Movement is viewed as a historical and cultural artifact and probed for its ability to capture and convey the ethos and issues of the era. As Jeffries emphasized above about "broadening definitions of leaders" and "plac[ing] ordinary Black folk . . . at the center of study," in what follows rhythm & blues-cum-soul and funk musicians are situated "at the center of study" and reinterpreted as furtive movement leaders, participants, and allies.

African American social and political movements typically produce several signposts to signify their emergence, and the Black Power Movement was no exception to this rule. One of the major indicators of the Black Power Movement's advent can be detected in the pervasive sense of social misery plaguing many parts of Black America by the mid-1960s. Whether it was a response to the innumerable acts of anti-Black racist violence or most police departments' inability or outright unwillingness to protect Black lives and property, Black America's relationship with law enforcement was dramatically altered by both the successes and the failures of the Civil Rights Movement. After bearing witness to White violence against students sitting-in, freedom riders, and nonviolent protesters; the assassination of Medgar Evers; the bombing of Addie Mae Collins, Cynthia Wesley, Carole Robertson, and Carol Denise McNair in the 16th Street Baptist Church; or the murders of James Chaney, Andrew Goodman, and Michael Schwerner, by the mid-1960s Black America held out little hope that local law enforcement or even federal government officials would "serve and protect" them.[11]

Another major indicator that the Black Power Movement was coming into being by the mid-1960s can be easily observed in Malcolm X's increasing influence on the Black masses. Perhaps more than any other figure in African American history, Malcolm X with his fiery words helped to spearhead the Black Power Movement. In speech after speech, he admonished African Americans to "stop singing and start swinging." "This is part of what's wrong with you," Malcolm intoned, "you do too much singing." He went on, "[t]oday it's time to stop singing and start swinging. You can't sing up on freedom, but you can swing up on some freedom."[12] It was not merely Angela Davis, the Black Panthers, and the Republic of New Afrika who sought to continue Malcolm X's Black consciousness-raising mission in the aftermath of his assassination on February 21, 1965. Whether consciously or unconsciously, by the mid-1960s Black popular music, especially rhythm & blues-cum-soul and funk, increasingly came to mirror the ethos and ideals of the emerging Black Power Movement. From Martha Reeves & the Vandellas' "Dancing in the Street" and James Brown's "Say It Loud – I'm Black and I'm Proud" to the Impressions' "We're a Winner" and the Temptations' "Message to a Black Man," a lot of Black popular music during the Black Power Movement evolved into a kind of message music that expressed the militant mood of Black America.[13]

It was not merely movement militants who took Malcolm's words to heart, but, as many members of the Black Arts Movement have attested, his words also hit home for myriad Black artists, including musicians, from the mid-1960s to the mid-1970s.[14] His unapologetic Black radicalism and emphasis on intellectual independence appealed to African American youth in ways that Martin Luther King's seemingly incessant invocation of the "founding fathers" and other White political figures did not in the dire period immediately after the March on Washington.

Ideologically, the Black Power Movement embraced and articulated a wider range of thought and practices when compared with the Civil Rights Movement.[15] In spite of the fact that all Black Power advocates and organizations believed that African Americans should control their own communities, in their efforts to achieve community control they employed a diverse array of approaches. Indeed, the NAACP, CORE, SCLC, and SNCC collectively struggled to dismantle desegregation and garner the right to vote. To achieve these goals they primarily employed nonviolence, passive resistance, and civil disobedience. However, for almost all Black Power proponents, nonviolence and its corollary concepts were completely out of the question, and integration was virtually a nonissue.[16]

Seeming to fly in the face of the Civil Rights Movement's consensus surrounding nonviolence, passive resistance, and civil disobedience, the Black Power Movement's ideological universe ran the gamut from Black nationalism and Pan-Africanism to Black separatism and Marxist-Leninism. For example, the Republic of New Africa (RNA) were Black separatists who sought to establish an independent Black America in five Southern states: Louisiana, Mississippi, Alabama, Georgia, and South Carolina. Later they argued that counties with African American majorities adjacent to the five aforementioned states in Arkansas, Texas, North Carolina, Tennessee, and Florida should also be considered part of Black America.[17] Led by the charismatic and at times controversial Maulana Karenga, the Us Organization (also known as the Organization Us) were the most prominent cultural nationalists of the Black Power Movement, emphasizing African Americans' cultural connections to Africa and its diaspora. The Us Organization also had a paramilitary cadre called the Simba Wachanga (the Young Lions) and consistently articulated their preference for self-defense over nonviolence.[18] Moreover, during their peak period (circa 1967–1977) the Black Panther Party could be characterized as nationalist and Marxist-Leninist, while some Panthers even embraced Pan-Africanism and feminism.[19] All of that being said, it is also important to emphasize that some Black Power Movement participants' beliefs, thoughts, and practices cut across a number of conventional ideological categories, while others simply are not easily ideologically labeled.

Much like the music that provided a soundtrack for the Black Power Movement, a survey of the major Black Power organizations will reveal that they were, ideologically speaking, fluctuating – in a constant state of evolution. The music of the Black Power Movement is incredibly revealing because it was produced during one of the most provocative periods in African American history, a period where Black folk, seemingly for the first time, announced that they were "Black and proud." When we move beyond the beautiful "sweet soul music" and heavenly harmonies of the Black Power Movement and turn our attention instead to its protest songs and message music, we are presented with an alternative history of the movement – a history not written by the heavy hands of highbrow historians or focused on the charismatic and often misogynist male leaders of the movement. On the contrary, presented here is a history of the Black Power Movement as told through its protest songs and message music, songs and music produced by both famous and virtually unknown, male and female, Northern and Southern, Western and Midwestern musicians. Ultimately what connects their work is its ability, whether blatantly, surreptitiously, or even unwittingly, to provide us with historical snapshots, cultural portraits, social commentary, and political critique. In other words, Black Power music was, and remains, more than merely music.

Similar to the Civil Rights Movement, the Black Power Movement offered up its own distinct soundtracks, specifically soul and funk. Placing a greater emphasis on rhythm & blues' gospel roots, soul was partly a musical and partly a political response to the whitening and lightening of both rhythm & blues and rock & roll. Moving away from the pop elements and the obsession with crossing over so common in rhythm & blues in the early 1960s, at its emergence in the mid-1960s soul privileged gospel over blues and jazz. Where classic rhythm & blues could be said to have electrified and amplified the blues, classic soul could be said to have intensified the spiritual, sexual, social, political, and cultural components of classic rhythm & blues. Indeed, all of these elements were present in classic rhythm & blues, but they were most often buried beneath a barrage of pop chart-obsessed pretensions, which ultimately whitewashed the music and made it sound like little more than Black singers imitating White singers.[20] Soul, as with its sister sound funk, was a sonic challenge that openly emphasized the "African" elements of African Americans' musical and cultural history.[21]

Moreover, soul music also expressed African Americans' growing disillusionment with both the broken and the unfulfilled promises of American democracy during its peak years between 1965 and 1975. After more than a decade of nonviolent sitting-in, marching, freedom-riding, demonstrating, and protesting, many African Americans, especially Black ghetto youth, observed that little had actually changed in American society. Even after the signing of high-sounding Civil Rights legislation – for example, *Brown v. the Board of Education* in 1954, *Gideon v. Wainwright* in 1963, *Heart of Atlanta v. the United States* in 1964, the Civil Rights Act of 1964, the Twenty-Fourth Amendment in 1964, and the Voting Rights Act of 1965 – American apartheid seemed as alive and pernicious as ever.[22] As a consequence, soul lyrics reflected the spiritual, sentimental, and sensual, as well as – in clear contrast to most classic rhythm & blues – the social, political, and cultural. Inspired by both the Civil Rights Movement and the Black Power Movement, then, soul lyrics carried over classic rhythm & blues' focus on love, lust, and loss but distinctively expanded Black popular music's sonic palette to include social commentary, political critique, and copious cultural references. In this sense soul music is distinguished from rhythm & blues in both its broadened lyrical content and grittier, gospel-influenced musical elements.[23]

Soul was the unsanctioned sound of primarily Black ghetto youth expressing not only their adolescent love (à la Motown-styled rhythm & blues), but also their discontent with both American democracy and the increasingly placid moderatism of the Civil Rights Movement.[24] Serving as a major mouthpiece for the rhetoric, politics, and aesthetics of the Black Power Movement, classic soul sought to decolonize and re-politicize Black popular music, if not Black people more generally. Essentially mirroring the Black Power Movement's efforts to radicalize African American politics in the aftermath of the mixed results and mostly disappointing outcomes of the Civil Rights Movement, soul represented a radicalization and, truth be told, a *re-African Americanization* of Black popular music in the 1960s and 1970s. Because of the often overtly political nature of a lot of soul music, and considering the ways in which all post-soul Black popular music drew from classic soul aesthetics and Black Power politics, it is important to understand the larger social, political, and cultural landscape in which soul emerged.

The "soul aesthetic" was essentially the musical expression of the much-celebrated "Black aesthetic" that was propagated by the members of the Black Arts

Movement. However, most discussions of classic soul, even those that claim to be "scholarly," frequently fail to acknowledge or critically engage either the Black Arts Movement or the Black aesthetic. What is more, there is a longstanding tendency to disassociate soul music's politics from the wider political world of the Black Power Movement. Similar to rhythm & blues in relationship to the Civil Rights Movement, soul expressed the lives, loves, and struggles of African Americans during the Black Power Movement years. Because soul emerged at the intersection of two movements, the Black Power Movement *and* the Black Arts Movement, any serious discussion of soul music should situate it in the milieux of these movements, as well as connect the soul aesthetic with the broader Black aesthetic. Consequently, this chapter will provide snapshot histories of the Black Power Movement, Black Arts Movement, and Black aesthetic in an effort to historically and culturally ground readers in the ideals and ethos of the era in which Black Power music emerged.

The Black Power Movement

In order to critically understand the Black Arts Movement and the Black aesthetic, it is important, first and foremost, to engage the myriad meanings of the Black Power Movement, its central message, and its mission. However, identifying the essential message and mission of the Black Power Movement has proved to be extremely difficult in light of the fact that "Black Power" actually meant many different things to many different individuals and organizations.[25] As a matter of fact, one could go so far as to say that there was no such thing as the Black Power Movement, singular, but rather something more akin to Black Power Movements, plural. Within the larger, macro-Black Power Movement there were several smaller, micro-Black Power Movements, for example, the Black Arts Movement, Black Women's Liberation Movement, Black Studies Movement, Modern Black Convention Movement, and Black Prisoners' Rights/Prison Power Movement.[26] *Black Power studies* is an emerging, discursively diverse, and conceptually contentious arena within African American studies that seeks to document and develop a critical reevaluation of the Black Power Movement. Because of the wide range of issues Black Power Movement members and organizations addressed, Black Power studies is a highly heterogeneous field, one that, much like the Black Power Movement itself, challenges the homogenization of the interpretation and appreciation of African American history, culture, and struggles in general, and Black Power Movement histories, cultures, and struggles in particular. Needless to say, even with all of its discursive diversity, several central questions and concerns, recurring themes and theories emerge that have enabled Black Power studies scholars and students to capture the contours of the movement.[27]

In *New Day in Babylon: The Black Power Movement and American Culture, 1965–1975*, William Van Deburg declared: "Black Power was a revolutionary cultural concept that demanded important changes in extant patterns of American cultural hegemony. Its advocates hoped that this revolution eventually would reach the very core of the nation's value system and serve to alter the social behavior of White Americans."[28] In order to challenge and change "American cultural hegemony," however, Black Power advocates – faithfully following Malcolm X and Frantz Fanon – argued that African Americans needed *psychological liberation* and to undergo a *protracted process of decolonization and re-education*. Before they could "alter the social behavior of White Americans," Black Power advocates asserted, Black folk "had to be awakened, unified, and made to see that if they were to succeed they must define and establish their own values while rejecting the cultural prescriptions of their oppressors."[29]

All of this is to say that *self-discovery, self-definition, self-determination*, and *self-defense* were at the heart of the Black Power Movement, its central message and mission.[30] In fact, we could go so far as to say that the Black Power Movement might be more properly called *the Black Empowerment Movement*, because it was not a movement that had as its end goal "Black supremacy" – an oxymoron if ever there was one – but a bona fide multiracial and multicultural democracy.[31] For example, in arguably one of the most widely read works of the movement, *Black Power: The Politics of Liberation in America*, Stokely Carmichael and Charles V. Hamilton strongly stressed that the "ultimate values and goals" of the Black Power Movement "are not domination or exploitation of other groups, but rather an effective share in the total power of society."[32]

The early advocates of Black Power came to the conclusion that the *nonviolence, civil disobedience*, and *passive resistance* strategies and tactics of the Civil Rights Movement had been exhausted and that the time for masking and muting ongoing Black suffering and Black social misery, as well as Black anger and Black outrage aimed at racial and economic injustice, had long passed. After centuries of anti-Black racist oppression, exploitation, and violence, Black Power advocates decided it was time for *Black solidarity, Black self-love*, and *Black self-defense*. "They proclaimed that Blacks were indeed beautiful." And also claimed, Van Deburg wrote, "was the right to define Whites."[33] It is difficult at this point to determine what caused White America of the 1960s and 1970s more angst and ire: Blacks' radical redefinition of themselves and their Blackness, or Blacks' radical redefinition of Whites and their Whiteness.

In *Waiting 'Til the Midnight Hour: A Narrative History of Black Power in America*, Peniel Joseph contended that Stokely Carmichael's "calls for Blacks to organize a national Black Panther political party . . . placed racial solidarity ahead of interracial alliances – he dared White and Black liberals to 'prove that coalition and integration are better alternatives.'"[34] Carmichael's critique of the increasing obsolescence of Civil Rights strategies and tactics had a resounding – indeed, *Black radicalizing* – effect on Black Power political culture. After all, Carmichael not only issued the call for the formation of "a national Black Panther political party," but he and his Student Nonviolent Coordinating Committee (SNCC) comrades also provided the Black Power Movement with its name. To reiterate, it was Carmichael who popularized the "Black Power" slogan during an impassioned speech delivered in the course of the 1966 March Against Fear in Mississippi.[35] However, as Joseph's judicious research highlights, throughout the Black Power period Carmichael went through great pains to explain that "Black Power" *was not about hating White people, but about loving Black people.*[36]

Whites, to put it plainly, were not the focus of Black Power, and most Black Power proponents believed that Whites' narrow-minded and knee-jerk reactions to the movement had more to do with their own, whether conscious or unconscious, deep-seated hatred of and historical amnesia concerning African Americans, their history, culture, and post-Civil Rights Movement struggles. What is more, Black Power radicals exclaimed, Whites' histrionic and hyper-negative reactions to the Black Power Movement also seemed to be symptomatic of their unacknowledged uneasiness about the epoch-making calls for *Black solidarity*, *Black self-love*, and *Black self-defense* coming from African Americans coast to coast.[37] With respect to Carmichael's conception of Black Power, Joseph astutely observed:

> For Carmichael, Black Power did indeed promote universalism, but it did so in Black. That is to say, Black Power recognized power's ability to shape politics, identity, and civilization, and sought to extend these privileges to African Americans – a group that was too often excluded from even the broadest interpretations of whose interests constituted those of humanity. While critics feared that Black Power hinted at a perverse inversion of America's racial hierarchies, Carmichael envisioned something both more and less dangerous – a Black community with the resources, will, and imagination to define the past, present, and future on its own terms.[38]

When one takes a long and hard look at the history of the Black Power Movement it is easy to see it as the logical evolution of the Civil Rights Movement's efforts to attain liberty, dignity, and equality for Black folk in America. To be sure, Black Power militants greatly differed in semantics and tactics when compared with the Civil Rights moderates, but it must be borne in mind that in the final analysis the core concerns of the two movements were more congruous and complementary than conflictual and contradictory. Where the Civil Rights Movement was reformist and moderate, the Black Power Movement was radical and militant. In fact, the Black Power Movement ushered in a whole new age of unprecedented *Black radicalism* in the wake of the woes of the Civil Rights Movement. Its goals extended well beyond Civil Rights Movement conceptions of "integration" and "assimilation," and it was not preoccupied with the reaffirmation of African Americans' Civil Rights and the U.S. government's public admission that it had a legal and ethical obligation to protect the constitutional rights of its Black citizens.[39]

Black Power proponents daringly demanded access to the fundamental operative force in U.S. history, culture, society, and politics: *power* – physical and psychological, social and political, economic and educational, cultural and aesthetic. Following Malcolm X, they argued that they would gain *power* "by any means necessary."[40] Moreover, Malcolm X admonished Blacks to focus their energies and resources on improving their own conditions rather than exhorting Whites to allow them to integrate into mainstream America. He also preached Black self-defense, repeatedly reminding his audiences that Blacks have a constitutional right to retaliate against anti-Black racist violence.[41] Black Power radicals challenged Whites' constant claims that they (i.e., Black Power radicals) had essentially reversed America's racial hierarchy by deconstructing the "myth of Black racism." From Malcolm X to Stokely Carmichael, Maulana Karenga to Amiri Baraka, and the Black Panther Party to the Republic of New Africa, the Black Power period offered up innumerable contestations of the "myth of Black racism," and William Van Deburg's weighted words continue to capture this quandary best:

> To the militant mind, White racism had no valid Black analogue. By definition, racism involved not only exclusion on the basis of race, but exclusion for the purpose of instituting and maintaining a system of arbitrary subjugation. Throughout American history, Whites, not Blacks, had been the chief supporters of this corrupt ideology. Black people had not lynched Whites, murdered their children, bombed their churches, or manipulated the nation's laws to maintain racial hegemony. Nor would they. To adopt the ways of the White racist as their own would be counterproductive and, for a minority group, self-destructive. What Whites called Black racism was only a healthy defense reflex on the part of Afro-Americans attempting to survive and advance in an aggressively hostile environment.[42]

It is important here to emphasize, once again, that Black Power was not about *hating* White people, but about *loving* Black people and defending them against anti-Black racist assaults (again, both physical and psychological). When the history of anti-Black racist violence in the U.S. is taken into serious consideration, then, and perhaps only then, does Van Deburg's contention that Black Power proponents' stance on self-defensive violence as "a healthy defense reflex on the part of Afro-Americans attempting to survive and advance in an aggressively hostile environment" make any sense. Even though Malcolm X's words on Black self-love and Black self-defensive violence were held as prophecy by most Black Power radicals, more often than not, in practice the activist expressions of their movement followed more carefully defined and, for the most part, more familiar African American socio-political movement methods (e.g., boycotts, direct-action protests, street rallies, marches, demonstrations, conferences, concerts, etc.). In fact, according to Van Deburg, although the Black Power Movement "was not exclusively cultural . . . it was essentially cultural. It was a revolt in and of culture that was manifested in a variety of forms and intensities."[43]

The Black Arts Movement

In so many words, it could be said that at its core the Black Power Movement was essentially an *African American cultural revolution*.[44] This, of course, is where the cultural aesthetic radicalism of the Black Arts Movement comes into play. Mirroring the Harlem Renaissance in relationship to the New Negro Movement, the

Black Arts Movement was the artistic wing of the Black Power Movement, but it also served a role that seemed to situate it within a distinct historical and cultural continuum. It would seem that there is a discernable pattern with respect to African American cultural aesthetic movements. Recall that the Harlem Renaissance only emerged when the younger "New Negroes" of the New Negro Movement believed that an embourgeoisement of the movement had taken place and that Booker T. Washington and W.E.B. Du Bois' articulations of New Negro politics had run their course. There was, indeed, a discernable shift away from politics in the traditional Civil Rights sense and greater emphasis placed on New Negro culture, poetics, and aesthetics. This is extremely telling insofar as the emphasis on cultural aesthetics appears to arise only after what is perceived to be a political impasse in the more mainstream African American Civil Rights and social justice struggle. Clearly something very similar occurred when we consider that the young militants of the Black Arts Movement were extremely frustrated with the Civil Rights Movement's strategies and tactics of nonviolence, civil disobedience, and passive resistance in light of seemingly ever-increasing displays of White supremacy and anti-Black racist exploitation, oppression, and violence by the mid-1960s.[45]

In African American studies it is generally accepted that the Black Arts Movement represented the cultural aesthetic arm of the Black Power Movement. As with recent studies that challenge the commonly held notion that the Harlem Renaissance only took place in Harlem or that the Civil Rights Movement mostly took place in the South, it is important to observe that the Black Arts Movement blossomed in a wide range of locations.[46] In fact, virtually every community and college campus with a substantial African American presence between 1965 and 1975 offered up its own unique Black Arts Movement-inspired organizations, cultural centers, theaters, art galleries, and recording studios, with neo-Black nationalist writers, actors, dancers, musicians, and visual artists.[47] For instance, noted Black Arts Movement organizations and institutions of the era included the Umbra Poets Workshop, the New Lafayette Theater, and the Black Arts Repertory Theater and School in New York, New York; the Committee for a Unified Newark and the Spirit House in Newark, New Jersey; BLKARTSOUTH, the Free Southern Theater, and the Southern Black Cultural Alliance in New Orleans, Louisiana; the Sudan Arts South/West in Houston, Texas; the Theater of Afro-Arts in Miami, Florida; the Black Arts Workshop in Little Rock, Arkansas; the Black Belt Cultural Center and the Children of Selma Theater in Selma, Alabama; the Blues Repertory Theater in Memphis, Tennessee; the Last Messengers in Greenville, Mississippi; the Kuumba Theater, the Association for the Advancement of Creative Musicians, the Organization of Black American Culture, and the African Commune of Bad Relevant Artists in Chicago, Illinois; Broadside Press in Detroit, Michigan; the Black Arts Group in Saint Louis, Missouri; Black Arts/West and the Black House in San Francisco, California; and the Watts Writers Workshop, the Underground Musicians Association, the Union of God's Musicians and Artists Ascension, and the Pan-Afrikan Peoples Arkestra in Los Angeles, California.[48]

Where many Black Power Movement radicals conceived of a movement for Black political and economic independence, others understood it to be more of a revolutionary political struggle against racism, capitalism, and other forms of imperialism in the United States and throughout the wider world.[49] However, yet another wing of the Black Power Movement interpreted it as a Black consciousness-raising and cultural nationalist movement, emphasizing *African roots* and *African American fruits*. It is this latter group of Black Power proponents who created and crusaded on behalf of the Black Arts Movement. Similar to the Black Power Movement, Black Arts intellectuals, artists, and activists embraced a wide range of political and cultural ideologies: from pre-colonial or indigenous African worldviews and religions to revolutionary Pan-Africanism; from Malcolm X-styled Islamic radicalism to Frantz Fanon-inspired revolutionary decolonization; and from Maulana Karenga's articulation of Kawaida philosophy-informed cultural nationalism to the Black Panther Party's emphasis on self-defense and Marxist-Leninism in the interest of African Americans. As Van Deburg perceptively put it:

> Despite an observable tendency for differing factions to claim the entire movement as their own, the multifaceted nature of Black Power was one of its most significant characteristics. One important mode of Black Power expression was cultural. Playwrights, novelists, songwriters, and artists all had their chance to forward a personalized vision of the militant protest sentiment. They used cultural forms as weapons in the struggle for liberation and, in doing so, provided a much-needed structural underpinning for the movement's more widely trumpeted political and economic tendencies.[50]

This means, then, that despite the jaw-dropping range of what would be otherwise considered conflicting ideological positions, Black Arts advocates generally held a collective belief in African American liberation and African Americans' right to self-definition and self-determination. However, in order to really and truly define or, rather, *redefine* themselves, ironically, 1960s and 1970s Black cultural aesthetes came to the startling conclusion that Blacks would have to radically deconstruct Whites and their much-vaunted Whiteness.[51] Here, we have come back to the diabolical dialectic of White superiority and Black inferiority and the precise reason why Black Arts advocates, almost as a rule, employed their "cultural forms as weapons in the struggle for liberation." Black Arts radicals sought to either recover or discover an authentic African American culture free from White capitalist commodification and consumer culture. This authentic African American culture was believed to be buried in African American folk philosophy and popular culture because the masses of Black folk were understood to have had little or no lasting contact with the dominant White bourgeois culture and values.[52]

The Black aesthetic

Obviously from the point of view of people who are critically conscious of their oppression, politics and aesthetics are frequently combined, in a sense searingly synthesized in ways often unimaginable and/or incomprehensible to people, particularly politicians, artists, and critics, who know nothing about the kinds of half-lived lives and dire struggles that oppression and incessant exploitation breed. This is precisely why the discourse on the development of a *Black aesthetic* specific to the special needs of African Americans during the 1960s and 1970s was such a major preoccupation for the Black Arts Movement.[53] It could be argued that at the conceptual core of the Black Arts Movement was an incendiary effort to, literally, *decolonize* every aspect of African American expressive culture or, rather, *the art of Black expression*.[54]

Although a heatedly debated concept between 1965 and 1975, with often widely differing definitions, the Black aesthetic could be said to collectively include a corpus of oral and written fiction and non-fiction that proclaimed the distinctiveness, beauty, and sometimes the supposed superiority of African American thought, culture, and aesthetics; an assemblage of radical political principles openly opposed to American apartheid and anti-Black racism, which promoted Black unity and solemn solidarity with other oppressed non-Whites, such as Native Americans, Asian Americans, Mexican Americans, and other Latinx folk; and an ethical exemplar and aesthetic criteria outlining "authentic" and "inauthentic" African American literature and art. Above all else, the Black aesthetic strongly stressed that "authentic" Black art has always been and must remain *historically grounded*, *politically engaged*, *socially uplifting*, and *consciousness-raising*.[55]

There is widespread consensus that the Black aesthetic provided the major theoretical thrust of the Black Arts Movement. The unrelenting search for, and definition and redefinition of, the Black aesthetic gave way to a set of distinctive discursive formations and discursive practices that continue to reverberate through hip hop soul (aka neo-soul), rap, and the wider Hip Hop Movement (e.g., see the work of Public Enemy, KRS-One, X Clan, Poor Righteous Teachers, Paris, the Jungle Brothers, A Tribe Called Quest, De La Soul, Queen Latifah, Brand Nubian, Arrested Development, Digable Planets, Meshell Ndegeocello, the Coup, Lauryn Hill, Wyclef Jean, Michael Franti & Spearhead, Erykah Badu, NaS, Common, Mos Def, Talib Kweli, Jill Scott, the Roots, India.Arie, Dead Prez, Kanye West, Georgia Anne Muldrow, Lupe Fiasco, J. Cole, Rapsody, Kendrick Lamar, and Jamila Woods). In fact, one of the more innovative aspects of the discourse on the Black aesthetic revolved around its unambiguous critique of "Western cultural aesthetics."[56] For instance, in "The Black Arts Movement," Larry Neal articulated the collective ambitions of the advocates of the Black aesthetic:

> The Black Arts Movement is radically opposed to any concept of the artist that alienates him from his community. This movement is the aesthetic and spiritual sister of the Black Power concept. As such, it envisions an art that speaks directly to the needs and aspirations of Black America. In order to perform this task, the Black Arts Movement proposes a radical reordering of the Western cultural aesthetic. It proposes a separate symbolism, mythology, critique, and iconology. The Black Arts and the Black Power concepts both relate broadly to the Afro-American's desire for self-determination and nationhood. Both concepts are nationalistic. One is concerned with the relationship between art and politics; the other with the art of politics.[57]

Emphasis should be placed on the fact that the Black Arts activists understood their movement to be the "aesthetic and spiritual sister of the Black Power concept," which is also to say, there was a deliberate division of labor between those who were primarily "concerned with the relationship between art and politics" (i.e., the Black Arts Movement) and those who were preoccupied with "the art of politics" (i.e., the Black Power Movement). This is an extremely important point, not simply because it reveals the sophistication of 1960s and 1970s African American aesthetic and political culture but, even more, because it highlights one of the major differences between the Black Arts Movement and the Harlem Renaissance: Black Arts Movement members' artistry was not a reaction to the nadir of "Negro" life or leadership between 1965 and 1975, but an audacious call to action that was inextricable from the radical politics of the broader Black Power Movement – a social and political movement that arose in the aftermath of the Civil Rights Movement, which many consider, in light of the signing of the Civil Rights Act of 1964 and the Voting Rights Act of 1965, the most successful social justice movement in African American history. In fact, James Smethurst has eloquently argued in *The Black Arts Movement: Literary Nationalism in the 1960s and 1970s*, "[i]t is a relative commonplace to briefly define Black Arts as the cultural wing of the Black Power Movement." However, "one could just as easily say that Black Power was the political wing of the Black Arts Movement."[58]

Here it is equally important to understand that when Neal wrote that the Black Arts Movement was the "aesthetic and spiritual sister of the Black Power concept," he was also hinting at the ways in which the two movements overlapped virtually from their inceptions. This is to say, going back to Smethurst's comment, during the Black Power period "Black radical politics" was not automatically privileged over "Black art," but Black politics and Black art were understood to be complementary. As a matter of fact, between 1965 and 1975 there was a kind of synergy and symmetry between "art and politics" and the "art of politics" in Black America that had not been achieved before, and has not been achieved since, the Black Power Movement and Black Arts Movement. Directly commenting on the overlap between the Black Power Movement and Black Arts Movement, Larry Neal shared:

> Recently, these two movements have begun to merge: the political values inherent in the Black Power concept are now finding concrete expression in the aesthetics of Afro-American dramatists, poets, choreographers, musicians, and novelists. A main tenet of Black Power is the necessity for Black people to define the world in their own terms. The Black artist has made the same point in the context of aesthetics. The two movements postulate that there are in fact and in spirit two Americas – one Black, one White. The Black artist takes this to mean that his primary duty is to speak to the spiritual and cultural needs of Black people. Therefore, the main thrust of this new breed of contemporary writers is to confront the contradictions arising out of the Black man's experience in the racist West. Currently, these writers are reevaluating Western aesthetics, the traditional role of the writer, and the

social function of art. Implicit in this reevaluation is the need to develop a "Black aesthetic." It is the opinion of many Black writers, I among them, that the Western aesthetic has run its course: it is impossible to construct anything meaningful within its decaying structure. We advocate a cultural revolution in art and ideas. The cultural values inherent in Western history must either be radicalized or destroyed, and we will probably find that even radicalization is impossible. In fact, what is needed is a whole new system of ideas.[59]

The Black Arts Movement sought to offer "a whole new system of ideas" that would complement the radical politics of the Black Power Movement. It was, as Neal explicitly stated, a "cultural revolution in art and ideas" that took very seriously the notion that *Black artists' work should be historically rooted, be socially relevant, be politically radical, and reflect the ongoing struggles of the Black community (or, rather, the Black nation)*. In fact, it could be said that the Black Arts Movement in several senses represented the 1960s' and 1970s' blossoming of the aspirations of the radical New Negroes of the Harlem Renaissance of the 1920s and 1930s insofar as the radical New Negroes were more or less the African American avant-garde of their era.[60] It is relatively easy to see, as the work of GerShun Avilez, Cheryl Clarke, Margo Crawford, Fred Moten, Aldon Nielsen, Carmen Phelps, Mike Sell, James Smethurst, and David Widener emphasizes, that the Black Arts Movement was the Black Power Movement's avant-garde.[61]

Neal's words also provide us with a conceptual framework in which to explore the ways the Black aesthetic was translated into the "soul aesthetic" that seemed to influence every major form of Black popular music during the Black Power period: from gospel and blues to jazz and rhythm & blues.[62] In several senses soul music can be taken as a deconstruction of Western European and European American musical aesthetics. It can also be viewed as a deconstruction and reconstruction of the aesthetic principles of rhythm & blues that emerged and were codified between roughly 1945 and 1965.[63] In line with Black Arts Movement members' emphasis on art serving a "social function" by "speak[ing] to the spiritual and cultural needs of Black people," increasingly Black musicians developed their own distinct aesthetic, *the soul aesthetic*, which was essentially a musical offshoot of the Black aesthetic. By the middle of the 1960s the soul aesthetic was influential enough to make the most successful African American-owned record company in U.S. history, the Motown Record Corporation, take notice and eventually alter both its sonic *and* its social vision.

Notes

1 On Carmichael's introduction of the Black Power slogan, see Stokely Carmichael, *Ready for Revolution: The Life and Struggles of Stokely Carmichael*, ed. Michael Thelwell (New York: Scribner, 2003), 501–19; and Peniel E. Joseph, *Stokely: A Life* (New York: Basic Civitas, 2014), 101–24. For further discussion of the Meredith March Against Fear, see Aram Goudsouzian, *Down to the Crossroads: Civil Rights, Black Power, and the Meredith March Against Fear* (New York: Farrar, Straus and Giroux, 2014).

2 William L. Van Deburg, *New Day in Babylon: The Black Power Movement and American Culture, 1965–1975* (Chicago: University of Chicago Press, 1992); Jeffrey Ogbar, *Black Power: Radical Politics and African American Identity* (Baltimore: Johns Hopkins University Press, 2004); Judson L. Jeffries, ed., *Black Power in the Belly of the Beast* (Urbana: University of Illinois Press, 2006); Ashley D. Farmer, *Remaking Black Power: How Black Women Transformed an Era* (Chapel Hill: University of North Carolina Press, 2017); Rhonda Y. Williams, *Concrete Demands: The Search for Black Power in the 20th Century* (New York: Routledge, 2015); and Peniel E. Joseph, *Waiting 'Til the Midnight Hour: A Narrative History of Black Power in America* (New York: Henry Holt, 2006).

3 Jacquelyn Dowd Hall, "The Long Civil Rights Movement and the Political Uses of the Past," *Journal of American History* 91, no. 4 (2005): 1233–263.

4 On the Pan-African pantheon that many members of the Black Power Movement drew inspiration from, see Scott Brown, *Fighting for Us: Maulana Karenga, the US Organization, and Black Cultural Nationalism* (New York: New York University Press, 2003), 6–37; Theodore Draper, *The Rediscovery of Black Nationalism* (New York: Penguin, 1970); Joseph, *Waiting 'Til the Midnight Hour*; Edward Onaci, *Free the Land: The Republic of New Afrika and the Pursuit of a Black Nation-State* (Chapel Hill: University of North Carolina Press, 2020), 15–42; Timothy B. Tyson, *Radio Free Dixie: Robert F. Williams and the Roots of Black Power* (Chapel Hill: University of North Carolina Press, 1999); Van Deburg, *New Day in Babylon*; Williams, *Concrete Demands*; and Komozi Woodard, *A Nation within a Nation: Amiri Baraka (LeRoi Jones) and Black Power Politics* (Chapel Hill: University of North Carolina Press, 1999), 49–68.

5 With regard to the contention that the Civil Rights Movement was as Northeastern, Midwestern, and Western as it was Southern, and each region developed distinct programs and practices to challenge racial segregation and bring about integration, see Stanley Keith Arnold, *Building the Beloved Community: Philadelphia's Interracial Civil Rights Organizations and Race Relations, 1930–1970* (Jackson: University Press of Mississippi, 2014); Shana Bernstein, *Bridges of Reform: Interracial Civil Rights Activism in Twentieth-Century Los Angeles* (New York: Oxford University Press, 2011); Martha Biondi, *To Stand and Fight: The Struggle for Civil Rights in Postwar New York City* (Cambridge: Harvard University Press, 2006); Matthew Countryman, *Up South: Civil Rights and Black Power in Philadelphia* (Philadelphia: University of Pennsylvania Press, 2007); Emilye Crosby, ed., *Civil Rights History from the Ground Up: Local Struggles, a National Movement* (Athens: University of Georgia Press, 2011); Sidney Fine, *"Expanding the Frontiers of Civil Rights": Michigan, 1948–1968* (Detroit: Wayne State University Press, 2000); Mary Lou Finley, Bernard LaFayette, James R. Ralph, and Pam Smith, eds., *The Chicago Freedom Movement: Martin Luther King Jr. and Civil Rights Activism in the North* (Lexington: University Press of Kentucky, 2016); Douglas Flamming, *Bound for Freedom: Black Los Angeles in Jim Crow America* (Berkeley: University of California Press, 2005); Patrick D. Jones, *The Selma of the North: Civil Rights Insurgency in Milwaukee* (Cambridge: Harvard University Press, 2009); Elaine K'Meyer, *Civil Rights in the Gateway to the South: Louisville, Kentucky, 1945–1980* (Lexington: University Press of Kentucky, 2011); Sonia Song-Ha Lee, *Building a Latino Civil Rights Movement: Puerto Ricans, African Americans, and the Pursuit of Racial Justice in New York City* (Chapel Hill: University of North Carolina Press, 2014); Peter B. Levy, *Civil War on Race Street: The Civil Rights Movement in Cambridge, Maryland* (Gainesville: University Press of Florida, 2003); Robert B. McKersie, *A Decisive Decade: An Insider's View of the Chicago Civil Rights Movement during the 1960s* (Carbondale: Southern Illinois University Press, 2013); Paul T. Miller, *The Postwar Struggle for Civil Rights: African Americans in San Francisco, 1945–1975* (New York: Routledge, 2010); Abigail Perkiss, *Making Good Neighbors: Civil Rights, Liberalism, and Integration in Postwar Philadelphia* (Ithaca: Cornell University Press, 2016); James R. Ralph, *Northern Protest: Martin Luther King, Chicago, and the Civil Rights Movement* (Cambridge: Harvard University Press, 1994); Todd E. Robinson, *A City within a City: The Black Freedom Struggle in Grand Rapids, Michigan* (Philadelphia: Temple University Press, 2013); Thomas J. Sugrue, *Sweet Land of Liberty: The Forgotten Struggle for Civil*

Rights in the North (New York: Penguin/Random House, 2009); Clarence Taylor, *Reds at the Blackboard: Communism, Civil Rights, and the New York City Teachers Union* (New York: Columbia University Press, 2011); Clarence Taylor, ed., *Civil Rights in New York City: From World War II to the Giuliani Era* (New York: Fordham University Press, 2011); Jeanne Theoharis, *A More Beautiful and Terrible History: The Uses and Misuses of Civil Rights History* (Boston: Beacon Press, 2018); Jeanne Theoharis and Komozi Woodard, eds., *Freedom North: Black Freedom Struggles Outside the South, 1940–1980* (New York: Palgrave Macmillan, 2003); Jeanne Theoharis and Komozi Woodard, eds., *Groundwork: Local Black Freedom Movements in America* (New York: New York University Press, 2005); and Yohuru R. Williams, *Black Politics/White Power: Civil Rights, Black Power and the Black Panthers in New Haven* (St. James, NY: Brandywine Press, 2000).

6 Hall, "The Long Civil Rights Movement," 1233.

7 Ibid., 1235–236. For further discussion of the ways in which the Civil Rights Movement and postwar mass media developed along parallel paths, see William Barlow, *Voice Over: The Making of Black Radio* (Philadelphia: Temple University Press, 1999); Maurice Berger, *For All the World to See: Visual Culture and the Struggle for Civil Rights* (New Haven: Yale University Press, 2010); Aniko Bodroghkozy, *Equal Time: Television and the Civil Rights Movement* (Urbana: University of Illinois Press, 2013); Steven D. Classen, *Watching Jim Crow: The Struggles over Mississippi TV, 1955–1969* (Durham: Duke University Press, 2004); Allison Graham, *Framing the South: Hollywood, Television, and Race during the Civil Rights Struggle* (Baltimore: Johns Hopkins University Press, 2003); Thomas Cripps, *Making Movies Black: The Hollywood Message Movie from World War II to the Civil Rights Era* (New York: Oxford University Press, 1993); Matthew F. Delmont, *Why Busing Failed: Race, Media, and the National Resistance to School Desegregation* (Berkeley: University of California Press, 2016); Mary L. Dudziak, *Cold War Civil Rights: Race and the Image of American Democracy* (Princeton: Princeton University Press, 2011); Kay Mills, *Changing Channels: The Civil Rights Case that Transformed Television* (Jackson: University Press of Mississippi, 2004); Ellen C. Scott, *Cinema Civil Rights: Regulation, Repression, and Race in the Classical Hollywood Era* (New Brunswick: Rutgers University Press, 2015); Sasha Torres, *Black, White, and in Color: Television and Black Civil Rights* (Princeton: Princeton University Press, 2003); Brain Ward, ed., *Media, Culture, and the Modern African American Freedom Struggle* (Gainesville: University Press of Florida, 2001); Brian Ward, *Radio and the Struggle for Civil Rights in the South* (Gainesville: University Press of Florida, 2004); David J. Wallace, *Massive Resistance and Media Suppression: The Segregationist Response to Dissent During the Civil Rights Movement* (El Paso: LFB Scholarly Publishing, 2013); and Mary Ann Watson, *The Expanding Vista: American Television in the Kennedy Years* (Durham: Duke University Press, 1994).

8 Hall, "The Long Civil Rights Movement," 1236.

9 Hasan Kwame Jeffries, "Searching for a New Freedom," in *A Companion to African American History*, ed. Alton Hornsby (Malden: Blackwell, 2005), 505.

10 Ibid., 505.

11 On the Black Power Movement, anti–Black racist violence, and police collusion with both White vigilante and state violence against Blacks, see Curtis J. Austin, *Up Against the Wall: Violence in the Making and Unmaking of the Black Panther Party* (Fayetteville: University of Arkansas Press, 2006); Nancy K. Bristow, *Steeped in the Blood of Racism: Black Power, Law and Order, and the 1970 Shootings at Jackson State College* (New York: Oxford University Press, 2020); Goudsouzian, *Down to the Crossroads*; Kenneth Robert Janken, *The Wilmington Ten: Violence, Injustice, and the Rise of Black Politics in the 1970s* (Chapel Hill: University of North Carolina Press, 2015); Yasuhiro Katagiri, *Black Freedom, White Resistance, and Red Menace: Civil Rights and Anti-Communism in the Jim Crow South* (Baton Rouge: Louisiana State University Press, 2014); J. Todd Moye, *Let the People Decide: Black Freedom and White Resistance Movements in Sunflower County, Mississippi, 1945–1986* (Chapel Hill: University of North Carolina Press, 2004); Donna Jean Murch, *Living for the City: Migration, Education, and the Rise of the Black Panther Party in*

Oakland, California (Chapel Hill: University of North Carolina Press, 2010); Onaci, *Free the Land*; James D. Robenalt, *Ballots and Bullets: Black Power Politics and Urban Guerrilla Warfare in 1968 Cleveland* (Chicago: Lawrence Hill Books, 2018); Christopher B. Strain, *Pure Fire: Self-Defense as Activism in the Civil Rights Era* (Athens: University of Georgia Press, 2005); Simon Wendt, *The Spirit and the Shotgun: Armed Resistance and the Struggle for Civil Rights* (Gainesville: University Press of Florida, 2007); and Akinyele Omowale Umoja, *We Will Shoot Back: Armed Resistance in the Mississippi Freedom Movement* (New York: New York University Press, 2014).

12 Malcolm X, "The Ballot or the Bullet" (speech delivered at King Solomon Baptist Church, Detroit, Michigan, April 12, 1964) http://americanradioworks.publicradio. org/features/blackspeech/mx.html. On Malcolm X, see Peter L. Goldman, *The Death and Life of Malcolm X* (Urbana: University of Illinois Press, 1979); Malcolm X, *The Auto-biography of Malcolm X*, with Alex Haley (New York: Ballantine Books, 1999); Manning Marable, *Malcolm X: A Life of Reinvention* (New York: Penguin, 2011); Manning Marable and Garrett Felber, eds., *The Portable Malcolm X Reader: A Man Who Stands for Nothing Will Fall for Anything* (New York: Penguin, 2013); Les Payne and Tamara Payne, *The Dead Are Arising: The Life of Malcolm X* (New York: Liveright, 2020); William W. Sales, *From Civil Rights to Black Liberation: Malcolm X and the Organization of Afro-American Unity* (Boston: South End Press, 1994); Robert E. Terrill, *Malcolm X: Inventing Racial Judgment* (East Lansing: Michigan State University Press, 2007); and Robert E. Terrill, ed., *The Cambridge Companion to Malcolm X* (Cambridge: Cambridge University Press, 2012).

13 Doug Bradley and Craig Werner, *We Gotta Get Out of This Place: The Soundtrack of the Vietnam War* (Amherst: University of Massachusetts Press, 2015), 91–144; Michael Haralambos, *Soul Music: The Birth of a Sound in Black America* (New York: Da Capo, 1975), 135–55; Brian Ward, *Just My Soul Responding: Rhythm & Blues, Black Conscious-ness, and Race Relations* (Berkeley: University of California Press, 1998), 388–416; Craig Werner, *Higher Ground: Stevie Wonder, Aretha Franklin, Curtis Mayfield, and the Rise and Fall of American Soul* (New York: Crown Publishers, 2004), 63–187; and Craig Werner, *Change Is Gonna Come: Music, Race & the Soul of America* (Ann Arbor: University of Michigan Press, 2006), 103–73.

14 Amy Abugo Ongiri, *Spectacular Blackness: The Cultural Politics of the Black Power Movement and the Search for a Black Aesthetic* (Charlottesville: University of Virginia Press, 2009), 108–9; Van Deburg, *New Day in Babylon*, 2–9; and Woodard, *A Nation within a Nation*, 49–68.

15 On the various ideologies of the Black Power Movement, see Jeffries, *Black Power in the Belly of the Beast*, 1–11, 297–308; Peniel E. Joseph, ed., *The Black Power Movement: Rethinking the Civil Rights-Black Power Era* (New York: Routledge, 2006), 1–25; John T. McCartney, *Black Power Ideologies: An Essay in African American Political Thought* (Phila-delphia: Temple University Press, 1993), 111–90; Ogbar, *Black Power*, 37–67; and Van Deburg, *New Day in Babylon*, 112–91.

16 For further discussion of Black Power proponents' emphasis on self-defensive violence over nonviolence, see Austin, *Up Against the Wall*; Strain, *Pure Fire*; Wendt, *The Spirit and the Shotgun*; and Umoja, *We Will Shoot Back*.

17 On the Republic of New Africa, see Donald Cunnigen, "The Republic of New Africa in Mississippi," in *Black Power in the Belly of the Beast*, ed. Judson L. Jeffries (Urbana: Uni-versity of Illinois Press, 2006), 93–115; Imari Abubakari Obadele, *Revolution and Nation-Building: Strategy for Building the Black Nation in America* (Detroit: House of Songhay, 1970); Imari Abubakari Obadele, "The Republic of New Africa: An Independent Black Nation," *Black World* 20 (1971): 81–89; Imari Abubakari Obadele, "The Struggle Is for Land," *The Black Scholar* 3, no. 6 (1972): 24–36; Imari Abubakari Obadele, *Foundations of the Black Nation* (Detroit: House of Songhay, 1975); and Onaci, *Free the Land*.

18 On Karenga and the Us Organization, see Molefi Kete Asante, *Maulana Karenga: An Intellectual Portrait* (Cambridge: Polity Press, 2009); Brown, *Fighting for Us*; Floyd W.

Hayes and Judson L. Jeffries, "*Us* Does Not Stand for United Slaves!" in *Black Power in the Belly of the Beast*, ed. Judson L. Jeffries (Urbana: University of Illinois Press, 2006), 67–92; Maulana Karenga, "Us, Kawaida, and the Black Liberation Movement in the 1960s: Culture, Knowledge, and Struggle," *Engines of the Black Power Movement: Essays on the Influence of Civil Rights Actions, Arts, And Islam,* ed. James L. Conyers (Jefferson, NC: McFarland & Co., 2007), 95–133; and Keith A. Mayes, *Kwanzaa: Black Power and the Making of the African American Holiday Tradition* (New York: Routledge, 2009).

19 There is a significant body of secondary literature on the Black Panther Party, some of the most noteworthy sources include Paul Alkebulan, *Survival Pending Revolution: The History of the Black Panther Party* (Tuscaloosa: University of Alabama Press, 2012); Joshua Bloom and Waldo E. Martin, *Black Against Empire: The History and Politics of the Black Panther Party* (Berkeley: University of California Press, 2016); Kathleen Cleaver and George Katsiaficas, eds., *Liberation, Imagination, and the Black Panther Party: A New Look at the Panthers and Their Legacy* (New York: Routledge, 2001); Judson L. Jeffries, ed., *The Black Panther Party in a City Near You* (Athens: University of Georgia Press, 2018); Judson L. Jeffries, ed., *Comrades: A Local History of the Black Panther Party* (Bloomington: Indiana University Press, 2007); Judson L. Jeffries, ed., *On the Ground: The Black Panther Party in Communities across America* (Jackson: University Press of Mississippi, 2010); Charles E. Jones, ed., *The Black Panther Party [Reconsidered]* (Baltimore: Black Classic Press, 1998); Jama Lazerow and Yohuru Williams, eds., *In Search of the Black Panther Party: New Perspectives on a Revolutionary Movement* (Durham: Duke University Press, 2006); Sean L. Malloy, *Out of Oakland: Black Panther Party Internationalism during the Cold War* (Ithaca: Cornell University Press, 2017); Murch, *Living for the City*; Donna Jean Murch, *Revolution in Our Lifetime: A Short History of the Black Panther Party* (London: Verso, 2017); Jane Rhodes, *Framing the Black Panthers: The Spectacular Rise of a Black Power Icon* (Urbana: University of Illinois Press, 2017); Bobby Seale, *Power to the People: The World of the Black Panthers*, with photographs by Stephen Shames (New York: Abrams, 2016); Robyn C. Spencer, *The Revolution Has Come: Black Power, Gender, and the Black Panther Party in Oakland* (Durham: Duke University Press, 2016); Williams, *Black Politics/White Power*; Yohuru R. Williams and Jama Lazerow, eds., *Liberated Territory: Untold Local Perspectives on the Black Panther Party* (Durham: Duke University Press, 2009).

20 Nelson George, *Where Did Our Love Go?: The Rise and Fall of the Motown Sound* (Urbana: University of Illinois Press, 2007), 50–147.

21 Mark Anthony Neal, *What the Music Said: Black Popular Music and Black Public Culture* (New York: Routledge, 1998), 33–36.

22 *Brown v. the Board of Education* (1954), as is well known, desegregated public schools. *Gideon v. Wainwright* (1963) granted accused individuals the right to an attorney. Prior to *Gideon v. Wainwright* an attorney was provided by the state only in cases that could result in the death penalty. *Heart of Atlanta v. the United States* (1964) stipulated that any business which participated in interstate commerce was required to observe all federal Civil Rights legislation. The Civil Rights Act of 1964 stopped racial segregation and discrimination in all public accommodations, gave the U.S. Attorney General the authority to intervene on behalf of the victims of Civil Rights violations, and forbade employers to discriminate against people based on their race. The Twenty-Fourth Amendment (1964) outlawed poll taxes in all fifty states. In other words, states could no longer charge people for exercising their right to vote. And, finally, the Voting Rights Act of 1965 essentially guaranteed the Fifteenth Amendment to the U.S. Constitution, which prohibited U.S. citizens from being denied the right to vote based on their race. The Voting Rights Act also ended literacy tests and provided the U.S. Attorney General with the authority to intervene on behalf of those voters who had been discriminated against based on their race. For further discussion of 1950s, 1960s, and 1970s Civil Rights legislation and its impact on post-Civil Rights Movement America, and for the most noteworthy works that informed my interpretation here, see Megan Ming Francis, *Civil Rights and the Making of the Modern American State* (Cambridge: Cambridge University Press, 2014); Jeffrey

D. Gonda, *Unjust Deeds: The Restrictive Covenant Cases and the Making of the Civil Rights Movement* (Chapel Hill: University of North Carolina Press, 2015); Jack Greenberg, *Crusaders in the Courts: Legal Battles of the Civil Rights Movement* (New York: Twelve Tables Press, 2004); and Timothy J. Minchin, "Making Best Use of the New Laws: The NAACP and the Fight for Civil Rights in the South, 1965–1975," *Journal of Southern History* 74, no. 3 (2008): 669–702.

23 Claudrena N. Harold, *When Sunday Comes: Gospel Music in the Soul and Hip Hop Eras* (Champaign: University of Illinois Press, 2020); Neal, *What the Music Said*, 36–53.

24 Neal, *What the Music Said*, 44–45.

25 Joseph, *Waiting 'Til the Midnight Hour*, 132–73; Ogbar, *Black Power*, 123–25; Van Deburg, *New Day in Babylon*, 11–28.

26 Dan Berger, *Captive Nation: Black Prison Organizing in the Civil Rights Era* (Chapel Hill: University of North Carolina Press, 2016); Lisa M. Corrigan, *Prison Power: How Prison Influenced the Movement for Black Liberation* (Jackson: University Press of Mississippi, 2016); Farmer, *Remaking Black Power*; Joseph, *The Black Power Movement*, 1–25; Kwasi Konadu, *View from the East: Black Cultural Nationalism and Education in New York City* (Syracuse: Syracuse University Press, 2009); Leonard N. Moore, *The Defeat of Black Power: Civil Rights and the National Black Political Convention of 1972* (Baton Rouge: Louisiana State University Press, 2018); Fabio Rojas, *From Black Power to Black Studies: How a Radical Social Movement Became an Academic Discipline* (Baltimore: Johns Hopkins University Press, 2007); Michael Simanga, *Amiri Baraka and the Congress of African People: History and Memory* (New York: Palgrave Macmillan, 2015); James Edward Smethurst, *The Black Arts Movement: Literary Nationalism in the 1960s and 1970s* (Chapel Hill: University of North Carolina Press, 2005); Kimberly Springer, *Living for the Revolution: Black Feminist Organizations, 1968–1980* (Durham: Duke University Press, 2005), 1–44; Heather Ann Thompson, *Blood in the Water: The Attica Prison Uprising of 1971 and Its Legacy* (New York: Pantheon, 2016); Donald F. Tibbs, *From Black Power to Prison Power: The Making of Jones v. North Carolina Prisoners' Labor Union* (New York: Palgrave Macmillan, 2012); Van Deburg, *New Day in Babylon*, 63–111; Tom Wicker, *A Time to Die: The Attica Prison Revolt* (Chicago: Haymarket Books, 2011); Daniel Widener, *Black Arts West: Culture and Struggle in Post-War Los Angeles* (Durham: Duke University Press, 2010); Woodard, *A Nation within a Nation*, 1–3, 202–18.

27 On Black Power studies, see Joseph, *The Black Power Movement*, 1–25; Peniel Joseph, ed., "Black Power Studies: A New Scholarship," *The Black Scholar* 31, no. 3/4 (2001): 1–84; Peniel Joseph, ed., "Black Power Studies II," *The Black Scholar* 32, no. 1 (2002): 1–68; Peniel Joseph, ed., "The New Black Power History: A *Souls* Special Issue," *Souls* 9, no. 4 (2007); Peniel Joseph, "Historians and the Black Power Movement," *OAH Magazine of History* 22, no. 3 (2008): 8–15; Peniel Joseph, "The Black Power Movement: A State of the Field," *Journal of American History* 96, no. 3 (2009): 751–76.

28 Van Deburg, *New Day in Babylon*, 27.

29 Ibid., 27.

30 Brown, *Fighting for Us*, 49–51.

31 Van Deburg, *New Day in Babylon*, 11–28.

32 Stokely Carmichael and Charles V. Hamilton, *Black Power: The Politics of Liberation in America* (New York: Vintage, 1992; orig. pub. 1967), 47.

33 Van Deburg, *New Day in Babylon*, 27.

34 Joseph, *Waiting 'Til the Midnight Hour*, 163.

35 Ibid., 142–62.

36 Ibid., 152–53.

37 Ogbar, *Black Power*, 145–53.

38 Joseph, *Waiting 'Til the Midnight Hour*, 172.

39 On the unprecedented Black radicalism of the Black Power Movement, see Farmer, *Remaking Black Power*; Herbert H. Haines, *Black Radicals and the Civil Rights Mainstream, 1954–1970* (Knoxville: University of Tennessee Press, 1988); Ogbar, *Black Power*;

Rhodes, *Framing the Black Panthers*; Robenalt, *Ballots and Bullets*; Hettie V. Williams, *We Shall Overcome to We Shall Overrun: The Collapse of the Civil Rights Movement and the Black Power Revolt* (Lanham: University Press of America, 2009).

40 Malcolm X, *By Any Means Necessary*, ed. George Breitman (New York: Pathfinder, 1992).

41 Richard D. Benson, *Fighting for Our Place in the Sun: Malcolm X and the Radicalization of the Black Student Movement 1960–1973* (New York: Peter Lang, 2015); Marable, *Malcolm X*; Terrill, *Malcolm X*.

42 Van Deburg, *New Day in Babylon*, 21.

43 Ibid., 9.

44 On the Black Power Movement as essentially a cultural revolution, see GerShun Avilez, *Radical Aesthetics and Modern Black Nationalism* (Urbana: University of Illinois Press, 2016), 1–94; Konadu, *View from the East*, xix–xxxiii, 1–25; Mayes, *Kwanzaa*, 1–134; Ogbar, *Black Power*, 106–22; Van Deburg, *New Day in Babylon*, 192–291.

45 Smethurst, *The Black Arts Movement*, 1–22.

46 For work that challenges the notion that the Harlem Renaissance only took place in Harlem, see Davarian L. Baldwin, *Chicago's New Negroes: Modernity, the Great Migration, and Black Urban Life* (Chapel Hill: University of North Carolina Press, 2007); Davarian L. Baldwin and Minkah Makalani, eds., *Escape from New York: The New Negro Renaissance beyond Harlem* (Minneapolis: University of Minnesota Press, 2013); Bruce A. Glasrud and Cary D. Wintz, eds., *The Harlem Renaissance in the American West: The New Negro's Western Experience* (New York: Routledge, 2012); Darlene Clark Hine and John McCluskey, eds., *The Black Chicago Renaissance* (Urbana: University of Illinois Press, 2012); Anne Meis Knupfer, *The Chicago Black Renaissance and Women's Activism* (Urbana: University of Illinois, 2006); Steven C. Tracy, ed., *Writers of the Black Chicago Renaissance* (Urbana: University of Illinois Press, 2012). And for work that challenges the contention that the Civil Rights Movement mostly took place in the South, see the above-cited Arnold, *Building the Beloved Community*; Bernstein, *Bridges of Reform*; Biondi, *To Stand and Fight*; Countryman, *Up South*; Fine, *"Expanding the Frontiers of Civil Rights"*; Finley, et al, *The Chicago Freedom Movement*; Jones, *The Selma of the North*; Lee, *Building a Latino Civil Rights Movement*; Levy, *Civil War on Race Street*; Miller, *The Postwar Struggle for Civil Rights*; Perkiss, *Making Good Neighbors*; Ralph, *Northern Protest*; Sugrue, *Sweet Land of Liberty*; Theoharis and Woodard, *Freedom North*; Theoharis and Woodard, *Groundwork*; Williams, *Black Politics/White Power*.

47 Smethurst, *The Black Arts Movement*, 100–366.

48 For further discussion of the Black Arts Movement, see Avilez, *Radical Aesthetics and Modern Black Nationalism*; John H. Bracey, Sonia Sanchez, and James Edward Smethurst, eds., *SOS–Calling All Black People: A Black Arts Movement Reader* (Amherst: University of Massachusetts Press, 2014); Susan E. Cahan, *Mounting Frustration: The Art Museum in the Age of Black Power* (Durham: Duke University Press, 2016); Cheryl Clarke, *"After Mecca": Women Poets and the Black Arts Movement* (New Brunswick: Rutgers University Press, 2005); Lisa Gail Collins and Margo Natalie Crawford, eds., *New Thoughts on the Black Arts Movement* (New Brunswick: Rutgers University Press, 2006); Margo Natalie Crawford, *Black Post-Blackness: The Black Arts Movement and Twenty-First-Century Aesthetics* (Urbana: University of Illinois Press, 2017); Robert L. Douglas, *Resistance, Insurgence, and Identity: The Art of Mari Evans, Nelson Stevens, and the Black Arts Movement* (Trenton: Africa World Press, 2008); Gene Andrew Jarrett, "The Black Arts Movement and Its Scholars," *American Quarterly* 57, no. 4 (2005): 1243–51; Kellie Jones, *South of Pico: African American Artists in Los Angeles in the 1960s and 1970s* (Durham: Duke University Press, 2017); Larry P. Neal, "The Black Arts Movement," *Drama Review* 12, no. 4 (1968): 29–39; Larry P. Neal, *Visions of a Liberated Future: Black Arts Movement Writings*, ed. Michael Schwartz (New York: Thunder's Mouth Press, 1989); Ongiri, *Spectacular Blackness*; Carmen L. Phelps, *Visionary Women Writers of Chicago's Black Arts Movement* (Jackson: University Press of Mississippi, 2012); Howard Rambsy, *The Black*

Arts Enterprise and the Production of African American Poetry (Ann Arbor: University of Michigan Press, 2011); Kalamu ya Salaam, *The Magic of Juju: An Appreciation of the Black Arts Movement* (Chicago: Third World Press, 2016); Mike Sell, *Avant-Garde Performance and the Limits of Criticism: Approaching the Living Theatre, Happenings/Fluxus, and the Black Arts Movement* (Ann Arbor: University of Michigan Press, 2008); David Lionel Smith, "The Black Arts Movement and Its Critics," *American Literary History* 3, no. 1 (1991): 93–110; Julius E. Thompson, *Dudley Randall, Broadside Press, and the Black Arts Movement in Detroit, 1960–1995* (Jefferson: McFarland, 2005); Eleanor W. Traylor, "Women Writers of the Black Arts Movement," in *The Cambridge Companion to African American Women's Literature*, eds. Angelyn Mitchell and Danille K. Taylor (Cambridge: Cambridge University Press, 2009), 50–70; Widener, *Black Arts West*; Zoé Whitley, Susan E. Cahan, and Mark Godfrey, eds., *Soul of a Nation: Art in the Age of Black Power* (New York: Distributed Art Publishers/Tate, 2017).

49 For conceptions of the Black Power Movement as a revolutionary political struggle against racism, capitalism, and other forms of imperialism in the United States and throughout the wider world, see Alkebulan, *Survival Pending Revolution*; Bloom and Martin, *Black Against Empire*; Cleaver and Katsiaficas, *Liberation, Imagination, and the Black Panther Party*; Jones, *The Black Panther Party [Reconsidered]*; Lazerow and Williams, *In Search of the Black Panther Party*; Malloy, *Out of Oakland*; Kate Quinn, ed., *Black Power in the Caribbean* (Gainesville: University Press of Florida, 2015); Nico Slate, ed., *Black Power beyond Borders: The Global Dimensions of the Black Power Movement* (New York: Palgrave Macmillan, 2012); Quito Swan, *Black Power in Bermuda: The Struggle for Decolonization* (New York: Palgrave Macmillan, 2010); Robert Vitalis, *White World Order, Black Power Politics: The Birth of American International Relations* (Ithaca: Cornell University Press, 2015).

50 Van Deburg, *New Day in Babylon*, 9.

51 On the Black Arts Movement's deconstructions of Whiteness, see Avilez, *Radical Aesthetics and Modern Black Nationalism*, 29–60; Collins and Crawford, *New Thoughts on the Black Arts Movement*, 1–22; Van Deburg, *New Day in Babylon*, 260–72.

52 Van Deburg, *New Day in Babylon*, 192–247.

53 For further discussion of the Black aesthetic, especially as an outgrowth of the Black Arts Movement, and for the most noteworthy works that informed my interpretation here, see Avilez, *Radical Aesthetics and Modern Black Nationalism*; Houston A. Baker, *The Journey Back: Issues in Black Literature and Criticism* (Chicago: University of Chicago Press, 1980); Houston A. Baker, *Afro-American Poetics: Revisions of Harlem and the Black Aesthetic* (Madison: University of Wisconsin Press, 1988); Amiri Baraka and Larry Neal, eds., *Black Fire: An Anthology of Afro-American Writing* (New York: William Morrow & Co./Apollo, 1969); Melba Joyce Boyd, *Wrestling with the Muse: Dudley Randall and the Broadside Press* (New York: Columbia University Press, 2003); Collins and Crawford, *New Thoughts on the Black Arts Movement*; Crawford, *Black Post-Blackness*; Addison Gayle, ed., *Black Expression: Essays By and About Black Americans in the Creative Arts* (New York: Weybright & Talley, 1969); Addison Gayle, ed., *Black Situation* (New York: Horizon Press, 1970); Addison Gayle, ed., *The Black Aesthetic* (Garden City, NY: Doubleday, 1972); Iton, *In Search of the Black Fantastic*; Maulana Karenga, "Black Art: A Rhythmic Reality of Revolution," *Negro Digest* 3 (1968): 5–9; Maulana Karenga, "Black Cultural Nationalism," in *The Black Aesthetic*, ed. Addison Gayle (Garden City, NY: Doubleday, 1972), 32–38; Maulana Karenga, "Black Art: Mute Matter Given Force and Function," in *The Norton Anthology of African American Literature*, eds. Henry Louis Gates and Nellie Y. McKay (New York: Norton, 1997), 1972–977; Neal, "The Black Arts Movement"; Neal, *Visions of a Liberated Future*; Ongiri, *Spectacular Blackness*; Dudley Randall, *Roses and Revolutions: The Selected Writings of Dudley Randall*, ed. Melba Joyce Boyd (Detroit: Wayne State University Press, 2009); Evie Shockley, *Renegade Poetics: Black Aesthetics and Formal Innovation in African American Poetry* (Iowa City: University of Iowa Press, 2011); Paul C. Taylor, *Black is Beautiful: A Philosophy of Black Aesthetics* (Hoboken, NJ:

John Wiley & Sons, 2016); Thompson, *Dudley Randall, Broadside Press, and the Black Arts Movement*.

54 Smethurst, *The Black Arts Movement*, 57–99. See also Waldo E. Martin, *No Coward Soldiers: Black Cultural Politics in Postwar America* (Cambridge: Harvard University Press, 2005), 10–43.

55 Avilez, *Radical Aesthetics and Modern Black Nationalism*, 1–28; Collins and Crawford, *New Thoughts on the Black Arts Movement*, 1–22; Gayle, *The Black Aesthetic*; Karenga, "Black Art: Mute Matter Given Force and Function"; Aaron Myers, "The Black Aesthetic," in *Africana: The Encyclopedia of the African and African American Experience*, eds. Kwame Anthony Appiah and Henry Louis Gates (New York: Basic Civitas, 1999), 239; Neal, "The Black Arts Movement"; Ongiri, *Spectacular Blackness*, 7–17, 97–100, 111–17; Smethurst, *The Black Arts Movement*, 57–84, Van Deburg, *New Day in Babylon*, 170–71, 181–91.

56 Avilez, *Radical Aesthetics and Modern Black Nationalism*, 29–60; Emily Bernard, "A Familiar Strangeness: The Spectre of Whiteness in the Harlem Renaissance and the Black Arts Movement," in *New Thoughts on the Black Arts Movement*, eds. Lisa Gail Collins and Margo Natalie Crawford (New Brunswick: Rutgers University Press, 2006), 255–72.

57 Neal, "The Black Arts Movement," 29. See also Collins and Crawford, *New Thoughts on the Black Arts Movement*, 1–22.

58 Smethurst, *The Black Arts Movement*, 14. See also Van Deburg, *New Day in Babylon*, 181–91.

59 Neal, "The Black Arts Movement," 29.

60 On the Harlem Renaissance as an expression of African American avant-gardism during the 1920s and 1930s, see Geneviève Fabre and Michel Feith, eds., *Temples for Tomorrow: Looking Back at the Harlem Renaissance* (Bloomington: Indiana University Press, 2001); George Hutchinson, *The Harlem Renaissance in Black and White* (Cambridge: Harvard University Press, 1995); George Hutchinson, ed., *The Cambridge Companion to the Harlem Renaissance* (New York: Cambridge University Press, 2007); David Levering Lewis, *When Harlem Was in Vogue* (New York: Oxford University Press, 1989); Fionnghuala Sweeney and Kate Marsh, eds., *Afromodernisms: Paris, Harlem and the Avant-Garde* (Edinburgh: Edinburgh University Press, 2013).

61 Avilez, *Radical Aesthetics and Modern Black Nationalism*; Clarke, *"After Mecca"*; Crawford, *Black Post-Blackness*; Fred Moten, *In the Break: The Aesthetics of the Black Radical Tradition* (Minneapolis: University of Minnesota Press, 2003); Aldon Lynn Nielsen, *Black Chant: Languages of African American Postmodernism* (Cambridge: Cambridge University Press, 1997); Phelps, *Visionary Women Writers of Chicago's Black Arts Movement*; Mike Sell, *Avant-Garde Performance and the Limits of Criticism: Approaching the Living Theatre, Happenings/Fluxus, and the Black Arts Movement* (Ann Arbor: University of Michigan Press, 2008); Smethurst, *The Black Arts Movement*; Widener, *Black Arts West*.

62 On the pervasive influence of the soul aesthetic, see Michael Awkward, *Soul Covers: Rhythm & Blues Remakes and the Struggle for Artistic Identity (Aretha Franklin, Al Green, Phoebe Snow)* (Durham: Duke University Press, 2007), 1–24; Samuel A. Floyd, *The Power of Black Music: Interpreting its History from Africa to the United States* (New York: Oxford University Press, 1995), 183–211; William L. Van Deburg, *Black Camelot: African American Culture Heroes in Their Times, 1960–1980* (Chicago: University of Chicago Press, 1997), 197–242.

63 Nelson George, *The Death of Rhythm & Blues* (New York: Pantheon Books, 1988), 59–94; Neal, *What the Music Said*, 25–53; Ongiri, *Spectacular Blackness*, 124–58.

2

MOTOWN AND THE EMERGENCE OF MESSAGE MUSIC

Motown: more than "sell-out" soul and superficial funk

Over the years scholarly engagements of Motown Records' classic years between 1959 and 1979 have most often interpreted the company and its artists as purveyors of "pop-R&B" or "sell-out" soul music. However, any serious treatment of classic Motown must acknowledge that along with its preoccupation with placing hit singles on the pop charts was a burgeoning undercurrent of Black consciousness that musically matured during the Black Power Movement era, roughly between 1965 and 1975. For instance, and flying in the face of those critics who quickly dismiss Motown as "sell-out" soul music, between 1965 and 1975 the company released dozens of "message" soul and funk songs from Marvin Gaye's immortal "What's Going On?" and Eddie Kendricks' "My People . . . Hold On" to Stevie Wonder's "Living for the City" and the Temptations' "Message from a Black Man." It was not merely the men of Motown who made message music during the Black Power period. Alongside the soul brothers, Motown soul sisters such as Martha Reeves & the Vandellas checked in with "I Should be Proud," Gladys Knight & the Pips with "Friendship Train," and Syreeta with "Black Maybe." Even the iconic Diana Ross & the Supremes caught the message song bug and released "I'm Livin' in Shame," "The Young Folks," and "Shadows of Society," among others.[1]

Obviously, Motown's music was more complex during the Black Power period than most fans and critics have previously understood. And although often facile correlations have been made between Motown's music serving as a soundtrack for the Civil Rights Movement, it is incredibly important for fans and critics to seriously consider the ways in which Motown was influenced by, and, in fact, came to influence, the protest songs and message music of the Black Power Movement. The fans and critics who downplay Motown's impact on the soundtracks of the Black Power Movement have failed to fully comprehend the meaning of Motown

DOI: 10.4324/9781003254492-3

for African Americans, especially those active in the movement, between 1965 and 1975. These same fans and critics also seem to be overlooking the fact that Black economic nationalism was one of the core concerns of Black Power proponents, from Elijah Muhammad, Malcolm X, and the Nation of Islam to Huey Newton, Bobby Seale, and the Black Panther Party. The fact that Motown was the most well-known independent record company during its classic era and undoubtedly the most successful African American-owned company in the United States by the 1970s was not lost on most members of the Black Power Movement, even if they thought much of Motown's output during the 1970s was merely "sell-out" soul and superficial funk.[2]

It is relatively easy to comprehend how Marvin Gaye's *What's Going On?* (1971) or Stevie Wonder's *Innervisions* (1973) resonated with the radical tenor of the Black Power Movement. For example, on *What's Going On?* Gaye's meditative lyrics touched on Black politics on "What's Going On?," "What's Happening Brother?" and "Right On!"; spirituality on "God is Love," "Wholy Holy," and "Right On!"; poverty on "Inner-City Blues (Makes Me Wanna Holler)"; drug abuse on "Flyin' High (In the Friendly Sky)"; child protection on "Save the Children"; police brutality on "What's Going On?"; and the Vietnam War on "What's Going On?" and "What's Happening Brother?"[3] Likewise, on *Innervisions* Wonder's introspective lyrics dealt with racism and the rising prison industrial complex on "Living for the City," drug abuse on "Too High," the aftermath of the Civil Rights Movement on "Visions," love on "All is Fair in Love," religious hypocrisy on "Jesus Children of America," and government corruption, specifically President Richard Nixon's ailing administration, on "He's Misstra Know-It-All."[4] However, it was not only Motown's A-list artists like Gaye and Wonder whose music served as a soundtrack for the Black Power Movement.

During the 1970s Motown's music was seemingly ubiquitous, most often placing higher on the R&B (read: Black) charts than on the pop (read: White) charts. Songs by second-tier and even obscure Motown artists, such as Edwin Starr with "Stop the War Now!," Junior Walker & the All-Stars with "Right on Brothers and Sisters," the Undisputed Truth with "Ungena Za Ulimwengu (Unite the World)," and Willie Hutch with "Brother's Gonna Work it Out," clearly demonstrate that even as the mastermind behind Motown, Berry Gordy, was chomping at the bit to garner a larger share of pop chart profits with certain high-profile Motown artists during the late 1960s and throughout the 1970s, he and his bevy of producers kept taking the pulse of the people, which is to say *Black* people. Consequently, the above songs, with their copious references to "the struggle," "the movement," and "the people," harbored a multiplicity of meanings: Perhaps, one set of meanings for the producers of the music and, again perhaps, a whole set of other, different meanings for the consumers of the music. The cultural, social, and political meaning of art produced by oppressed and economically exploited groups has a long history of being misinterpreted by the established order's art critics and scholars (which includes the established order's music critics, music historians, and other music scholars), who most often and in the most myopic manner imaginable only engage the history and culture of the said groups via their artistic expressions.[5]

At this point it seems relatively easy to ascertain the host of problems involved in approaching African Americans exclusively from the point of view of Black popular music, or Black popular culture more generally. Much must be understood about the turbulent history, culture, and struggle of Black people in America in order to adequately interpret *the dialectic of tradition and innovation at the heart of African American musical history and musical culture*. But, yet and still, whitewashed, sanitized study after study seems to almost as a rule disassociate African American musical history and musical culture from African American social history and political culture. All of this is to say Motown did not exist in a vacuum during its golden age between 1959 and 1979, and history, culture, and socio-political movements influenced its artists and producers in ways that may not be readily apparent to those who do not acknowledge or critically understand the extra-musical elements of Black popular music during both the Civil Rights Movement and Black Power Movement eras. Even those music fans and critics who are inclined to accept the contention that Motown served as a soundtrack for the Civil Rights Movement have a hard time coming to terms with the equally true assertion that Motown, even if only with certain songs, in fact espoused and was emblematic of the ethos of the Black Power Movement between 1965 and 1975.[6]

On the one hand, slightly before the beginning of the Black Power Movement Martha Reeves & the Vandellas' 1964 classic "Dancing in the Street" was adopted as an anthem during the waning years of the Civil Rights Movement and served in the minds of many as a tacit, sonic symbol of Motown's support for the emerging Black Power Movement.[7] On the other hand, as late as 1976, a year after the understood end of the Black Power Movement, many interpreted Stevie Wonder's *Songs in the Key of Life* double album as arguably Motown's coda to the movement. On *Songs in the Key of Life* classics such as "Love's in Need of Love Today," "Have a Talk with God," "Village Ghetto Land," "Sir Duke," "Ebony Eyes," and, of course, "Black Man" seemed to capture the mindset of Black America at the end of an epoch-making movement.[8] However, if the mostly White *and* male music critics and scholars either erase or diminish the ways in which Motown artists and producers borrowed from, and ultimately contributed to, the Black aesthetic at the heart of the artistic arm of the Black Power Movement, which is to say, the Black Arts Movement, then misinterpretations of Motown's message music are almost guaranteed to abound.

Truth be told, most Motown scholarship has had a tendency to almost completely overlook Motown's relationship with the Black Power Movement, preferring instead to focus on the Detroit-based record company's connections to the Civil Rights Movement. However, when we take into consideration the discourse on the "long Civil Rights Movement," which extends far beyond the 1954 *Brown vs. the Board of Education* Supreme Court decision to the assassination of Martin Luther King in 1968, the over-focus on Motown in relationship to the Civil

Rights Movement is a bit odd, if not disconcerting, because classic, game-changing Motown songs and albums such as the Temptations' *Cloud Nine* (1969), *Puzzle People* (1969), and *Psychedelic Shack* (1970); Edwin Starr's "War" (1970); the Undisputed Truth's eponymous 1971 debut album and *Face to Face with the Truth* (1972); Marvin Gaye's *What's Going On?* (1971); Syreeta's eponymous 1972 debut album; Stevie Wonder's *Music of My Mind* (1972), *Talking Book* (1972), and *Innervisions* (1973); and Eddie Kendricks' "My People . . . Hold On" (1972), among others, are left in the lurch. Obviously, then, the Civil Rights Movement-centered approach to Motown's music leaves much to be desired, because many of Motown's most remarkable songs and albums evaporate into the ether and suffer historical erasure and depoliticization.[9]

Between 1965 and 1975 Motown's music changed, and many of these changes, in fact, reflect general trends in Black popular music during that decade. However, there are other aspects of the changes in Motown's music that simply cannot be accounted for without linking musicology with history, sociology, politics, and economics. As will be discussed in greater detail in the following pages, Motown made music based on an assembly-line model, something Berry Gordy picked up from his days working in Detroit's auto industry. In considering the assembly line-like specified roles the vocalists, musicians, producers, songwriters, arrangers, and innumerable others played in producing Motown music, it is important to never lose sight of the fact that the end product of Motown's assembly line was simultaneously a musical *and* a cultural product.[10] Even more, as mentioned above, from the release of Martha Reeves & the Vandellas' 1964 classic "Dancing in the Street" to Stevie Wonder's groundbreaking 1976 double album *Songs in the Key of Life*, at least some of the end product of Motown's assembly line was understood by its core audience – which is to say, working-class and underclass Black folk – to be not merely a musical and cultural product, but also a product with social and political implications. Here these musical and cultural products with social and political implications emerging from Motown are reinterpreted in relationship to the politics and aesthetics of the Black Power Movement. The primary goal of this approach is to reveal the ways in which Motown's message music was in many ways emblematic of the complications and contradictions endemic to the Black Power Movement in particular, and Black people in general, between the late 1960s and the late 1970s.

Because of its corporate success, there has been a longstanding tendency to decry Motown, as Andrew Flory emphasized in *I Hear a Symphony: Motown and Crossover R&B*, initially as "pop-R&B," and then "sell-out" soul music and superficial funk.[11] As a matter of fact, in most general histories of classic rhythm & blues, and certainly those centered on classic soul, Motown is typically taken as the paradigmatic example of "cross-over" Black popular music during the 1960s and 1970s and, consequently, mercilessly criticized for essentially peddling Black pop to suburban White teens, if not White America more generally. In other words, a dismissive attitude toward Motown pervades Black popular music scholarship. Without entering into the debate about whether Motown was "soft," White folk-friendly soul, compared to the "hard," more authentic soul of, for example, James Brown, Aretha Franklin, and Otis Redding, the analysis here is interested in the relationship of Motown's message music to Black people and the Black Power Movement. Too often in the context of discussions of African American art and culture, White patronage and White perceptions are privileged. Here, by purposely focusing on the message music of the Black Power Movement – a movement that focused on Black culture, Black community, Black love, and Black liberation – White consumption and White interpretations of Black popular music are placed in a secondary position, and Black patronage and Black perceptions of Black popular music are brought front and center.

Even with all of that being said, there simply is no way to get around the fact that a dismissive attitude toward Motown seems to be lodged in the minds of most African American music scholars. For example, in *Race Music: Black Cultures from Bebop to Hip Hop*, acclaimed African American musicologist Guthrie Ramsey only makes passing mention of the "conservative and historically important Motown label" in the midst of a very brief discussion of Stevie Wonder's *Songs in the Key of Life*.[12] As a matter of fact, Motown is only mentioned on one page of Ramsey's renowned volume. However, as I stated above, Ramsey's snub of Motown is hardly out of the ordinary in African American music scholarship. Sadly, in his study, like those of countless others, Motown is marginalized, and an opportunity to critically engage its musical *and* extra-musical impact on African American musical history and culture, not to mention African American history and culture more generally speaking, during Motown's peak period in the 1960s and 1970s is sorely missed.

So that there is no misunderstanding, I would like to state outright that it is not my intention to criticize Ramsey for the book he did not write. In fact, I consider his work, along with the work of Eileen Southern, Samuel Floyd, Portia Maultsby and Mellonee Burnim, and Earl Stewart, arguably one of the most important contributions in the history of African American music scholarship, and it is a body of work to which I am indelibly indebted. However, it would be negligent in a study such as *Black Power Music!* not to emphasize that frequently in musicological inquiry concerning the Black popular music tradition, ironically the most "popular" Black popular music is often critically engaged the least, at best, or almost completely ignored, at worst.[13] To reiterate, Ramsey's omission of Motown is not at all out of the ordinary and is, in fact, in keeping with standard African American musicology. My work here, if not throughout this volume, is earnestly intended to provide a window into the world of Black popular music during the Black Power Movement and the ways in which much of the music that was "popular" during this period was popular precisely because it captured and conveyed aspects of the social, political, and cultural character of the movement. In other words, this chapter, among other things, critically engages the persistent propensity among African American music scholars to either outright erase or politely ignore Motown music and any other music deemed "pop-R&B," "sell-out" soul, or superficial funk, when and where they historicize and analyze Black popular music during the 1960s and 1970s. The real rub here lies in the simple fact that Motown's music was among the most audible and omnipresent *popular* music at the core of Black popular culture, if not American popular culture, during the later years of the Civil Rights Movement and certainly throughout the Black Power Movement era.[14]

A corollary concern at the heart of my work here revolves around an impulse to reinterpret Motown in relationship to the politics and aesthetics of the Black Power Movement, and to clearly demonstrate that although many Black popular music scholars have long dismissed Motown variously as "pop-R&B," "sell-out" soul, or superficial funk, Motown, in fact, produced protest songs and message music. Unfortunately, it would seem that many African American music scholars have conflated popularity with apoliticality or depoliticization. In other words, Motown's popularity beyond Black America during the Civil Rights Movement and Black Power Movement years means that it was somehow inauthentic, which is to say classic Motown was *not authentically Black* at a time when claiming a Black identity carried a great deal of political baggage with it and, equally importantly, connoted a commitment to a Black popular movement, whether the Civil Rights Movement or the Black Power Movement.[15]

As though there is some sort of Black musical measuring tape, from what I can gather from African American music scholarship, classic Motown was not really "Black music" because it was ironically as meaningful and popular among White folk as it was among Black folk during one of the most racially charged and tumultuous periods in American history. Here I would like to sidestep the debate about the Black authenticity or inauthenticity of Motown's music by focusing instead on the ways in which some of Motown's music, in fact, seemed to embrace and articulate the ideals and ethos of initially the Civil Rights Movement and then ultimately the Black Power Movement. Bearing in mind the pride of place given to classic Motown music in some musicological quarters and its almost visceral, complete disavowal in others, my work here will not be overly concerned with proving that classic Motown was, in fact, "real" or "authentic" Black music.[16]

Classic Motown music, literally, speaks – or, rather, *sings* – for itself. It needs no apologists. I honestly believe that the depth of the music is actually demonstrated by the fact that it resonated with both Black *and* White (among other) folk at a time when the dream-destroying rules and regulations of American apartheid were strictly enforced. Instead of constantly comparing Motown to other classic R&B, soul, and funk, here I am more interested in analyzing the ways in which Motown music refracted and put polish on some of the "hardest" and "heaviest" sounds emerging from Black America during the Civil Rights Movement and Black Power Movement years.[17] This approach to classic Motown music will enable me to avoid the Black authenticity game altogether and to importantly acknowledge that classic Motown not only harbored multiple meanings for Black folk during the Civil Rights Movement and Black Power Movement years, but it also had myriad meanings for the mostly Black working-class and underclass vocalists, musicians, producers, songwriters, arrangers, and innumerable others involved in the creation and production of the music. In other words, in spite of Berry Gordy's bourgeois pretensions and sonic conservatism, Motown music was meaningful to the activists and broader Black masses who were integral to the Black popular movements of the 1960s and 1970s. Consequently, in most instances in what follows, Motown's message music is taken on its own terms and not in constant comparison with the supposedly "Blacker" Black popular music emerging from, first, the Civil Rights Movement and, then later, the Black Power Movement. In fact, when the almost incessant comparative approach to classic Motown is set aside, Motown's contributions to the soundtracks of the Civil Rights Movement can be comprehended as actually helping to set the stage for what came to be called the "protest songs" or "message music" of the Black Power Movement, what I am currently calling *Black Power music*.

In order to critically comprehend Motown's contributions to the "protest songs" and "message music" of the Black Power Movement, a brief survey of its contributions to the message music of the Civil Rights Movement is necessary. There simply is no way to adequately understand the groundbreaking message-oriented music of the Temptations, Marvin Gaye, or Stevie Wonder, among others, without first understanding the extra-musical meanings attached to Motown music during the Civil Rights Movement. In other words, "Black Power music" is virtually incomprehensible without first critically engaging and understanding "Civil Rights music" and especially the ways in which Motown's *sonic integration* of the pop charts served as a metaphor for African Americans' quest for desegregation and authentic integration into American society.[18]

Motown and the Civil Rights Movement: the sound of social segregation and sonic integration

At this point it might be safe to say that in terms of rhythm & blues serving as one of the major soundtracks for the Civil Rights Movement, nothing drives this point home better than the triangular relationships between the Civil Rights Movement, the rise of Motown Records, and the inroads they both made in integrating Black America into White America. The Motown story has been recounted on so many occasions that it hardly seems necessary to rehearse it here. However, considering my ultimate aim of reinterpreting Motown in relationship to the Black popular movements of the 1950s, 1960s, and 1970s, a qualitatively different kind of history of Motown is called for here. Whether the Motown story has been told by "insiders, outsiders, mud-slingers," or "tribute-bringers," as Ward put it, the constant in the various narratives seems to revolve around the record company's remarkable ability to make meaningful music for people from all walks of life while it simultaneously expressed the ethos of Black America.[19]

The iconic founder of Motown Records, Berry Gordy, was born in 1929 into an upwardly mobile middle-class African American family with roots in rural Georgia. The Gordy family had moved from Oconee, Georgia, to Detroit, Michigan, in 1922 in search of better work and some relief from the restrictions of racial segregation. Although he came from a family that placed a great deal of emphasis on education, Gordy dropped out of high school in the eleventh grade with dreams of becoming a professional boxer. His boxing career was short-lived because he was drafted by the U.S. Army to serve in the Korean War in 1950. It was in the army that Gordy obtained his General Educational Development (GED) certificate.[20]

Discharged from the army in 1953, Gordy gravitated toward music, especially jazz, regularly frequenting clubs and eventually opening a record store, the 3-D Record Mart. In the 1950s jazz was becoming more and more an acquired taste, being eclipsed first by jump blues and then ultimately by rhythm & blues. Needless to say, Gordy's "old hat" jazz-centered record store did not last long. However, it did pique his interest in songwriting, music production, and music promotion. Financially devastated by the failure of his record store, Gordy was forced to take a job working at the Ford Motor Company, manufacturing cars on the assembly line. It was a pivotal experience for him, and later he would model his record company on Detroit's auto industry, attempting to achieve the same level of ingenuity, productivity, and efficiency.[21]

Even as he worked at the auto plant, Gordy stubbornly refused to let go of his dream of a career in the music industry. He began writing songs and shopping them around Detroit's music scene. After writing a string of hits for Jackie Wilson (e.g., "Reet Petite," "That Is Why [I Love You So]," "I'll Be Satisfied," and "Lonely Teardrops"), Gordy created Anna Records in 1959 along with two of his sisters, Anna and Gwen Gordy, and his friend Billy Davis. In quick succession after Anna Records, he established Tamla Records and later Jobete Music Publishing (aptly named in honor of his daughters: Joy, Betty, and Terry). On April 14, 1960, he incorporated his many music business ventures under the name the Motown Record Corporation ("Motown," being a portmanteau of *motor* and *town*, is a well-known African American colloquialism for Detroit). Because Motown ultimately placed 110 records in the Top Ten of the *Billboard* Hot 100 record chart between 1961 and 1971, it was duly dubbed "Hitsville."[22]

Beginning with an artist roster that boasted classic rhythm & blues luminaries such as Smokey Robinson & the Miracles, Marv Johnson, Barrett Strong, Mable John, Eddie Holland, Mary Wells, and the Marvelettes, Gordy created what has been repeatedly referred to as "clean" or, rather, "polished" rhythm & blues records that increasingly owed as much to White pop as they did Black pop. Gordy and his Hitsville production team paid as much attention to the White pop chart as they did the ostensibly "Black" rhythm & blues chart. Even though he greatly respected the raunchier and more mature aspects of 1950s rhythm & blues, Motown Records' rhythm & blues would emphasize anodyne youthful singers and songs, in effect deconstructing and reconstructing rhythm & blues to make it more palatable to a wider, Whiter, and younger audience.[23]

Motown artists in the 1960s were in many ways the antithesis of 1950s rhythm & blues artists. For instance, the contrasts between Smokey Robinson and Howlin' Wolf, or Mary Wells and Big Maybelle, or Marvin Gaye and Muddy Waters are obvious to anyone with eyes to see and ears to hear. But, and this hits at the heart of the matter here, Motown's music was more than chocolate-covered pop fluff. By synthesizing Black and White pop music, by coloring Motown songs with gospel beats and subdued church choir background singing, throbbing jazz-influenced bass lines, and blues-soaked guitar licks, Gordy ingeniously revolutionized rhythm & blues' sonic palette. Whatever he lacked in terms of technical proficiency at singing or playing a musical instrument, there simply was no denying Gordy's gargantuan sonic vision. In the 1960s Motown produced a wide range of music, all of which seemed to appeal to a broad audience and several different demographics. Ultimately, Motown created an extremely fluid and flexible sound – the much vaunted "Motown sound" – which, in the most unprecedented manner imaginable, allowed its music to appeal to, and have special meaning for, mainstream pop music lovers and discerning Black music lovers across the contentious regional, racial, cultural, social, political, and generational chasms afflicting America in the 1960s.[24]

According to Nelson George in *Where Did Our Love Go?: The Rise & Fall of the Motown Sound*, Gordy "preferred jazz musicians for his sessions, believing that they were both more technically assured and more creative than their blues-based counterparts."[25] Consequently, most of Motown's session musicians were local luminaries from Detroit's jazz scene. For example, some of the major moonlighting jazz musicians who performed on classic Motown recordings include trumpeters Marcus Belgrave, Russell Conway, Eddie Jones, John Trudell, Floyd Jones, John Wilson, and Herbie Williams; saxophonists Thomas "Beans" Bowles, Teddy Bucker, Henry "Hank" Cosby, Charles "Lefty" Edwards, Eli Fontaine, Williams "Wild Bill" Moore, Norris Patterson, Bernie Peacock, Andrew Terry, Dan Turner, and Ronnie Wakefield; trombonists George Bohannon, Bob Cousar, Patrick Lanier, Carl Raetz, and Paul Riser; flutists Dayna Hartwick, Thomas "Beans" Bowles, and Henry "Hank" Cosby; pianists Joe Hunter, Richard "Popcorn" Wylie, Earl Van Dyke, Johnny Griffith, James Gittens, Ted Sheely, and Joe Weaver; guitarists Dennis Coffey, Dave Hamilton, Joe Messina, Marvin Tarplin, Melvin "Wah-Wah Watson" Raglin, Robert White, Eddie Willis, Cornelius Grant, and Larry Veeder; bassists James Jamerson, Clarence Isabell, Bob Babbitt, Michael Henderson, Eddie Watkins, Prof. Beard, Joe James, and Tony Newton; drummers William "Benny" Benjamin, Uriel Jones, Richard "Pistol" Allen, George McGregor, Frederick Waites, Andrew Smith, Clifford Mack, and Larry London; and percussionists Eddie "Bongo" Brown, Jack Ashford, and Jack Brokensha.[26] To complement the supper club soul or uptown jazzy soul sound Gordy was going for, as early as 1960 he "hired members of the Detroit Symphony Orchestra to achieve the upscale R&B sounds" made popular by Nat King Cole, Ray Charles, Jackie Wilson, Sam Cooke, and Aretha Franklin during her Columbia Records years.[27] The strings had the "Whitening and lightening" effect, smoothing out the rough edges of Motown's rhythm & blues and providing it with an identifiable sound virtually at the outset.

From Gordy's point of view, Black popular music, much like Black people in the U.S. in the 1950s and 1960s, represented the recording industry's "bastard child and mother lode, an aesthetic and economic contradiction that was institutionalized by White record executives."[28] Hence, Motown's music became a metaphor for urban African American life, culture, and struggle in the 1960s. Gordy demonstrated to the American music industry, and eventually to the world, that African American youths were just like the "clean-cut" boy or girl next door, which was one of the major motifs of Motown's music, and especially classic recordings by Smokey Robinson & the Miracles, the Supremes, the Temptations, Mary Wells, Marvin Gaye, Tammi Terrell, Stevie Wonder, Kim Weston, the Marvelettes, the Four Tops, Gladys Knight & the Pips, and Martha Reeves & the Vandellas.[29]

As George observed, Motown made it clear that beneath the "glistening strings, Broadway show tunes, and relaxed vocal styles was a music of intense feeling."[30] Rhythm & blues, even the most "pop soul" sounding (à la Roy Hamilton, Dionne Warwick, Walter Jackson, Barbara Lewis, Chuck Jackson, Maxine Brown, and Freddie Scott), was more than mere background music. It was a tool that could be used to break down barriers: musical, cultural, social, political, and economic barriers. Paralleling the emergence of the Civil Rights Movement, the rise of Motown Records sent a clear message to the White-dominated music industry: African Americans would no longer tolerate any form of segregation, neither social nor musical segregation. The message Motown sent to Black America was equally provocative. Here was a company owned and operated by an African American armed only with a GED who challenged White corporate interests and White America's perception of African Americans, especially African American youths.[31]

There is a certain kind of sick and twisted irony at play when one seriously ponders the parallels between the emergence of the Civil Rights Movement and the rise of classic rhythm & blues, specifically Motown and Motown sound-derived rhythm & blues. In a nutshell, both the Civil Rights Movement and classic rhythm & blues, for all intents and purposes, were *African American youth issues-centered* and *African American youth activism-centered*. In terms of the Civil Rights Movement, the 1954 *Brown vs. the Board of Education* victory obviously focused on African American youth, as it desegregated public schools; the March 1955 arrest of fifteen-year-old Claudette Colvin, who was the first person on record to resist bus segregation in Montgomery, Alabama, alerted many African American adults to the adverse impact that segregation was having on African American youth and made many commit to the then inchoate Civil Rights Movement; the August 1955 lynching of fourteen-year-old Emmett Till in Money, Mississippi, enraged even the most moderate African American adults, providing yet another reason to rise up against American apartheid; the September 1957 display of courage on the part of the "Little Rock Nine" (Melba Pattillo Beals, Minnijean Brown, Elizabeth Eckford, Ernest Green, Gloria Ray Karlmark, Carlotta Walls LaNier, Thelma Mothershed, Terrence Roberts, and Jefferson Thomas) as they integrated the all-White Central High School in Little Rock, Arkansas, flanked by gun-toting National Guardsmen, clearly made even more freedom-loving folk commit to the principles and practices of the Civil Rights Movement; the August 1958 sit-ins spearheaded by Clara Luper and the NAACP Youth Council accented the brimming youth activism of the Civil Rights Movement, as did the 1960 emergence of a full-blown Sit-In Movement led by African American college students (Diane Nash, James Bevel, Bernard Lafayette, and C.T. Vivian); the May 1961 initiation of the Freedom Riders Movement, primarily led by the Congress of Racial Equality (CORE) and the Student Nonviolent Coordinating Committee (SNCC), ratcheted up youth radicalism during the movement years; the May 1963 Children's Crusade, led by James Bevel in Birmingham, Alabama, accented even more youth issues and youth activism in the Civil Rights Movement; and certainly the September 1963 bombing of the 16th Street Baptist Church that took the lives of the schoolgirls Addie Mae Collins, Denise McNair, Cynthia Wesley, and Carole Robertson two weeks after the March on Washington sent shock waves through Black America and helped to kick the Civil Rights Movement into an even higher gear. Again, African American youth – their lives and struggles – were squarely at the center of the Civil Rights Movement.[32]

During the same turbulent years that witnessed the backlash against African American youth and their valiant struggle for human, civil, and voting rights, Motown was tapping the teenage talent pool of Detroit's Brewster-Douglass Housing Projects. According to Nelson George, the Brewster-Douglass Housing Projects were "low-rent yet well-kept public housing that served as home for the children of Detroit's post-World War II migration. For all intents and purposes, it was a ghetto, but for Detroit's Blacks it was one with hope."[33] Gordy's first great discovery from Detroit's public housing projects was Smokey Robinson & the Miracles, followed soon thereafter by a group of guys called the "Primes" and their companion girl group called the "Primettes." The Motown machine quickly polished and rechristened the guy group as "The Temptations" and their sister group as "The Supremes."

Hence, similar to several contemporary rap stars (e.g., Jay-Z, NaS, Marley Marl, Kool G Rap, MC Shan, Roxanne Shanté, Mobb Deep, Trina, Lil' Wayne, Juvenile, Soulja Slim, and Jay Electronica, among countless others), the ghetto, and public housing projects in particular, provided classic rhythm & blues with the raw talent, tall tales, and innovative subaltern aesthetic that fueled much of its success. But, unlike rap, the ghetto origins or the otherwise humble beginnings of many classic rhythm & blues stars were masked to make them more appealing to middle-class and mainstream America, especially middle-class and mainstream White America.[34] As is well known, a lot of rap is unapologetically ghetto-centered and often celebrates ghetto life and culture. For the most part, classic rhythm & blues production and promotion teams, especially those at Motown in the 1960s, downplayed the humble beginnings of the bulk of their stars, preferring to present them decked out in the glitz and glam fashions of the era. Needless to say, rap music and hip hop culture's hyper-materialism and bold bourgeoisisms did not develop in a vacuum, and Motown and Motown-sound derived music and marketing have long served as a major point of departure for contemporary Black popular music, especially rap and neo-soul music.

Even though it was obviously an oppositional operation within the music industry of the 1960s, Motown was nonetheless deeply committed to the *modus operandi* and mechanisms of the U.S. mass market and, it should be strongly stressed, on the U.S. mass market's mostly anti-African American terms. This, of course, resembles most Civil Rights Movement members' open embrace of the "American Dream" without critically calling into question whether "American democracy" – as articulated by the wealthy, White, slaveholding men who are recognized as the "Founding Fathers" – was a viable goal for African Americans (and other non-Whites) in the second half of the twentieth century. Consider for a moment, if you will, Martin Luther King's famous "I Have a Dream" speech, with its scattered references to the Constitution and the Declaration of Independence.[35] King undeniably critiqued "the architects of our republic" (i.e., the wealthy, White, slaveholding men who are recognized as America's "Founding Fathers"), but he also passionately embraced *their* American dream. As a matter of fact, King's dream – to use his own words – was "a dream deeply rooted in the American dream."[36] For several of the unsung soldiers of the Civil Rights Movement, such as Ella Baker, Malcolm X, James Baldwin, and Robert F. Williams, King's articulation of the American dream did not sufficiently differentiate between White America's and non-White America's conflicting conceptions of the American dream. As Peniel Joseph's brilliant *The Sword and the Shield: The Revolutionary Lives of Malcolm X and Martin Luther King Jr.* emphasized, the militants of the Civil Rights Movement were not as interested in the American dream as they were concerned with ending the "American nightmare" – to employ Malcolm X's infamous phrase – in which Black America continued to be ensnared in the 1960s.[37]

In this sense, Berry Gordy's efforts to upset the White male-dominated music industry of the 1960s by drawing from the successful business models of White America was not out of the ordinary and perfectly mirrored the integrationist and middle-class mindset of most of the Black bourgeoisie during the Civil Rights Movement years. In the 1960s most African Americans were, as they remain today, largely working-class and working-poor. What Gordy and Motown provided the Black masses with were sonic slices of African American life and culture, not necessarily as they actually were at the time but as the Black bourgeoisie *and* the Black masses wished them to be. Indeed, it was these literally phantasmagoria or surreal songs that both Black and White America danced, romanced, partied, and politicked to during the Civil Rights Movement years.[38]

Working-class and working-poor Black folk – those humble human beings frequently treated like second-class citizens in segregated 1960s America – knew that Motown's music grew out of their loves, lives, and struggles. In short, they could genuinely relate to Motown music's timeless, clever, often tongue-in-cheek, and passionate stories of love, loss, loneliness, heartbreak, happiness, and community because in no uncertain terms these stories grew out of Black folklore. It really did not matter to them how Gordy managed to create one of the most successful businesses in African American history. Simply said, they did not care about the backstory with all of its tales of trials and tribulations. What was new, exciting, and inspiring about Motown in the 1960s was that it consistently presented African Americans in general, and African American youth in particular, in dignified and sophisticated ways that the White male-dominated music industry – indeed, White America in general – had never dreamed of.[39]

It could be said that Gordy challenged the mainstream American business model by deconstructing and reconstructing the received images of, and stereotypes about, African Americans in general and African American ghetto youth in particular. He literally refined, repackaged, and re-presented African Americans, and again African American ghetto youth in particular, employing business paradigms and procedures that were as far removed from African America, especially African American ghetto youth, as they were from the music business.[40] Here, it is important to accentuate African Americans' emphasis on cultural adaptation and the distinct ways in which Black folk practice creolization and hybridization.

No matter how far-fetched and mindboggling it might sound, the truth of the matter is that Berry Gordy meticulously modeled his record company on Detroit's auto industry, selling a sumptuous Black youthfulness, Black hipness, and Black sexiness employing one of the quintessential examples of mass production and mass consumption in America's market-driven economy. The Motown Record Corporation was simultaneously new and familiar to most middle-class and mainstream-minded Americans, both Black and White, because it utilized one of corporate America's most revered models. As Gerald Early explained in *One Nation Under a Groove: Motown and American Culture*, Gordy's work on the assembly line at the Ford factory was pivotal:

> His job at the Ford plant, as Nelson George and other critics have pointed out, made him aware of two things: how production can be efficiently organized and automated for the highest quality. At Motown during the sixties, producers could also write songs and songwriters could produce, but artists – either singers or session musicians – were not permitted to do either. With this type of control, Motown put out a highly consistent product. . . . From his auto plant experience, Gordy also became aware that to keep his company going, it was necessary to provide a series of attractive rewards and incentives for hard work, as well as an elaborate system of shaming for laziness. A record company, like an auto company, requires an almost unbearable atmosphere of competition. Gordy believed in competition with the fervor of a fanatic. (This intense sense of contest not only created a celebrity system within the company but became a point of celebration about the company, a virtual mark of internal and external prestige.) Thus, producers with hit records at Motown were given more studio time, and the others had to fight for what was left. The hottest songwriters were allowed to work with the hottest singers. At company meetings, Gordy bluntly criticized any song or performance he considered inferior, not permitting the song to be released, thereby angering his producers and songwriters, but also spurring them to do better in order to curry his favor and approval. This system produced an unprecedented number of hit records in relation to the number of records released.[41]

Here we have a Black record company owner utilizing the production techniques of a White car company owner, Henry Ford, to mass-produce a smoother, more or less White folk-friendly form of Black popular music. It was not only ingenious, but it was also indicative of the desegregationist and integrationist ethos sweeping across Black America in the late 1950s and early 1960s. By recreating and recasting African American ghetto youth in the anodyne and angelic image of mainstream and middle-class White youth, Motown was increasingly given entry into mainstream American popular culture at the exact same time that African Americans were desperately struggling to integrate into mainstream American society. In short, *1960s Motown music was implicitly Civil Rights Movement music without explicitly espousing traditional Civil Rights Movement themes, politics, and slogans.*[42] This is where we come back to the double entendres and cultural codes contained in Black popular culture in general, and Black popular music in particular. Motown's *implicit politics* mirrored the Civil Rights Movement's *explicit politics.*

It is not my intention to argue that Motown agreed with or supported each and every social struggle, political campaign, and cultural movement afoot in Black America in the 1960s. I am well aware of Berry Gordy's infamous reluctance to associate Motown with any organization or movement that could potentially negatively impact his company's commercial success. For instance, somewhat overstating his case, I believe, in *Motown: Music, Money, Sex, and Power,* Gerald Posner went so far to say that Gordy "had no interest in politics or history. He did not read newspapers or books and had little sense of social destiny or moral responsibility stemming from his remarkable success."[43]

However, it should be quickly pointed out that Posner's interpretation directly contradicts Brian Ward's brilliant work in *Just My Soul Responding: Rhythm & Blues, Black Consciousness, and Race Relations,* where he revealed that Gordy actually viewed "his own economic success as a form of progressive racial politics."[44] Bearing this in mind, it is not surprising that Gordy "did not wish to jeopardize his position" and the lucrative middle-of-the-road Motown brand by becoming "too closely associated with a still controversial Black Movement for civil and voting rights." Hence, Posner's interpretation flies in the face of the facts and is quite simply untenable, if not outright wrongheaded. Like most African Americans at the time, Berry Gordy was not free from "double-consciousness" and seemed to be an expert at *code-switching for capital gain* (including *cultural capital gain*), frequently saying one thing in public and another thing in private (à la most successful Black folk in White-dominated societies).[45]

In addition, Posner's analysis negates the simple fact that although Gordy was the chief executive officer of the Motown Record Corporation, it was, indeed, a "corporation" – which is to say, "a company or group of people authorized to act as a single entity (legally a person) and recognized as such in law," as defined by the *Merriam-Webster Dictionary.* Can Posner not comprehend that Gordy often purposely played the role of the mysterious point man or chief executive officer and allowed his surrogates to, even if only implicitly, mouth African American aspirations and frustrations during the Civil Rights Movement era via Motown's music? Can Posner not comprehend that legendary Motown singer-songwriters, producers, and musicians, such as Smokey Robinson, Marvin Gaye, Stevie Wonder,

Harvey Fuqua, William "Mickey" Stevenson, Richard "Popcorn" Wylie, Clarence Paul, Johnny Bristol, Norman Whitfield, Holland-Dozier-Holland, and, of course, the Funk Brothers perhaps felt deeply and often differently about the Civil Rights struggle than the big boss Berry Gordy? Autobiographical works by, and biographical works about, Motown singer-songwriters, producers, and musicians in most instances reveal that Motown was not completely out of touch with or, worse, dispassionate about, and divorced from, the Civil Rights Movement.[46]

Ward's painstaking research revealed that Gordy and Motown actually contributed to several 1960s Civil Rights organizations and causes, from the National Association for the Advancement of Colored People (NAACP) and the Congress of Racial Equality (CORE), to the Negro American Labor Council (NALC) and the 1963 March on Washington.[47] Moreover, in the liner notes for the compilation *Power to the Motown People!: Civil Rights Anthems and Political Soul, 1968–1975*, Peter Doggett observed that Motown's support of the Civil Rights Movement steadily, even if initially subtly, increased as the Civil Rights Movement 1960s gave way to the Black Power Movement 1970s. He matter-of-factly stated, "Motown never set out to be a political force."[48] In fact, he went on, "it was simply a stable of incredible musical talent, which earned its reputation as Hitsville USA" and the "Sound of Young America." However, Doggett importantly commented further,

> during that time of Civil Rights marches and ghetto riots, liberation armies and Black martyrs, all African Americans were inevitably sucked into the conflict. Motown Records was no exception. Berry Gordy himself was a strong supporter of the prince of the non-violent Civil Rights Movement, Martin Luther King; Motown even issued several albums of his speeches. As the racial heat increased, and Motown's home city of Detroit erupted into blazing riots in the summer of 1967, it became impossible for Gordy and his artists to avoid the call of the times. Over the next six years, Motown not only founded a subsidiary label entirely devoted to the struggle for Black Power (Black Forum Records); it also allowed its artists to comment directly on the situation of Black people in contemporary America. For the first time, you could hear the nation changing shape in the sounds that came out of Hitsville USA.[49]

What needs to be emphasized here is essentially a point that I made in *Civil Rights Music* concerning African American artists in relationship to the Civil Rights Movement, and that is that "all African Americans were inevitably sucked into the conflict" – "the conflict" meaning the struggle for human rights, civil rights, and voting rights during the Civil Rights Movement era – whether they were active members of the movement or not. As Doggett sternly stated, "Motown Records was no exception." As a matter of fact, as the moderate Civil Rights Movement 1960s evolved into the unapologetically militant Black Power Movement 1970s, "it became impossible for Gordy and his artists to avoid the call of the times." To reiterate, during the Civil Rights Movement Motown put into play the very same *"we can implicitly sing what we cannot explicitly say"* aesthetic at the heart of each and every major soundtrack of the Civil Rights Movement.[50] Perhaps summing up Gordy and Motown's Civil Rights Movement moderatism best, Nelson George wryly noted:

> Though he never spoke about the issue overtly, Berry's rise in the early 1960s linked him with the Civil Rights Movement. (Dr. Martin Luther King, Jr., once visited Motown briefly, and Berry would release his "I Have a Dream" speech, along with a few other Civil Rights-related albums throughout the decade.) Naïvely, some saw Motown as the entertainment-business equivalent of the National Association for the Advancement of Colored People, or the Southern Christian Leadership Conference. To them Motown wasn't just a job; it was part of a movement.[51]

This means, then, that I am not alone in conceiving of Black popular music, in this instance classic Motown, as having deeper, implicit political meanings and being connected to the explicit political expressions of a broader social and cultural movement. No matter how "naïve" I may appear to be to those folk who have little or no real relationship with the history, politics, sociology, *and* musicology of Black popular movements, similar to the African American youth of the 1950s and 1960s, I understand Black popular music to be more than merely music. To paraphrase George above, among other things, Motown was "part of a movement," the Civil Rights Movement, and, therefore, *Civil Rights music.*[52]

The truth of the matter is that Motown's music and its entrepreneurial acumen were culled from urban African American communities that had longstanding traditions of asserting their "implicit politics" through Black popular culture, Black popular music, and successful Black businesses. By eventually becoming one of Detroit's, and the country's, most successful producers of Black popular music and most successful Black businesses in the midst of a racially segregated American society, Motown was indeed perceived as "political," and that is regardless of whether or not we have consensus on whether Berry Gordy, Motown, or its individual artists comprehended it as such. As is the case in White America, Black America has its own unique interpretive communities, customs of cultural appropriation, and political practices, which do not cater to the whims and wishes of megastars, music industry moguls, musicologists, sociologists, political analysts, or cultural critics.[53] Speaking directly and eloquently to this issue in *Dancing in the Street: Motown and the Cultural Politics of Detroit*, Suzanne Smith offered remarkable insight:

> Motown's role as a producer of Black culture and its ambitions in the business world did not coexist without conflict and contradiction. At Hitsville, U.S.A., commercial concerns about the marketability of a recording often stalled and sometimes canceled projects that management deemed too politically controversial. The political climate at Motown Records was highly variable. Throughout the Civil Rights era the company wavered between

willingness and caution when asked to produce recordings – musical or spoken-word – that involved overt political or racial messages. Sometimes an atmosphere of race consciousness prevailed, and other times a politically conservative ethos dominated.

Motown's internal ambivalence about its relationship to the Civil Rights Movement was, however, only one side of the story. On the other side were popular music audiences, local artists, and national Civil Rights leaders, who had their own ideas and disagreements about the meanings of Motown's music and commercial success for the movement. At the national level debates about Motown's role in the struggle for racial justice mirrored larger divisions within the movement itself. From 1963 to 1973 . . . the national Civil Rights campaign shifted from the unified fight for integration – exemplified by the March on Washington – to a more fractious battle for Black Power. Given these transitions, Motown could not avoid becoming a contested symbol of racial progress. Motown's music symbolized the possibility of amicable racial integration through popular culture. But as a company, Motown represented the possibilities of Black economic independence, one of the most important tenets of Black nationalism.[54]

By bringing so many diverse groups together, at least in terms of a shared aural experience, classic Motown music foreshadowed and laid a foundation for every major form of Black popular music that followed. It captured the comedy and tragedy, and sonically signified the dancing and romancing of 1960s segregated Black America in the process of desegregating and integrating into mainstream America.[55] Moreover, Motown also symbolized Black powerbrokers and Black businesses in the process of desegregating and integrating into corporate America. With its increasing young White clientele, in the 1960s Motown was both a metaphor for and one of the major Black popular music soundtracks of the Civil Rights Movement. Its challenge to America's musical segregation mirrored African Americans' social and political challenges to America's racial segregation.[56] Touching on this point in his classic essay "Crossing Over: 1939–1989," Reebee Garofalo importantly observed:

> In its early stages, the Civil Rights Movement, as embodied by Dr. Martin Luther King, Jr., had two predominant themes: non-violence and integration. As other, more militant tendencies developed in the Black community, such a stance would soon appear to be quite moderate by comparison. At the time, however, it seemed to many that the primary task facing Black people was to become integrated into the mainstream of American life. It was in this context that Motown developed and defined itself. . . . Gordy once commented that any successful Motown hit sold at least 70% to White audiences. Working closely with Smokey Robinson on the label's early releases, he laid rich gospel harmonies over extravagant studio work with strong bass lines and came up with the perfect popular formula for the early Civil Rights era:

upbeat Black pop, that was acceptable to a White audience, and irresistibly danceable. This was the "Motown sound."[57]

In spite of classic Motown's more or less apolitical lyrics, many of its songs contained metaphors and came to have alternative meanings within the cultural, social, and political context of the Civil Rights Movement. Even the most apolitical lyrics can take on new meanings unfathomed by songwriters, singers, musicians, and record companies when the lyrics resonate with the cultural conventions, social sensibilities, and political praxes of a brutally oppressed people determined to rescue and reclaim their human, civil, and voting rights. For instance, a short list of classic Motown's songs that took on special socio-political meanings within the context of the Civil Rights Movement would most certainly include Martha Reeves & the Vandellas' "Dancing in the Street," "Heat Wave," "Quicksand," and "Nowhere to Run"; Smokey Robinson & the Miracles' "I Gotta Dance to Keep from Crying," "The Tracks of My Tears," "Going to a Go-Go," "Abraham, Martin, and John," "Whose Gonna Take the Blame?," and "Tears of a Clown"; Marvin Gaye's "Can I Get a Witness?," "I'll Be Doggone," "Ain't That Peculiar?," and "I Heard It Through The Grapevine"; the Supremes' "Where Did Our Love Go?," "Stop in the Name of Love," "Love Child," "I'm Livin' in Shame," and "The Young Folks"; the Temptations' "Ain't Too Proud to Beg," "Beauty Is Only Skin Deep," and "Ball of Confusion (That's What the World is Today)"; and, finally, the Four Tops' "It's the Same Old Song" and "Reach Out I'll Be There."[58]

Given the social and political situation during the early 1960s, Gordy's idea to create crossover "upbeat Black pop" that was "irresistibly danceable" was yet another mark of his managerial and musical genius. Motown's predominantly White consumer base eventually made it one of the most influential record companies of the 1960s. When viewed from the "implicit politics" of Black popular culture perspective, we witness that as it increasingly exerted its influence on mainstream American popular music and popular culture, Motown was transformed into a glowing symbol of the unprecedented economic and cultural opportunities available to African Americans during the Civil Rights Movement years. In this sense, Motown stars were understandably appropriated by most members of the Civil Rights Movement, who viewed them as more than musicians but also as strategic cultural, social, and political icons. The fact that megastars such as Diana Ross, Smokey Robinson, Eddie Kendrick, and Mary Wells were all working-class and working-poor Black youth raised in the often-brutal Brewster-Douglass Housing Projects prior to their Motown fame and fortune made them, for all intents and purposes, *icons of integration*. However, the success stories of the handful of African American ghetto youth that Motown took from rags to riches were frequently redeployed by White America in its efforts to quell legitimate critiques coming from the Civil Rights Movement concerning the mistreatment that the Black masses continued to experience throughout the 1960s.[59]

This means that America's culture wars are not new, and the utilization of Black popular music and Black popular culture as a political football, as it were, is not new either. Culture wars were a major part of the Civil Rights Movement. Going against the conventions of mainstream American society in the 1960s, Motown gave Black ghetto youth an opportunity to more or less express their views and values. In capturing the creativity of working-class and underclass African American youth, Motown opened a window to an often-ignored world, and much of what has been identified as the "Motown sound" is frequently little more than the pent-up sound of Black working-class and underclass suffering and celebration. Moreover, it was this distinct sound that increasingly became more and more audible on Motown classics as the Civil Rights Movement morphed into the Black Power Movement and the collective mood of Black America changed from one of moderatism to militantism.[60]

The emergence and early evolution of the Motown sound

Even though there has been a tendency to almost over-focus on Berry Gordy when and where we come to Motown, it is important to bear in mind that during its classic period (circa 1959 to 1979) Motown was a record *company*; actually it was incorporated as the "Motown Record Corporation" in 1960. That is to say, even though Gordy was the acknowledged head of the emerging music empire, he relied heavily on singers, musicians, producers, songwriters, arrangers, and the like to achieve his goals. Although Gordy had a Black bourgeois mindset, many of the vocalists, musicians, producers, songwriters, arrangers, and others who contributed to the company's success did not, and they were, as a consequence, often more in tune with what was happening in Black America and with what was on the minds of the mostly working-class and underclass Black masses. This may go far to explain why Motown serves as such an ideal point of departure to explore the emergence of the message music of the Black Power Movement. In spite of Gordy's middle-of-the-road, almost obsessive middle-class mindset, Motown artists like the Temptations, Marvin Gaye, and Stevie Wonder deeply desired to create music for and about Black America, the majority of which was not middle-class and, in fact, harbored a healthy resentment against what E. Franklin Frazier called the "make-believe world of the Black bourgeoisie." As a matter of fact, what has been repeatedly referred to in music scholarship as the "Motown sound" actually has its origins in the lives and struggles of the working-class and underclass Black communities from which most Motown employees emerged in the 1960s and 1970s.[61]

Truth be told, the Motown sound has proved to be difficult to adequately describe. As a matter of fact, Motown fans, scholars, and critics have not come to any kind of clear-cut consensus as to what the Motown sound is and isn't. Many believe that the classic sound had to do with a combination of the following: playful and often ironically insightful lyrics; catchy, seemingly homespun hummable melodies; distinctive, gospel-styled lead vocals draped by sophisticated harmonizing and clever call-and-response background vocals; and the instrumental innovations of the Funk Brothers, Motown's legendary studio band of mostly moonlighting jazz musicians.[62] Motown scholar Charles Sykes emphasized that it is important to bear in mind that the Motown sound was equally rooted in the metamorphosis and ongoing synthesis of various gospel, jazz, rhythm & blues, rock & roll, and mainstream pop styles between 1945 and 1965:

> Future Motown artists, writers, and producers, born during World War II, were teenagers during the 1950s and consumer-participants in a new popular culture. American popular music, formally defined by mainstream pop, had become redefined as rhythm & blues or rock & roll. Teenagers were the target market of record companies and broadcast media who disseminated and propagated this new music. Like Berry Gordy, the new generation of Detroit's Black teenagers was exposed to diverse forms of music. In church, they would hear and sing gospel. In Glee Club and other school music classes they studied European-based classical and folk traditions under the tutelage of White teachers. Broadcast media, primarily radio and to a lesser but growing extent television, provided access to a broad array of musical offerings and was the core source of exposure to the current forms of music that future Motown personnel would listen to, dance to, buy on record, and emulate.[63]

Moreover, highlighting the doo-wop vocal tradition, "with its 'ooos,' 'ahhs,' and vocal riffs," Sykes pointed out that these elements were prevalent throughout rhythm & blues "through the mid-1960s." He also noted a number of "blues elements" scattered throughout the Motown sound.[64] Indeed, while relatively easy to identify by ear, the Motown sound has long escaped simple synopsis.

Some Motown fans and critics believe that the distinctiveness of the Motown sound stemmed from the driving backbeat of most classic Motown songs, which percussionists literally drummed up and beat out on everything from tambourines, wood blocks, and timpani to jug band-inspired makeshift instruments such as chains, trash cans, and Coke bottles.[65] Other Motown aficionados strongly believe that the music's remarkable panache is attributable to James Jamerson's inventive and ever-bubbling bass lines combined with the dynamic drumming of Benny Benjamin, Uriel Jones, or Richard "Pistol" Allen.[66] Jamerson, according to Flory in *I Hear a Symphony*, "helped to make the bass another vital element of Motown records." In particular, Flory went further:

> Jamerson created active lines that often used syncopation across the bar and downward leaps followed by ascending passing tones to create linear passages that evoked gospel harmonization. Rather than using a microphone to capture the sound of an amplifier, Jamerson's performances were recorded through direct input, which helped to shape his sound. After 1964, Motown's eight-track apparatus recorded bass performances on a separate track, which allowed for further enhancement and placement in final mixes. Jamerson's playing was revolutionary in popular music at the time, and others who performed at Motown, such as Bob Babbitt and Tony Newton, emulated his style. Before the early 1960s the bass had been relegated to a purely

supportive role in most popular music, but Jamerson helped to change this. His performances inspired many other bassists in the R&B and rock communities to command a new sense of freedom.[67]

According to Sykes, the Motown sound actually went through three phases between 1959 and 1972: Phase I, the "formative years," ran from 1959 to 1963; Phase II, the "classic period," went from 1964 to 1967, and it was during this phase that the Motown sound "crystallized"; and Phase III, which was "a period of diversification and transition to the post-Detroit era," stretched from 1968 to 1972.[68] Even though Sykes asserted that the "works of other writer-producer-artist combinations made different but no less vital contributions to shaping [Motown's] legacy," he nonetheless emphasized that the formation of the Holland-Dozier-Holland songwriting team, which consisted of Lamont Dozier and brothers Brian and Eddie Holland, and which eventually composed twenty-five top-ten pop hits for Motown, were the architects behind the emergence and maturation of the Motown sound.[69] Flory, among many other Motown fans, scholars, and critics, appears to agree with Sykes' assessment.[70]

In his autobiography, *To Be Loved: The Music, the Magic, the Memories of Motown*, Berry Gordy, perhaps tongue-in-cheek but tellingly nonetheless, remarked that Motown's distinctive sound was a consequence of a crude combination of "rats, roaches, soul, guts, and love." He strongly stressed the love free-floating through Motown, stating: "The love we felt for each other when we were playing is the most undisputed truth about our music."[71] Observe Gordy's imaginative yet insightful definition of the Motown sound. According to Gordy, the Motown sound had nothing to do with lyrics, backbeats, or chord changes, but an unmistakable extra-musical ambition ironically inspired by life in the ghetto ("rats" and "roaches") and expressed through audible – albeit often seemingly controlled – passion, determination, and deep affection ("soul, guts, and love"). Gordy's emphasis on the social and cultural environment that Motown music emerged from, and was created in, was not part of Motown's marketing campaign. Motown vocalists and instrumentalists developed their skills with individuals and in institutions endemic to their then highly segregated inner-city/urban environments. Chief among the individuals who helped Motown artists hone their musical talents were family members, preachers, teachers, older musicians, and the segregated audiences who offered encouragement and constructive criticism. Among the institutions of the Black public sphere that assisted Motown musicians in ultimately creating the distinctive sound that provided a soundtrack for both the Civil Rights Movement and Black Power Movement were Black churches, blues bars, jazz clubs, street corners, public schools, and public housing projects.[72]

Both public and private segregated housing provided the space where Motown music was created, and this seemingly inconsequential fact is central to any understanding of the development of what we now know as the Motown sound. For instance, in 1958 a scuffling Gordy established the Rayber Music Company with the woman who would become his second wife, Raynoma Liles. Rayber, a contraction of *Raynoma* and *Berry*, was run out of Berry's sister Gwen's home and later Raynoma's humble apartment, not rented office space like other independent record companies at the time.[73] To keep operating costs at the minimum, Rayber's modus operandi revolved around home production. Needless to say, recording demo tapes in Raynoma's cramped apartment invariably presented a number of problems. In *Berry, Me, and Motown*, Raynoma – writing under the name Raynoma Gordy Singleton as a consequence of her subsequent marriage to Eddie Singleton – observed: "Creating an efficient routine was necessary . . . to make the most of our somewhat limited resources. . . . there was, after all, only one piano and one tape recorder." She explained further, "[w]e kept the tape recorder in the hallway. And when we were ready to do a demo, I gathered everyone around the piano."[74] Soon Gordy, Raynoma, and their cohort of music-making characters outgrew the apartment and home production process. It was Raynoma who located a "two-story house at 2648 West Grand Boulevard with a big picture window in the front and a photography studio in the back," Gordy recalled.[75]

What we now think of as the majestic Motown actually began in a humble two-story house Raynoma found at 2648 West Grand Boulevard in Detroit; the house was later lovingly dubbed "Hitsville U.S.A." because Motown produced an unprecedented number of hit records there between 1959 and 1972. Gordy established "Studio A," as it was grandly called, in the basement of the house. Motown musicians dubbed Studio A the "snake-pit" because it was incredibly cramped and had reverberating hardwood floors with tiny isolation booths for vocalists built into the wall. As with the makeshift setup at Raynoma's little apartment, the snake-pit's close quarters presented all kinds of audio engineering difficulties. For instance, issues surrounding sound isolation were incessant. In the midst of a recording session, the sounds from different instruments frequently bled into multiple microphones. In an effort to steer clear of such issues musicians frequently did not use amplifiers, which ironically created an intimate, atmospheric sound.[76]

According to Allan Slutsky in *Standing in the Shadows of Motown*, another issue endemic to Studio A had to do with its constantly shifting climate. "With a dozen or more singers and musicians in the same small room, the climate, as well as the music being played, could heat up very quickly."[77] Because Studio A's air conditioning and heating systems produced a great deal of background noise, producers typically turned them on and off between rehearsals and recording sessions. The studio's fluctuating temperature meant that instruments frequently went out of tune, causing serious intonation issues that understandably irked the musicians. Motown guitarist Joe Messina wanted Slutsky to know that "poor ventilation was the culprit, as opposed to bad ears or shoddy tuning habits." And Motown pianist Early Van Dyke jokingly said to Slutsky, "hey, why don't you try and see if you can keep your guitar or horn in tune when the temperature is changing plus or minus fifteen degrees every half hour?"[78]

All of this is to say that Motown began with homespun or "in-house" productions. Eventually it turned its seemingly cursed and cramped quarters and its hit-or-miss, more or less makeshift sound booths into a musical blessing. Motown musicians seem to have sensed early on that whatever the inconveniences of record-ing in a cobbled-together and crowded studio, they were worth the end result, which was a remarkably organic and atmospheric sound that evidently proved impossible to replicate in high-tech recording studios anywhere else. Tellingly, even after "cleaner," more stereophonic recordings were made possible in light of technological advances, Motown went to great lengths not to tinker with the magical sound emanating from all of the blood, sweat, and tears poured into the snake-pit over the years. Slutsky related that when Motown moved from Detroit to Los Angeles in 1972, Berry Gordy seriously considered carefully dismantling and rebuilding Studio A in California in an effort to maintain the magical Motown sound.[79] Hence, even the great Gordy seems to have understood that the environ-ment that music is created in influences the music in myriad extra-musical ways.[80]

Picking up on a theme touched on above, another extra-musical element that factored into the origins and evolution of the Motown sound was low-income public housing projects, specifically the Brewster-Douglass Housing Projects (offi-cially named the Frederick Douglass Homes and alternately named Frederick Douglass Projects, Frederick Douglass Apartments, Brewster-Douglass Homes, and Brewster-Douglass Projects). Innumerable Motown vocalists experienced their earliest informal singing lessons in doo-wop groups they formed in the housing projects. As a matter of fact, the Supremes – Diana Ross, Mary Wilson, and Flor-ence Ballard – initially met each other in the Brewster-Douglass Housing Pro-jects.[81] Brewster-Douglass residents considered their housing projects a relatively pleasant place to live during the segregated 1950s. "Moving to the Brewster Pro-jects in 1956 was a turning point in my life," Mary Wilson observed in *Dreamgirl: My Life as a Supreme*.[82] She continued, "Many people would have considered a move to the Projects a step down." But for Wilson, "having already stepped down from a middle-class neighborhood to various apartments in the inner-city, this was a step back up. I felt like I just moved into a Park Avenue skyscraper. . . . It was quite crowded compared to suburbia, but I loved it."[83] It may be hard for many to understand why Wilson would say that she "loved" living in the projects, especially after she had lived in a "middle-class neighborhood." But it is important to bear in mind that those of us who have lived in the projects may in many instances have a qualitatively different understanding of the positives and negatives of project life. As Wilson's autobiography emphasized, the Brewster-Douglass Housing Projects furnished many of its tenants with a distinct conception of community and spaces to develop their vocal talents that upscale apartments or single-family homes did not easily offer.

As made mention of above, before they were rechristened the Supremes by Berry Gordy in 1961, high schoolers Diana Ross, Mary Wilson, and Florence Ballard called themselves the Primettes. The Primettes used the Brewster-Douglass recreation building to rehearse their early songs. "We spent hours at the Brewster Center learning the intricate harmonies of the Mills Brothers and the Four Fresh-men," Wilson remembered.[84] Along with the Brewster-Douglass recreation build-ing, the young singers who would be future Motown stars frequently requisitioned

Brewster-Douglass Housing Projects roof tops, hallways, and stairwells to sharpen their vocal abilities. Wilson vividly remembered:

> Some groups used the roof for a stage, others the hallways in the Projects buildings. Because of their smooth hard walls and echo, these spots were prized for their acoustics. The lucky kids had access to parent-free apartments, which served as rehearsal studios between the last school bell and dinner time.
>
> Competition among members of rival groups and their fans could be fierce. They were competing for attention, competing for a choice space to sing in, competing for some kind of recognition in a place that didn't offer too much hope to any of them. You didn't need any formal training; all you needed was heart and the courage to take some chances and do something with whatever God gave you that would make your singing different or better. Friends, neighbors, and passersby made up a critical and vocal audience. If you didn't have a good sound, or if the group wasn't up to par, the audience and your rivals would ask you – in quite unflattering terms – to vacate the spot. The more cherished the spot – say, a building stairwell – the tougher it was to keep it.[85]

The competition for temporary rehearsal spaces extended beyond the boundaries of the housing projects and spilled over into other parts of Detroit. These struggling young singers transformed every open nook and cranny of public buildings into prized performance oases. Prefiguring much of the musical ingenuity they would later display at Motown, these housing project youths personalized and revolutionized unwelcoming institutions and environments, and in the process they produced a unique musical and extra-musical culture.

Included in Berry Gordy's fanciful definition of the Motown sound was not only a nod to "rats" and "roaches," as well as other ghettocentric references, but, perhaps even more importantly, an emphasis on "soul, guts, and love." The "soul, guts, and love" at the center of the Motown sound was an important source of pride and inspiration for African Americans as the Civil Rights Movement morphed uneasily into the Black Power Movement. In the midst of the emerging Black Power Movement in the mid-1960s, Motown's music took on a number of extra-musical meanings, many of which, it should be stated outright, Gordy vociferously disagreed with. The public meanings of the Motown sound multiplied many times over during the Black Power Movement. Arguments and counterarguments about what Motown music meant and what it did not mean reveal much about collective struggles within the company and the country concerning trite definitions of what "Negro" music should sound like, what "Negro" singers ought to be singing about, and what, if anything, this new, "Blacker" sounding music might do to the hearts *and* minds of the Black masses. This "heavier" and "harder"-sounding Black popular music was obviously not the "nice," White folk-friendly "Negro" music Motown had come to prominence with.[86] There was something deeper and "darker" lurking in the lyrics. The sound, although not always easily audible, could be interpreted as sinister.[87]

As the Civil Rights Movement morphed into the Black Power Movement, as the mood and mindset of Black America began to grow impatient with the slow pace of the non-violent and integrationist ethos of the Civil Rights Movement, it is relatively easy to understand how Motown music came to mean much more than music to many African Americans. It would have been surprising if the Motown sound, with its inner-city origins and its "soul, guts, and love" attitude, had not been raised up and roiled as a contested symbol of the power of Black popular music to raise Black cultural consciousness and contribute to efforts aimed at either uniting or further dividing Black folk, first and foremost, and then Black folk with Black folk-friendly others, including progressive Whites. Berry Gordy's obsession with placing hits on the pop charts while keeping a keen eye on the R&B charts almost guaranteed that Motown's music would come to mean many different things to many different people. His deep desire to create a kind of pop music, even though primarily sung and backed by musicians from Detroit's public housing projects and low-income Black neighborhoods, that appealed to an incredibly wide audience across racial, gender, class, and generational lines further complicated Motown's meaning within and without Black America in the 1960s and 1970s.[88]

The Black Power sound of Motown

Where many have a dismissive attitude toward any assertion that Motown's music captured elements of the ethos of the Black Power Movement, there are others who hear echoes of the turbulent ten-year period that began as the Civil Rights Movement came to end. No one contends that each and every tune that Motown released roughly between 1965 and 1975 was some sort of sonic call to arms. However, a small but steadily growing group of Motown fans, scholars, and critics believe that select classic Motown songs, even if only implicitly in most instances, reflect aspects of the radical tenor at the heart of the Black Power Movement. For instance, in his liner notes for *The Complete Motown Singles, Vol. 5: 1965*, Herb Boyd shared:

> Motown Records leapt into the national consciousness in 1965. The outlook was sunny for a Black-owned company. Yet all was not bright. Sam Cooke's tragic murder in a seedy motel in December 1964 foreshadowed the gloom of the following year; a gloomy year of death and dismay that even the joyful noise from Motown couldn't brighten. In fact, in several ways the company's music seemed to presage or accentuate the year's setbacks.[89]

A week before Malcolm X was assassinated on February 21, 1965, Junior Walker & the All-Stars' "Shotgun" made its debut on *Billboard*'s R&B chart. After opening with the unmistakable crackle of a shotgun burst, the song then leaps into a rowdy and saw-toothed saxophone-led instrumental, peppered with Walker's half-hollered, hoarse-voiced bluesy lyrics. Something of a break with what was then understood to be the "Motown sound," especially the Motown *hit* sound, the fact that it didn't sound like a Motown song appears to have only increased its popularity. A month after its release, "Shotgun" rose to number one on the R&B chart on March 13, 1965, and it stayed on the chart for seventeen weeks.[90] It was the first release on Motown's subsidiary Soul label to reach the top spot on the charts. Berry Gordy established the label in 1964 to market Motown's "heavier" and "harder" sounding rhythm & blues, which eventually evolved into what came to be called "soul music."[91]

It is interesting to observe Gordy's prescience and impeccable timing when he bestowed the Soul Records imprint with an obviously excellent name that no one else had the foresight to snap up and copyright prior to 1964. Granted, Soul Records was never considered one of Motown's most prestigious imprints (à la its "big three" subsidiaries Tamla Records, Motown Records, and Gordy Records, formed in 1959, 1960, and 1962, respectively).[92] However, the fact of the matter is that Soul Records rostered many of Motown's most outstanding artists and produced some of the best songs in the classic Motown catalogue. For instance, along with the prevoiusly mentioned Junior Walker & the All-Stars, Gladys Knight & the Pips, Edwin Starr, Barbara Randolph, Jimmy Ruffin, the Velvelettes, Shorty Long, the Originals, Frank Wilson, and the Fantastic Four were all signed to Soul Records. As a result, an argument could be made that Soul Records was in many ways on the same level as the "big three," except it had a lower profile and did not receive the kind of marketing campaigns lavished on the Tamla, Motown, and Gordy labels.[93]

After the demise of Motown's short-lived Workshop Jazz Records imprint, which was only in existence from 1962 to 1964 and which was intended as an outlet for jazz sides with a pop soul slant, Gordy formed Soul Records with an eye on releasing material with limited pop appeal.[94] At the time Motown believed that releasing more "soulful," R&B chart-friendly songs would give it some much-needed street credibility in the Black community. Although often overlooked in Motown scholarship, Soul Records was an incredibly important venture and positive proof that Motown, in fact, was as interested in producing meaningful music for Black folk as it was pop dance ditties and innocuous love songs for suburban White folk. A lot more successful than most Motown critics and fans may realize, Soul Records went on to become one of Motown's longest-lived subsidiaries. By 1976 its output had decreased considerably, and it only released a trickle of singles before finally coming to a grinding halt during the flamboyant, disco-dominated days of 1978.[95]

Back in 1965, when "Shotgun" not only rose to number one on the R&B chart but also raced up the pop charts to the number four position, Gordy was, to say the least, surprised. He sensed that music tastes were changing, not merely for Black America, but for White America as well. Motown fans and critics seemed to crave a more creative, ostensibly "heavier" and "harder" sounding music with possibly deeper and "darker" lyrics. For Gordy and his minions at Motown, "Shotgun's" success was a harbinger of the "heavier" and "harder" sounding rhythm & blues-cum-soul music with deeper and "darker" lyrics to come.[96]

"Shotgun's" surprise success wasn't only a shock to Motown, it also sent reverberations through the mid-1960s music industry. Along with James Brown's "Papa's Got a Brand New Bag," the Impressions' "People Get Ready," Otis Redding's "I've Been Loving You Too Long (To Stop Now)," Wilson Pickett's "In the Midnight Hour," Fontella Bass' "Rescue Me," the Ramsey Lewis Trio's "The 'In' Crowd," and Little Milton's "We're Gonna Make It," all hitting the charts in 1965, the "heavier" and "harder" sounding rhythm & blues-cum-soul music with deeper and "darker" lyrics challenged longstanding conceptions of what "race," "Negro," or "Black" music was or would sound like in the future.[97] Initially calling Black popular music "race records" in the 1920s, American music industry executives first took notice and identified a market for African American music when blues queens such as Ma Rainey, Bessie Smith, Sarah Martin, Maggie Jones, Lucille Bogan, Mamie Smith, Mildred Bailey, and Alberta Hunter, among others, achieved widespread popularity. Monitored by magazines such as *Billboard*, *Cashbox*, and *Music Vendor*, the ever-watchful and always-eager-to-make-a-dollar American music industry inaugurated "race records" charts between the 1920s and the mid-1940s to keep track of trends in "race music," which included a variety of Black popular music genres, such as blues, jazz, and gospel, as well as comedy. From 1942 to 1945 *Billboard* devoted its first chart to Black popular music, dubbing it the "Harlem Hit Parade." From 1945 to 1949 *Billboard* returned to the "race records" designation to track African American music. In June 1949, at the suggestion of *Billboard* journalist and future Atlantic Records producer Jerry Wexler, the magazine changed the name of the "race records" chart to the "Rhythm & Blues" chart. The chart has since undergone further name changes, becoming the Soul chart in 1969, the Black chart in 1982, the R&B chart in 1990, and the R&B/Hip Hop chart in December 1999.[98]

Observe that through all of the name changes, the "rhythm & blues" moniker seems to have had the most staying power. A catch-all phrase if ever there was one for Black popular music, beginning in the immediate post-war period, circa 1945, rhythm & blues has defined every form of Black popular music, if not American popular music, since its emergence. Its relationship to soul and funk during the Black Power period can hardly be questioned. Consequently, in the aftermath of the Civil Rights Movement and in the midst of the emerging Black Power Movement Motown established its Soul Records subsidiary to unambiguously indicate to its fans and critics that it was still producing rhythm & blues as opposed to pop records. Listeners had a tendency to define "Black" music as music made *by African Americans for African Americans*. In the minds of many during the Black Power Movement years, "Black" music was music that unambiguously emphasized African American musical genres such as gospel, blues, jazz, and, of course, rhythm & blues. When Motown's Soul Records sent "Shotgun" to the top of the pop charts, the incongruity, the oddness of such a raucous, juke joint-sounding song making it big showed how flimsy and indefinite sonic segregationist or, rather, racialized music categories were at the moment of soul music's emergence.[99]

Efforts to define, and in some instances redefine, "Black" music and evaluate its role in African American culture, and American culture more generally, increased as the Civil Rights Movement morphed into the Black Power Movement. Much of White America became nostalgic about the "Negro" past, the "good old days" when "Negroes knew their place," and the good old "Negro" music that was purely entertainment and free from furtive Black radicalism.[100] Motown held a special place in the hearts and minds of Whites who advanced these kinds of ahistorical arguments because it was a phenomenal crossover success and fit within the apolitical rags-to-riches "American dream" framework.[101] For all of the fanfare surrounding "Shotgun," in the aftermath of Malcolm X's assassination a week after the song made its *Billboard* debut it seemed that the real violence rocking Black America transmuted the jostling but jocular violence of the song. No matter how desperately White America wanted Motown to stay stuck in the past and continue producing those incredibly catchy pop dance ditties and innocuous love songs, even Motown's new "soul" music simply could not avoid the social, political, and cultural meanings the turbulent historical happenings during the Black Power Movement thrust upon it.[102]

In many ways Berry Gordy was obsessed with keeping Motown a middle-of-the-road and middlebrow music brand. He shrewdly understood what the purchasing power of suburban White America, especially suburban White youth, meant to Motown. As a consequence, Motown expended a great deal of its energy and public relations dollars in its efforts to transcend the crude and often incredibly offensive categories and stereotypes associated with "race" or "Negro" music. Frequently in its efforts to transcend the baggage that came along with the "Negro music" moniker Motown ironically distanced itself from unmistakably Black musical styles that it pioneered and helped to popularize in the first half of the 1960s. However, in spite of all of its attempts to rise above the "Negro music" label, Motown continued to produce music – songs such as "Shotgun," "Dancing in the Street," "Nowhere to Run," "The Tracks of My Tears," and "It's the Same Old Song" – which were frequently infused with social, political, and cultural meanings as a result of the shift from the moderatism of the Civil Rights Movement to the militantism of the Black Power Movement. Moreover, no record company, not even the great Motown Record Corporation, could control the ways in which the music it produced during one of the most turbulent periods in American history was imbued with extra-musical meanings. Whether Berry Gordy wanted to concede it or not, Motown was always enmeshed in the hidden histories of the sonic segregation, musical colonization, and economic exploitation of Black popular music. In other words, Motown's much-celebrated "Sound of Young America" motto was deeply rooted in, and understood by many to be, a reflection of the racial, historical, cultural, social, and political conditions of the era it was created in.[103]

In the minds of many African Americans who witnessed or actually participated in the Watts rebellion that rocked Los Angeles, it was not a coincidence that a 1964 classic like "Dancing in the Street" was repurposed and put to use in the midst of the 1965 urban unrest.[104] Obviously, the mood and mindset of Black America transmuted in the aftermath of both the 1963 March on Washington and the passage of the 1964 Civil Rights Act, and the popular music emerging out of Black America at the time served as a sort of soundtrack. In 1963 and 1964 songs such as the Impressions' "It's All Right," Etta James' "Pushover," Ruby & the Romantics' "Our Day Will Come," Irma Thomas' "I Wish Someone Would Care," and the Larks' "The Jerk" seemed to represent the overarching, more or less moderate mood of Black America. However, by 1965 a "harder" and "heavier" sound with an echoing immediacy and audible militancy crept into Black popular music and expressed the sonic hearts and minds of Black America. Whether we turn to Junior Walker & the All-Stars' "Shotgun" and Little Milton's "We're Gonna Make It," Wilson Pickett's "In the Midnight Hour" and Fontella Bass' "Rescue Me," or, most obviously, James Brown's "Papa's Got a Brand New Bag" and "I Got You (I Feel Good)," all number-one hits in 1965, Black popular music was increasingly commenting on what was happening in and to Black America in the aftermath of the Civil Rights Movement.[105]

We should be clear here: In 1965 Motown was not consciously producing music aimed at advocating radical actions or eliciting any kind of revolutionary thought. For example, by the end of 1965 the Motown albums creating the most buzz in the music industry were Stevie Wonder's *Up-Tight*, the Supremes' *The Supremes at the Copa*, and Marvin Gaye's *Tribute to the Great Nat King Cole*. On the one hand, with his cover of Bob Dylan's "Blowin' in the Wind," Wonder hinted at the kinds of social commentary his music would make in the 1970s, but almost all of the other tracks on the *Up-Tight* album were rather run-of-the-mill Motown love songs.[106] On the other hand, on *The Supremes at the Copa* and *Tribute to the Great Nat King Cole* the Supremes and Marvin Gaye, respectively, paid tribute to Nat King Cole, who died of lung cancer on February 15, 1965. Cole, for all of his pioneering work in the 1940s and 1950s, was a sonically safe, middle-of-the-road crooner by the 1960s. Consequently, Motown's tributes to Cole in the wake of his death would not ruffle any White, middle-class American feathers, although, truth be told, Cole had endured a great deal of racism throughout his storied career.[107]

From the mid-to-late 1960s Motown's music would be repeatedly interpreted as expressing more than mere "love" or introducing a new dance craze. The Black Power Movement enabled African Americans to view Motown music as culturally coded music that surreptitiously said in song what African Americans could not say otherwise. However, it was not only Motown that African Americans perceived of as part of the broader soundtrack of the Black Power Movement. As rhythm & blues morphed into soul music simultaneously as the Civil Rights Movement transmuted into the Black Power Movement, Black popular music, whether soul or funk, was understood to be more than merely music. It was seen as a "weapon," as an instrument in the fight for Black freedom, and often the more oblique the sonic critique – à la much of Motown's music in the 1960s – the more meaningful and popular the music was.

Notes

1 For discussion of Motown and its artists as purveyors of "pop-R&B" or "sell-out" soul music, see Tim Brown, "The Northern Soul of Berry Gordy," in *Calling Out Around the World: A Motown Reader*, ed. Abbott, Kingsley (London: Helter Skelter, 2000), 223–25; Gerald L. Early, *One Nation Under a Groove: Motown and American Culture* (Ann Arbor: University of Michigan Press, 2004), 79–105; Jon Fitzgerald, "Motown Crossover Hits 1963–1966 and the Creative Process," *Popular Music* 14, no. 1 (1995): 1–11; Jon Fitzgerald, "Black Pop Songwriting, 1963–1966: An Analysis of U.S. Top Forty Hits by Cooke, Mayfield, Stevenson, Robinson, and Holland-Dozier-Holland," *Black Music Research Journal* 27, no. 2 (2007): 97–140; Andrew Flory, *I Hear a Symphony: Motown and Crossover R&B* (Ann Arbor: University of Michigan Press, 2017), 20–40, 69–82; Reebee Garofalo, "Crossing Over: 1939–1989," in *Split Image: African Americans in the Mass Media*, eds. Jannette L. Dates and William Barlow (Washington, D.C.: Howard University Press, 1990), 90–102; Reebee Garofalo, "Popular Music and the Civil Rights Movement," in *Rockin' the Boat: Mass Music and Mass Movements*, ed. Reebee Garofalo (Boston: South End, 1992), 234–38; Nelson George, *The Death of Rhythm & Blues* (New York: Pantheon Books, 1988), 87–89; Nelson George, *Where Did Our Love Go?: The Rise and Fall of the Motown Sound* (Urbana: University of Illinois Press, 2007), 127–28; Gerri Hirshey, *Nowhere to Run: The Story of Soul Music* (New York: Times Books, 1984), 117–227; Martin Lüthe, "Color-line and Crossing-Over: Motown and Performances of Blackness in 1960s American Culture" (Ph.D. dissertation, Justus Liebig University, 2010); Arnold Shaw, *The World of Soul: Black America's Contributions to the Pop Music Scene* (New York: Cowles Book Co., 1970), 165–80; Arnold Shaw, *Black Popular Music in America: From the Spirituals, Minstrels, and Ragtime to Soul, Disco, and Hip Hop* (New York: Schirmer Books, 1986), 223–36; Brian Ward, *Just My Soul Responding: Rhythm & Blues, Black Consciousness, and Race Relations* (Berkeley: University of California Press, 1998), 266–68.

2 Garofalo, "Popular Music and the Civil Rights Movement," 234–38; Suzanne E. Smith, *Dancing in the Street: Motown and the Cultural Politics of Detroit* (Cambridge: Harvard University Press, 1999), 67–93; Ward, *Just My Soul Responding*, 393–400.

3 On Marvin Gaye's *What's Going On?*, see Michael Eric Dyson, *Mercy, Mercy Me: The Art, Loves, and Demons of Marvin Gaye* (New York: Basic Civitas, 2004), 47–96; Ben Edmonds, *What's Going On?: Marvin Gaye and the Last Days of the Motown Sound* (Edinburgh: Mojo Books, 2001); Ben Edmonds, "A Revolution in Sound and Spirit: The Making of *What's Going On?*," liner notes for Marvin Gaye, *What's Going On?: 30th Anniversary Deluxe Edition* (Motown, 440 013 404–2, 2001, CD), 3–10; Ben Edmonds, "How," liner notes for Marvin Gaye, *What's Going On?: 40th Anniversary Deluxe Edition* (Motown, B0015552–02, 2011, CD), 5–10; David Ritz, *Divided Soul: The Life of Marvin Gaye* (New York: McGraw-Hill, 1985), 131–62; David Ritz, "Marvin's Miracle," liner notes for Marvin Gaye, *What's Going On?* (Motown, 31453–0022–2, 1994, CD), 4–16; David Ritz, "Why," liner notes for Marvin Gaye, *What's Going On?: 40th Anniversary Deluxe Edition* (Motown, B0015552–02, 2011, CD), 2–4.

4 On Stevie Wonder's *Innervisions*, see Sharon Davis, *Stevie Wonder: Rhythms of Wonder* (London: Robson, 2003), 90–102; Steve Lodder, *Stevie Wonder: A Musical Guide to the Classic Albums* (San Francisco: Backbeat Books, 2005), 87–93; James E. Perone, *The Sound of Stevie Wonder* (Westport, CT: Praeger, 2006), 47–56; Mark Ribowsky, *Signed, Sealed, and Delivered: The Soulful Journey of Stevie Wonder* (Hoboken, NJ: John Wiley & Sons, 2010), 228–36; Craig Werner, *Higher Ground: Stevie Wonder, Aretha Franklin, Curtis Mayfield, and the Rise and Fall of American Soul* (New York: Crown Publishers, 2004), 192–98.

5 James C. Scott, *Domination and the Arts of Resistance: Hidden Transcripts* (New Haven: Yale University Press, 1990), 17–44, 136–82.

6 Ward, *Just My Soul Responding*, 258–88; Craig H. Werner, *Change Is Gonna Come: Music, Race & the Soul of America* (Ann Arbor: University of Michigan Press, 2006), 15–27.

7   On Martha Reeves & the Vandellas' "Dancing in the Street" as a movement anthem, see Mark Kurlansky, *Ready for a Brand-New Beat: How "Dancing in the Street" Became the Anthem for a Changing America* (New York: Riverhead Books, 2013); Smith, *Dancing in the Street*, 1–4; Werner, *Change Is Gonna Come*, 27–28.

8   On Stevie Wonder's *Songs in the Key of Life*, see Lodder, *Stevie Wonder*, 93–103; Zeth Lundy, *Stevie Wonder's Songs in the Key of Life* (New York: Continuum, 2007); Perone, *The Sound of Stevie Wonder*, 63–71; Ribowsky, *Signed, Sealed, and Delivered*, 261–69; Werner, *Higher Ground*, 223–29.

9   On the "long Civil Rights Movement," see Eric Arnesen, "Reconsidering the 'Long Civil Rights Movement'," *Historically Speaking* 10, no. 2 (2009): 31–34; Lauren Elizabeth Beaupre, "Saints and the 'Long Civil Rights Movement'," *Journal of Urban History* 38, no. 6 (2012): 971–1002; Kevin Boyle, "Labor, the Left, and the Long Civil Rights Movement," *Social History* 30, no. 3 (2005): 366–72; Sundiata Keita Cha-Jua and Clarence Lang, "The 'Long Movement' as Vampire: Temporal and Spatial Fallacies in Recent Black Freedom Studies," *Journal of African American History* 92, no. 2 (2007): 265–88; Jacquelyn Dowd Hall, "The Long Civil Rights Movement and the Political Uses of the Past," *Journal of American History* 91, no. 4 (2005): 1233–263; Larry Isaac, "Movement of Movements: Culture Moves in the Long Civil Rights Struggle," *Social Forces* 87, no. 1 (2008): 33–63; John Salmond, "The Long Civil Rights Movement," *Agora* 44, no. 4 (2009): 20–24.

10 Smith, *Dancing in the Street*, 1–20.

11 Jonathan Andrew Flory, "I Hear a Symphony: Making Music at Motown, 1959–1979" (Ph.D. dissertation, University of North Carolina at Chapel Hill, 2006), 1–14.

12 Guthrie P. Ramsey, *Race Music: Black Cultures from Bebop to Hip Hop* (Berkeley: University of California Press, 2003), 1–2.

13 Flory, "I Hear a Symphony," 14.

14 Ibid., 14–15.

15 Ward, *Just My Soul Responding*, 262–66.

16 George, *The Death of Rhythm & Blues*, 86–89; George, *Where Did Our Love Go?*, 127–28.

17 With regard to the "hard" and "heavy" sounds emerging from Black America during the Civil Rights Movement and Black Power Movement years that Motown put its special spin on, see Samuel A. Floyd, *The Power of Black Music: Interpreting its History from Africa to the United States* (New York: Oxford University Press, 1995), 183–211; Peter Guralnick, *Sweet Soul Music: Rhythm & Blues and the Southern Dream of Freedom* (New York: Harper & Row, 1986); Michael Haralambos, *Soul Music: The Birth of a Sound in Black America* (New York: Da Capo, 1975), 94–155; Hirshey, *Nowhere to Run*, 117–347; Shaw, *The World of Soul*, 61–216; Werner, *Change Is Gonna Come*, 56–191.

18 For further discussion of my conception of "Civil Rights music," see Reiland Rabaka, *Civil Rights Music: The Soundtracks of the Civil Rights Movement* (Lanham, MD: Rowman & Littlefield Publishers, 2016).

19 Ward, *Just My Soul Responding*, 259. Major sources on the history of Motown utilized here include Kingsley Abbott, ed., *Calling Out Around the World: A Motown Reader* (London: Helter Skelter, 2000); Al Abrams, *Hype & Soul: Behind the Scenes at Motown* (Lilleshall, UK: TempleStreet, 2011); Jack Ashford, *Motown: The View from the Bottom*, ed. Charlene Ashford (New Romney: Bank House Books, 2003); Peter Benjaminson, *The Story of Motown* (New York: Grove Press, 1979); Graham Betts, *Motown Encyclopedia* (London: AC Publishing, 2014); David Bianco, *Heat Wave: The Motown Fact Book* (Ann Arbor: Pierian Press, 1988); Dennis Coffey, *Guitars, Bars, and Motown Superstars* (Ann Arbor: University of Michigan Press, 2009); Bill Dahl, *Motown: The Golden Years, The Stars and Music That Shaped a Generation* (Iola, WI: Krause, 2001); Sharon Davis, *Motown: The History* (Enfield, UK: Guinness Publishing, 1988); Early, *One Nation Under a Groove*; Flory, *I Hear a Symphony*; Ben Fong-Torres, *The Motown Album: The Sound of Young America* (London: Virgin Books, 1990); Graham Fuller and Lorrie Mack, eds., *The Motown Story* (London: Orbis, 1985); George, *Where Did Our Love Go?*; Pete McKenna, *Motown: Celebrating 60 Years of Amazing Music* (Nottinghamshire, UK: New Haven

Publishing, 2020); Pat Morgan, *Motown Artist by Artist: A Compilation of the 100 Greatest Motown Artists* (Hextabel, Kent: G2 Entertainment, 2015); David Morse, *Motown and the Arrival of Black Music* (New York: Macmillan, 1971); Gerald L. Posner, *Motown: Music, Money, Sex, and Power* (New York: Random House, 2002); Keith Rylatt, *Hitsville! The Birth of Tamla Motown* (Belper, UK: Modus, 2016); Jack Ryan, *Recollections, The Detroit Years: The Motown Sound by the People Who Made It* (Whitmore Lake, MI: Glendower Media, 2012); Smith, *Dancing in the Street*; J. Randy Taraborrelli, *Motown: Hot Wax, City Cool, Solid Gold* (Garden City: Doubleday, 1986); Harold Keith Taylor, *The Motown Music Machine* (Detroit: Jadmeg Music, 2003); Don Waller, *The Motown Story* (New York: Scribner, 1985); Susan Whitall, *Women of Motown: An Oral History*, 2nd ed. (New York: Devault Graves, 2017); Adam White, *The Motown Story* (Boston: Bedford Press, 1985); Adam White, *Motown: The Sound of Young America*, ed. Barney Ales (London: Thames & Hudson, 2016); Terry Wilson, *Tamla Motown: The Stories Behind the UK Singles* (London: Cherry Red, 2009); Vickie Wright, Louvain Demps, Marlene Barrow-Tate, and Jackie Hicks, *Motown from the Background: The Authorized Biography of the Andantes* (New Romney: Bank House Books, 2007).

20 Berry Gordy, *To Be Loved: The Music, the Magic, the Memories of Motown: An Autobiography* (New York: Warner Books, 1994), 1–107.

21 Gordy, *To Be Loved*, 59–77.

22 Ibid., 84–123.

23 Portia K. Maultsby, "Rhythm & Blues/R&B," in *African American Music: An Introduction*, 2nd ed., eds. Mellonee V. Burnim, and Portia K. Maultsby (New York: Routledge, 2015), 257–60.

24 On the much-celebrated "Motown sound," see Benjaminson, *The Story of Motown*, 28–35; John Covach and Andrew Flory, "Motown Pop and Southern Soul," in John Covach and Andrew Flory, *What's That Sound?: An Introduction to Rock and Its History*, 3rd ed. (New York: Norton, 2012), 223–26; Dahl, *Motown*, 10–43; Davis, *Motown*, 29–48; Flory, *I Hear a Symphony*, 41–68; Shaw, *The World of Soul*, 165–80; Charles E. Sykes, "Motown," in *African American Music: An Introduction*, eds. Mellonee V. Burnim and Portia K. Maultsby (New York: Routledge, 2006), 440–50; Waller, *The Motown Story*, 136–53; Ward, *Just My Soul Responding*, 262–66.

25 George, *Where Did Our Love Go?*, 37.

26 Flory, *I Hear a Symphony*, 43–44.

27 Ibid., 45–46.

28 George, *Where Did Our Love Go?*, 50.

29 Benjaminson, *The Story of Motown*, 36–41; Flory, *I Hear a Symphony*, 41–68; George, *Where Did Our Love Go?*, 27–49; Neal, *What the Music Said*, 42–46; White, *Motown*, 42–67.

30 George, *Where Did Our Love Go?*, 50.

31 Neal, *What the Music Said*, 42–46; Ward, *Just My Soul Responding*, 266–68; White, *Motown*, 68–127.

32 Several youth-centered or, at the least, youth issues-sensitive historical works on the Civil Rights Movement informed my narrative here. For example, see Rebecca de Schweinitz, *If We Could Change the World: Young People and America's Long Struggle for Racial Equality* (Chapel Hill: University of North Carolina Press, 2009); Ellen S. Levine, *Freedom's Children: Young Civil Rights Activists Tell Their Own Stories* (New York: Putnam, 1993); Andrew B. Lewis, *The Shadows of Youth: The Remarkable Journey of the Civil Rights Generation* (New York: Hill & Wang, 2009); James P. Marshall, *Student Activism and Civil Rights in Mississippi: Protest Politics and the Struggle for Racial Justice, 1960–1965* (Baton Rouge: Louisiana State University Press, 2016); Jeffrey A. Turner, *Sitting In and Speaking Out: Student Movements in the American South, 1960–1970* (Athens: University of Georgia Press, 2010).

33 George, *Where Did Our Love Go?*, 80.

34 Benjaminson, *The Story of Motown*, 64–75; Davis, *Motown*, 29–48; Neal, *What the Music Said*, 45; Waller, *The Motown Story*, 43–58.

35 Martin Luther King, Jr., "I Have a Dream," in Martin Luther King, *A Testament of Hope: The Essential Writings of Martin Luther King, Jr.*, ed. James Melvin Washington (San Francisco: Harper & Row, 1986), 217.

36 Ibid., 219.

37 Peniel E. Joseph, *The Sword and the Shield: The Revolutionary Lives of Malcolm X and Martin Luther King Jr.* (New York: Basic Books, 2020), 157–98.

38 Early, *One Nation Under a Groove*, 41–65; Flory, *I Hear a Symphony*, 29–44; Smith, *Dancing in the Street*, 67–93.

39 Flory, *I Hear a Symphony*, 69–99; George, *Where Did Our Love Go?*, 50–147; Neal, *What the Music Said*, 43.

40 Neal, *What the Music Said*, 43–45; Posner, *Motown*, 60–97.

41 Early, *One Nation Under a Groove*, 53–54. See also George, *Where Did Our Love Go?*, 55–65; Posner, *Motown*, 42–54; Sykes, "Motown," 442–44.

42 George, *Where Did Our Love Go?*, 54–55; Smith, *Dancing in the Street*, 50–53, 83–93; White, *Motown*, 79–80.

43 Posner, *Motown*, 172.

44 Ward, *Just My Soul Responding*, 268.

45 In *One Nation Under a Groove*, Gerald Early offered insight on Gordy's distinct brand of double-consciousness. See Early, *One Nation Under a Groove*, 46–49.

46 For examples of autobiographical works by, and biographical works about, Motown singer-songwriters, producers, and musicians that make, however muted, connections between 1960s Motown and the Civil Rights Movement, see Ashford, *Motown*; Peter Benjaminson, *The Lost Supreme: The Life of Dreamgirl Florence Ballard* (Chicago: Lawrence Hill Books, 2008); Peter Benjaminson, *Mary Wells: The Tumultuous Life of Motown's First Superstar* (Chicago: Chicago Review Press, 2012); Peter Benjaminson, *Super Freak: The Life of Rick James* (Chicago: Chicago Review Press, 2017); Sharon Davis, *Marvin Gaye: I Heard It Through the Grapevine* (Edinburgh: Mainstream, 2001); Sharon Davis, *Lionel Richie: Hello* (London: Equinox, 2009); Dyson, *Mercy, Mercy Me*; Edmonds, *What's Going On?*; Gordy, *To Be Loved*; Rick James, *Glow: The Autobiography of Rick James*, with David Ritz (New York: Simon & Schuster, 2014); Gladys Knight, *Between Each Line of Pain and Glory: My Life Story* (New York: Hyperion, 1997); Perone, *The Sound of Stevie Wonder*; Martha Reeves, *Dancing in the Street: Confessions of a Motown Diva*, with Mark Bego (New York: Hyperion, 1994); Ribowsky, *The Supremes*; Ribowsky, *Ain't Too Proud to Beg*; Ribowsky, *Signed, Sealed, and Delivered*; Ritz, *Divided Soul*; Smokey Robinson, *Smokey: Inside Life* (New York: McGraw-Hill, 1989); Ryan, *Recollections*; Richard Street, *Ball of Confusion: My Life as a Temptin' Temptation*, with Gary Flanigan (Mustang, OK: Tate Publishing, 2014); Richard Street, *Richard Street: My Life as a Temptation*, with Toi Moore (New York: TM Publications, 2017); J. Randy Taraborrelli, *Diana Ross: A Biography* (New York: Citadel Press/Kensington Publishing, 2014); Marc Taylor, *The Original Marvelettes: Motown's Mystery Girl Group* (Jamaica, NY: Aloiv Publishing, 2004); Steve Turner, *Trouble Man: The Life and Death of Marvin Gaye* (New York: Ecco Press, 1998); Otis Williams, *Temptations*, with Patricia Romanowski Bashe (New York: Putnam, 1988); Mary Wilson, *Dreamgirl: My Life as a Supreme* (New York: St. Martin's Press, 1986); Mary Wilson, *Supreme Faith: Someday We'll Be Together*, with Patricia Romanowski Bashe (New York: HarperCollins, 1990); Susan Whitall, *Women of Motown*; Vickie Wright, et al., *Motown from the Background*.

47 Ward, *Just My Soul Responding*, 268–75.

48 Peter Doggett, "Liner Notes," in *Power to the Motown People!: Civil Rights Anthems and Political Soul, 1968–1975* (Motown, 980 090–1, 2007, CD), 2.

49 Ibid., 2–3. Regarding Martin Luther King's Motown releases, see Martin Luther King, *The Great March to Freedom: Detroit June 23, 1963* (Gordy, 906, 1963, LP); Martin Luther King et al., *The Great March on Washington* (Gordy, 908, 1963, LP); Martin Luther King, *Free at Last* (Gordy, 929, 1968, LP); Martin Luther King, *I Have a Dream* (Tamla Motown, SJET-8062, 1968, LP); Martin Luther King, *Why I Oppose the War in Vietnam* (Black Forum, BF451, 1970, LP). And for more detailed discussion of Motown's Black

Forum subsidiary label, see Charles E. Sykes, "The Black Forum Label: Motown Joins the Revolution," *ARSC Journal* 46, no. 1 (2015): 1–41; Pat Thomas, "The Movement, Motown, and Popular Music," in Pat Thomas, *Listen, Whitey!: The Sights and Sounds of Black Power, 1965–1975* (New York: Norton, 2012), 11–53.

50 Rabaka, *Civil Rights Music*, 71–85.
51 George, *Where Did Our Love Go?*, 54.
52 Rabaka, *Civil Rights Music*, 138–53.
53 Smith, *Dancing in the Street*, 21–53.
54 Ibid., 18.
55 Neal, *What the Music Said*, 42–46.
56 Smith, *Dancing in the Street*, 54–93.
57 Garofalo, "Crossing Over," 90.
58 Doggett, "Liner Notes," 2–6; Neal, *What the Music Said*, 44–45; Smith, *Dancing in the Street*, 135–38; Ward, *Just My Soul Responding*, 181–216.
59 Smith, *Dancing in the Street*, 67–93.
60 Flory, *I Hear a Symphony*, 29–40; Smith, *Dancing in the Street*, 5–20; Sykes, "Motown," 431–42.
61 E. Franklin Frazier, *Black Bourgeoisie* (New York: Free Press, 1969), 153–238. On Berry Gordy's middle-of-the-road, almost obsessive middle-class mindset, see Early, *One Nation Under a Groove*, 35–65; Flory, *I Hear a Symphony*, 22–40; George, *Where Did Our Love Go?*, 139–40; Michael Goldberg, "Berry Gordy: Motown's Founder Tells the Story of Hitsville, U.S.A.," in *Calling Out Around the World: A Motown Reader*, ed. Kingsley Abbott (London: Helter Skelter, 2000), 27–35; Posner, *Motown*, 114–25; Ward, *Just My Soul Responding*, 258–62; White, *Motown*, 128–65.
62 Benjaminson, *The Story of Motown*, 28–35; Dahl, *Motown*, 10–43; Davis, *Motown*, 29–68; Flory, *I Hear a Symphony*, 43–44; George, *Where Did Our Love Go?*, 102–3, 107–8; Gordy, *To Be Loved*, 125–26; Shaw, *The World of Soul*, 165–80; Smith, *Dancing in the Street*, 154–55; Sykes, "Motown," 444–50; Taraborrelli, *Motown*, 3–6; Ward, *Just My Soul Responding*, 262–66.
63 Sykes, "Motown," 436–37. See also Marie McCarthy, "The Young Musicians of Motown: A Success Story of Urban Music Education," *Music Educators Journal* 99, no. 3 (2013): 35–42.
64 Sykes, "Motown," 444–45. For further discussion of the various music genres that Motown incorporated into its sonic DNA to develop its classic sound, see Flory, *I Hear a Symphony*, 29–37.
65 Flory, *I Hear a Symphony*, 58–64; George, *Where Did Our Love Go?*, 102–3; Smith, *Dancing in the Street*, 155; Sykes, "Motown," 444–50.
66 Betts, *Motown Encyclopedia*, 15, 35, 219–20, 229–30; Per Elias Drabløs, *The Quest for the Melodic Electric Bass: From Jamerson to Spenner* (Farnham, Surrey: Ashgate, 2016), 14–17, 27–30, 72–74, 118–20; Dan Forte, "James Jamerson: Preeminent Motown Bassist," *Guitar Player* 6 (1979): 44–45; Ed Friedland, *R&B Bass Masters: The Way They Play* (San Francisco: Backbeat Books, 2005), 7–14; Gordy, *To Be Loved*, 124–26; Allan Slutsky, *Standing in the Shadows of Motown: The Life and Music of Legendary Bassist James Jameson* (Milwaukee: Hal Leonard Publishing, 1989); Smith, *Dancing in the Street*, 155; Waller, *The Motown Story*, 154–67; Brain F. Wright, "Reconstructing the History of Motown Session Musicians: The Carol Kaye/James Jamerson Controversy," *Journal of the Society for American Music* 13, no. 1 (2019): 78–109; Joshua Andrew Zarbo, "James Jamerson: From Jazz Bassist to Popular Music Icon" (Master's thesis, Texas State University, 2014).
67 Flory, *I Hear a Symphony*, 61–62. See also Slutsky, *Standing in the Shadows of Motown* 3–83; Zarbo, "James Jamerson," 1–20.
68 Sykes, "Motown," 444–50.
69 Sykes, "Motown," 448. See also Lamont Dozier, *How Sweet It Is: A Songwriter's Reflections on Music, Motown, and the Mystery of the Muse*, with Scott B. Bomar (New York: BMG Books, 2019); Brian Holland and Edward Holland, *Come and Get These Memories: The Genius of Holland-Dozier-Holland*, with Dave Thompson (London: Omnibus Press,

2019); Adam White, "The Master in Them: The Story of Holland/Dozier/Holland," liner notes for Holland/Dozier/Holland, *Heaven Must Have Sent You: The Holland/Dozier/Holland Story* (Hip-O Records, B0004845–02, 2005, CD) 1–21.

70 Flory, *I Hear a Symphony*, 49–64. See also George, *Where Did Our Love Go?*, 114–20; Smith, *Dancing in the Street*, 155; Taraborrelli, *Motown*, 5–6.

71 Gordy, *To Be Loved*, 125.

72 Marilyn Bond and S.R. Boland, *The Birth of the Detroit Sound, 1940–1964* (Charleston: Arcadia, 2002); Early, *One Nation Under a Groove*, 67–105; Smith, *Dancing in the Street*, 155; Sykes, "Motown," 435–40.

73 Gordy, *To Be Loved*, 99–100, 112–13, 117–20; Posner, *Motown*, 34–36.

74 Betts, *Motown Encyclopedia*, 256–57; Raynoma Gordy Singleton, *Berry, Me, and Motown: The Untold Story*, with Bryan Brown and Mim Eichler (Chicago: Contemporary Books, 1990), 90; Smith, *Dancing in the Street*, 155–56.

75 Gordy, *To Be Loved*, 118.

76 Dahl, *Motown*, 23–26; Flory, *I Hear a Symphony*, 44–49.

77 Slutsky, *Standing in the Shadows of Motown*, 16.

78 Ibid., 16.

79 Ibid., 81–83.

80 For a more detailed discussion of Motown's recording process during its Detroit years between 1959 and 1972, see Flory, *I Hear a Symphony*, 44–49.

81 Ribowsky, *The Supremes*, 7–10.

82 Wilson, *Dreamgirl*, 24.

83 Ibid., 24–25.

84 Ibid., 59.

85 Ibid., 24–25.

86 George, *Where Did Our Love Go?*, 43–49.

87 Dahl, *Motown*, 33–43; Flory, *I Hear a Symphony*, 69–99; Posner, *Motown*, 172–78; Taraborrelli, *Motown*, 52–72.

88 Early, *One Nation Under a Groove*, 107–35; Flory, *I Hear a Symphony*, 100–34; George, *Where Did Our Love Go?*, 148–89; Taraborrelli, *Motown*, 52–133.

89 Herb Boyd, "Nothing but Heartaches," liner notes for Various Artists, *The Complete Motown Singles, Vol. 5: 1965* (Hip-O Select, B0006775–02, 2006, CD), 11.

90 Bill Dahl and Keith Hughes, "The Songs: Track-By-Track Annotations," liner notes for Various Artists, *The Complete Motown Singles, Vol. 5: 1965* (Hip-O Select, B0006775–02, 2006, CD), 20–21.

91 Betts, *Motown Encyclopedia*, 520–23; Boyd, "Nothing But Heartaches," 13–15; Bill Dahl, "Junior Walker: Motown's Screaming Sax Star," in *Calling Out Around the World: A Motown Reader*, ed. Kingsley Abbott (London: Helter Skelter, 2000), 121–26; Dahl, *Motown*, 174–83; Davis, *Motown*, 65–67; Ben Edmonds, "Liner Notes," liner notes for Junior Walker and the All-Stars, *Nothin' but Soul: The Singles* (Motown, 37463–6270–2, 1994, CD), 3–19; Flory, *I Hear a Symphony*, 77–79; George, *Where Did Our Love Go?*, 127–31.

92 Betts, *Motown Encyclopedia*, 145, 303–4, 461–62; Flory, *I Hear a Symphony*, 120–34; George, *Where Did Our Love Go?*, 28–29.

93 Betts, *Motown Encyclopedia*, 418; Harry Weinger, "The Indexes," liner notes for Various Artists, *The Complete Motown Singles, Vol. 5: 1965* (Hip-O Select, B0006775–02, 2006, CD), 139–43.

94 On Motown's short-lived Workshop Jazz Records imprint, see Betts, *Motown Encyclopedia*, 575; Bill Dahl and Keith Hughes, "The Songs: Track-By-Track Annotations," liner notes for Various Artists, *The Complete Motown Singles, Vol. 2: 1962* (Hip-O Select, B0004402–02, 2005, CD), 32–33; Bill Dahl and Keith Hughes, "The Songs: Track-By-Track Annotations," liner notes for Various Artists, *The Complete Motown Singles, Vol. 3: 1963* (Hip-O Select, B0005352–02, 2005, CD), 18, 25–29; Flory, *I Hear a Symphony*, 33.

95 Betts, *Motown Encyclopedia*, 418; Flory, *I Hear a Symphony*, 77–79.

96 Benjaminson, *The Story of Motown*, 158–63; Flory, *I Hear a Symphony*, 79–88; George, *Where Did Our Love Go?*, 127–31; Smith, *Dancing in the Street*, 163–64.

97 Smith, *Dancing in the Street*, 163–65.

98 Tim Brooks, *Lost Sounds: Blacks and the Birth of the Recording Industry, 1890–1919* (Urbana: University of Illinois Press, 2004); Karl Hagstrom Miller, *Segregating Sound: Inventing Folk and Pop Music in the Age of Jim Crow* (Durham: Duke University Press, 2010); Arnold Shaw, *Honkers and Shouters: The Golden Years of Rhythm & Blues* (New York: Macmillan, 1978); David Suisman, *Selling Sounds: The Commercial Revolution in American Music* (Cambridge: Harvard University Press, 2009), esp. 204–39; Ward, *Just My Soul Responding*, 19–55.

99 Betts, *Motown Encyclopedia*, 418; Flory, *I Hear a Symphony*, 77–79; Smith, *Dancing in the Street*, 164; Ward, *Just My Soul Responding*, 173–216.

100 Ward, *Just My Soul Responding*, 232–43.

101 Early, *One Nation Under a Groove*, 67–105; Shaw, *The World of Soul*, 165–80; Sykes, "The Black Forum Label," 3–11; Thomas, "The Movement, Motown, and Popular Music," 12–15; White, *Motown*, 90–127.

102 Smith, *Dancing in the Street*, 165; Sykes, "The Black Forum Label," 26–53.

103 Smith, *Dancing in the Street*, 164–65; Thomas, "The Movement, Motown, and Popular Music," 12–15; Ward, *Just My Soul Responding*, 262–68.

104 On the Watts rebellion of 1965, see Paul Bullock, ed., *Watts: The Aftermath: An Inside View of the Ghetto* (New York: Grove Press, 1970); Jerry Cohen and William S. Murphy, *Burn, Baby, Burn!: The Los Angeles Race Riot, August, 1965* (New York: Avon Books, 1967); Mike Davis and Jon Wiener, *Set the Night on Fire: L.A. in the Sixties* (London: Verso Books, 2020), 203–98; Robert M. Fogelson, *The Los Angeles Riots* (New York: Arno Press, 1969); Gerald Horne, *Fire This Time: The Watts Uprising and the 1960s* (New York: Da Capo Press, 1997); Della Rossa, *Why Watts Exploded: How the Ghetto Fought Back* (New York: Merit Publishers, 1969); David O. Sears and John B. McConahay, *The Politics of Violence: The New Urban Blacks and the Watts Riot* (Washington, DC: University Press of America, 1973).

105 George, *The Death of Rhythm & Blues*, 95–119; Haralambos, *Soul Music*, 93–135; Neal, *What the Music Said*, 46–53; Thomas, *Listen, Whitey!*, passim; Ward, *Just My Soul Responding*, 181–216; Werner, *Change Is Gonna Come*, 103–20.

106 On Stevie Wonder's sonic social commentary in the 1970s, see Davis, *Stevie Wonder*, 71–144; Lodder, *Stevie Wonder*, 58–217; Lundy, *Stevie Wonder's Songs in the Key of Life*, passim; Perone, *The Sound of Stevie Wonder*, 25–84; Ribowsky, *Signed, Sealed, and Delivered*, 179–275; Werner, *Higher Ground*, 188–235.

107 See Inger L. Stole, "Nat King Cole and the Politics of Race and Broadcasting in the 1950s," *Communication Review* 1, no. 3 (1996): 349–71; Brian Ward, "Civil Rights and Rock & Roll: Revisiting the Nat King Cole Attack of 1956," *OAH Magazine of History* 24, no. 2 (2010): 21–24.

3

SOUL MEN, MUSICAL MACHISMO, AND THE BLACK POWER MOVEMENT

Soul: deepening and darkening Black popular music

Much like Motown from the mid-1960s to the mid-1970s, as the wider world of rhythm & blues morphed into soul music it shifted from implicitly raising Civil Rights Movement issues to explicitly articulating the ideals and ethos of the Black Power Movement. As a matter of fact, from the mid-1960s to the mid-1970s Black popular song after Black popular song unambiguously referenced the ongoing post-Civil Rights Movement struggle.[1] Initially, early proto-soul and then ultimately bona fide soul singer-songwriters openly commented on everything from Black history and Black culture to Black politics and Black economics. War and peace, community and family, spirituality and sexuality, crime and poverty, and alcoholism and drug addiction were among the plethora of other issues consistently raised in the radical new form of rhythm & blues being increasingly called "soul music" by the mid-1960s.[2] Similar to several of the Motown artists who would make the transition from rhythm & blues to soul, other Black singer-songwriters who began their careers as rhythm & blues recording artists evolved into soul singer-songwriters whose work often echoed and offered a distinctive public voice for many of the collective beliefs of the Black Power Movement.[3]

Almost all of the major changes in rhythm & blues-cum-soul in the mid-1960s can be connected to the changes taking place in Black America as a consequence of a rising collective Black cultural consciousness. That is to say, important musical changes in lyrics, sound, instrumentation, presentation, and performance practices coincided with social, political, and cultural changes afoot in Black America from the mid-1960s to the mid-1970s. While it is undeniable that the Civil Rights Act of 1964 and the Voting Rights Act of 1965 were historic triumphs that seemed to call into being a desegregated and integrated, pluralistic America with equal opportunity and justice for all, the truth of the matter is that by the end of the

DOI: 10.4324/9781003254492-4

1960s these momentous victories seemed like little more than empty words on pretty pieces of paper.[4]

When all of the smoke cleared and all of the dust settled surrounding the 1963 March on Washington, the Civil Rights Act of 1964, and the Voting Rights Act of 1965, many in Black America could clearly see that the arduous efforts and landmark legislation of the mid-to-late 1960s had at best moderated but hardly eradicated the undeniably destructive effects of racial segregation and ongoing systematic discrimination. Furthermore, the introduction of statutory equality in and of itself did very little, if anything at all, to curtail the demoralizing effects of centuries of racial terrorism and post-enslavement American apartheid. In addition, neither the Civil Rights Act of 1964 nor the Voting Rights Act of 1965 helped to prepare or actually provided African Americans with tools to compete on a level playing field with Whites. Inferior education, inadequate housing, second-class healthcare, skyrocketing poverty rates, incessant unemployment, and paltry political power collectively continued to afflict most of Black America in the decade immediately following the Civil Rights Movement, and the protest songs and message music of the period creatively chronicled and critiqued African Americans' aspirations and frustrations in ways that were both old and new: *old* in the sense that they often built on the foundation that rhythm & blues laid, and *new* in that they almost as a rule broke the rules of rhythm & blues record-making by *deepening and darkening the sound of Black popular music.*[5]

As if responding to the seemingly concerted efforts, especially by many at Motown (Berry Gordy chief among them), to *whiten and lighten* rhythm & blues, soul burst on the mid-1960s scene with *deeper lyrics* and *a darker, undeniably Black sound.* It was a sound that captured and frequently conveyed not merely the ideals and ethos of the Black Power Movement but also the complex and often contradictory spiritual, sexual, and ideological thought that emerged in the immediate aftermath of the Civil Rights Movement. The Black Power Movement was characterized by the simultaneous dense and tense interplay of Black insurgency and Black apathy, Black empowerment and Black disenfranchisement, Black pragmatism and Black dogmatism, all of which was coupled with a distinct post-Civil Rights Movement Black cultural consciousness that was one of the hallmarks and lasting legacies of the movement. On the one hand, the Black Power Movement allowed African Americans to collectively articulate some of the most penetrating critiques of American racism and set into motion some of the most inspirational, progressive, and creative efforts to economically, socially, politically, culturally, and intellectually empower African Americans since the New Negro Movement and its artistic offshoot, the Harlem Renaissance. On the other hand, the Black Power Movement also gave rise to some of the most ignominious, pessimistic, exploitative, misogynist, homophobic, and outright reactionary impulses passing themselves off as Black Power politics.[6] At both its best and its worst, soul seemed to express this tangle of paradoxes, enabling African Americans to intensify and radicalize the *"we can implicitly sing what we cannot explicitly say" aesthetic* carried over from the soundtracks of the Civil Rights Movement. Indeed, this *lyrically deeper and sonically darker music* gave voice to both the progressive and retrogressive ethos of the Black Power Movement.[7]

Musical Africanisms: on the Africanization and radicalization of rhythm & blues

The sonic range of Black popular music during the Black Power Movement reflected both the musical *and* the political paradoxes besetting Black America from the mid-1960s to the mid-1970s. In terms of the political paradoxes, Black popular music increasingly incorporated elements of what could be broadly conceived of as both integrationist and nationalist sentiments – sentiments, it should be emphasized, which had consistently collided with each other in collective Black consciousness throughout African American history, from Frederick Douglass and Martin Delany to Martin Luther King and Malcolm X. And for those who continue to believe that it was something new in the 1960s and 1970s, Roderick Bush reminded us that Black nationalism "has been a significant component of African American social thought for more than two hundred years, varying in intensity according to time, place, and circumstance."[8] As a matter of fact, Bush continued, the call for Black Power "was based precisely on Black people's awareness that the Civil Rights Movement did not address the key issues that would result in genuine empowerment. What was needed was not more 'Civil Rights,' but human rights." Then, echoing Malcolm X, Bush stated, "the problem facing African Americans was not a 'Negro' problem or an American problem, but a human problem that could not be solved merely by the attainment of Civil Rights." Indeed, he went even further, "it required a long-range strategy for independence and self-determination."[9]

According to William Van Deburg in *Modern Black Nationalism*, the origins of Black nationalism can be traced back to African American enslavement when the enslaved first began to (1) "question and then reject their presumed status as 'inferior' vis-à-vis the Whites"; (2) "recognize the need for intraracial solidarity"; (3) "proclaim their intellectual independence"; and (4) "employ shared experiences with bondage, caste, and folk culture to shape countervisions of the racial future."[10] During the Black Power Movement years African Americans came to question integrationism and embrace nationalism because in many ways their conditions continued to mirror those of their enslaved ancestors, although without shackles, chains, and whips. Again, it was not merely active members of the Black Power Movement who were indelibly influenced by its ideology. Countless preachers and teachers, doctors and lawyers, construction workers and college students, athletes and artists fell under the spell of Black nationalism between the mid-1960s and mid-1970s.[11] Consequently, musicians were not immune to the ideological influence of the Black Power Movement and latent Black nationalism in particular. This means that it is important for us to understand the particular kind of Black nationalism that was prevalent during the Black Power Movement if we are to critically comprehend Black Power music.

It was nationalist themes, not desegregationist or integrationist themes à la Civil Rights music, that both lyrically and sonically distinguished 1960s and 1970s soul and funk as unmistakable forms of Black Power music. Discussing the rise and rationale of Black nationalism during the Black Power Movement, Van Deburg importantly explained:

> The Black nationalist worldview of these tumultuous years can be encapsulated as follows: White power, as manifested in the workings of U.S. institutional life, had long been a major impediment to the African American's attainment of the good life. In order to challenge and ultimately dissolve this oppressive monopoly, Blacks had to mobilize, close ranks, and build group strength. This difficult process involved all aspects of Black life – political, economic, psychological, and cultural. Once unity had been achieved in these areas, Blacks would form a significant power bloc and move toward realizing the ideal expressed in the concept "consent of the governed." Able to exercise true freedom of choice for the first time, they might then choose to go it alone, either in "liberated" urban enclaves, in a separate Black-run nation-state, or simply in the realm of the psyche.
>
> Whatever the specific nationalist format, the new Black American would be a transformed, self-actualized individual. Central to the Black Power/ Black nationalist experience, the concept of self-definition was a fundamental component of the "revolution of the mind" that many activists believed was a prerequisite for the successful implementation of their (numerous and varied) plans for revolutionizing society. To become self-directed, to be assertive, to take pride in skin color and heritage was to remove the negative connotations of race that had long served as a constraining psychological and social force. Whites, of course, might still factor supposed racial limitations into their own plans for continued societal domination, but Black people endowed with a "national" consciousness no longer would agree to play by the old rules. Instead of meekly responding to White stimuli or linking arms with paternalistic White liberals, they would dare to be pro-Black – to look, feel, be and *do* Black. It was the nationalists' hope and expectation that this revolutionary psychological process of *becoming* Black would initiate and support a social revolution of considerable magnitude.[12]

It was against this political backdrop that Civil Rights music morphed into Black Power music, and integrationist themes in Black popular music increasingly gave way to nationalist themes in the music. Van Deburg not only emphasized the "revolutionary psychological process of *becoming* Black" that was integral to the Black Power Movement, but also the fact that "[t]his difficult process involved all aspects of Black life – political, economic, psychological, and cultural." When he invoked the "cultural" aspects of the African American experience that were utilized in the "revolutionary psychological process of *becoming* Black" during the Black Power Movement, Black popular music should be considered a key element of Black cultural expression. In fact, Black music should be considered one of the primary conveyors of Black culture, both in the past and in the present.[13] And, just as Black culture increasingly incorporated aspects of nationalist or "pro-Black" ideology during the Black Power Movement, Black music also came to incorporate "pro-Black" elements and messages. Hence, whether we turn to Donny Hathaway's *Everything Is Everything* (1970), Funkadelic's *Free Your Mind . . . And Your Ass Will Follow* (1970), Marvin Gaye's *What's Going On?* (1971), Sly & the Family Stone's *There's a Riot Goin' On* (1971), James Brown's *Revolution of the Mind: Live at the Apollo, Volume III* (1971), or Stevie Wonder's *Innervisions* (1973), nationalist themes provided a subtext for much of the message music of the era.

With regard to the musical paradoxes at play in the Black popular music of the Black Power Movement, it is important to observe the ways in which consecutive rhythm & blues styles arranged and rearranged, extended and expanded conventionally conceived "Black" and "White" musical techniques. The manipulation of these ostensibly "Black" and "White" musical techniques assisted not only in further sonically desegregating the American soundscape and broader American music industry, but also in sonically deconstructing and reconstructing Black popular music from the mid-1960s to the mid-1970s.[14]

In essence, the major musical mouthpieces of the Black Power Movement, soul and its sibling sound funk, frequently blurred the lines between what had previously been conceived of as "Black" and "White" music. The lyrics and sonics of soul and funk provided a crude kind of analogue, predicated on distinctively Black symbols and Black sounds, that seemed to capture and convey the mood of Black America between the mid-1960s and the mid-1970s. Soul and funk also offered a medium through which African American musicians could innovatively assert cultural pride and a general commitment to the Black freedom struggle, regardless of whether their lyrics explicitly espoused Black liberation or active membership in a specific Black Power Movement organization. What needs to be understood here is that unlike most forms of political protest, *aesthetic protest* is very rarely a direct call to action, and this is where there is considerable overlap between soul and funk as forms of musical protest during the Black Power Movement. Even so, critical aesthetic representation of socio-political problems, political aesthetics, and social realism in the context of African American artistic traditions must be comprehended as constituting extremely powerful socio-political ideas and acts.

Most musicologists might interpret instances of protest in classic soul as mere "complaint," but by the very fact that the alleged "complaint" is publicly articulated to such an eloquent extent that even Black popular music's most ahistorical, apolitical, and often incredibly uninformed interpreters understand it to be "complaint" illustrates that musical protest, indeed, is a form of contestation of oppressive and exploitive conditions even when it does not directly translate into concrete political organization and public demonstration. This is part of the distinct power of Black popular music, if not Black popular culture in general. Indirectly responding to Black popular music critics' de-politicization of Black song and helping to drive my point home about classic soul as a form of protest even though it may not have translated into "protest" in the conventional Black Power Movement sense of the word, in *Black Culture and Black Consciousness: Afro-American Folk Thought from Slavery to Freedom*, Lawrence Levine offered remarkable insight:

> To state that Black song constituted a form of Black protest and resistance does not mean that it necessarily led to or even called for any tangible and specific actions, but rather that it served as a mechanism by which Negroes could be relatively candid in a society that rarely accorded them that privilege, could communicate this candor to others whom they would in no other way be able to reach, and, in the face of the sanctions of the White majority, could assert their own individuality, aspirations, and sense of being. Certainly, if nothing else, Black song makes it difficult to believe that Negroes internalized their situation so completely, accepted the values of the larger society so totally, or manifested so pervasive an apathy as we have been led to believe. . . . The African tradition of being able to verbalize publicly in song what could not be said to a person's face, not only lived on among Afro-Americans throughout slavery but continued to be a central feature of Black expressive culture in freedom.[15]

It is Levine's last sentence that directly connects with classic soul and funk songs. When he reminded us that the "African tradition of being able to verbalize publicly in song what could not be said to a person's face, not only lived on among Afro-Americans throughout slavery but continued to be a central feature of Black expressive culture in freedom," he hinted at how generation after jostling generation of African American musicians have literally utilized music as a medium to constructively critique their enslavers, oppressors, and abusers. From Billie Holiday's "Strange Fruit" and Nina Simone's "Mississippi Goddam" to James Brown's "Say It Loud – I'm Black and I'm Proud" and Parliament's "Chocolate City," much like the message music of the Civil Rights Movement, with the protest songs and message music of the Black Power Movement African Americans were able to sing what many believed they could not unambiguously say "in the face of the sanctions of the White majority."[16]

It is also important for us to keep in mind that the contention that "Black song constituted a form of Black protest and resistance does not mean that it necessarily led to or even called for any tangible and specific actions." As with rhythm & blues during the Civil Rights Movement, classic soul's "protest and resistance" may not have nicely and neatly paralleled the "protest and resistance" emerging from the dominant African American socio-political movement of its epoch (i.e., the Black Power Movement). But, make no mistake about it, soul sisters and brothers, as Levine noted, indeed did protest and resist by way of Black popular music and Black popular culture, among other social, political, and aesthetic avenues. In hindsight, then, the wide number of efforts aimed at deepening the lyrics and darkening the sound of Black popular music from the mid-to-late 1960s should not be glossed over, because, above all else, they symbolized African Americans' unapologetic embrace and celebration of the African elements of their highly hybrid heritage.[17]

Although not much discussion is given to it today, from the mid-1960s to the mid-1970s African Americans' increasing preoccupation with the African roots of the African American experience revived interest in African history, cultures, struggles, and languages. This interest eventually gave way to intense interests in African music. Iconic African musicians, such as Miriam Makeba, Hugh Masekela, Babatunde Olatunji, Manu Dibango, Abdullah Ibrahim (aka Dollar Brand), and of course Fela Kuti, all benefitted from the Black Power Movement's seeming interest in all things African. Between the mid-1960s and the mid-1970s African American jazz musicians in particular drew a great deal of musical, cultural, and spiritual inspiration from Africa, frequently fusing this inspiration with myriad other "world music" and "world religion" influences. As detailed in important works such as Norman Weinstein's *A Night in Tunisia: Imaginings of Africa in Jazz*, Ingrid Monson's *Freedom Sounds: Civil Rights Call Out to Jazz and Africa*, Robin Kelley's *Africa Speaks, America Answers: Modern Jazz in Revolutionary Times*, Karlton Hester's *African Roots of the Jazz Evolution*, and Gerhard Kubik's *Jazz Transatlantic: The African Undercurrent in Twentieth Century Jazz Culture*, legendary jazz artists like Sun Ra, Art Blakey, Ahmed Abdul-Malik, John Coltrane, Randy Weston, Yusef Lateef, Max Roach, June Tyson, Pharoah Sanders, McCoy Tyner, Abbey Lincoln, Archie Shepp, Lonnie Liston Smith, Gary Bartz, and Horace Tapscott collectively conceived of Africa as much more than a musical source of inspiration. Indeed, for many African American musicians, jazz musicians or otherwise, Africa was also a spiritual and cultural source of inspiration.[18] As Gregory Freeland asserted in " 'We're a Winner': Popular Music and the Black Power Movement":

> With the application of the Black Power metaphor, as well as the representation of Black pride in the lyrics, the music, particularly as performed and produced by African Americans, connected political goals and artistic desires of progressive Blacks, and forged them into a more unified force for political change, cultural infusion, and social justice. The Black cultural themes of jazz musicians such as John Coltrane and Archie Shepp aided in their Black political and cultural immersion. Their song titles, for example John Coltrane's "Afro-Blue" and Archie Shepp's "Malcolm, Malcolm – Semper Malcolm," illustrate the Black cultural themes that jazz musicians delved into. The importance of non-lyrical musical forms and the lifestyles of its adherents are discussed by observers as being important to deciphering the role of music. Steven Isoardi, for example, wrote that Horace Tapscott, jazz pianist and supporter of Black Arts, didn't want just the voice of the instrument but also the life of the player expressed in the music he played. Because Tapscott resided in the Black community and made the community the focus and inspiration for his work, listeners felt that the music he was playing represented many of the trials and tribulations that came from living in political,

social and economic exclusion. . . . And Tapscott's use of instruments and musical themes was also a constant reminder to his listeners of the African culture connections. In songs with African themes, such as "Lumumba" and "Dar es Salaam," Tapscott employed polyrhythms characteristic of African music and a heavy use of drums. Pianist Bobby West described Tapscott's music as incorporating the entire history of the Black experience in his performances in that you could hear everything from field hollers to tin roof church revivals, to the earliest origins of the blues.[19]

Similar to the jazz musicians of the era, soul musicians amplified echoes of not only Africa but also African Americans' more immediate national spiritual and cultural homeland: the Southern states of the U.S., stretching from Florida through Texas. If Africa was African Americans' homeland abroad, then the American South was their homeland at home, so to speak. With the deepening of the lyrics and the darkening of the sound of Black popular music, by the mid-to-late 1960s rhythm & blues returned to its church roots and *the characteristic call-and-response, cry, scream, and shout sound* that defined the golden age of gospel and gave birth to rhythm & blues, which sparked rock & roll and ultimately sired soul. Slightly behind the curve when it came to the mercurial rise of soul music in the mid-1960s, Motown initially struggled to keep up with the other rhythm & blues labels that began to increasingly turn to Southern recording studios and musicians to create a rawer and realer, less polished, seemingly secular gospel sound. Consequently, Berry Gordy and the super-successful Motown machine began to experiment with a rawer and realer, less polished sound on some of its recordings. Motown artists, such as Martha Reeves & the Vandellas, Brenda Holloway, Shorty Long, Jimmy Ruffin, Junior Walker & the All-Stars, Gladys Knight & the Pips, the Originals, the Fantastic Four, the Temptations, and, most obviously, Edwin Starr, collectively benefitted from the more organic, bare-bones, sonically southward productions in the mid-to-late 1960s, and their work was instrumental in helping Motown make the pivotal transition from rhythm & blues to soul.[20]

What could be called "musical Africanisms" seemed almost ubiquitous in soul music, including Motown's mid-to-late 1960s rhythm & blues-cum-soul. For instance, when producer Norman Whitfield assumed the primary writing and production duties for the Temptations in 1966, he almost immediately began to experiment with elaborate African-inspired polyrhythms and a bevy of percussion instruments. The Temptations' Whitfield-produced songs, including classic soul ballads such as the string-ladened "You're My Everything" and even the incredibly popular "Ain't Too Proud to Beg," have audible Africanisms, specifically flashes of percussion that clearly distinguish these songs from anything the Temptations had previously recorded and released. With songs such as "Message from a Black Man," "Ball of Confusion (That's What the World Is Today)," "You Make Your Own Heaven and Hell Right Here on Earth," "Smiling Faces Sometimes," and "Ungena Za Ulimengu (Unite the World)," among others, Whitfield brought the deeper lyrics and darker sound of mid-to-late 1960s Black popular music to Motown and in the process successfully extended and expanded Motown's sonic palette. Because of the phenomenal popularity of Motown, the more Whitfield tinkered with the Motown sound and was successful, the more the musical Africanisms he peppered his productions with increasingly came to define the sound of soul, if not funk as well. When Whitfield pushed the envelope by adding seemingly more and more African-inspired sounds, particularly percussion, and coupled them with elements of free jazz, psychedelic rock, and the then-emerging funk sound (Sly & the Family Stone's music in particular), his deconstructed and reconstructed Motown sound opened up a seemingly brand-new sonic universe for soul and funk musicians.[21]

Musical Africanisms, especially congas, bongos, and wood-blocks, increasingly became omnipresent in soul. However, even though a number of soul and funk groups, such as the Temptations, Earth, Wind & Fire, Mandrill, and Kool & the Gang seemed sincere in their explorations (and celebrations) of African Americans' musical and cultural links to Africa, a number of other soul and funk acts seemed more interested in cashing in on African Americans' fascination with Africa than with making real cultural connections. This is to say, much of what was passed off as "African" in a lot of the soul and funk of the Black Power Movement was little more than staid, racial romanticizations and wild imaginations of "African sounds" that very rarely resembled authentic African music, specifically the myriad African musics that were in vogue between the mid-1960s and the mid-1970s. But the fact that much of what was being peddled to soul and funk audiences as "African" was not, for the most part, was completely irrelevant. When viewed from an African American perspective, these musical Africanisms in soul and funk gave the music a clearly understood cultural provenance in Africa and a profoundly symbolic resonance for an exiled people collectively seeking to make connections with their African ancestral homeland. In the most pragmatic manner imaginable, the musical Africanisms in much of the soul and funk emerging in the midst of the Black Power Movement helped to move the Black popular music of the period in a lyrically deeper and sonically darker direction that, for the most part, eschewed crossover and pop chart pretensions in favor of reflecting the aspirations and frustrations of Black America in the decade immediately following the Civil Rights Movement.

"Is It Because I'm Black?": the soul aesthetic, soul music, and post-Civil Rights Movement Black popular culture

Emerging within the context of the Black Arts Movement's re-evaluation of the social function of art, soul music was a sonic expression of the aspirations and frustrations of the Black Power Movement. It was an integral part of African Americans' post-Civil Rights Movement efforts to radically redefine the world on their own terms. It was the sound of African American musicians embracing a distinct sense of duty to speak to the post-Civil Rights Movement Black struggle. In stark contrast to the pop chart-obsessed and increasingly bland-sounding rhythm & blues of the mid-1960s, soul refocused Black popular music on the "spiritual and cultural needs of Black people."[22]

By focusing on the "spiritual and cultural needs of Black people," similar to rap and neo-soul for many contemporary Black ghetto youth, soul was more than merely music. It was a way of life and emblematic of the wide spectrum of Black popular culture between 1965 and disco music's rise to national prominence in the late 1970s. Thus, beyond its musical meanings, soul had several extra-musical expressions and was frequently associated with a wide range of Black popular cultural forms between 1965 and 1977, including Black Power Movement and Black Arts Movement-influenced language, literature, theater, dance, visual art, fashion, hairstyles, television, film, and food, among others.[23]

For instance, soul fashions included either African or African-derived clothing and accessories, khaki safari jackets, leisure suits, colorful bell-bottom pants, berets, leather jackets and vests, platform shoes, and wide-brimmed hats. Soul was also associated with natural hairstyles, including Afros, cornrows, blowout combs, fist picks, colorful hair beads, and African-based crops. Moreover, soul was connected with African American non-verbal communication practices, which encompassed rhythmic greeting rituals, complex and coded handshakes, swagger-filled walking styles, and other inimitable and dynamic body motions. And, lastly, with respect to language, as Geneva Smitherman observed in *Black Language and Culture: Sounds of Soul*, soul was said to be at the heart of the coded colloquialisms of Black ghetto youth and the radical rhetoric of Black Power Movement militants.[24]

Soul musicians and DJs popularized not only the word "soul," but also several key phrases that supposedly expressed the "soul aesthetic."[25] Both within everyday language use and in musical contexts, *soul sociolinguistics* seemed to be heavily based on the African American preaching and gospel singing traditions, especially both traditions' use of call-and-response. For example, soul musicians' lyrical and overall musical delivery frequently reflected the dramatic performance styles of African American preachers, who regularly utilize a wide range of improvisatory techniques – including vocal inflections, varying timbres, word and riff repetition, and the punctuation of the end of phrases with shouts, grunts, groans, and moans – to systematically build the intensity to an unfathomed degree that transfigures what began as a sermon into an epic *sermon-song*. Hence, the preacher and congregation paradigm, with its patented call-and-response tradition so prevalent in African American church culture and gospel music, was secularized and popularized by soul musicians (especially in the work of icons such as Ray Charles, Etta James, James Brown, Aretha Franklin, Curtis Mayfield, Donny Hathaway, Otis Redding, Wilson Pickett, Solomon Burke, the Temptations, Gladys Knight & the Pips, and the Staples Singers). Furthermore, just as Sunday morning sermons were peppered with spirited interjections such as "Amen brother, God be praised!" and "Tell the truth and shame the devil!," classic soul music – especially live performances – was augmented with exclamations such as "Tell it like it is!," "Ain't it the truth!," "Can you dig it?," and "Right on!"

Soul was obviously more than music. It was the first post-Civil Rights Movement Black popular culture, and as such it was part of African Americans' ongoing efforts to deconstruct and reconstruct what it meant to be unapologetically "Black" or "African American" as opposed to "Negroes" or "colored people." In this sense, *soul signified the views and values of arguably the first generation of Black ghetto youth since the radical New Negroes of the Harlem Renaissance to be in open revolt against the middle-aged, middle-class, and middle-of-the-road establishments of both White and Black America.* To be a "soul man" (à la Sam & Dave) or "a natural woman" (à la Aretha Franklin) or to be, more generally speaking, a "soul brother" or "soul sister" meant that one identified with the ongoing struggles of working-class and underclass African Americans, among other non-White working-poor people.[26]

With the politicization of Black popular culture came the politicization of Black popular music and, as Brian Ward asserted, during soul's heyday "popular music and its heroes did help to shape the ways in which people – especially young people – perceived the world, sorted out its heroes from its villains, and evaluated the relationship between its rights and its wrongs."[27] Hence, no matter how preoccupied White America is with soul love songs, it is equally important to acknowledge that for most African American youth, past and present, soul music is in equal measures concerned with both *Black love* and *Black liberation.* Having roots in the early gospel-influenced rhythm & blues experiments of Ray Charles, James Brown, and Sam Cooke, among others, soul music's politics can be traced back to the late 1950s and early 1960s love songs sung in a secularized gospel style that often subtly depicted the hardships of African American life and romance as a consequence of segregation, poverty, poor education, and sub-standard housing (e.g., Ray Charles' "The Sun's Gonna Shine" and "The Midnight Hour"; James Brown's "Why Does Everything Happen To Me?" and "Messin' with the Blues"; and Sam Cooke's "Wonderful World"). However, soul music's politics also have roots in the more obvious early gospel-influenced rhythm & blues songs that are not love songs and that unambiguously express the hardships and horrors of African American life in light of American apartheid (e.g., Ray Charles' "Greenbacks," "Hard Times," and "Losing Hand"; Sam Cooke's "Chain Gang" and "A Change Is Gonna Come"; Lloyd Price's "Stagger Lee"; and Jerry Butler's "I'm Telling You").[28]

Many Black popular music scholars have argued that Sam Cooke's "A Change Is Gonna Come" marked the transition from rhythm & blues to soul. Growing out of years of quiet reflection on segregation and other Civil Rights abuses, Cooke was inspired to compose and record "A Change Is Gonna Come" after hearing Bob Dylan's epochal "Blowin' in the Wind." Touching on everything from poverty to segregation, the simultaneously gospel-tinged vocals and orchestral/pop sounding background music made "A Change Is Gonna Come" a harbinger of a new genre of Black popular music.[29]

Musically speaking, soul obviously continued the evolution of rhythm & blues, which reached back to the early 1940s and synthesized elements of gospel, blues, jazz, and doo-wop. But vocally and lyrically speaking, soul was something altogether new: *Vocally*, it secularized the gospel sound, bringing a spirit-filled folksiness to Black popular music, and *lyrically*, it extended the topical range and political character of Black popular music. "If you're going to come away from a party singing the lyrics of a song," Curtis Mayfield contended in *Soul* magazine in 1969, "it is better that you sing of self-pride like 'We're A Winner' instead of 'Do the Boo-ga-loo!'"[30]

Prior to the release of Cooke's "A Change Is Gonna Come" in December of 1964, in July of that year Curtis Mayfield & the Impressions released an album entitled *Keep On Pushing* that featured two falsetto-filled tracks that were almost immediately adopted as "movement songs": the title track, "Keep On Pushing," and the immortal "Amen." The next year Mayfield & the Impressions released *People Get Ready*, which featured a set of songs that further developed the soul aesthetic, including the title track, "People Get Ready," "Woman's Got Soul," and "Just Another Dance." As adept at composing love songs as he was at penning "protest songs" (e.g., "Gypsy Woman," "Minstrel and Queen," "I'm So Proud," "We're a Winner," "Little Brown Boy," "This Is My Country," "Choice of Colors," "Mighty Mighty [Spade & Whitey]"), Mayfield provided one of the major models for soul musicians.[31]

By the mid-1960s Black popular music was being used to express more than merely love and do more than popularize the latest dance craze. Chart-topping songs such as Martha Reeves & the Vandellas' "Dancing in the Street" and Little Milton's "We're Gonna Make It" were emblematic of African Americans' increasing desire for music that openly engaged the key issues confronting Black America in the aftermath of the Civil Rights Movement. Between 1964 and 1967 there was an astonishing increase in the level of lyrical engagement with the Black freedom struggle by rhythm & blues-cum-soul artists. As the Civil Rights Movement morphed into the Black Power Movement, Black popular music reflected this epoch-making metamorphosis, and intracommunal concerns collided with artistic integrity, street credibility, and commercial success. The American music industry seemed to recognize that African Americans' demand for more explicit political critique and social commentary in soul lyrics was not only a necessity to successfully sell records to Black America, but also that Black freedom struggle-inspired protest songs and message music would not inevitably alienate the ever-increasing mostly suburban White consumers of Black popular music. On the contrary, the amplification of lyrical engagement with the Black freedom struggle by soul artists corresponded with an intense period of unprecedented crossover success for African American entertainers, especially recording artists.[32]

Arguably more than any other classic soul song, it was Aretha Franklin's 1967 dramatic remake of Otis Redding's "Respect" that turned the tide and opened the floodgates for overtly Black freedom struggle-inspired protest songs and message music. In many ways, Franklin's "Respect" provided the perfect transitional rhythm & blues-cum-soul song, because it was emblematic of the ways in which Black America would imaginatively politicize Black popular music between the mid-1960s and the mid-1970s. For instance, even though many in Black America, especially African American women, conceived of "Respect" as a new, post-Civil Rights Movement Black national anthem, frequently in interviews at the time Franklin asserted that it was not her intention to offer an anthem or make any sort of political statement with the song, although in many of the same interviews she openly acknowledged that she appreciated that her music could mean one thing to her and wholly another for her fans. Franklin told Gerri Hirshey if her fans found pain or anger in her music, or a certain song of hers moved them to activism, "that has to be their personal interpretation."[33] Franklin went further:

> What I feel singing it, and where it comes from, is something I keep to myself. Music, especially the kind I make, is a very emotional thing. And as an artist you're happy when people get *involved*, you know? But what they hear and what I feel when I sing can be very, very different. Sometimes I wish I could make them understand that.[34]

In the aftermath of the phenomenal success of "Respect" in 1967, soul was soon inundated with outright lyrical expressions of Black pride and the popularization of the soul aesthetic. Franklin's listeners cared very little that "Respect" was essentially an appeal for respect in her own home and that this topic had a particular personal resonance for her as a consequence of her tumultuous marriage to her manager, Ted White. Flying in the face of all of that, in an act of Black creative consumption, "Respect" was understood to be lyrically and musically ideal for appropriation as an anthem, as a battle cry in the midst of the ongoing Black freedom struggle. Falling fast on the heels of the artistic and commercial success of "Respect," songs such as James Brown's "Say It Loud – I'm Black and I'm Proud," Sam & Dave's "Soul Man," Charles Wright & the Watts 103rd Street Rhythm Band's "Express Yourself," Curtis Mayfield & the Impressions' "We're a Winner," the Staple Singers' "Respect Yourself," Sly & the Family Stone's "Dance to the Music," and the Temptations' "Cloud Nine" were among the myriad songs that provided African American listeners with unmistakable certainty that their lives mattered and their culture was worthy of respect.[35]

Expressions of Black pride were not limited to song lyrics, as many soul and funk groups' names reflected the influence of the broader Black Power Movement and Black aesthetic. As discussed in Chapter 1, the Black aesthetic emphasized *Black self-determination*, *Black self-definition*, and *Black self-naming*. Consequently, the music of groups such as Black Heat, Black Ivory, the Ebonys, Funk Inc., S.O.U.L. (aka "Sounds of Unity & Love"), the Soul Children, the Soul Searchers, the Natural Four, the Undisputed Truth, the People's Choice, Brothers of Soul, Brother to Brother, and New Birth is essentially incomprehensible without some significant understanding of the Black Power Movement, Black Arts Movement, and Black aesthetic. It is also interesting to observe that the iconography of soul artists, whether on album covers, stage, or television, reflected the influence of the Black aesthetic. Between the mid-1960s and the mid-1970s, most soul acts swapped out their sleek uptown attire and processed hair styles for ghetto chic and natural hair styles. Many funk musicians went outer space by sporting elaborate space suits and thigh-high metallic platform boots, and still other soul and funk artists donned dashikis and African-inspired clothing.[36]

All of this decidedly Black iconography translated into an intense declaration of Black pride and increasing cultural consciousness on the part of these artists in particular and African Americans in general. Along with the succession of blaxploitation films that followed the breakout success of *Sweet Sweetback's Baadasssss Song* in 1971, Black style, whether expressed via music, film, or fashion, seemed to sit at the heart of the Black Power Movement. Perhaps more than any other Black aesthetic-influenced TV show at time, Don Cornelius' nationally networked *Soul Train* virtually guaranteed that new Black popular music, dances, and fashions spread throughout Black America at a rapid-fire rate. During and even in the aftermath of the Black Power Movement, *Soul Train* helped African Americans evolve a sense of a national Black popular culture centered around music, dance, film, and fashion that undeniably influenced the emergence of rap music and hip hop culture in the late 1970s and early 1980s.[37]

Along with soul musicians' myriad songs dedicated to Black pride and Black style were an increasing number of topical tunes devoted to documentary-style descriptions of Black poverty, social misery, crime, addiction, and often brutal betrayal by the American established order. Songs such as the Temptations' "Ball of Confusion," Syl Johnson's "Is It Because I'm Black?," Les McCann's "Compared to What?," Marvin Gaye's "Right On!," Stevie Wonder's "Living for the City," War's "The World Is a Ghetto," and the Whatnauts' "Message from a Black Man" collectively expressed Black pride and a heightened Black political consciousness. However, an argument could be made about the ways in which soul was centered on racial harmony and brotherhood and sisterhood, just as much as it was focused on expressing Black pride. Songs such as Sly & the Family Stone's "Everyday People," Harold Melvin & the Bluenotes' "Wake Up Everybody," Bill Withers' "Lean on Me," the O'Jays' "Love Train," and the Isley Brothers' "Harvest for the World" all touched on the radical humanism and emphasis on racial harmony that was actually at the heart of the best of the Black Power Movement. Still, it is important to observe that the increase in racial harmony-themed songs seemed to parallel the increase in songs about denial and betrayal, within and without the Black community. For instance, the Temptations' "Papa Was a Rolling Stone" touched on abandonment and betrayal, and Eddie Kendricks' "My People . . . Hold On," with its discussion of falling hawks and flying doves, pleaded with African Americans to not only live together, but to learn to love one another. In "Backstabbers" the O'Jays also emphasized denial and betrayal, as did the Undisputed Truth in "Smiling Faces Sometimes (Tell Lies)." James Brown's "Talkin' Loud and Sayin' Nothing" simultaneously critiqued the radical rhetoric of many Black Power activists and the empty, often left-leaning, liberal rhetoric of many White politicians who seemed to incessantly speak of racial justice without sufficiently socially and politically committing to racial and economic justice.[38]

During the declining years of the Black Power Movement, Black communalism was replaced with Black individualism, and songs such as James Brown's "I Don't Want Nobody to Give Me Nothing," Jerry Butler's "Only the Strong Survive," Marvin Gaye's "Trouble Man," Aaron Neville's "Hercules," and War's "Slippin' into Darkness" cast off the communalism of the soundtracks of the Civil Rights Movement, especially gospel and freedom songs, and embraced an impassioned, rugged individualism that reached back to the blues tradition. By the early 1970s the romanticizations of soul brotherhood, soul sisterhood, and Black communalism that had shaped and shaded soul music up to that point were replaced by a new emphasis on self-reliance and the kind of cutthroat and callous thought and behavior that many soul brothers and soul sisters believed was necessary to navigate through, and indeed survive, the increasingly violent and unsavory urban environments most African Americans remained quarantined to in the aftermath of the Civil Rights Movement. Many soul artists tried hard to strike a balance between documentary-style descriptions of the abject poverty, crime, and addiction plaguing Black America, on the one hand, and sonically celebrating the new expressive culture African Americans created in an effort to survive it, on the other hand.[39]

To be sure, the lion's share of these songs were merely descriptive. Very seldom were they ever instructive. However, when we turn to James Brown's "Get Up, Get into It, Get Involved," Curtis Mayfield's "Move On Up," Sly & the Family Stone's "You Can Make It If You Try," and the Staple Singers' "Respect Yourself," we have obvious examples of the ways in which some soul artists sought to utilize their music for inspirational and educational purposes. Interestingly, not all of the critiques emerging from soul music were aimed at the established order. With hard-hitting songs such as "Niggers Are Scared of Revolution," "Wake Up, Niggers," "When the Revolution Comes," "Run, Nigger," and "Black People, What Y'all Gon' Do?," East Coast spoken-word legends the Last Poets lambasted Black America for acquiescing to the often anti-Black racist whims and wishes of White America. Much like the Last Poets, with searing songs such as "There's a Difference Between a Black Man and a Nigger," "Hello Niggers," "I'll Stop Calling You Niggers," "Response to a Bourgeois Nigger," and "Amerikkka," West Coast spoken-word icons the Watts Prophets simultaneously critiqued both Black and White America: Black America for internalizing Eurocentric and anti-Black racist conceptions of Black folk and Blackness, and White America for its ongoing racial colonization and economic exploitation of Black folk.

Undoubtedly, the most renowned of the soul-centered poets was Gil Scott-Heron, whose "The Revolution Will Not Be Televised" popularized soul poetry and evolved the genre in ways that have led many musicologists to observe its obvious connections to the emergence of rap music in the mid-to-late 1970s. Scott-Heron's innovative albums such as *Small Talk at 125th and Lenox* (1970), *Pieces of a Man* (1971), *Free Will* (1972), *Winter in America* (1974), *The First Minute of a New Day* (1975), *From South Africa to South Carolina* (1976), and *It's Your World* (1976) were not merely among the most creative syntheses of poetry, jazz, soul, and funk ever produced, but his body of work also articulated the range and reach of African Americans' social, political, and cultural concerns during the Black Power Movement. His syntheses of poetry, jazz, soul, and funk critiqued the media ("The Revolution Will Not Be Televised"), paid homage to the jazz tradition ("Lady Day and John Coltrane" and "Trane"), dealt with drug addiction ("Home Is Where the Hatred Is" and "Speed Kills"), lamented alcoholism ("The Bottle"), painted candid portraits of ghetto life ("The Get Out of the Ghetto Blues"), touched on Black sexuality ("Sex Education: Ghetto Style"), delivered blistering analyses of mainstream politics ("H2O Blues" and "Pardon Our Analysis [We Beg Your Pardon]"), and regularly denounced racism ("Winter in America," "The Liberation Song [Red, Black and Green]," "Johannesburg," and "South Carolina [Barnwell])."[40]

Considering all that the Black Power Movement meant to African Americans, it should not come as a complete shock to anyone that soul musicians increasingly came to paint candid sonic portraits of the ongoing hardships and horrors of Black life in the immediate aftermath of the Civil Rights Movement. As mentioned above, the Black Power Movement was indicative of a widespread change in the collective consciousness of African Americans between the mid-1960s and mid-1970s, and this change in consciousness logically led to changes in African American culture, which in turn translated into social and political changes that significantly impacted African Americans' desire for music that reflected their post-Civil Rights Movement lives and struggles. To state the obvious, African American vocalists, musicians, songwriters, arrangers, producers, deejays, club owners, and concert promoters were all members of the broader Black community. As a consequence, African American music industry professionals frequently shared the pervasive sense of frustration and pessimism circulating throughout Black America as the euphoria and optimism of the Civil Rights Movement steadily declined in the late 1960s.[41]

With that being said, one would be remiss not to point out that there was an increased desire for social commentary and political songs amongst White rock artists and fans that ran parallel to the message music and protest songs emerging from the Black Power Movement. A number of White rock artists produced legendary songs that engaged some of the most important social and political issues of the era. For instance, songs such as Bob Dylan's "Masters of War," Buffalo Springfield's "For What It's Worth," the Beatles' "Revolution," the Rolling Stones' "Street Fighting Man," Creedence Clearwater Revival's "Fortunate Son," Crosby, Stills, Nash & Young's "Ohio," Jefferson Airplane's "Volunteers," the Who's "Won't Get Fooled Again," and Bob Dylan's "Hurricane" demonstrate that the protest songs and message music of the Black Power Movement coincided with the wider politicization of American popular music that took place between the mid-1960s and the mid-1970s.

African American musicians produced countless protest songs in the decade immediately following the Civil Rights Movement, and, much like that of their White counterparts, their work touched on national and international pressing issues and political problems. As with many White rock musicians, African American soul artists were particularly critical of the Vietnam War and made several major contributions to the overarching soundtrack of the Anti-War Movement that took place between the mid-1960s and mid-1970s. Coinciding with the end of the Civil Rights Movement and the beginning of the Black Power Movement in the mid-1960s, African Americans became increasingly involved in the opposition to the Vietnam War. Along with disillusionment with the decline of the Civil Rights Movement and the empty rhetoric surrounding the Civil Rights Act of 1964 and Voting Rights Act of 1965, American militarism in Vietnam only intensified a growing Black bitterness toward the government. Just as had been the case with World War II, African Americans were being called on to fight for "freedom and democracy" abroad but continued to experience racism, political disenfranchisement, and economic exploitation at home.[42]

In sizing up the situation, African Americans came to clearly understand that they were being disproportionately drafted, maimed, and murdered in the Vietnam War, and no amount of righteous-sounding government-sanctioned rhetoric could curtail the grief and anger that ensued as countless body bags with bullet-riddled Black corpses flooded the ghettoes. This, understandably, enraged a long-beleaguered and brutally oppressed people, and soul musicians provided a mouthpiece, a kind of musical megaphone, for Black America to express its views on America's bloody misadventures and outright mayhem in Vietnam. Songs such as Edwin Starr's "Stop the War Now," Freda Payne's "Bring the Boys Home," Bill Withers' "I Can't Write Left-Handed," Joe Tex's "I Believe I'm Gonna Make It," Curtis Mayfield's "Back to the World," Big Amos' "Going to Vietnam," Tiny Watkins' "A Soldier's Sad Story," and Jimmy Holiday's "I'm Gonna Help Hurry My Brothers Home" collectively provide a snapshot of the range and reach of anti-war songs produced by soul artists.[43] Moreover, the politicization of American popular music that took place in the period following the Civil Rights Movement had a wide-ranging impact, and that impact went well beyond social and political issues and eventually registered its influence on African American gender and sexual politics.

Many male soul artists' music seemed to sonically mirror the problematic gender and sexual politics emerging from the Black Power Movement. After all, music is one of the most prominent African American art forms – some have gone so far as to say that music sits at the heart of Black art. It has consistently enabled African Americans to speak their special truths to each other and to the wider world, from slavery to freedom. It has helped Black folk express some "good" truths and some brutally honest, often sad, and very "bad" truths. And, just as there were Black Power women who critiqued the movement from within, there were soul women who countered and critiqued expressions of masculinism and misogyny in male soul music. What were some of the major themes of male soul music, sexist or otherwise? What were some of the major themes of female soul music, womanist or otherwise? And how did soul music in general reflect many of the broader concerns of Black America between the mid-1960s and the mid-1970s?[44]

Soul brothers, the masculinization of the soul aesthetic, and musical machismo: soul men on social, political, and sexual power

The politicization of American popular music that took place between the mid-1960s and mid-1970s played itself out in unique ways within Black America. Soul artists not only engaged many of the most pressing social and political problems of the era, but they also often coupled *social commentary* with *sexual commentary*. In other words, frustrations about what was happening, or not happening, in the broader American society and Black community seemed to be redirected to critiques of what was happening, or not happening, in the domestic sphere and the bedroom. For example, as many Black men increasingly felt socially impotent and irrelevant, they began to assert their "manhood" in incredibly sexist ways – as if fearing that social impotence would translate into sexual impotence. Seeming to mirror the prickly gender politics of Martin Luther King, Malcolm X, Stokely Carmichael, Amiri Baraka, and many of the men of the Black Panther Party, many male soul artists often combined dreamy romance with raunchy desire. Much of their work had an almost schizophrenic quality, simultaneously invoking love and lust, fidelity and infidelity, respect and disrespect.[45]

Indeed, a lot of the soul music produced by men consistently expressed an often mercurial mixture of the self-confidence and self-reliance that they believed was missing in the public sphere coupled with most often tacit expressions of emotional vulnerability and outright reverence for "soul sisters" and "natural women." Take, for example, the work of Wilson Pickett and Otis Redding. On the one hand, part of what made Pickett so "wicked" was the fact that many conceived of him as some sort of sexual superman. Indeed, he played up his public persona as a smooth "Midnight Mover" and "A Man and a Half," who was eagerly awaiting his female fans' call at "634–5789." With songs such as "Mustang Sally," "In the Midnight Hour," "That's a Man's Way," "I Need a Lot of Lovin'," "Stagger Lee," and "Mini-Skirt Minnie," Pickett came to personify the machismo and misogyny many African American men embraced during the Black Power Movement.[46] On the other hand, for the most part Redding articulated the gentle, more respectable side of African American masculinity during the Black Power Movement, and after his untimely death at 26 his more sensitive version of soul became a key point of departure for iconic artists such as Isaac Hayes, William Bell, Eddie Floyd, James Carr, Percy Sledge, Arthur Alexander, Jimmy Hughes, Big John Hamilton, O.V. Wright, Otis Clay, and, of course, arguably Redding's greatest musical heir, Al Green. The epitome of emotional vulnerability and sensual sensitivity, Redding produced several tender love songs that helped to define soul balladry. With songs such as "These Arms of Mine," "Pain in My Heart," "That's How Strong My Love Is," "I've Been Loving You Too Long," "Just One More Day," and "Try a Little Tenderness," Redding complicates one-dimensional interpretations of masculinity during the Black Power Movement that claim that all African American men embraced machismo and misogyny.[47]

Consequently, as helpful as *the dreamy romance/raunchy desire dichotomy* is for engaging male soul music, it oversimplifies often incredibly complicated artists and their equally complex artistry. For instance, Pickett was also a soul balladeer of some distinction, with songs such as "It's Too Late," "It's All Over," "I'm in Love," and "I Found a True Love" quickly coming to mind. Likewise, Redding could leave his pleading love songs in the lurch at a moment's notice and rival Pickett with the passion and vocal pyrotechnics with which he expressed his deepest desires in songs such as "I Can't Turn You Loose," "Hard to Handle," and "Love Man." Comparing and contrasting Pickett with Redding helps us clearly see that *the dreamy romance/ raunchy desire dichotomy* is actually not a dichotomy at all. Most male soul singers plying their crafts between the mid-1960s and mid-1970s produced music that was at times sensitive and romantic (à la Sam Cooke) and, at other times, macho and misogynistic (à la James Brown). Often this tension permeated the entirety of soul men's repertoires and frequently found its way into a single song or performance (again, à la James Brown's soul-cum-funk amalgam).[48]

Even with all of that being said, it would be hard to overlook the fact that a lot of male soul music between the late 1960s and mid-1970s seems to suggest that sexual conquest was much more than merely a path for Black men to achieve personal prestige and power. It also suggests, considering the void left by the assassinations of Malcolm X and Martin Luther King, that the domination and objectification of women in male soul seems to have served as some sort of sick and twisted proxy for social and political power. In other words, if the "Black man" (a phrase that seemed to roll off the tip of most Black males' tongues during the Black Power Movement) could not command respect within the White world, he would get respect from Black women – second-wave feminism and the Women's Liberation Movement be damned. Many Black males' quest for respect, and their subsequent frustration with ongoing disrespect within the White world, frequently caused them to violently reduce African American women to sex objects to be conquered and sexually colonized. As a matter of fact, many of the songs celebrating soul men's sexual facility and power expressed verbal violence against women, which means that a good number of male soul songs served as soundtracks for the sexual colonization of Black women during the Black Power Movement. In keeping with the colonial metaphor, it could be said that these soundtracks for the sexual colonization of African American women in essence reduced them to sexual servants, to colonial concubines, much like they had been reduced to sexual servants and concubines by White male enslavers during the antebellum era.[49]

Obviously, male soul music has been interpreted in myriad ways, and it is important to tease out both the positives and negatives ensconced within this genre of music. That is to say, much like Pickett and Redding, male soul music had both a romantic and a misogynistic side. It would seem that for every misogynistic song, soul men produced a sensitive, "sweet soul" ballad. Consequently, it would be incredibly erroneous to flatly conceive of male soul music as *musical machismo* and merely the musical expression of the ultra-macho and super-sexist wave that rolled across Black America during the Black Power Movement. All African American men did not succumb to sexism during the Black Power Movement. As a matter of fact, there is ample evidence that demonstrates that many male soul artists expressed vulnerability, fidelity, reciprocity, respect, and affection in ways that served to counter the over-the-top and increasing rudeness and lewdness, phallocentrism and priapism, and male supremacy and misogyny articulated by some soul men.

Soul brothers, such as Percy Sledge, Smokey Robinson, Joe Simon, Tyrone Davis, the Delfonics, the Chi-Lites, and the Stylistics, largely focused on joy and blues, love and loss, but for the most part steered clear of the bitterness, pessimism, and sexual paranoia that seemed to haunt a lot of male soul music during the period. Other soul men, such as Marvin Gaye, Al Green, Isaac Hayes, Barry White, and Teddy Pendergrass, offered up a plethora of sex-centered songs but typically expressed more equitable and reciprocal relationships. On the whole, in their music sex was not reduced to some kind of conquest, and ultimately their music was conceived of as serving as a soundtrack for an elaborate form of foreplay that was incredibly attentive to women's sexual needs, desires, and fantasies. Seeming to expand on Curtis Mayfield & the Impressions' 1965 celebration of the special beauty of African American women in "Woman's Got Soul," myriad soul men composed and passionately performed songs that praised the inner strength and outer beauty of African American women without necessarily resorting to crude and overt kinds of sexual objectification.[50]

Countless male soul songs told tales of nagging and unnerving girlfriends, wives, and lovers full of resentment-filled rhymes, but for the most part mothers were praised. In essence, these soul men saw girlfriends, wives, and lovers both as opponents of, and impediments to, their exercise of social, political, and sexual power. Ironically, these same soul men saw mothers as revered repositories of, most obviously, mother wit, but also African American culture and struggle. In myriad soul men's songs mothers symbolize stability and ingenuity in the absence of fathers. Mothers could also represent all of the conventional conceptions associated with motherhood in a patriarchal society. In other words, mothers were primarily conceived of as the bearers and nurturers of children in many male soul songs. Interestingly, there is ample statistical data that demonstrates that between 1950 and 1970 the number of Black female-headed households doubled. Consequently, many soul men composed and produced songs that mirrored an increasing intracommunal trend in Black America by the middle years of the Black Power Movement.[51]

Another irony of male soul and funk was that much like mothers, for the most part prostitutes escaped criticism. Even with all of the angst intensely expressed in male soul music surrounding ego-shattering female infidelity or any form of female sexual freedom or sexual power, a lot of male soul and funk seemed to give prostitutes a pass. As with so many other things that occurred during the Black Power Movement era, there is indeed a psychological and cultural logic to soul men exempting prostitutes from fault-finding. Prostitutes epitomized traditional gender roles in the sadistic value system of the patriarchal world. From this point of view, prostitutes do not in any way challenge male supremacy, and, in fact, they allow men to define, rate, rank, and exploit women exclusively based on patriarchal conceptions of how women should look and sexually behave. Plain and simple, in male supremacist societies prostitutes are the epitome of a sexual commodity, which is to say they can literally be bought and sold, owned like one does a piece of furniture or a pet. This situation creates little or no guilt surrounding the incredibly sexist and economically exploitive aspects of prostitution. When we emphasize the combination of both patriarchal and capitalist aspirations among many Black men during the Black Power Movement, it helps to explain the twisted logic that led to the glorification of pimps in a number of the most noted blaxploitation films and their soundtracks (e.g., *Superfly, The Mack, Willie Dynamite, Dolemite, The Candy Tangerine Man*, etc.).[52]

None of the above is meant to imply that soul men did not sometimes critically engage male figures, especially fathers, drug dealers, pimps, and preachers, in their songs. The most obvious example of a father-centered soul song is, of course, "Papa Was a Rolling Stone" by the Temptations. As a matter of fact, it is quite fascinating to compare and contrast soul men's mother-centered songs with their father-centered songs. Some songs, such as O.C. Smith's "Daddy's Little Man," Clarence Carter's "Patches," Joe Tex's "Papa's Dream," the Chi-Lites' "Let Me Be the Man My Daddy Was," and the Winstons' "Color Him Father," painted sonic portraits of responsible fathers who protected and provided for their families to the best of their abilities. Other father-centered soul songs, like the Temptations' "Papa Was a Rolling Stone," exposed the damage done to Black America as a consequence of ongoing economic exploitation, racism, and Black machismo. "Papa Was a Rolling Stone," arguably the most superlative song Motown produced during its storied psychedelic soul phase, demonstrates that male soul could offer up hard-hitting critiques, rather than merely senseless celebrations, of Black machismo.[53]

Male soul music was more than merely a sonic metaphor celebrating Black machismo. It captured and conveyed the spiritual, social, and sexual thought of African American men between the mid-1960s and mid-1970s. Some of that thought was obviously connected to the rabid forms of sexism that rose in the aftermath of the Civil Rights Movement. Sadly, some male soul songs often unrepentantly proclaimed sexist views and values that preceded both the Civil Rights Movement and the Women's Liberation Movement that emerged in its aftermath. Seemingly, as the Women's Liberation Movement increased its public presence and political power, many male soul artists' songs appear to have waged an ideological war against the rise of the modern women's movement. Against the backdrop of both the Black Power Movement and the Women's Liberation Movement many soul sisters collectively countered the sonic sexism of many of their soul brothers and the rampant racism ravaging America. Consequently, as with soul men's music, soul women's music touched on a wide variety of topics and should not be simply conceived of as love songs. Even when singing about love, many soul women's songs had deep cultural, social, political, and economic implications.

Notes

1 For key examples of the wide spectrum of message music and protest songs that articulated the ideals and ethos of the Black Power Movement, see Various Artists, *Black Power: Music of a Revolution* (Shout! Factory, D2K 37398, 2004, CD); Various Artists, *Change Is Gonna Come: The Voice of Black America, 1963–1973* (Kent Soul, CDKEND 270, 2007, CD); Various Artists, *Listen, Whitey!: The Sounds of Black Power, 1967–1974* (Light In The Attic, LITA 081, 2012, CD).

2 For further discussion of the origins and early evolution of soul music, see Nelson George, *The Death of Rhythm & Blues* (New York: Pantheon Books, 1988), 95–146; Peter Guralnick, *Sweet Soul Music: Rhythm & Blues and the Southern Dream of Freedom* (New York: Harper & Row, 1986), 1–75; Portia K. Maultsby, "Soul Music: Its Sociological and Political Significance in American Popular Culture," *Journal of Popular Culture* 17, no. 2 (1983): 51–57; Portia K. Maultsby, "Soul," in *African American Music: An Introduction*, eds. Mellonee V. Burnim, and Portia K. Maultsby (New York: Routledge, 2006), 277–79; Brian Ward, *Just My Soul Responding: Rhythm & Blues, Black Consciousness, and Race Relations* (Berkeley: University of California Press, 1998), 339–45.

3 Gregory Freeland, "Music and the Civil Rights Movement, 1954–1968," in *Teaching the American Civil Rights Movement: Freedom's Bittersweet Song*, ed. Julie Buckner Armstrong (New York: Routledge, 2012), 125–46; Gregory Freeland, "'We're a Winner': Popular Music and the Black Power Movement," *Social Movement Studies* 8, no. 3 (2009): 261–88; Mark Anthony Neal, *What the Music Said: Black Popular Music and Black Public Culture* (New York: Routledge, 1998), 36–42, 46–53.

4 Waldo E. Martin, *No Coward Soldiers: Black Cultural Politics in Postwar America* (Cambridge: Harvard University Press, 2005), 44–81.

5 George, *The Death of Rhythm & Blues*, 95–146; Peniel E. Joseph, *Waiting 'Til the Midnight Hour: A Narrative History of Black Power in America* (New York: Henry Holt, 2006), 68–131; Jeffrey Ogbar, *Black Power: Radical Politics and African American Identity* (Baltimore: Johns Hopkins University Press, 2004), 37–67; William L. Van Deburg, *New Day in Babylon: The Black Power Movement and American Culture, 1965–1975* (Chicago: University of Chicago Press, 1992), 112–91; Gayle Wald, "Soul Vibrations: Black Music and Black Freedom in Sound and Space," *American Quarterly* 63, no. 3 (2011): 673–96; Craig Werner, *Change Is Gonna Come: Music, Race & the Soul of America* (Ann Arbor: University of Michigan Press, 2006), 103–73.

6 Waldo E. Martin, "'Be Real Black for Me': Representation, Authenticity, and the Cultural Politics of Black Power," in *The Cultural Turn in U.S. History: Past, Present, and Future*, eds. James W. Cook, Lawrence B. Glickman, and Michael O'Malley (Chicago: University of Chicago Press, 2008), 243–66; Ogbar, *Black Power*, 93–122; Amy Abugo Ongiri, *Spectacular Blackness: The Cultural Politics of the Black Power Movement and the Search for a Black Aesthetic* (Charlottesville: University of Virginia Press, 2009), 124–85; James Edward Smethurst, *The Black Arts Movement: Literary Nationalism in the 1960s and 1970s* (Chapel Hill: University of North Carolina Press, 2005), 57–99; Van Deburg, *New Day in Babylon*, 248–91.

7 Maultsby, "Soul Music," 54–57; Neal, *What the Music Said*, 55–84; Robert W. Stephens, "Soul: A Historical Reconstruction of Continuity and Change in Black Popular Music," *The Black Perspective in Music* 12, no. 1 (1984): 21–43; Pat Thomas, *Listen, Whitey!: The Sights and Sounds of Black Power, 1965–1975* (New York: Norton, 2012), 89–131; Ward, *Just My Soul Responding*, 339–45; Werner, *Change Is Gonna Come*, 103–73.

8 Roderick D. Bush, *We Are Not What We Seem: Black Nationalism and Class Struggle in the American Century* (New York: New York University Press, 1999), 3.

9 Ibid., 7–8.

10 William L. Van Deburg, ed., *Modern Black Nationalism: From Marcus Garvey to Louis Farrakhan* (New York: New York University Press, 1997), 5.

11 Theodore Draper, *The Rediscovery of Black Nationalism* (New York: Penguin, 1970); Joseph, *Waiting 'Til the Midnight Hour*, 118–204; Ogbar, *Black Power*, 145–58; Van Deburg, *New Day in Babylon*, 63–111.

12 Van Deburg, *Modern Black Nationalism*, 14–15, all emphasis in original.

13 Samuel A. Floyd, *The Power of Black Music: Interpreting its History from Africa to the United States* (New York: Oxford University Press, 1995), 183–96; Reiland Rabaka, *Hip Hop's Inheritance: From the Harlem Renaissance to the Hip Hop Feminist Movement* (Lanham: Rowman & Littlefield, 2011); Reiland Rabaka, *Hip Hop's Amnesia: From Blues and the Black Women's Club Movement to Rap and the Hip Hop Movement* (Lanham: Rowman & Littlefield, 2012); Reiland Rabaka, *The Hip Hop Movement: From R&B and the Civil Rights Movement to Rap and the Hip Hop Generation* (Lanham: Rowman & Littlefield, 2013); Guthrie P. Ramsey, *Race Music: Black Cultures from Bebop to Hip Hop* (Berkeley: University of California Press, 2003), 29; Denise Sullivan, *Keep on Pushing: Black Power Music from Blues to Hip Hop* (Chicago: Lawrence Hill Books, 2011), 57–98.

14 Andrew Flory, *I Hear a Symphony: Motown and Crossover R&B* (Ann Arbor: University of Michigan Press, 2017), 69–134; Floyd, *The Power of Black Music*, 183–211; Ramsey, *Race Music*, 149–62.

15 Lawrence Levine, *Black Culture and Black Consciousness: Afro-American Folk Thought from Slavery to Freedom* (New York: Oxford University Press, 1977), 239–40, 247.

16 For further discussion of the long African American protest song and message music tradition that soul and funk emerged out of, see Jeffrey Eugene Baumann, "Chords of Discord: Songs of Dissonance, Violence, and Faith in the Civil Rights Movement" (M.A. thesis, San Diego State University, 2011); Guy Carawan and Candie Carawan, eds., *We Shall Overcome!: Songs of the Southern Freedom Movement* (New York: Oak Publications, 1963); Guy Carawan and Candie Carawan, *Freedom Is a Constant Struggle: Songs of the Freedom Movement* (New York: Oak Publications, 1968); Guy Carawan and Candie Carawan, eds., *Sing for Freedom: The Story of the Civil Rights Movement Through its Songs* (Montgomery, AL: NewSouth Books, 2007); Mario Dunkel, *Aesthetics of Resistance: Charles Mingus and the Civil Rights Movement* (Zürich: LIT-Verlag, 2012); Mary Ellison, *Lyrical Protest: Black Music's Struggle Against Discrimination* (New York: Praeger, 1989); Nathaniel Frederick, "Praise God and Do Something: The Role of Black American Gospel Artists as Social Activists, 1945–1960" (Ph.D. diss., Pennsylvania State University, 2009); Greg Kot, *I'll Take You There: Mavis Staples, the Staple Singers, and the Music that Shaped the Civil Rights Era* (New York: Scribner, 2014); George H. Lewis, "Social Protest and Self-Awareness in Black Popular Music," *Popular Music & Society* 2, no. 4 (1973): 327–33; Portia K. Maultsby and Mellonee V. Burnim, eds., *Issues in African American Music: Power, Gender, Race, Representation* (New York: Routledge, 2017); Anne S. McCanless, "Uniting Voices in Song: The Music of the Civil Rights Movement" (M.A. thesis, University of South Florida, 1997); Ingrid Monson, *Freedom Sounds: Civil Rights Call Out to Jazz and Africa* (New York: Oxford University Press, 2007); Burton W. Peretti, "Signifying Freedom: Protest in Nineteenth Century African American Music," in *The Routledge History of Social Protest in Popular Music*, ed. Jonathan C. Friedman (New York: Routledge, 2013), 3–18; Rabaka, *Civil Rights Music*; Bernice Johnson Reagon, "Songs of the Civil Rights Movement, 1955–1965: A Study in Culture History" (Ph.D. diss., Howard University, 1975); Bernice Johnson Reagon, "Civil Rights and Black Protest Music," in *Civil Rights Since 1787: A Reader on the Black Struggle*, eds. Jonathon Birnbaum and Clarence Taylor (New York: New York University Press, 2000), 24–28; Kerran L. Sanger, *When the Spirit Says Sing!: The Role of Freedom Songs in the Civil Rights Movement* (New York: Garland, 1995); Pete Seeger and Bob Reiser, *Everybody Says Freedom: A History of the Civil Rights Movement in Songs and Pictures* (New York: Norton, 1989); James Smethurst, "A Soul Message: R&B, Soul, and the Black Freedom Struggle," in *The Routledge History of Social Protest in Popular Music*, ed. Jonathan C. Friedman (New York: Routledge, 2013), 108–20; Jon Michael Spencer, *Protest & Praise: Sacred Music of Black Religion* (Minneapolis: Fortress Press, 1991); Katherine L. Turner, "Sonic Opposition: Protesting Racial Violence before Civil Rights," in *The Routledge History of Social Protest in Popular Music*, ed. Jonathan C. Friedman (New York: Routledge, 2013), 44–56; Wyatt Tee Walker, *"Somebody's Calling My Name": Black Sacred Music and Social Change* (Valley Forge, PA: Judson Press, 1979).

17 For further discussion of Africanisms in the music of the African diaspora and African American popular music in particular, see Ashenafi Kebede, *Roots of Black Music: The Vocal, Instrumental, and Dance Heritage of Africa and Black America* (Trenton: Africa World Press, 1995); Portia K. Maultsby, "West African Influences and Retentions in U.S. Black Music: A Sociocultural Study," in *More Than Dancing: Essays on Afro-American Music and Musicians*, ed. Irene V. Jackson (Westport: Greenwood, 1985), 25–57; Portia K. Maultsby, "Africanisms in African American Music," in *Africanisms in American Culture*, ed. Joseph E. Holloway (Indianapolis: Indiana University Press, 2005), 326–55; Richard Alan Waterman, "African Influence on the Music of the Americas," in *Write Me a Few of Your Lines: A Blues Reader*, ed. Steven C. Tracy (Amherst: University of Massachusetts Press, 1999), 17–27; Olly Wilson, "The Significance of the Relationship Between Afro-American Music and West African Music," *The Black Perspective in Music* 2, no. 1 (1974): 3–22; Olly Wilson, " 'It Don't Mean a Thing if It Ain't Got That Swing': The Relationship Between African and African American Music," in *African Roots/American Cultures: Africa in the Creation of the Americas*, ed. Sheila S. Walker (Lahman: Rowman & Littlefield, 2001), 153–68.

18 Norman C. Weinstein, *A Night in Tunisia: Imaginings of Africa in Jazz* (New York: Limelight, 1994); Monson, *Freedom Sounds*; Robin D.G. Kelley, *Africa Speaks, America Answers: Modern Jazz in Revolutionary Times* (Cambridge: Harvard University Press, 2012); Karlton E. Hester, *African Roots of the Jazz Evolution* (San Diego: Cognella, 2017); Gerhard Kubik, *Jazz Transatlantic, Volume I: The African Undercurrent in Twentieth Century Jazz Culture* (Jackson: University Press of Mississippi, 2017); Gerhard Kubik, *Jazz Transatlantic, Volume II: The African Undercurrent in Twentieth Century Jazz Culture* (Jackson: University Press of Mississippi, 2017).

19 Gregory Freeland, " 'We're a Winner': Popular Music and the Black Power Movement," *Social Movement Studies* 8, no. 3 (2009): 272–73. See also Steven Louis Isoardi, *The Dark Tree: Jazz and the Community Arts in Los Angeles* (Berkeley: University of California Press, 2006), 112–200.

20 Flory, *I Hear a Symphony*, 69–99; Nelson George, *Where Did Our Love Go?: The Rise and Fall of the Motown Sound* (Urbana: University of Illinois Press, 2007), 148–89; Suzanne E. Smith, *Dancing in the Street: Motown and the Cultural Politics of Detroit* (Cambridge: Harvard University Press, 1999), 139–208; Charles E. Sykes, "Motown," in *African American Music: An Introduction*, eds. Mellonee V. Burnim and Portia K. Maultsby (New York: Routledge, 2006), 446–50; Thomas, *Listen, Whitey!*, 11–53; Werner, *Change Is Gonna Come*, 116–24; Ward, *Just My Soul Responding*, 173–216.

21 For more on Norman Whitfield and his melding of the Motown sound and "musical Africanisms" with elements of free jazz, psychedelic rock, and the then-emerging funk sound (Sly & the Family Stone's music in particular), see Robert Fink, "Goal-Directed Soul?: Analyzing Rhythmic Teleology in African American Popular Music," *Journal of the American Musicological Society* 64, no. 1 (2011): 179–238; Flory, *I Hear a Symphony*, 93–99; George, *Where Did Our Love Go?*, 96–97, 168–72; Smith, *Dancing in the Street*, 233–36; Paul Zollo, "Norman Whitfield," in *Calling Out Around the World: A Motown Reader*, ed. Kingsley Abbott (London: Helter Skelter, 2000), 144–48.

22 Neal, "The Black Arts Movement," 29. It will be recalled in chapter 1, Larry Neal stated, "The black artist['s] . . . primary duty is to speak to the spiritual and cultural needs of black people."

23 Tanisha C. Ford, *Liberated Threads: Black Women, Style, and the Global Politics of Soul* (Chapel Hill: University of North Carolina Press, 2017), 1–122; Monique Guillory and Richard C. Green, eds., *Soul: Black Power, Politics, and Pleasure* (New York: New York University Press, 1998); Devorah Heitner, *Black Power TV* (Durham: Duke University Press, 2013); Van Deburg, *New Day in Babylon*, 192–247; Gayle Wald, *It's Been Beautiful: Soul! and Black Power Television* (Durham: Duke University Press, 2015).

24 Geneva Smitherman, *Black Language and Culture: Sounds of Soul* (New York: Harper & Row, 1975).

25 Maultsby, "Soul," 279–82.

26 Smethurst, *The Black Arts Movement*, 58–76.

27 Ward, *Just My Soul Responding*, 333.

28 Guralnick, *Sweet Soul Music*, 1–15; Shaw, *The World of Soul*, 165–216; Ward, *Just My Soul Responding*, 173–216.

29 Guralnick, *Sweet Soul Music*, 32–50; Shaw, *The World of Soul*, 85–87; Christopher Trigg, "A Change Ain't Gonna Come: Sam Cooke and the Protest Song," *University of Toronto Quarterly* 79, no. 3 (2010): 991–1003; Ward, *Just My Soul Responding*, 146–48; Werner, *Change Is Gonna Come*, 31–37, 40–44.

30 Curtis Mayfield quoted in *Soul*, September 22, 1969, 16.

31 Aaron Cohen, *Move On Up: Chicago Soul Music and Black Cultural Power* (Chicago: University of Chicago Press, 2019), 27–30, 48–51, 79–81; Freeland, "'We're a Winner'"; Robert Pruter, *Chicago Soul* (Urbana: University of Illinois Press, 1991), 30–33, 136–45; Werner, *Higher Ground*, 63–125.

32 John Covach and Andrew Flory, "Motown Pop and Southern Soul," in John Covach and Andrew Flory, *What's That Sound?: An Introduction to Rock and Its History*, 3rd ed. (New York: Norton, 2012), 223–26; Flory, *I Hear a Symphony*, 100–34; George, *The Death of Rhythm & Blues*, 95–120; Neal, *What the Music Said*, 85–100; Werner, *Change Is Gonna Come*, 103–202.

33 Aretha Franklin quoted in Hirshey, *Nowhere to Run*, 242.

34 Aretha Franklin quoted in Hirshey, *Nowhere to Run*, 242, emphasis in original.

35 Aretha Franklin, *Aretha: From These Roots*, with David Ritz (New York: Villard Books, 1999), 107–27; Neal, *What the Music Said*, 85–100; Ogbar, *Black Power*, 110–16; Ongiri, *Spectacular Blackness*, 124–39; Van Deburg, *New Day in Babylon*, 204–16; Ward, *Just My Soul Responding*, 388–416; Werner, *Higher Ground*, 126–87.

36 Ford, *Liberated Threads*; Heitner, *Black Power TV*; Neal, *What the Music Said*, 85–124; Joaquim Paulo and Julius Wiedemann, *Funk & Soul Covers* (Köln: Taschen, 2010); Thomas, *Listen, Whitey!*; Van Deburg, *New Day in Babylon*, 192–247; Wald, *It's Been Beautiful*.

37 For further discussion of *Soul Train*, see Nelson George, *The Hippest Trip in America: Soul Train and the Evolution of Culture & Style* (New York: William Morrow, 2014); Ahmir Khalib "Questlove" Thompson, *Soul Train: The Music, Dance, and Style of a Generation* (New York: HarperCollins, 2013).

38 George, *The Death of Rhythm & Blues*, 95–169; Neal, *What the Music Said*, 55–84; Ongiri, *Spectacular Blackness*, 124–58; Pruter, *Chicago Soul*, 235–356; Van Deburg, *New Day in Babylon*, 204–16; Ward, *Just My Soul Responding*, 388–416; Werner, *Higher Ground*, 126–87.

39 Maultsby, "Soul," 282–85; Neal, *What the Music Said*, 101–57; Werner, *Higher Ground*, 188–290.

40 For further discussion of Gil Scott-Heron, see Marcus Baram, *Gil Scott-Heron: Pieces of a Man* (New York: St. Martin's Press, 2014); Tony Bolden, *Groove Theory: The Blues Foundation of Funk* (Jackson: University Press of Mississippi, 2020), 147–81.

41 George, *The Death of Rhythm & Blues*, 95–170; Maultsby, "Soul," 272–79; Neal, *What the Music Said*, 25–100; Ongiri, *Spectacular Blackness*, 130–58.

42 For further discussion of African Americans' experiences in the Vietnam War, see Randall M. Fisher, *Rhetoric and American Democracy: Black Protest through Vietnam Dissent* (Lanham: University Press of America, 1985); Herman Graham, *The Brothers' Vietnam War: Black Power, Manhood, and the Military Experience* (Gainesville: University Press of Florida, 2003); Daniel S. Lucks, *Selma to Saigon: The Civil Rights Movement and the Vietnam War* (Lexington: University Press of Kentucky, 2014), 73–140; James E. Westheider, *Fighting on Two Fronts: African Americans and the Vietnam War* (New York: New York University Press, 1999); James E. Westheider, *The African American Experience in Vietnam: Brothers in Arms* (Lanham: Rowman & Littlefield, 2008).

43 For important examples of classic soul and funk anti-war protest songs, see Various Artists, *Soul of Vietnam* (Risky Business, AK 53917, 1993, CD); Various Artists, *A Soldier's*

Sad Story: Vietnam through the Eyes of Black America, 1966–1973 (Kent Soul, CDKEND 226, 2003, CD); Various Artists, *Does Anybody Know I'm Here?: Vietnam through the Eyes of Black America, 1962–1972* (Kent Soul, CDKEND 245, 2005, CD); Various Artists, *Stop the War: Vietnam Through the Eyes of Black America, 1965–1974* (Kent Soul, CDKEND 474, 2021, CD).

44 Mark Anthony Neal, "The Post-Civil Rights Period: The Politics of Musical Creativity," in *Issues in African American Music: Power, Gender, Race, Representation*, eds. Portia K. Maultsby and Mellonee V. Burnim (New York: Routledge, 2017), 368–80; Neal, *What the Music Said*, 55–84; Thomas, *Listen, Whitey!*, 11–54, 143–82; Ward, *Just My Soul Responding*, 360–69.

45 D'Weston L. Haywood, " 'A Superb Sales Force . . . The Men of Muhammad': The Nation of Islam, Black Masculinity, and Selling *Muhammad Speaks* in the Black Power Era," in *New Perspectives on the Nation of Islam*, eds. Dawn-Marie Gibson and Herbert Berg (New York: Routledge, 2017), 19–40; Kimberly Springer, "Black Feminists Respond to Black Power Masculinism," in *The Black Power Movement: Rethinking the Civil Rights-Black Power Era*, ed. Peniel E. Joseph (New York: Routledge, 2006), 105–18; Simon Wendt, " 'They Finally Found Out That We Really Are Men': Violence, Non-Violence, and Black Manhood in the Civil Rights Era," *Gender & History* 19, no. 3 (2007): 543–64.

46 Tony Fletcher, *In the Midnight Hour: The Life & Soul of Wilson Pickett* (New York: Oxford University Press, 2016), 71–186; Guralnick, *Sweet Soul Music*, 152–76.

47 For further discussion of Otis Redding's life and musical legacy, see Robert M. J. Bowman, *Soulsville, U.S.A.: The Story of Stax Records* (New York: Schirmer Books, 1997), 30–169; Geoff Brown, *Otis Redding: Try a Little Tenderness* (New York: Canongate Books, 2001); Scott Freeman, *Otis!: The Otis Redding Story* (New York: St. Martin's Press, 2001); Robert Gordon, *Respect Yourself: Stax Records and the Soul Explosion* (New York: Bloomsbury, 2015), 72–184; Jonathan Gould, *Otis Redding: An Unfinished Life* (New York: Random House, 2017); Guralnick, *Sweet Soul Music*, 133–51; Mark Ribowsky, *Dreams to Remember: Otis Redding, Stax Records, and the Transformation of Southern Soul* (New York: Liveright, 2015); Jane Schiesel, *The Otis Redding Story* (Garden City, NY: Doubleday, 1973).

48 E. Taylor Atkins, "The Funky Divas Talk Back: Dialogues about Black Feminism, Masculinity, and Soul Power in the Music of James Brown," *Popular Music and Society* 38, no. 3 (2015): 337–54; Guralnick, *Sweet Soul Music*, 220–307; Neal, "The Post-Civil Rights Period," 368–80; Ward, *Just My Soul Responding*, 339–87.

49 For further discussion of the centuries-spanning racial-sexual violence against and rape of enslaved African American women, see Marisa J. Fuentes, *Dispossessed Lives: Enslaved Women, Violence, and the Archive* (Philadelphia: University of Pennsylvania Press, 2016); Sowande M. Mustakeem, *Slavery at Sea: Terror, Sex, and Sickness in the Middle Passage* (Urbana: University of Illinois Press, 2016); Gregory D. Smithers, *Slave-Breeding: Sex, Violence, and Memory in African American History* (Gainesville: University Press of Florida, 2012); Ned Sublette and Constance Sublette, eds., *The American Slave Coast: A History of the Slave-Breeding Industry* (Chicago: Lawrence Hill Books, 2015).

50 Laurence Cole, *Deep Soul Ballads: From Sam Cooke to Stevie Wonder* (Farington: Libri, 2010), 144–236; Marc Taylor, *A Touch of Classic Soul, Vol. 1: Soul Singers of the Early 1970s* (New York: Aloiv Publishing, 1996), 22–43, 89–117, 263–72, 305–14; Marc Taylor, *A Touch of Classic Soul, Vol. 2: Soul Singers of the Late 1970s* (New York: Aloiv Publishing, 2001), 106–28, 159–76.

51 Kristin Clark Taylor, *Black Mothers: Songs of Praise and Celebration* (New York: Gramercy Books, 2006).

52 Katharine Bausch, "Superflies into Superkillers: Black Masculinity in Film from Blaxploitation to New Black Realism," *Journal of Popular Culture* 46, no. 2 (2013): 257–76; Stephane Dunn, *"Baad Bitches" and Sassy Supermamas: Black Power Action Films* (Urbana: University of Illinois Press, 2008), 55–84; Ongiri, *Spectacular Blackness*, 159–85; Novotny

Lawrence, *Blaxploitation Films of the 1970s: Blackness and Genre* (New York: Routledge, 2008), 62–77; Cedric J. Robinson, "Blaxploitation and the Misrepresentation of Liberation," *Race & Class* 40, no. 1 (1998): 1–12; Yvonne D. Sims, *Women of Blaxploitation: How the Black Action Film Heroine Changed American Popular Culture* (Jefferson: McFarland, 2006).

53 Flory, *I Hear a Symphony*, 93–97; Mark Ribowsky, *Ain't Too Proud to Beg: The Troubled Lives and Enduring Soul of the Temptations* (Hoboken, NJ: John Wiley & Sons, 2010), 230–35.

4

SOUL SISTERS, MUSICAL FEMINISM, AND THE BLACK WOMEN'S LIBERATION MOVEMENT

Soul sisters: architects of an unapologetically Black women-centered movement and music

The female soul singers of the classic soul period between the mid-1960s and mid-1970s created a distinct kind of cultural, social, and political expression that was ideologically situated somewhere between the Black Power Movement and the Women's Liberation Movement. In other words, soul sisters' music was frequently simultaneously *Black nationalist* and *Black feminist*, which distinguished it from both soul brothers' music and White pop rock divas' music. In many regards, soul sisters' music touched on a lot of the same topics as their soul brother and White pop rock diva counterparts. However, and this should be strongly stressed, soul sisters engaged these topics from *African American women's point of view*.

As previously noted by numerous music scholars, initially soul sisters' music thematically paralleled many of the love songs made famous during the golden age of the girl groups (circa 1955–1970). Most girl groups' music centered on meeting the perfect guy and celebrating the triumph of true love against all the odds. Some of the more noted songs in this genre include Mary Wells' "My Guy," the Supremes' "I Hear a Symphony," Carla Thomas' "B-A-B-Y," Barbara Lewis' "Baby, I'm Yours," Doris Troy's "Just One Look," Theola Kilgore's "The Love of My Man," Barbara Mason's "Yes, I'm Ready," Betty Swann's "Make Me Yours," and Betty Everett's "The Shoop Shoop Song (It's in His Kiss)." Much like the girl groups, soul women also had a wing of their work that lamented either the absence or the loss of idealized relationships, as in Doris Duke's "To the Other Woman (I'm the Other Woman)," Baby Washington's "That's How Heartaches Are Made," Irma Thomas' "I Wish Someone Would Care," Barbara Lynn's "You'll Lose a Good Thing," and Millie Jackson's "(If Loving You Is Wrong) I Don't Want to Be Right."[1]

DOI: 10.4324/9781003254492-5

A distinct lyrical shift can be detected in girl group music-cum-women's soul music by the mid-1960s, when indications of domestic discontent and a more intense assertiveness increasingly crept into the music. Seeming to usher in a new wave of feisty female soul, songs such as Martha Reeves & the Vandellas' "Come Get These Memories" signaled that soul sisters refused to wallow in the emotional aftermath of failed relationships. Betty Everett's evocative "I Can't Hear You No More" and "You're No Good" went far to put soul brothers on notice that a new, soulful, assertive, fiercely independent African American woman was on the scene. One of the most remarkable voices of the classic soul period, Mitty Collier contributed three undisputed classics to the feisty female soul canon with "I'm Your Part-Time Love," which boldly broached the subject of male infidelity; the no-nonsense, tell-it-like-it-is "I Had a Talk with My Man"; and, finally, the brutally honest "No Faith, No Love." The "soul queen of New Orleans," Irma Thomas provided a striking expression of women's sexual agency and erotic power on "Time Is on My Side," confidently and repeatedly telling her man, "you'll come running back." And when Thomas tired of her husband's unfaithfulness, she put all of her cards on the table and in no uncertain terms told the "other woman" "(You Can Take My Husband but Please) Don't Mess with My Man."[2]

It is interesting to observe that Thomas' "(You Can Take My Husband but Please) Don't Mess with My Man" was her first hit record when it was released in late 1959, clearly demonstrating that women-centered soul's roots antedate soul music's golden age between the mid-1960s and the mid-1970s. This is also to say the assertiveness found in women-centered soul did not spring up overnight but had been emerging, perhaps in response to the increasing masculinism in rhythm & blues and the one-dimensional caricatures of the "girl next door" image in girl group music, since the late 1950s and early 1960s.[3] It is also interesting to observe that during the exact same period when a more assertive strand of female soul was forming, African American women such as Ella Baker, Septima Clark, and Fannie Lou Hamer were increasingly moving from the background and sidelines of the Black freedom struggle to play more active and visible roles as the Civil Rights Movement morphed into the Black Power Movement.[4] African American women such as Frances Beale, Mary Ann Weathers, Linda La Rue, Pauli Murray, Angela Davis, and the members of the Combahee River Collective were integral to the emergence of the Women's Liberation Movement, which was also directly influenced by the women-centered leadership and activism of the Civil Rights Movement.[5]

As male soul and funk resuscitated Black machismo and embraced the *Moynihan Report's* myth of Black matriarchy in the late 1960s, female soul and funk registered the complicated and frequently conflicted responses of African American women to the simultaneous militantization and masculinization of the Black protest movement. African American women obviously took note of the resurgence of Black male militancy during the Black Power Movement. As African American men's exasperation with the system increased and often transformed itself into various kinds of new-fangled forms of machismo and misogyny, African American women largely ended up in the unpleasant position of having to choose between supporting the Black Power Movement, which was now largely defined and dominated by Black men, or supporting the Women's Liberation Movement, which had increasingly come to be defined and dominated by White women. Many African American women, understandably, found few connections with what they perceived to be the White women-centered, middle-class, college-educated, and career-oriented overarching agenda of the Women's Liberation Movement. Consequently, a contingent of Black women ultimately decided to create their own distinct movement that combined the struggle for racial justice emerging from the Black Power Movement with the struggle for gender justice emerging from the Women's Liberation Movement.[6]

At this point, there can be little doubt concerning African American women's alienation and marginalization in both the Black Power Movement and the Women's Liberation Movement. A spate of recent research has demonstrated that many Black women were participants in the aforementioned widely recognized movements, as well as their own often unrecognized movement: the Black Women's Liberation Movement. As with any other socio-political movement, the Black Women's Liberation Movement of the 1960s and 1970s had several major objectives, organizations, activists, theorists, and themes. Here it will be important to briefly discuss the Black Women's Liberation Movement with an eye on the ways it influenced, whether directly or indirectly, the tenor of female soul, and female soul, in turn, served as a musical mouthpiece for the movement.[7]

The Black Women's Liberation Movement and the emergence of musical feminism

Much like their soul sister counterparts, it is important to acknowledge that not all of the women who participated in the Black Women's Liberation Movement self-identified as "feminists." However, whether they identified as "Black feminists," "womanists," "women's liberationists," or not, it is important to emphasize that for the most progressive among them, their collective goal was *Black women's empowerment*, the liberation of all Black people (which, of course, includes Black men and Black boys), and more broadly human liberation.[8] Their social and political agenda included an emphasis on a comprehensive reconstruction of social relations and a radical redistribution of political power. Neither the Civil Rights Movement, the Black Power Movement, nor the wider Women's Liberation Movement adequately focused on African American women's issues and quest for liberation. As discussed in the previous chapter, as the Civil Rights Movement began its decline and transition into the Black Power Movement in the mid-1960s, African American women witnessed the rise of an unrelenting Black nationalist masculinism accompanied by a rhetoric of revolution and Black liberation that, at best, quarantined Black women to "traditional" gender roles and, at worst, excluded their lives and struggles from the overarching Black Power Movement agenda altogether.[9]

As the Civil Rights Movement came to a close Black women were increasingly being relegated to supportive roles behind the scenes, and with the rise of Black nationalist masculinist rhetoric during the early years of the Black Power Movement they came to understand that the Black male leaders of the movement, essentially in response to the infamous 1965 *Moynihan Report*, wanted Black women to embrace "traditional" gender roles based on White middle-class conceptions of womanhood, wifehood, and motherhood. The *Moynihan Report* disreputably revealed that the African American family was dominated and deformed by "Black matriarchs" who, in essence, emasculated Black men because they, Black women, supposedly had more economic power and greater access to social resources as a result of their greater employment opportunities in mid-twentieth-century America.[10]

Where Black women encountered issues revolving around sexism and hyper-masculinism in the Civil Rights Movement and Black Power Movement, respectively, in the White women-centered Women's Liberation Movement they were confronted with what social movement sociologist Steven Buechler has termed White feminists' "race and class unconsciousness."[11] White feminists' "race and class unconsciousness" caused many Black women to shun feminism and others who identified as feminists to be extremely reluctant to participate in a Women's Liberation Movement that was essentially destined to liberate White middle-class women only. Black women were as constricted because of racism and capitalism as they were because of sexism. And they understood White feminists' "race and class unconsciousness" to be yet another reminder of the yawning chasm between Black and White women's lives and struggles. Besides, many Black feminists asserted, joining the White women-centered Women's Liberation Movement would be another double-duty for Black women in that they would have to constantly deconstruct and reconstruct White feminist issues and incessantly educate White feminists about Black women's distinct lives and struggles, especially as they revolved around the political economy of race and anti-Black racism in a simultaneously White supremacist, patriarchal, and capitalist society.[12]

Instead of genuflecting to White feminists' gender obsession, and rather than kowtowing to the radical rhetoric of Black nationalist masculinists, Black women mobilized their own insurgent intersectional movement. As Benita Roth's *Separate Roads to Feminism: Black, Chicana, and White Feminist Movements in America's Second Wave* and Kimberly Springer's *Living for the Revolution: Black Feminist Organizations, 1968–1980* reveal, between 1966 and 1980 Black women established a number of autonomous Black women-led and Black women-centered organizations, including the Black Women's Liberation Committee of SNCC, which broke away from SNCC in 1968 to form an independent group initially named the Black Women's Alliance and later the Third World Women's Alliance (1968–1980); the National Black Feminist Organization (1973–1975); the National Alliance of Black Feminists (1976–1980); the Combahee River Collective (1975–1980); and Black Women Organized for Action (1973–1980).[13] There were also important debates and critical discussions concerning Black women's liberation that were undertaken within organizations not commonly perceived as sites for "feminist" or "womanist" mobilization, such as the Black Panther Party, the National Welfare Rights Organization, and the National Domestic Workers Union.[14]

Along with establishing activist-oriented organizations, the Black women of the 1960s and 1970s Black Women's Liberation Movement also developed Black feminist theory and praxis to speak to their special needs. For instance, the polymathic Toni Cade Bambara published her seminal edited volume, *The Black Woman*, in 1970; the Third World Women's Alliance published a newspaper, *Triple Jeopardy*, at least ten times between 1971 and 1975; Black Women Organized for Action published a monthly newsletter regularly between 1973 and 1980; in April of 1977 Barbara Smith, Beverly Smith, and Demita Frazier issued their groundbreaking "Combahee River Collective Statement"; and evolving out of the Combahee River Collective's Black Women's Network retreats, in 1980 Barbara Smith, Audre Lorde, and Cherríe Moraga, among others, co-founded Kitchen Table Women of Color Press, which published pioneering non-white feminist texts, such as *All the Women Are White, All the Men Are Black, But Some of Us Are Brave* edited by Gloria Hull, Patricia Bell Scott, and Barbara Smith; *Home Girls: A Black Feminist Anthology* edited by Barbara Smith; and *This Bridge Called My Back: Writings by Radical Women of Color* edited by Cherríe Moraga and Gloria Anzaldúa.[15] Several recurring themes surfaced in the writings of Black and other non-White feminists of the late 1960s, 1970s, and early 1980s that demonstrate their distinct deconstruction and reconstruction of the concept of consciousness-raising and the personal-as-political model: an emphasis on the intersection of race, gender, and class oppression as the only viable way to critically analyze and adequately articulate the lives and struggles of Black and other non-White women; the "feminist racism" and "race and class unconsciousness" of the White women-centered Women's Liberation Movement; homophobia and heterosexism; domestic violence; rape; reproductive rights; healthcare; political prisoners; alternative and women-centered education; and non-White women's leadership and activism, among others.[16]

Taken together, then, the overarching contributions of the Black Women's Liberation Movement to the Black feminist aesthetic found in select classic soul and funk songs stems from Black women's liberationists' innovative deconstruction and reconstruction of the "personal is political" paradigm into a more insurgent, inclusive, and intersectional Black women-centered theory and praxis. "Buoyed by the emergence of feminist fiction, nonfiction, and poetry by the likes of Toni Cade Bambara, Alice Walker, and Nikki Giovanni," Mark Anthony Neal noted, Black popular music "increasingly captured the tenor of the period regarding the centrality of gender concerns within the tradition."[17] Soul sisters' women-centered music drew from a long tradition of blues, jazz, and gospel women who articulated Black women's special truths in much the same way that Black women's liberationists drew from Black feminist foremothers to convey bittersweet truths about Black women's lives and struggles in the 1960s and 1970s. Drawing from blues queens, jazz chanteuses, and gospel divas from Ma Rainey and Bessie Smith to Billie Holiday and Dinah Washington to Mahalia Jackson and Clara Ward, and much like the Black women's liberationists of the Black Women's Alliance/Third World Women's

Alliance, National Black Feminist Organization, National Alliance of Black Feminists, Combahee River Collective, and Black Women Organized for Action, soul sisters "responded to the public silence accorded many of their defining issues." As Neal importantly observed, "[w]ithin the context of the male-dominated protest movement, Black women began to articulate their singular experiences with the external forces of racism, sexism, and exploitation," as well as the "internal forces of sexism, exploitation, and condescension."[18]

In many ways grounded within and innovatively building on and going beyond the long Black protest song and message music tradition, soul sisters "created the aesthetic and commercial space for a new generation of womanist voices within the Black popular music tradition." Moreover, they "infused public narratives of Black rage and militancy, with nuanced demands for human respect and human decency." Historically, it is important to note, Black women's "willingness to articulate the rich diversity of human emotions within Black popular culture, particularly given the lack of accessible language to articulate such emotions, has served to broaden the limits of Black popular expression."[19]

As this section has demonstrated, the Black Women's Liberation Movement of the late 1960s and 1970s was multidimensional and multiperspectival, not monolithic, and a similar radical political and discursive diversity undoubtedly marks the female soul music from the mid-1960s to the mid-1970s. For instance, in the liner notes for the compilation *Go Girl!: Soul Sisters Tellin' It Like It Is*, music journalist Tracey New essentially summarized the ways in which the Black feminist aesthetic emerging from the Black Women's Liberation Movement translated itself into song, stating, "[t]hese songs get the message across in basically three minutes or less. And each title practically explains the content of the song. The hooks on each song come quickly and leave little to the imagination."[20] Providing further insight into the incredible interplay between the Black feminist politics and Black feminist aesthetics of the era, New emphasized that each song on *Go Girl!* was "written from a woman's point of view," was released between the mid-1960s and mid-1970s, and covered the "relationship gamut – love had and lost, hearts broken and mended, affairs and their painful results, and even the price of marrying the wrong man." She concluded by observing that the "messages in every song bear strong resemblance to sound advice from a sister, and the soulful delivery helps bring every single point home."[21]

Much like the Black women's liberationists at the time, a great many soul sisters with unnamed Black feminist inclinations were incredibly cynical about the intense machismo free-floating through the Black Power Movement. Their cynicism only increased as it became clear that perpetual racism, poverty, and unemployment ultimately meant that Black men quite simply could not fulfill the role of the conventional patriarchal protector and provider. In other words, for most Black women it was painfully clear that Black men were frequently patriarchs in name (and bad behavior) only. Bearing all of this in mind, a lot of female soul and funk music began to offer blistering, brutally honest, and often darkly humorous critiques of Black male deficiencies. Attached to assertions of Black male inadequacies were many female soul singers' declarations of women's rights, especially women's right to equal and respectful treatment at work, at home, and in the bedroom. It is this women-centered subgenre within soul music that I maintain may be viewed as a form of *musical feminism* and that might more properly be called *Black musical feminism*.[22]

The most obvious example of female soul advocating for equal rights and respectful treatment is Laura Lee's 1971 classic "Woman's Love Rights," where she audaciously asserted her equal right to sexual satisfaction, among other things. Lee's "Wedlock Is a Padlock," with its "what's good for the goose is good for the gander" emphasis, put the womanizing Black macho man on notice that soul sisters had no hangups about getting their "love rights" and sexual satisfaction outside of marriage. Several of Lee's songs, such as "Love and Liberty," "It's Not What You Fall For, It's What You Stand For," "If I'm Good Enough to Love (I'm Good Enough to Marry)," and "I Need It Just as Bad as You," can be read as forms of *Black musical feminism* in line with the ideals and ethos of the Black Women's Liberation Movement.[23]

Arguably the "Queen of Infidelity" soul music, Millie Jackson produced an unprecedented series of albums that explored the emotional and sexual politics of "cheating," "creeping," and "two-timing." Her albums *Millie Jackson* (1972), *It Hurts So Good* (1973), *I Got to Try It One Time* (1974), *Caught Up* (1974), and *Still Caught Up* (1975) collectively provide superlative examples of the ways in which female soul singers synthesized elements of the Black aesthetic and soul aesthetic with the feminist aesthetic. Jackson would frequently sing from multiple points of view (e.g., wife, mother, mistress, seductress, etc.). For instance, on "I Got to Try It One Time" she sings as a woman seriously contemplating cheating, where on "How Do You Feel the Morning After?" she sings as a betrayed, broken-hearted lover.

Jackson's greatest commercial success came in the form of her controversial concept album *Caught Up*, where she put her own special spin on the love triangle (i.e., husbands, wives, and mistresses). On the widely popular "(If Loving You Is Wrong) I Don't Want to Be Right," she sings from the perspective of the mistress or "other woman." On "It's All Over but the Shouting," she provides listeners with a window into the wounded wife's mindset and rush of raw emotions. By the album's end, listeners are left with a clear sense of the pitfalls of love triangles and the politics of relationships during the Black Women's Liberation Movement era. On her follow-up to *Caught Up*, appropriately titled *Still Caught Up*, Jackson revisited the pleasure, pain, and politics of relationships, going even further to put "soul men" and "soul brothers" on notice. Songs such as "Making the Best of a Bad Situation," "The Memory of a Wife," and "Tell Her It's Over" enabled Jackson to once again assertively sing from various points of view and express many soul sisters' thoughts on "two-timing," "cheating," and "creeping."[24]

Jackson was not alone in singing this kind of assertive, hard-hitting Black women-centered soul. From Carla Thomas' "Some Other Man (Is Beating Your Time)" and Ann Peebles' "Breaking Up Somebody's Home" to Denise LaSalle's "Married, But Not to Each Other" and the Honey Cones' "While You Were Out

Looking for Sugar," soul sisters let misbehaving Black men know that they were no longer willing to quietly sit at home, wishing and waiting, hoping and praying for idealized girl group-styled romance to magically come to them. Consequently, the increase in more assertive Black women-centered soul seems to coincide with the emergence and evolution of the Black Women's Liberation Movement. And, once again, just as the Black feminists of the Black Women's Liberation Movement embraced and expressed a wide range of views and values, something similar could be said of the musical feminists of the movement – although, it should be noted, like many of the female rappers who rose in the wake of the Black Women's Liberation Movement, most soul sisters probably would be "uncomfortable with being labeled feminist" and very likely "perceived feminism as a signifier for a movement that related specifically to White women."[25]

As discussed above, beyond their issues with what Buechler called White feminists' "race and class unconsciousness" and what Winifred Breines termed "feminist racism," most soul sisters may have also thought feminism "involved adopting an anti-male position, and although they clearly express[ed] frustration with men, they did not want to be considered or want their work to be interpreted as anti-Black male."[26] This is to say, many soul sisters practiced a distinct kind of Black feminist/womanist artistry (predicated on full-throated expressions of Black women's empowerment) without ever self-describing as "feminists." In fact, "for Black women," Tricia Rose asserted, "feminism often reads *White feminism* and consequently represents a movement that has contributed to sustaining their oppression while claiming to speak on their behalf."[27] At issue here, then, should not be whether this or that soul sister self-identified as a "feminist" but what they articulated via their artistry.

If, as Kimberly Springer noted, many Black women – including Black women activists, those who identified as feminist or otherwise – during the Black Women's Liberation Movement era took issue with White women's perceived monopoly of the term "feminist," then it is unfair to expect their soul sister counterparts to adhere to, and embrace, quite often Eurocentric, White women-only, bourgeois, heteronormative, and rather romantic conceptions of feminism and feminist activism. As a matter of fact, Mavis Bayton observed that many White female pop rock musicians do not as a rule self-describe as "feminists," and they, on the whole, have very varied relationships with feminist theory and activism. She noted: "Feminism has meant different things to different people at different times. Many more women have been influenced by it and espouse its tenets than would readily call themselves 'feminists'."[28] I believe a similar statement may be made with respect to Black feminism in relation to soul sisters: "[Black] [f]eminism has meant different things to different people at different times. Many more [Black] women have been influenced by it and espouse its tenets than would readily call themselves [Black] 'feminists'," let alone *Black musical feminists*. But I honestly believe much of the hairsplitting surrounding whether Black women self-describe as "Black feminists" or "womanists" or otherwise is beside the point and a laborious academic exercise of no interest to anyone other than a handful of armchair revolutionaries.

A kind of *Black feminist ideological fluidity* seems to pervade the thought and practices of both the Black political feminists and Black musical feminists of the Black Women's Liberation Movement. That being said, the membership brochure of the Black Women Organized for Action (BWOA) organization arguably captures the kind of catch-all philosophy many Black political feminists and Black musical feminists put into practice in their work. The BWOA's recruitment and membership credo emphasized its openness to

> old sisters, young sisters, skinny sisters, fat sisters . . . the poor and the not so poor . . . you and me . . . from blue Black to high yellow. A bouquet of BLACK WOMEN – action oriented, composed of feminists and non-feminists concerned with the political and economic development of a total Black community.[29]

Consequently, when I write of Black musical feminism here I do not understand each and every soul sister discussed to embrace frequently bourgeois, Eurocentric, and academic 1960s and 1970s forms of feminism. On the contrary, I interpret them as adhering to, and articulating, a much more *sister-centered, Black womenfolk and Black mother-wit-informed philosophy and artistry* that is *simultaneously part womanist consciousness-raising and part spiritual, sexual, intellectual, and cultural art.*[30]

In keeping with many of the major themes of the Black Women's Liberation Movement discussed above, a lot of female soul emphasized sisterhood and solidarity. This sentiment could be said to have culminated with Sister Sledge's 1979 classic anthem "We Are Family," with its copious references to sisterhood, family, and other allusions to a discofied form of Black musical feminism. And because many Black women conceived of each other as family and, consequently, "sisters," two-timing "brothers" were typically dismissed as an abhorrent but unfortunate fact of Black life and relationships. Female soul songs such as Doris Duke's "To the Other Woman," Ann Peebles' "Part-Time Love," and Mitty Collier's "Sharing You" demonstrate the kind of care and sensitivity that Black women frequently treated each other with when confronted with womanizing Black men. Indeed, in many soul sisters' songs about being involuntarily involved in love triangles, they were often reluctant to outright accuse the other woman of any immorality. An obvious anomaly to this tendency was Betty Wright's 1971 classic "Clean Up Woman," with its "if you don't take care of your business in the bedroom somebody else will" message. "Clean Up Woman" pointed to many Black women's alleged inability to satisfy Black men's enormous sexual desires as one of the key reasons so many Black men were not monogamous. In essence, the song lyrically let womanizing Black men off the hook and put the real responsibility for the success or failure of relationships squarely on Black women. Here we witness a small sample of the diversity of thought contained in Black women-centered soul and the reason superficial, one-dimensional, or dismissive interpretations of this genre prove problematic.[31]

"Clean Up Woman," indeed, was an outlier, as most women-centered soul critical of "creeping" usually included sisterly warnings and advice not to trust men, as with Mary Wells' "Never Give a Man the World." Similarly, sharing that she had cooked for, cleaned for, clothed, and supported her man through thick and thin, in "Woman to Woman" Shirley Brown passionately warned the "other woman" that her man was a heartbreaker who could not be trusted. Some female soul singers advocated revenge against womanizing men, as Candi Staton did in "Evidence," Ann Peebles in "Tear Your Playhouse Down," Denise LaSalle in "Breaking up Somebody's Home," and Millie Jackson in "You Can't Stand the Thought of Another Me." Other female soul singers disparaged the hypermasculinity at the heart of seemingly most male soul music by broaching the incredibly taboo topic of male sexual failings.[32]

Indeed, a great many soul women bemoaned the big talk and small sexual satisfaction of jive-talking and smooth-walking soul brothers. In "Circuits Overloaded," Inez Foxx called out her man for playing the field so much that he was unable to "handle his business" in the bedroom. Jean Knight's "Mr. Big Stuff," Veda Brown's brazen "Short Stopping," and the Sweet Inspirations' tale of sexual frustration "(Gotta Find) A Brand New Lover" all touched on the same taboo topic. Lastly, in "Man-Sized Job," Denise LaSalle claimed that pleasing her was more than most men could handle and went further to state outright that for all their macho bragging and boasting, she had yet to encounter a man who fully sexually satisfied her.[33]

Feisty female soul and funk songs like the ones noted above and countless others produced during the Black Women's Liberation Movement demonstrate that soul women created what could be broadly conceived of as *Black feminist soul and funk* or, rather, *musical expressions of Black feminism* – forms of *Black musical feminism*. For the most part, these songs grew out of a fierce rejection of the helpless woman in love stereotype (à la the girl groups). From retaliatory infidelity to making known male sexual performance problems, even though soul women did not articulate any sort of clear-cut Black feminist program (à la their social, political, and cultural counterparts discussed earlier), their work offset longstanding images of African American women as willingly accepting Black machismo, musical or otherwise. As Shay Holiday's vengeful tale of infidelity in "Fight Fire with Fire" demonstrated, soul women could give as good as they got during the male-dominated Black Power Movement years. Ironically, some soul women sought to gain respect by beating men at their own deceitful game. In essence, if men could lie and cheat, so could women. But bad behavior is just that, *bad behavior*, no matter who engages in it. Women supposed heartlessly behaving like men (read: *patriarchal, misogynist, womanizing* men) is incredibly problematic on lots of different levels.[34]

We should avoid applying some sort of inverted sexual double-standard to this frequently raunchy and sexually assertive subgenre of Black women-centered soul and funk. While this work is, obviously, incredibly important, too often it was merely reactive and not proactive. Even though much of this music deconstructed stereotypes about African American women, it often failed to offer healthy alternatives. Women behaving like misogynist and philandering men is reactionary, not revolutionary (à la several of the forms of Black feminism discussed earlier). Here, then, there is a disconnect between female soul music and the Black Women's Liberation Movement. However, this incongruence is one that may be accounted for because the music may have been more cathartic rather than realistic or didactic. Just as soul men could sing of their wildest sexual fantasies, the same creative license should be extended to soul women and female funksters. During the Black Power Movement there was a real need for Black popular culture and Black popular music that, however problematically, empowered African American women, and this raunchy and sexually assertive subgenre of female soul may have enabled many Black women to rescue and reclaim themselves in ways not fully understood by those who are neither Black nor female nor living through the tumultuous late 1960s and 1970s.[35]

As discussed in the previous chapter, a number of criticisms can be leveled against a lot of male-centered soul. First, for instance, sundry male soul can be criticized for projecting "over-sexualized constructs of Black femininity" and the "reconstruction of patriarchal modes of Black masculinity," as well as for often intimating that Black women are the reason for a plethora of Black problems in the aftermath of the Civil Rights Movement.[36] Second, much male soul can be rightly critiqued for recurringly glorifying stereotypical images of reckless, rapacious promiscuousness and sexual adventurism. And, lastly, masculinist soul music can be criticized for obsessively playing up exploitative, abusive, and often sadistic relationships with Black women. Ensconced in a lot of male soul music, these repugnant lyrical leanings made it appear as though male chauvinism, misogyny, and two-timing were endemic to Black relationships during the Black Power Movement.[37] Needless to say, many of the messages in this music painted an extremely cynical, one-dimensional, and patriarchal picture of Black society during the exact same time period when calls for Black unity in the midst of Black diversity were unceasing. The truth of the matter is that most African Americans continued to struggle to live respectable, responsible, and productive lives despite the insidious influence of racial oppression, cultural degradation, and economic exploitation.[38]

Consequently, many of the same criticisms that have been made against many of the most misogynist male soul artists could be made against some of the soul women who essentially embraced and articulated off-kilter, inverted female versions of the philandering, sexually exploitative, and emotionally abusive soul man. As was stated earlier, *women behaving like misogynist and philandering men is reactionary, not revolutionary.* Instead of placing female soul and funk artists on a pedestal, it is important for us to acknowledge when and where they were progressive and challenged patriarchy and misogyny. Likewise, it is also important for us to observe when and where soul sisters made missteps and produced music that glorified and gave some Black women's two-timing, double-dealing, materialism, and sadism a pass.[39]

Similar to their soul men counterparts, many soul women and female funksters frequently depicted Black men as deficient, delinquent, deceitful, and ostentatious; as the key cause for Black women's misery; and as the real reason behind most of Black America's post-Civil Rights Movement social, political, and economic problems. Nonetheless, there has been a longstanding tendency to downplay and diminish these problematic preoccupations in female soul and funk. In fact, some music critics have come to conceive of these musings as authentic Black feminist responses to blatant expressions of sexism and the unambiguous quest for sexual and patriarchal power in much male soul and funk music. As observed above, the meaning of this music may seem esoteric to those who are not Black, female, and living through the tense times of the late 1960s and 1970s. It is relatively easy to understand how this music resonated with so many Black women during the Black male-dominated Black Power Movement era. Undoubtedly, there was something uplifting and empowering, perhaps even cathartic, about the unapologetic refusal of these soul sisters to give in to, or go along with, the rampant and flagrant forms of sexism and misogyny not merely in male soul music, but also pervasive throughout the Black Power Movement in particular, and Black America in general.[40]

The Queen of Soul: Aretha Franklin, musical feminism, and the movement

Among the soul sisters who challenged male domination and served as mouthpieces for the broadly conceived Black Women's Liberation Movement, Aretha Franklin and Nina Simone stand out and deserve special attention. Although she is primarily known for her soul love songs, similar to Curtis Mayfield and James Brown, Aretha Franklin's music also took on an increasingly political tone in the 1960s and 1970s. A list of several of the often overlooked protest songs Franklin released includes "Hard Times," "God Bless the Child," "Nobody Knows the Way I Feel This Morning," "If I Had a Hammer," "A Change Is Gonna Come," "Ain't Nobody (Gonna Turn Me Around)," "People Get Ready," "Son Of A Preacher Man," "When The Battle Is Over," "Young, Gifted and Black," "Border Song (Holy Moses)," "Bridge Over Troubled Water," and, many would argue, the entire *Amazing Grace* album. According to Brian Ward, Franklin's father, Reverend C.L. Franklin, was "a good friend of Martin Luther King," and it was King himself who coaxed Aretha into "Movement work."[41] Therefore, it should not come as a great surprise that Aretha's "presence in and around the Movement increased dramatically in the late 1960s."[42] Moreover, no one should be shocked that she consistently sang protest songs and supported both the Civil Rights Movement and the Black Power Movement.

As Jerry Wexler revealed in an interview quoted in Mark Bego's *Aretha Franklin: Queen of Soul*, Franklin "devoted an enormous piece of her life to Martin Luther King, yet she never became merely a sloganeer or polemicist. She acted out of the purest wellsprings of faith and belief."[43] Echoing Ward and Wexler, historian Craig Werner, in *Higher Ground: Stevie Wonder, Aretha Franklin, Curtis Mayfield, and the Rise and Fall of American Soul*, asserted:

> Because of her father's friendship with King and Detroit's Black political establishment, Aretha had more direct contact with the Movement. She

idolized King and took pride in Detroit's "Great March to Freedom," a Mid-western counterpart of the more famous 1963 March on Washington that her father helped to organize. Joining Mahalia Jackson and Dinah Washington at a Chicago benefit for the Birmingham Movement, Aretha mesmerized the overflowing audience at McCormack Place with a rendition of "Precious Lord (Take My Hand)."[44]

Consequently, although often erased or rendered invisible, Aretha Franklin's protest music began long before 1972 – the year she released both *Young, Gifted and Black* and *Amazing Grace*. As noted above, even during her early Columbia Records years between 1960 and 1966 she recorded and released several tracks that can certainly be considered protest songs when they are placed within the context of the Civil Rights Movement and, later, the Black Power Movement. Her early recordings such as "Hard Times," "God Bless the Child," "Nobody Knows the Way I Feel This Morning," and "If I Had a Hammer" were as much message music as anything Curtis Mayfield & the Impressions recorded and released during the same period. And, similar to Franklin, Mayfield's protest songs between 1960 and 1966 were often isolated efforts on albums that owed as much to the jazz, pop, and supper club singing traditions as they did to the emerging soul sound (e.g., see Mayfield & the Impressions' *The Impressions* [1963], *The Never Ending Impressions* [1964], *Keep On Pushing* [1964], *People Get Ready* [1965], *One By One* [1965], and *Ridin' High* [1966]). However, Franklin's gender and both the Civil Rights Movement's and Black Power Movement's embrace of simultaneously Eurocentric and patriarchal gender roles seems to have blinded most folk, especially Black popular music scholars and critics, from seeing her distinct, often understated brand of Black women-centered protest music.[45]

Franklin's politics and modes of protest may not mirror male soul musicians' politics and modes of protest, but that does not in any way negate the fact that she indeed did produce songs that offered social commentary and political critique. As a matter of fact, there is a sense in which Franklin's pioneering protest music went above and beyond the other mostly male architects of soul music when we seriously consider that her songs became anthems for the Black Women's Liberation Movement, as well as both the Civil Rights Movement and the Black Power Movement. Consequently, as Pamela Greene argued in "Aretha Franklin: The Emergence of Soul and Black Women's Consciousness in the Late 1960s and 1970s," along with her Civil Rights Movement- and Black Power Movement-associated songs, Franklin also released several songs that were adopted as anthems for the Black Women's Liberation Movement, including "Respect," "Do Right Woman, Do Right Man," "Satisfaction," "(You Make Me Feel Like) A Natural Woman," "Chain of Fools," and "Think."[46]

"I don't make it a practice to put my politics into my music," Franklin coyly contended in her acclaimed autobiography, *Aretha: From the Roots*.[47] However, she was all too aware of the fact that her chart-topping version of Otis Redding's "Respect" resonated with Blacks *and* Whites, males *and* females, businessmen *and* housewives across the country. At the time of its release, she recalled in her autobiography, the song touched the "need of a nation, the need of the average man and woman in the street, the businessman, the mother, the fireman, the teacher – everyone wanted respect. It was also one of the battle cries of the Civil Rights Movement. The song took on monumental significance. It became the 'Respect' women expected from men and men expected from women, the inherent right of all human beings."[48]

Situated at the intersection of three social and political movements (i.e., the Civil Rights Movement, the Black Power Movement, and the Women's Libera-tion Movement), "Respect," once again, demonstrates both the duality and the universality of Black popular music and Black popular movements. Remarking on the song's broad appeal and variable meanings in a *Rolling Stone* interview, famed Atlantic Records audio engineer Tom Dowd, who recorded and mixed the classic track, added that "[i]t could be a racial situation, it could be a political situation," or "it could be just the man-woman situation." But, no matter what the situation, it was a song that "[a]nyone could identify with it. It cut a lot of ground."[49] Even though "[a]nyone could identify with" "Respect," Jerry Wexler emphasized the song's special meaning for women, especially "minority" (read: Black) women, in the midst of the Black Women's Liberation Movement, stating:

> Aretha added another dimension to the song. . . . This is almost a feminist clarion. Whenever women heard the record, it was like a tidal wave of sororal [sorority-like] unity. "A little respect when you come home" doesn't only connote respect in the sense of having concern for another's position; there's also a little lubricity in there – respect acquires the notion of being able to perform conjugally in optimum fashion. It was just a very interesting mix: an intuitive feminist outcry, a sexual statement, and an announcement of dignity. And a minority person making a statement of pride without sloganeering.[50]

Similar to the apolitical stance and pop sheen Berry Gordy attempted to stamp Motown's music with throughout the 1960s, Aretha tried her best to avoid "put[ting] [her] politics into [her] music." But her magical melisma and unbridled *Übermensch* blending of gospel, blues, jazz, rhythm & blues, rock & roll, and coun-try & western vocalizations, not to mention the extremely turbulent nature of the times, made even her most middle-of-the-road and pop-sounding songs take on multiple socio-political meanings. Therefore, it wasn't merely the words Aretha sang but the Black church folk-influenced fervency with which she sang that gave her listeners the distinct impression that the power and passion in her voice was both the embodiment and the culmination of centuries of Black women's love, loss, and incessant struggle for liberation.[51]

Observe that prior to hinting at its anthemic status for the sister-soldiers of the Women's Liberation Movement, Franklin noted that "Respect" quickly became "one of the battle cries of the Civil Rights Movement." Her contention that the song "took on monumental significance" for many different people from many different walks of life was corroborated by Werner, who revealingly wrote:

> "Respect" burst like a howitzer shell over a nation braced for another round of summertime riots. Angry over the failure of the Movement's southern victories to translate into meaningful change in their own communities, rioters had taken to the streets in dozens of cities in the North and West the previous two years. The defeat of Martin Luther King's Chicago campaign transmitted an unambiguous message to the residents of Newark, Watts, and Paradise Valley as well as those manning the frontlines on the south shore of Lake Michigan. Many turned their backs on the Civil Rights Movement's nonviolent and interracial ideals in favor of the emerging Black Power Movement. But even many who weren't impressed with Black Power ideology responded powerfully to the emotional punch of slogans like "Black is Beautiful" and "Power to the People." "R-E-S-P-E-C-T" spelled the same thing to them, without the ideological baggage and with a gospel call to freedom on the backbeat.[52]

Not called the "Queen of Soul" for nothing, it seems that Aretha was right when she reluctantly admitted that "Respect" "took on monumental significance." In light of the deep disillusionment much of Black America experienced in the aftermath of the Civil Rights Movement, many knew that more needed to be done in order to achieve a real and lasting multiracial and multicultural democracy in America. As Dowd shared, the racial and political connotations of "Respect" were almost inherent in the song and the intense gospel-influenced manner in which it was sung – and that is whether Aretha intended those connotations or not. The truth of the matter is that most people hear what they want to hear in Black popular music. But I would heartily agree with those who hold that women's interpretation of women's art – in this instance, African American women's interpretation of an African American woman's artistry – is especially meaningful. As a result, along with the racio-cultural and socio-political interpretation of "Respect" there was the equally popular Black women-centered/womanist interpretation of the song.[53]

With regard to "Respect," in *Black Feminist Thought: Knowledge, Consciousness, and the Politics of Empowerment*, Patricia Hill Collins asserted that "[e]ven though the lyrics can be sung by anyone, they take on special meaning when sung by Aretha in the way that she sings them. On one level the song functions as a metaphor for the conditions of African Americans in a racist society."[54] This is obviously the way many Black Power Movement participants interpreted the song, as well as those African Americans "who weren't impressed with Black Power ideology" and all of its "ideological baggage," but who continued their commitments to the principles and practices of the waning Civil Rights Movement. On another level, however, "Respect" also serves as a metaphor for the conditions of African American women in a simultaneously racist *and* sexist society. "Aretha's being a Black woman enables the song to tap a deeper meaning," Collins continued. "Within the blues tradition, the listening audience of African American women assumes 'we' Black women, even though Aretha as the blues singer sings 'I'."[55]

The collective "I" of classic soul music – the musical "I" that was actually a socio-political "we" – should be borne in mind because it was soon inherited by female funksters and, even later, neo-soul sisters. This is to say, a very similar kind of "I"/"we" convergence – an individual artist serving as a symbol for the collective loves, lives, and struggles of African American women – continues to reverberate and boom in contemporary women-centered Black popular music. But, as it was with Aretha Franklin's classic soul songs, the political and unambiguously Black women-centered nature of African American women's music is often either down-played or erased altogether. In fact, the music criticism centered around African American women's work frequently mirrors the racial myth and sexual stereotype-styled approach to African American women's loves, lives, and struggles prevalent within the broader social, political, and cultural world.[56]

Consequently, whatever Aretha Franklin's music might have meant to the wider Women's Liberation Movement of the 1960s and 1970s, it had special meaning for the Black women of the period. Many African American women's deep iden-tification with Aretha grew out of their ability to relate to her life, music, and unapologetic commitment to the social and political movements of the era. As discussed above, Franklin enjoyed a close friendship with Martin Luther King and regularly sang at, and supported, Civil Rights Movement activities. According to Mark Bego, with her "sense of pride and her dignified stance," perhaps more than any other figure associated with soul music, the Civil Rights Movement, and the Black Power Movement, Aretha "represented the new Black woman of the late 1960s." He continued, "[i]n her own way she embodied the social and cultural change that was taking place in the country, merely by being herself without pre-tense. Respected by Black *and* White America, she was the 'natural woman' that she sang about."[57]

In terms of her personal life, many African American women in the 1960s and 1970s related to the fact that, as Franklin revealed in her autobiography, she had been an unwed teen mother. Making neo-soul divas Erykah Badu and Lauryn Hill's unwed and much-discussed pregnancies in the late 1990s look extremely tame in comparison (bear in mind that both Badu and Hill were over twenty-five at the time of their pregnancies and their children's births), Franklin had her first child, Clarence Franklin, on March 28, 1956, three days after her fourteenth birthday, and her second child, Edward Franklin, on January 5, 1957 at the age of fifteen. Franklin's much publicized abusive marriage to Ted White between 1961 and 1969 also endeared her to African American women, many of whom – very similar to "Sister Aretha" – knew firsthand the hardships of Black womanhood, Black wifehood, and Black motherhood, as well as the hurt and seemingly con-stant heartbreaks of unrewarding relationships. Therefore, Aretha's classic Atlantic Records albums have a special place within the world of Black popular music in general and Black women's popular music in particular.[58]

Instead of being the Motown and Brill Building "girl next door" – which always meant, however clandestinely, the *White girl* next door – Aretha's early Atlantic albums between 1967 and 1972 bristled with a gutsy, gospel-influenced intensity and unparalleled passion that were unmistakably *Black* and *womanist* in the sense that the sound of her voice seemed to capture and echo centuries of enslavement, hush harbors, ring shouts, tent revivals, healing crusades, brutal beatings, and incessant racialized sexual violence, as well as quiet determination, abolitionism, armed rebellion, Civil Rights struggle, and individual African American women's triumph over untold personal tragedies.[59] Her Atlantic albums *I Never Loved a Man the Way I Love You* (1967), *Aretha Arrives* (1967), *Lady Soul* (1968), *Aretha Now* (1968), *Aretha in Paris* (1968), *Soul'69* (1969), *This Girl's in Love with You* (1970), *Spirit in the Dark* (1970) *Aretha Live at Fillmore West* (1971), *Young, Gifted and Black* (1972), *Amazing Grace* (1972), and *Oh Me, Oh My: Aretha Live in Philly* (1972), a total of twelve music-history-making albums, endeared Aretha Franklin to African American women in the late 1960s and early 1970s in ways that few who are not African American *and* women fully understand. However, it could be argued even further that working-class and underclass African American women had an especially remarkable relationship with Aretha and her music because, in Werner's words:

> Those who'd grown up in the "Age of Aretha" kept right on living their lives to the rhythms of "Baby, I Love You," "Since You've Been Gone (Sweet Sweet Baby)," "Spirit in the Dark," and "Respect." That was especially the case for Black women, who'd always seen Sister Ree from a slightly different angle than anyone else. While feminists, revolutionaries, and Vietnam veterans all responded to the metaphorical possibilities of Aretha's music, the ghetto women whom Black novelist Paule Marshall called "poets in the kitchen" understood her as one of their own – if not quite a ghetto girl, certainly the voice of the girls in the ghetto. Aretha's struggles for self-acceptance, her fiery insistence that her man do the right thing, her melting sensuality, her never-easy knowledge that at the end of the day Jesus would give her the strength to weather the storm: all of it remained as real for Aretha's African American sisters in the late seventies as it had been five or ten years earlier. As the Black feminist (or womanist, to use Alice Walker's preferred term) movement emerged in the late seventies, Aretha became an icon. The first generation of Black women to articulate womanism's aims and values was Aretha's. They'd grown up with the Civil Rights Movement and benefited from the movement's assault on Jim Crow.[60]

It is important to understand that even though "feminists, revolutionaries, and Vietnam veterans all responded to the metaphorical possibilities of Aretha's music," it was the "ghetto women" who claimed her "as one of their own – if not quite a ghetto girl, certainly the voice of the girls in the ghetto." Franklin not only brought a grittier and heavier gospel-influenced sound to Black popular music in the late 1960s and early 1970s, but she also composed or appropriated and transposed songs that spoke directly to working-class and underclass African American women's loves, lives, and struggles. In this sense, one of the great ironies of Franklin's Atlantic albums between 1967 and 1972 is that even as they innovatively merged gospel inflections and non-verbal vocalizations (e.g., yelps, howls, moans, grunts, and groans) with the Stax Records-styled Southern soul sound, lyrically her music actually harked back and held on to themes and topics that were taken up by classic blues queens and classic jazz divas such as Ma Rainey, Bessie Smith, Billie Holiday, Dinah Washington, and Nina Simone. Needless to say, each of the forenamed are as famous for their protest songs as they are for their love songs.[61] As a matter of fact, similar to Franklin, as the 1960s rolled and raged on, Nina Simone blurred the lines between gospel, blues, folk, jazz, and soul, and increasingly peppered her albums with spirited protest songs.

The High Priestess of Soul: Nina Simone, musical feminism, and the movement

Nina Simone can be considered a "soul" singer when we observe her gospel-influenced singing and the sheer range of raw emotions she was able to capture and often conjure up, rather than strictly based on the unconventional but nonetheless "soulful" sound of her music. She synthesized gospel, blues, European classical, folk, jazz, pop, rhythm & blues, rock & roll, soul, and funk into her own distinct signature sound. Although often characterized as an innovative and eclectic jazz diva, Simone was as adept at folk and blues as she was at rhythm & blues and soul (e.g., see *Folksy Nina* [1964], *Broadway-Blues-Ballads* [1964], *Pastel Blues* [1965], *The High Priestess of Soul* [1967], *Nina Simone Sings the Blues* [1967], and *Nina Simone and Piano* [1968]). In *I Put a Spell on You: The Autobiography of Nina Simone* she stated, "[t]o me 'jazz' meant a way of thinking, a way of being, and the Black man in America was jazz in everything he did – in the way he walked, talked, thought and acted. Jazz music was just another aspect of the whole thing, so in that sense because I was Black I was a jazz singer, but in every other way I most definitely wasn't."[62]

Simone's words capture the ways in which African American music in general, and – even though she said the "Black *man* in America" – African American women's music in particular, has been consistently misnamed and forced to fit into mostly White male music critic-created categories. Along with condemning women's relegation to the " 'light' and seemingly 'feminine' frivolity of pop," and the general "lack of feminist writing on popular music," Mavis Bayton also importantly emphasized that "most [music] writers," which is to say, most music critics, "have been men."[63] I would go on to add that not only have most music critics been men, but they have been patently, for the most part, *White* men. Continuing to drive home the point that most music critics have been men who view and value women's music from a heteropatriarchal point of view, Bayton further maintained that because "most journalist are male, a hegemonic masculine view tends to predominate in the music press. Women, who are not presented as artists in the way that men are or to be taken seriously as musicians, are often viewed as just puppets, molded by record companies, rarely asked about playing their instruments and often presented in sexual terms rather than as craftswomen, serious about their work."[64]

Like Aretha Franklin, Etta James, Tina Turner, Esther Phillips, Roberta Flack, and a whole host of past and present Black divas, Nina Simone eschewed the lazy labeling so often associated with Black popular music. In fact, she was especially peeved by the constant comparisons between her music and that of other Black divas that, from her point of view, always seemed to rob her and whoever she was being compared with of the distinctiveness and magic of their music. Directly addressing this issue in her autobiography, Simone asserted:

> Because of "[I Loves You,] Porgy" people often compared me to Billie Holiday, which I hated. That was just one song out of my repertoire, and anybody who saw me perform could see we were entirely different. What made me mad was that it meant people couldn't get past the fact we were both Black: if I had happened to be White nobody would have made the connection. And I didn't like to be put in a box with other jazz singers because my musicianship was totally different, and in its own way superior. Calling me a jazz singer was a way of ignoring my musical background because I didn't fit into White ideas of what a Black performer should be. It was a racist thing; "if she's Black she must be a jazz singer." It diminished me, exactly like Langston Hughes was diminished when people called him a "great Black poet." Langston was a great poet period, and it was up to him and him alone to say what part the color of his skin had to do with that.[65]

It is important to note that Simone "didn't like to be put in a box with other jazz singers" because, she strongly stressed, "my musicianship was totally different." This is an important theme that runs throughout African American women musicians' interviews and autobiographies, from Billie Holiday's classic *Lady Sings the Blues* all the way to Tina Turner's *I, Tina: My Life Story*, Etta James' *Rage to Survive: The Etta James Story*, Aretha Franklin's *Aretha: From These Roots*, and Simone's own *I Put a Spell on You: The Autobiography of Nina Simone*.[66] In this sense, then, many African American women musicians' contestation of the lazy labeling that often diminished their distinctiveness could be understood as a form of protest against an anti-Black racist *and* sexist society that frequently fails to acknowledge African American women on their own terms, as opposed to Eurocentric terms that see Black women as nothing more than White women in Blackface or chocolate-covered White women. However, similar to Franklin, Simone's sonic protest registered on both the *personal* level and the *political* level, to play on the "personal is political" slogan of the Women's Liberation Movement. In other words, Simone's sonic protest was simultaneously and amazingly *Black women-centered* and *Civil Rights Movement-cum-Black Power Movement-centered*.[67]

Simone's growing commitment to the Civil Rights Movement led her to record some of the most incendiary protest music of the 1960s and 1970s. Under contract to record for Columbia Pictures' subsidiary Colpix Records between 1959 and 1963, Simone recorded several protest songs that mirrored the major issues and events of the Civil Rights Movement. For instance, *The Amazing Nina Simone* (1959) featured a stunning rendition of the gospel song "Children Go Where I Send You," which many took as a coded message of encouragement to Civil Rights workers; *Nina Simone at Town Hall* (1959) featured the folk song "Black Is the Color of My True Love's Hair" and an original composition "Under the Lowest"; *Forbidden Fruit* (1960) featured "Work Song," which critiqued chain gangs; *Nina Simone at the Village Gate* (1962) featured "House of the Rising Sun," "Brown Baby," and "Zungo," each of which unambiguously painted sonic portraits of African American life and culture in the early 1960s.[68]

When Simone signed a new recording contract with the Netherlands-based Philips Records in 1964 her music took on an even greater political tone and sense of social commentary. For instance, in response to the brutal murder of NAACP field secretary Medgar Evers on June 12, 1963, and the 16th Street Baptist Church bombing on September 15, 1963, in Birmingham, Alabama, which claimed the lives of Addie Mae Collins (age 14), Denise McNair (age 11), Carole Robertson (age 14), and Cynthia Wesley (age 14) and injured two dozen other churchgoers, Simone's first Philips album, *Nina Simone in Concert* (1964), featured two new subversive songs, "Mississippi Goddam" and "Old Jim Crow."[69] Her *Pastel Blues* (1965) featured "Strange Fruit" and "Sinnerman." Her album *Let It All Out* (1966) featured "The Ballad of Hollis Brown" and the Black working-class women-centered song "Images." Moreover, Simone's albums *Wild is the Wind* (1966), *The High Priestess of Soul* (1967), and *Nina Simone Sings the Blues* (1967) contained several tracks that reflected her and Black America's embrace of aspects of the more militant politics that characterized the Black Power Movement in the late 1960s and early 1970s.[70]

As a matter of fact, in *The Sound of Soul*, Phyl Garland quoted H. Rap Brown – one of the most noted and controversial militants of the Black Power Movement and, more specifically, the new chairman of the revamped SNCC – in 1967 lionizing Simone as the "singer of the Black Revolution because there is no other singer who sings real protest songs about the race situation."[71] Essentially corroborating Brown's contention, Brain Ward's painstaking scholarship in *Just My Soul Responding* painted a very vivid picture of Simone's music and politics in relationship to the Civil Rights Movement and its evolution into the Black Power Movement:

> Simone's level of involvement was unmatched by any of the major figures of rhythm & blues in the early-to-mid 1960s, and it was probably not coincidental that she was actually outside the main run of soul artists. Simone was a classically trained singer-pianist; a Julliard graduate whose predilection for mixing Bach fugues, jazz, blues, folk and gospel frequently confounded attempts by critics, record label executives, producers, and nightclub owners

to assign her to any of the stylistic slots routinely reserved for Black artists. "I didn't fit into White ideas of what a Black performer should be. It was a racist thing," she later wrote. Her distinctive hybrid stylings also meant that her principal Black audience comprised mainly intellectuals and Movement workers who appreciated her candid lyrics and personal commitment. Her other fans were mostly White folk, jazz, and blues aficionados, many of whom were Northern college students or budding bohemians. They also tended to be racial liberals and as such were untroubled by Simone's politics.[72]

To reiterate, Nina Simone's sonic protest registered on both the *personal* level and the *political* level, and part of her personal protest as a recording artist "frequently confounded attempts by critics, record label executives, producers, and nightclub owners to assign her to any of the stylistic slots routinely reserved for Black artists." Obviously, Simone's sonic protest grew more complex and, at times, more direct as the social, political, and cultural struggles engulfing her epoch further unfolded.

"After the murder of Medgar Evers, the Alabama bombing and 'Mississippi Goddam' the entire direction of my life shifted," Simone importantly recounted.[73] She further stated, "for the next seven years I was driven by Civil Rights and the hope of Black Revolution. I was proud of what I was doing and proud to be part of a movement that was changing history." Moving her music even further away from the unchallenging and unrewarding music favored by much of mainstream America in the 1960s, Simone shared, "although being a performing artist sounded like something grand and wonderful, up to then it felt like just another job." But, "[t]hat changed when I started singing for the movement. . . . It made what I did for a living something much more worthwhile." Instead of the world of popular music seeming like a "nothing world" where she "didn't have much respect for popular audiences because they were so musically ignorant," after she began to record Civil Rights Movement-centered music her relationship with her music, her audiences, and the movement drastically changed. Performing her music no longer felt like "just another job." Describing the far-reaching changes that took place in her life and music during the Civil Rights Movement and Black Power Movement years, Simone observed:

> As I became more involved in the movement this attitude I had towards my audiences changed, because I admired what they were achieving for my people so much that the level of their music education didn't come into it anymore. They gave me respect too, not only for my music – which they loved – but because they understood the stand I was making. They knew I was making sacrifices and running risks just like they were, and we were all in it together. Being a part of this struggle made me feel so good. My music was dedicated to a purpose more important than classical music's pursuit of excellence; it was dedicated to the fight for freedom and the historical destiny of my people. I felt a fierce pride when I thought about what we were

all doing together. So, if the movement gave me nothing else, it gave me self-respect.[74]

Simone's "fierce pride" and new sense of "self-respect" were documented in most of the songs she recorded in the mid-to-late 1960s and early 1970s. As a matter of fact, by the time she signed with RCA Records in 1967 she had produced a patchwork of political songs that were virtually unrivaled in Black popular music. However, like Franklin's music, Simone's new sense of "self-respect" embedded in her mid-to-late 1960s and early 1970s music seemed to resonate with the emerging Black Women's Liberation Movement just as much as it did the Civil Rights Movement and Black Power Movement. Songs such as "Images" (from *Let It All Out*) and "Four Women" (from *Wild Is the Wind*) endeared Simone to African American women in a special way: "Images" emphasized working-poor Black women's beauty and need for self-love and self-respect in spite of their dream-destroying jobs and the overall ugliness of most of their lives; and "Four Women" was an epic musical counter-history of stereotypical anti-Black racist and sexist images of African American women from enslavement to the Black Power Movement.[75]

By broaching the subject of Black women's brutal treatment during and after African American enslavement, with "Four Women" Simone made one of her greatest contributions to Black women's protest song tradition. For instance, "Aunt Sarah" is the first of the four women described in the song. Simone's "Aunt Sarah" is obviously a critique of the supposedly asexual and apolitical "Aunt Jemima" character, which was inspired by Billy Kersands' popular 1875 Blackface minstrel song "Old Aunt Jemima."[76] In a sense the allegedly asexual and unappealing "Aunt Sarah" is the mother of "Safronia," the second woman depicted in "Four Women." Simone details how Safronia's "father was rich and White" and he "forced [her] mother late one night." The racial *and* sexual violence of African American enslavement and its aftermath during the Reconstruction years produced an incredibly creolized, multiracial, and multicultural people who were forced to live "between two worlds," as Simone bitterly sang. As if putting Du Bois' analysis of double-consciousness, the color-line, and second-sight in *The Souls of Black Folk* to music, by giving the second of the four women the name "Safronia" – moving beyond the more obvious interpretation that connects the name to the lavender-colored saffron flower and linking it to "sapphire," as in the name of the precious blue stone – Simone connects the hardships and horrors of enslaved Black foremothers with the blues of the classic blues queens of the Jazz Age and the rhythm & blues-cum-soul divas of her own epoch during the Civil Rights Movement and Black Power Movement years.[77]

Safronia's life and struggles "between two worlds" led to "Sweet Thing," the third character Simone depicts in "Four Women." Sweet Thing conceptually captures the centuries of racial oppression, economic exploitation, and sexual violence against African American women. While she is, to a certain extent, accepted by both Whites and Blacks because her skin is "fair" and her hair is "fine," ultimately Sweet Thing is a reminder of the centuries of anti-Black racist rape Black women endured, as well as their ongoing misuse and abuse. Sweet Thing, as her name clearly implies ("sweet thing" is an African American colloquialism for the vagina), is almost completely reduced to her sexuality, to her body, and to her ability to tease and please men. Similar to Safronia, Sweet Thing is caught "between two worlds," and it is her foremothers' and mothers' sexuality and their sexual violation and sexual exploitation that continues to haunt her identity and sexuality.[78]

Recalling the "tragic mulatto," because even though her skin is "fair" and her hair is "fine," Sweet Thing is accepted neither in White nor in Black America because she has been hyper-sexualized, objectified, and reduced to a life of prostitution. As a result, in the end her life is extremely tragic. As with the "tragic mulatto" characters in Nella Larsen's *Passing*, Fannie Hurst's *Imitation of Life*, and Harper Lee's *To Kill a Mockingbird*, Simone's Sweet Thing is ultimately rejected by both White and Black America as a result of the very "miscegenation" and the same sordid inter-racial sex that produced her and, truth be told, the bastardization of the bulk of Black America.[79] The fourth and final woman Simone depicts in "Four Women" is named "Peaches." A peach is typically thought of as being soft and sweet. Simone's Peaches openly admits, "I'm awfully bitter these days,' cause my parents were slaves." Coming full circle with her narrative and essentially painting a sonic picture of Black women as being in bondage both during enslavement and afterwards in "freedom," Peaches invokes violence against enslavement and Black women's continued colonization: "I'll kill the first mother [as in "motherfucker"] I see!" Peaches' abrasive language, impertinence, and audible impatience link her to the militance and irreverence of the Black Power Movement, which was known for literally cursing the established order and referring to police officers as "pigs" and racist Whites as "honkies," "crackers," "rednecks," and "peckerwoods."

Simone's sonic protests did not go unnoticed by classic soul artists, who considered her an antecedent and extremely eclectic soul sister. Building on her Colpix and Philips years, Simone's RCA years between 1967 to 1974 produced even more searing message music which seemed to be perfectly in tune with many aspects of the Black Power Movement and Black Women's Liberation Movement.[80] For example, on *Nina Simone Sings the Blues* (1967), she recorded a hard-hitting protest poem written by her close friend Langston Hughes entitled "Backlash Blues"; *Silk & Soul* (1967) featured the Civil Rights anthem "I Wish I Knew How It Would Feel to Be Free" and the critique of racism "Turning Point";' *Nuff Said* (1968), which was recorded three days after Martin Luther King's assassination on April 4, 1968, featured a song dedicated to the slain Civil Rights leader entitled "Why? (The King of Love Is Dead)"; *To Love Somebody* (1969) featured "I Shall Be Released," as well as the epic "Revolution (Part 1)" and "Revolution (Part 2)"; and, finally, *Black Gold* (1970) featured the epochal "To Be Young, Gifted and Black," which was dedicated to her recently deceased confidante, playwright and political essayist Lorraine Hansberry.[81]

Of all of Simone's protest songs, it was "To Be Young, Gifted and Black" that seemed to resonate most with the classic soul crowd. For instance, almost immediately after hearing Simone's version of the song, one of the true unsung heroes of classic soul, Donny Hathaway, recorded a version of "To Be Young, Gifted and Black" that was featured on his debut album *Everything Is Everything* in 1970.[82] Two years later Aretha Franklin, the undisputed "Queen of Soul," not only recorded a jaw-dropping version of "To Be Young, Gifted and Black," but she titled her Grammy Award-winning 1972 album *Young, Gifted and Black*. Consequently, even if most music critics refuse to acknowledge Nina Simone as a classic soul chanteuse, her contemporaries did. Soul was more than merely Atlantic, Chess, Motown, Stax, and Philadelphia International Records. Indeed, classic soul was more than even the iconic artistry of James Brown, Aretha Franklin, Curtis Mayfield, Etta James, Otis Redding, Marvin Gaye, and Stevie Wonder. It was a broad cultural and musical category that often defied nice and neat definitions, which may be one of the main reasons the soul aesthetic, replete with its deeper lyrics and darker sound, remains relevant in the twenty-first century.[83]

The commercialization and further militantization of Black musical protest: from soul to funk

Here it is important to emphasize the ways in which Black popular music has consistently revealed the social, political, and cultural desires of African Americans, as well as the astonishing irony that these sonically registered desires remain largely overlooked and under-theorized in a wide range of academic disciplines, including African American studies, American studies, cultural studies, ethnic studies, and popular music studies. An equally indicting observation could be made about the ways in which classic soul queens' protest and, more specifically, African American women's protest in popular music and popular culture has been largely overlooked and under-theorized in women's studies. All of this is to say very few critics have critically engaged the ways in which blues women, jazz women, rhythm & blues women, rock & roll women, soul women, funk women, disco women, neo-soul women, and hip hop women, as well as their legions of female fans, have historically contributed and currently continue to contribute to Black feminism/womanism and produce public records of African American women's deep-seated social, political, cultural, spiritual, and sexual desires.[84] In other words, African American women's musical subcultures – from classic blues all the way to contemporary neo-soul – insist that we take them a lot more seriously in light of the fact that they – however "unconventionally" from Eurocentric, bourgeois, and heteropatriarchal points of view – actually articulate overt and covert common desires and shared dreams that run like a fast-flowing river through the peaks and valleys, the high points and low points, of African American history, culture, and struggle.

In many ways mirroring the interstitial expressive culture surrounding soul, although not nearly as female-friendly as the classic soul discussed above, in the late 1960s and throughout the 1970s classic funk provided Black America with a unique mouthpiece through which to articulate *alternative, post-Civil Rights Movement and post-soul views and values*. Growing out of both the Black aesthetic and the soul aesthetic, classic funk and the funk aesthetic expressed the disdain and desperation of African American youth in the aftermath of Martin Luther King's assassination and the demise of the Civil Rights Movement. As prone to partying as it was to politicking, funk brazenly built on every form of Black popular music that preceded it: from the spirituals and the blues to rock & roll and soul. However, like rhythm & blues in relationship to the Civil Rights Movement, it also – often tongue-in-cheek – expressed the evolving politics and social visions of the Black Power Movement. As soul began to soften as a consequence of its commercialization in the mid-to-late 1970s, funk captured the harder and heavier, the bolder and decidedly Blacker intra-communal politics and social visions that were being increasingly muted in soul as the 1970s progressed and disco rose to national (and international) prominence.

Notes

1 For further discussion of the golden age of the girl groups (circa 1955–1970) and their enormous influence on female soul singers and their musical feminism, see Alan Betrock, *Girl Groups: The Story of a Sound* (New York: Omnibus Press, 1982); John Clemente, *Girl Groups: Fabulous Females Who Rocked the World* (Iola, WI: Krause Publications, 2013); Charlotte Greig, *Will You Still Love Me Tomorrow?: Girl Groups from the 50s On . . .* (London: Virago, 1989); Rosa Hawkins and Steve Bergsman, *Chapel of Love: The Story of New Orleans Girl Group the Dixie Cups* (Jackson: University Press of Mississippi, 2021); Gerri Hirshey, "The Butterflies & Banshees of L-O-V-E: When the Girls Ruled the Airwaves," liner notes for Various Artists, *One Kiss Can Lead to Another: Girl Group Sounds Lost and Found* (Rhino, R2 74645, 2005, CD), 10–31; Gerri Hirshey, *Nowhere to Run: The Story of Soul Music* (New York: Times Books, 1984), 140–83; Sean Macleod, *Leaders of the Pack: Girl Groups of the 1960s and Their Influence on Popular Culture in Britain and America* (Lanham: Rowman & Littlefield, 2015); Jacqueline Warwick, *Girl Groups, Girl Culture: Popular Music and Identity in the 1960s* (New York: Routledge, 2013).
2 For further discussion of relationships in rhythm & blues-cum-soul in the 1960s and 1970s, see James B. Stewart, "Relationships between Black Males and Females in Rhythm & Blues Music of the 1960s and 1970s," *Western Journal of Black Studies* 3, no. 3 (1979): 186–96.
3 Macleod, *Leaders of the Pack*, 11–64; Stewart, "Relationships between Black Males and Females in Rhythm & Blues Music of the 1960s and 1970s," 189–93; Warwick, *Girl Groups, Girl Culture*, 13–92, 153–62, 181–202.
4 See Katherine Mellen Charron, *Freedom's Teacher: The Life of Septima Clark* (Chapel Hill: University of North Carolina Press, 2009); Chana Kai Lee, *For Freedom's Sake: The Life of Fannie Lou Hamer* (Urbana: University of Illinois Press, 1999); Barbara Ransby, *Ella Baker and the Black Freedom Movement: A Radical Democratic Vision* (Chapel Hill: University of North Carolina Press, 2003).
5 For further discussion of the ways in which African American women's Civil Rights Movement leadership and activism was integral to the emergence of the Women's Liberation Movement, see Bernice McNair Barnett, "Invisible Southern Black Women Leaders in the Civil Rights Movement: The Triple Constraints of Gender, Race, and Class," *Gender & Society* 7, no. 2 (1993): 162–82; Janet Dewart Bell, *Lighting the Fires of Freedom: African American Women in the Civil Rights Movement* (New York: New Press, 2018); Winifred Breines, *The Trouble Between Us: An Uneasy History of White and Black Women in the Feminist Movement* (New York: Oxford University Press, 2006), 19–49; Betty Collier-Thomas and V. P. Franklin, eds., *Sisters in the Struggle: African American Women in the Civil Rights-Black Power Movement* (New York: New York University Press, 2001); Vicki L. Crawford, Jacqueline Anne Rouse, and Barbara Woods, eds.,

Women in the Civil Rights Movement: Trailblazers and Torchbearers, 1941–1965 (Blooming-ton: Indiana University Press, 1990); Davis W. Houck and David E. Dixon, eds., *Women and the Civil Rights Movement, 1954–1965* (Jackson: University Press of Mississippi, 2009); Sara Evans, *Personal Politics: The Roots of Women's Liberation in the Civil Rights Movement* (New York: Vintage Books, 1979); Lynne Olson, *Freedom's Daughters: The Unsung Heroines of the Civil Rights Movement, 1830–1970* (New York: Simon & Schuster, 2002); Belinda Robnett, *How Long? How Long?: African American Women in the Struggle for Civil Rights* (New York: Oxford University Press, 1997); Benita Roth, *Separate Roads to Feminism: Black, Chicana, and White Feminist Movements in America's Second Wave* (New York: Cambridge University Press, 2004), 76–128.

6 Rosalyn Baxandall, "Re-Visioning the Women's Liberation Movement's Narrative: Early Second-Wave African American Feminists," *Feminist Studies* 27, no. 1 (2001): 225–45; Breines, *The Trouble Between Us*, 51–78; Robnett, *How Long? How Long?*, 173–89; Roth, *Separate Roads to Feminism*, 76–128; Kimberly Springer, "Black Feminists Respond to Black Power Masculinism," in *The Black Power Movement: Rethinking the Civil Rights-Black Power Era*, ed. Peniel E. Joseph (New York: Routledge, 2006), 113–18.

7 Kimberly Springer, *Living for the Revolution: Black Feminist Organizations, 1968–1980* (Durham: Duke University Press, 2005), 1–64.

8 Sheila Radford-Hill, *Further to Fly: Black Women and the Politics of Empowerment* (Min-neapolis: University of Minnesota Press, 2000), 1–24.

9 Springer, "Black Feminists Respond to Black Power Masculinism," 105–18; Rhonda Y. Williams, "Black Women and Black Power," *The OAH Magazine of History* 22, no. 3 (2008): 22–26; Rhonda Y. Williams, "Black Women, Urban Politics, and Engendering Black Power," in *The Black Power Movement: Rethinking the Civil Rights-Black Power Era*, ed. Peniel E. Joseph (New York: Routledge, 2006), 97–101.

10 For more on the *Moynihan Report* and the Black matriarchy thesis, see Herbert J. Gans, "The Moynihan Report and Its Aftermaths: A Critical Analysis," *Du Bois Review: Social Science Research on Race* 8, no. 2 (2011): 315–27; Daniel Geary, *Beyond Civil Rights: The Moynihan Report and Its Legacy* (Philadelphia: University of Pennsylvania Press, 2015); Susan D. Greenbaum, *Blaming the Poor: The Long Shadow of the Moynihan Report on Cruel Images about Poverty* (New Brunswick: Rutgers University Press, 2015); James T. Patter-son, *Freedom Is Not Enough: The Moynihan Report and America's Struggle over Black Family Life* (New York: Basic Books, 2010), 87–128; Robert Staples, "The Myth of the Black Matriarchy," *The Black Scholar* 1, no. 3–4 (1970): 8–16.

11 Steven M. Buechler, *Women's Movements in the United States: Woman Suffrage, Equal Rights, and Beyond* (New Brunswick: Rutgers University Press, 1990), 134. See also Roth, *Separate Roads to Feminism*, 1–17.

12 Ashley D. Farmer, *Remaking Black Power: How Black Women Transformed an Era* (Chapel Hill: University of North Carolina Press, 2017), 50–92; Carol Giardina, *Freedom for Women: Forging the Women's Liberation Movement, 1953–1970* (Gainesville: University Press of Florida, 2010), 100–25; Springer, *Living for the Revolution*, 88–112; Rebecca Tuuri, *Strategic Sisterhood: The National Council of Negro Women in the Black Freedom Strug-gle* (Chapel Hill: University of North Carolina Press, 2018), 80–148; Anne M. Valk, *Radical Sisters: Second-Wave Feminism and Black Liberation in Washington, D.C.* (Urbana: University of Illinois Press, 2008), 13–37, 110–34.

13 Roth, *Separate Roads to Feminism*, 76–128; Springer, *Living for the Revolution*; Stephen Ward, "The Third World Women's Alliance: Black Feminist Radicalism and Black Power Politics," in *The Black Power Movement: Rethinking the Civil Rights-Black Power Era*, ed. Peniel E. Joseph (New York: Routledge, 2006), 119–44.

14 Farmer, *Remaking Black Power*, 50–92; Roth, *Separate Roads to Feminism*, 86–98; Robyn C. Spencer, *The Revolution Has Come: Black Power, Gender, and the Black Panther Party in Oakland* (Durham: Duke University Press, 2016).

15 Toni Cade Bambara, ed., *The Black Woman: An Anthology* (New York: New American Library, 1970); Combahee River Collective, "A Black Feminist Statement," in *All the*

Women Are White, All the Blacks Are Men, But Some of Us Are Brave: Black Women's Studies, eds. Gloria T. Hull, Patricia Bell Scott, and Barbara Smith (New York: The Feminist Press at CUNY, 1982), 13–23; Gloria T. Hull, Patricia Bell Scott, and Barbara Smith, eds., *All the Women Are White, All the Blacks Are Men, But Some of Us Are Brave: Black Women's Studies* (New York: The Feminist Press at CUNY, 1982); Barbara Smith, ed., *Home Girls: A Black Feminist Anthology* (New York: Kitchen Table and Women of Color Press, 1983); Cherríe Moraga and Gloria Anzaldúa, eds., *This Bridge Called My Back: Writings by Radical Women of Color* (New York: Kitchen Table and Women of Color Press, 1984).

16 Dorothy Roberts, "Complicating the Triangle of Race, Class, and State: The Insights of Black Feminists," *Ethnic and Racial Studies* 37, no. 10 (2014): 1776–782; Benita Roth, "Race, Class, and the Emergence of Black Feminism in the 1960s and 1970s," *Womanist Theory and Research* 2, no. 1 (1999): 3–9; Sharon Smith, "Black Feminism and Intersectionality," *International Socialist Review* 91 (2013): 6–24; Kimberly Springer, "The Interstitial Politics of Black Feminist Organizations," *Meridians: Feminism, Race, Transnationalism* 1, no. 2 (2001): 155–91.

17 Neal, *What the Music Said*, 74.

18 Ibid., 75.

19 Ibid., 74–75. See also Angela Y. Davis, *Blues Legacies and Black Feminism: Gertrude "Ma" Rainey, Bessie Smith, and Billie Holiday* (New York: Vintage Books, 1999); Ruth Feldstein, *How It Feels to Be Free: Black Women Entertainers and the Civil Rights Movement* (New York: Oxford University Press, 2013), 3–21; Daphne Duval Harrison, *Black Pearls: Blues Queens of the 1920s* (New Brunswick: Rutgers University Press, 1988), 3–15, 63–112; Shana L. Redmond, *Anthem: Social Movements and the Sound of Solidarity in the African Diaspora* (New York: New York University Press, 2014), 141–220.

20 Tracey New, "Go Girl!: Liner Notes," liner notes for Various Artists, *Go Girl!: Soul Sisters Tellin' It Like It Is*, (Rhino Records, 8122–72506–2, 1996, CD), 2.

21 Ibid., 2–3.

22 Neal, *What the Music Said*, 73–77; Stewart, "Relationships between Black Males and Females in Rhythm & Blues Music of the 1960s and 1970s," 188–96; Ward, *Just My Soul Responding*, 383–85. For more on musical feminism, see Mavis Bayton, "Out on the Margins: Feminism and the Study of Popular Music," *Women: A Cultural Review* 3, no. 1 (1992): 51–59; Mavis Bayton, "Feminist Musical Practice: Problems and Contradictions," in *Rock and Popular Music: Politics, Policies, Institutions*, eds. Tony Bennett, Simon Furth, Lawrence Grossberg, John Shepherd, and Graeme Turner (New York: Routledge, 2005), 177–92; Lori Burns and Mélisse Lafrance, *Disruptive Divas: Feminism, Identity, and Popular Music* (New York: Routledge, 2013); Susan C. Cook and Judy S. Tsou, eds., *Cecilia Reclaimed: Feminist Perspectives on Gender and Music* (Urbana: University of Illinois Press, 1994); Davis, *Blues Legacies and Black Feminism*; Cynthia Mahabir, "The Rise of Calypso Feminism: Gender and Musical Politics in the Calypso," *Popular Music* 20, no. 3 (2001): 409–30; Jo Reger, "Where Are the Leaders?: Music, Culture, and Contemporary Feminism," *American Behavioral Scientist* 50, no. 10 (2007): 1350–369; Pieter C. Van den Toorn, "Politics, Feminism, and Contemporary Music Theory," *Journal of Musicology* 9, no. 3 (1991): 275–99; Gayle Wald, "Just a Girl?: Rock Music, Feminism, and the Cultural Construction of Female Youth," *Signs: Journal of Women in Culture and Society* 23, no. 3 (1998): 585–610. For examples of female soul songs that capture and convey elements of what could be loosely called "musical feminism," see Various Artists, *Atlantic Sisters of Soul* (Rhino Records, R2 71037, 1992, CD); Various Artists, *Atlantic Unearthed: Soul Sisters* (Rhino Records/Atlantic, R 77626, 2006, CD); Various Artists, *Cheatin': From a Woman's Point of View* (Soul Classics, SCL 2507–2, 1995, CD); Various Artists, *Chess Soul Sisters* (Chess, 9830155, 2005, CD); Various Artists, *The Girls Got Soul: Atlantic Records Soul Sisters* (Kent Soul, CDKEND 186, 2000, CD); Various Artists, *Go Girl!: Soul Sisters Tellin' It Like It Is* (Rhino Records, 8122–72506–2, 1996, CD); Various Artists, *Hi Girls: Hi Records Soul Divas* (Hi Records,

HILOCD 7, 1994, CD); Various Artists, *Soul Shots, Vol. 4: Tell Mama – Screamin' Soul Sisters* (Rhino Records, RNLP 70040, 1987, CD); Various Artists, *Southern Soul Sisters: The Sound Stage Seven Series* (Charly R&B, CRB 1155, 1987, CD); Various Artists, *The Stax Soul Sisters* (Stax, SCD-8543–2, 1988, CD); Various Artists, *Super Soul Sisters* (Not Now Music, NOT3CD243, 2016, CD); Various Artists, *Troubles, Heartaches & Sadness: Hi Records' Deep Soul Sisters, 1966–1976* (Hi Records, HILO 188, 2002, CD); Various Artists, *What More Can a Woman Do?: Brunswick and Chi-Sound Sisters of Soul* (Westside, WESM 602, 1999, CD).

23 Ward, *Just My Soul Responding*, 383–85. For further discussion of Laura Lee and her musical legacy, see Howard Priestley, "Women's Love Rights: Liner Notes," liner notes for Laura Lee, *Women's Love Rights: The Hot Wax Anthology* (Sanctuary Records/Castle Music, CMDDD 600, 2002, CD), 3–12; Tony Rounce, "Laura Lee: Liner Notes," liner notes for Laura Lee, *Women's Love Rights/I Can't Make It Alone/Two Sides of Laura Lee* (Edsel Records, EDSD 2050, 2010, CD), 8–18; Lois Wilson, "The Chess Collection: Liner Notes," liner notes for Laura Lee, *The Chess Collection, 1966–1969* (Chess, 983 229–4, 2006, CD), 2–5.

24 Randall Grass, "Totally Unrestricted!: Liner Notes," liner notes for Millie Jackson, *Totally Unrestricted!: The Millie Jackson Anthology* (Rhino Records, R2 72862, 1997, CD), 2–22; Sean Hampsey, "The Moods of Millie Jackson: Liner Notes," liner notes for Millie Jackson, *The Moods of Millie Jackson: Her Best Ballads* (Kent Records, CDKEND 391, 2013, CD), 3–10; David Nathan, "Caught Up/Still Caught Up: Liner Notes," liner notes for Millie Jackson, *Caught Up/Still Caught Up* (Hip-O Records, HIPD-40143, 1999), 3–6; David Nathan, *The Soulful Divas: Personal Portraits of Over a Dozen Divine Divas, from Nina Simone, Aretha Franklin & Diana Ross to Patti LaBelle, Whitney Houston & Janet Jackson* (New York: Billboard Books, 1999), 247–71; James B. Stewart, "Perspectives on Black Families from Contemporary Soul Music: The Case of Millie Jackson," *Phylon* 41, no. 1 (1980): 57–71; Marc Taylor, *A Touch of Classic Soul, Vol. 1: Soul Singers of the Early 1970s* (New York: Aloiv Publishing, 1996), 124–31.

25 Tricia Rose, *Black Noise: Rap Music and Black Culture in Contemporary America* (Hanover: Wesleyan University, 1994), 176.

26 Buechler, *Women's Movements in the United States*, 134; Breines, *The Trouble Between Us*, 6; Rose, *Black Noise*, 176.

27 Rose, *Black Noise*, 181, emphasis added.

28 Bayton, "Feminist Musical Practice," 178.

29 "Black Women Organized for Action Membership Brochure" cited in Springer, *Living for the Revolution*, 79.

30 For further discussion of women-centered soul being simultaneously part womanist consciousness-raising and part spiritual, sexual, intellectual, and cultural art, see the insightful interviews in David Freeland, *Ladies of Soul* (Jackson: University Press of Mississippi, 2001); Gillian G. Gaar, *She's a Rebel: The History of Women in Rock & Roll* (New York: Seal Press, 2002), 63–104, 159–76; Nathan, *The Soulful Divas*, 42–271.

31 David Nathan, "The Very Best of Betty Wright: Liner Notes," liner notes for Betty Wright, *The Very Best of Betty Wright* (Rhino Records, R2 79861, 2000, CD), 3–13; Taylor, *A Touch of Classic Soul, Vol. 1*, 332–38; Marc Taylor, *A Touch of Classic Soul, Vol. 2: Soul Singers of the Late 1970s* (New York: Aloiv Publishing, 2001), 265–76; Ward, *Just My Soul Responding*, 383–85.

32 Peter Benjaminson, *Mary Wells: The Tumultuous Life of Motown's First Superstar* (Chicago: Chicago Review Press, 2012), 153–59; Candi Staton, *This Is My Story* (Bakersfield, CA: Pneuma Life Publishing, 1994); Candi Staton, *Young Hearts Run Free: First Lady of Southern Soul* (Monterey, CA: Heritage Builders Publishing, 2016); Ward, *Just My Soul Responding*, 383–85.

33 Dennis Garvey, "Trapped by a Thing Called Love/On the Loose: Liner Notes," liner notes for Denise LaSalle, *Trapped by a Thing Called Love/On the Loose* (Westbound Records, CDSEWD 018, 2011, CD), 8–11; Ward, *Just My Soul Responding*, 384–85.

34 Ward, *Just My Soul Responding*, 384–85.
35 Danielle L. McGuire, *At the Dark End of the Street: Black Women, Rape, and Resistance – A New History of the Civil Rights Movement from Rosa Parks to the Rise of Black Power* (New York: Vintage Books, 2011), 212–78; Springer, "Black Feminists Respond to Black Power Masculinism," 113–16; Ward, *Just My Soul Responding*, 384–85; Williams, "Black Women and Black Power," 22–26; Williams, "Black Women, Urban Politics, and Engendering Black Power," 97–101.
36 Neal, *What the Music Said*, 67.
37 See, for example, Various Artists, *Cheatin': From a Man's Point of View* (Soul Classics, SCL 2508-2, 1995, CD); Various Artists, *Cheatin' Soul and the Southern Dream of Freedom* (Trikont, US-0337, 2005, CD); Various Artists, *If Loving You Is Wrong: 20 Cheatin' Heartbreakers* (Kent Soul, CDKEND 208, 2002, CD); Various Artists, *Motel Lovers: Southern Soul from the Chitlin' Circuit* (Trikont, US-0363, 2007, CD).
38 George, *The Death of Rhythm & Blues*, 121–46; Neal, *What the Music Said*, 101–12; Ward, *Just My Soul Responding*, 384–85.
39 Ward, *Just My Soul Responding*, 384–85.
40 Ibid., 384–85.
41 Ward, *Just My Soul Responding*, 400. For further discussion of C.L. Franklin, see C. L. Franklin, *Give Me This Mountain: Life History and Selected Sermons*, ed. Jeff Todd Titon (Urbana: University of Illinois Press, 1989); Nick Salvatore, *Singing in a Strange Land: C.L. Franklin, the Black Church, and the Transformation of America* (Urbana: University of Illinois Press, 2006).
42 Ward, *Just My Soul Responding*, 400.
43 Jerry Wexler cited in Mark Bego, *Aretha Franklin: The Queen of Soul* (New York: Skyhorse Publishing, 2012), 108–9.
44 Craig Werner, *Higher Ground: Stevie Wonder, Aretha Franklin, Curtis Mayfield, and the Rise and Fall of American Soul* (New York: Crown Publishers, 2004), 67.
45 Neal, *What the Music Said*, 74–75. For further discussion of Aretha Franklin's life and legacy, see Michael Awkward, *Soul Covers: Rhythm & Blues Remakes and the Struggle for Artistic Identity (Aretha Franklin, Al Green, Phoebe Snow)* (Durham: Duke University Press, 2007), 25–80; Stephen Barnard, *Aretha Franklin* (London: Unanimous, 2001); Bego, *Aretha Franklin*; Aaron Cohen, *Aretha Franklin's Amazing Grace* (New York: Bloomsbury, 2011); Matt Dobkin, *I Never Loved a Man the Way I Love You: Aretha Franklin, Respect, and the Making of a Soul Music Masterpiece* (New York: Macmillan, 2004); Aretha Franklin, *Aretha: From These Roots*, with David Ritz (New York: Villard Books, 1999); Nathan, *The Soulful Divas*, 66–97; David Ritz, *Respect: The Life of Aretha Franklin* (New York: Little, Brown & Company, 2015); Werner, *Higher Ground*, 89–99, 129–39.
46 Pamela J. Greene, "Aretha Franklin: The Emergence of Soul and Black Women's Consciousness in the Late 1960s and 1970s" (Ph.D. diss., Bowling Green State University, 1995), 85–127.
47 Franklin, *Aretha*, 155.
48 Ibid. See also Phyl Garland, *The Sound of Soul* (Chicago: H. Regnery Book Co, 1969), 191–203; Werner, *Higher Ground*, 126–39.
49 Tom Dowd cited in Bego, *Aretha Franklin*, 70. See also Franklin, *Aretha*, 105–17.
50 Jerry Wexler cited in Bego, *Aretha Franklin*, 70. See also Dobkin, *I Never Loved a Man the Way I Love You*, 164–73.
51 Cohen, *Aretha Franklin's Amazing Grace*, 1–29; Dobkin, *I Never Loved a Man the Way I Love You*, 155–225; Garland, *The Sound of Soul*, 191–203; Greene, "Aretha Franklin," 117–22, 180–92.
52 Werner, *Higher Ground*, 134.
53 Garland, *The Sound of Soul*, 191–203; Greene, "Aretha Franklin," 117–22; Victoria Malawey, "'Find Out What It Means to Me': Aretha Franklin's Gendered Re-Authoring of Otis Redding's 'Respect'," *Popular Music* 33, no. 2 (2014): 185–207.

54 Patricia Hill Collins, *Black Feminist Thought: Knowledge, Consciousness, and the Politics of Empowerment* (New York: Routledge, 1991), 108.
55 Ibid. See also Angela Y. Davis, "Black Women and Music: A Historical Legacy of Struggle," in *Wild Women in the Whirlwind: African American Culture and the Contemporary Literary Renaissance*, eds. Joanne M. Braxton and Andrée Nicola McLaughlin (New Brunswick: Rutgers University Press, 1990), 3–21; Eileen M. Hayes, *Songs in Black and Lavender: Race, Sexual Politics, and Women's Music* (Urbana: University of Illinois Press, 2010); Eileen M. Hayes and Linda F. Williams, eds., *Black Women and Music: More than the Blues* (Urbana: University of Illinois Press, 2007).
56 See Daphne A. Brooks, *Liner Notes for the Revolution: The Intellectual Life of Black Feminist Sound* (Cambridge: Harvard University Press, 2021); Davis, "Black Women and Music"; Greene, "Aretha Franklin"; Hayes, *Songs in Black and Lavender*; Hayes and Williams, *Black Women and Music*.
57 Bego, *Aretha Franklin*, 86, emphasis in original.
58 Bego, *Aretha Franklin*, 25–100; Franklin, *Aretha*, 57–62, 70–78.
59 Dobkin, *I Never Loved a Man the Way I Love You*, 1–14; Garland, *The Sound of Soul*, 191–203; Greene, "Aretha Franklin," 85–125, 177–95.
60 Werner, *Higher Ground*, 213. See also Greene, "Aretha Franklin," 85–125, 177–95.
61 Cohen, *Aretha Franklin's Amazing Grace*, 30–35; Dobkin, *I Never Loved a Man the Way I Love You*, 65–132; Guralnick, *Sweet Soul Music*, 332–52.
62 Nina Simone, *I Put a Spell on You: The Autobiography of Nina Simone*, with Stephen Cleary (New York: Pantheon Books, 1991), 68–69. For further discussion of Nina Simone's life and legacy, and for the most noteworthy works that informed my interpretation here, see Kerry Acker, *Nina Simone* (Philadelphia: Chelsea House Publishers, 2004); David Brun-Lambert, *Nina Simone: The Biography* (London: Aurum, 2009); Nadine Cohodas, *Princess Noire: The Tumultuous Reign of Nina Simone* (New York: Pantheon Books, 2010); Richard Elliott, *Nina Simone* (Sheffield: Equinox, 2013); Sylvia Hampton, *Nina Simone: Break Down & Let It All Out*, with David Nathan (London: Sanctuary, 2004); Alan Light, *What Happened, Miss Simone?: A Biography* (New York: Crown Archetype, 2016); Florence Noiville and Mathilde Hirsch, *Nina Simone: Love Me or Leave Me* (Paris: Tallandier, 2019); Andy Stroud, *Nina Simone: "Black Is the Color"* (Philadelphia: Xlibris, 2005); Jennifer Warner, *Keeper of the Flame: A Biography of Nina Simone* (Anaheim: Golgotha Press, 2014); Richard Williams, *Nina Simone: Don't Let Me Be Misunderstood* (Edinburgh: Canongate Books, 2002).
63 Bayton, "Out on the Margins," 55.
64 Mavis Bayton, *Frock Rock: Women Performing Popular Music* (New York: Oxford University Press, 1998), 3.
65 Simone, *I Put a Spell on You*, 69.
66 Franklin, *Aretha*; Billie Holiday, *Lady Sings the Blues*, with William Dufty (New York: Penguin, 1956); Etta James, *Rage to Survive: The Etta James Story*, with David Ritz (New York: Villard Books, 1995); Tina Turner, *I, Tina: My Life Story*, with Kurt Loder (Harmondsworth: Penguin, 1987).
67 Feldstein, *How It Feels to Be Free*, 84–112. See also Ruth Feldstein, "'I Don't Trust You Anymore': Nina Simone, Culture, and Black Activism in the 1960s," *Journal of American History* 91, no. 4 (2005): 1349–379; Garland, *The Sound of Soul*, 169–95; Tammy L. Kernodle, "'I Wish I Knew How It Would Feel to Be Free': Nina Simone and the Redefining of the Freedom Song of the 1960s," *Journal of the Society for American Music* 2, no. 3 (2008): 295–317.
68 Cohodas, *Princess Noire*, 80–132; Feldstein, *How It Feels to Be Free*, 93–99; Kernodle, "'I Wish I Knew How It Would Feel to Be Free,'" 295–99.
69 Simone, *I Put a Spell on You*, 88–89. For further discussion of Medgar Evers and the 16th Street Baptist Church bombing, see Glenn T. Eskew, *But for Birmingham: The Local and National Movements in the Civil Rights Struggle* (Chapel Hill: University of North Carolina Press, 2000), 53–152; Medgar Evers, *The Autobiography of Medgar Evers: A Hero's Life and*

Legacy Revealed Through His Writings, Letters, and Speeches, eds. Myrlie Evers-Williams and Manning Marable (New York: Basic Civitas, 2005); Minrose Gwin, *Remembering Medgar Evers: Writing the Long Civil Rights Movement* (Athens: University of Georgia Press, 2013); Diane McWhorter, *Carry Me Home: Birmingham, Alabama: The Climactic Battle of the Civil Rights Revolution* (New York: Simon & Schuster, 2002); Adam Nossiter, *Of Long Memory: Mississippi and the Murder of Medgar Evers* (Cambridge: Da Capo Press, 2002); Frank Sikora, *Until Justice Rolls Down: The Birmingham Church Bombing Case* (Tuscaloosa: University of Alabama Press, 2005); Michael Vinson Williams, *Medgar Evers: Mississippi Martyr* (Fayetteville: University of Arkansas Press, 2011).

70 Cohodas, *Princess Noire*, 133–274; Kernodle, " 'I Wish I Knew How It Would Feel to Be Free,' " 299–315.

71 H. Rap Brown quoted in Garland, *The Sound of Soul*, 183.

72 Ward, *Just My Soul Responding*, 303.

73 Simone, *I Put a Spell on You*, 91.

74 Ibid., 91. See also Cohodas, *Princess Noire*, 206–49.

75 Feldstein, *How It Feels to Be Free*, 106–11; Ashley Kahn, "Four Women: Liner Notes," liner notes for Nina Simone, *Four Women: The Nina Simone Philips Recordings* (Verve Records, 440 065 021–2, 2003, CD), 18–50; Kernodle, " 'I Wish I Knew How It Would Feel to Be Free,' " 310–12.

76 For further discussion of Aunt Jemima and the mammy archetype, and for the most noteworthy works that informed my interpretation here, see Lisa M. Anderson, *Mammies No More: The Changing Image of Black Women on Stage and Screen* (Lanham: Rowman & Littlefield, 1997); Brian D. Behnken and Gregory D. Smithers, *Racism in American Popular Media: From Aunt Jemima to the Frito Bandito* (Santa Barbara: Praeger, 2015); Kenneth W. Goings, *Mammy and Uncle Mose: Black Collectibles and American Stereotyping* (Bloomington: Indiana University Press, 1994); Marilyn Kern-Foxworth, *Aunt Jemima, Uncle Ben, and Rastus: Blacks in Advertising, Yesterday, Today, and Tomorrow* (Westport: Greenwood Press, 1994); Maurice M. Manring, *Slave in a Box: The Strange Career of Aunt Jemima* (Charlottesville: University Press of Virginia, 1998); Micki McElya, *Clinging to Mammy: The Faithful Slave in Twentieth Century America* (Cambridge: Harvard University Press, 2007); Diane Roberts, *The Myth of Aunt Jemima: Representations of Race and Region* (New York: Routledge, 1994); Patricia Morton, *Disfigured Images: The Historical Assault on Afro-American Women* (New York: Praeger, 1991); Kimberly Wallace-Sanders, *Mammy: A Century of Race, Gender, and Southern Memory* (Ann Arbor: University of Michigan Press, 2008).

77 W. E. B. Du Bois, *The Souls of Black Folk: Essays and Sketches* (Chicago: A.C. McClurg, 1903). See also Davis, *Blues Legacies and Black Feminism;* Harrison, *Black Pearls;* Buzzy Jackson, *A Bad Woman Feeling Good: Blues and the Women Who Sing Them* (New York: Norton, 2005).

78 The scholarly literature on African American women's sexual violation and sexual exploitation during enslavement is extensive. The following sources have been helpful here: Kathleen M. Brown, *Good Wives, Nasty Wenches, and Anxious Patriarchs: Gender, Race, and Power in Colonial Virginia* (Chapel Hill: University of North Carolina, 1996); Stephanie M.H. Camp, *Closer to Freedom: Enslaved Women and Everyday Resistance in the Plantation South* (Chapel Hill: University of North Carolina Press, 2004); Elizabeth Fox-Genovese, *Within the Plantation Household: Black and White Women of the Old South* (Chapel Hill: University of North Carolina Press, 1988); David Barry Gaspar and Darlene Clark Hine, eds., *More Than Chattel: Black Women and Slavery in the Americas* (Bloomington: Indiana University Press, 1996); Jacqueline Jones, *Labor of Love, Labor of Sorrow: Black Women, Work, and the Family, from Slavery to the Present* (New York: Basic Books, 2010), 9–42; Catherine M. Lewis and J. Richard Lewis, eds., *Women and Slavery in America: A Documentary History* (Fayetteville: University of Arkansas Press, 2011); Jessica Millward, *Finding Charity's Folk: Enslaved and Free Black Women in Maryland* (Athens: University of Georgia Press, 2015); Patrick N. Minges, ed., *Far More Terrible for Women:*

Personal Accounts of Women in Slavery (Winston-Salem, NC: John F. Blair, 2006); Jennifer L. Morgan, *Laboring Women: Reproduction and Gender in New World Slavery* (Philadelphia: University of Pennsylvania Press, 2004); Sowande M. Mustakeem, "'Make Haste & Let Me See You With A Good Cargo of Negroes': Gender, Power, and the Centrality of Violence in the Eighteenth Century Atlantic Slave Trade," in *Gender, Race, Ethnicity, and Power in Maritime America*, ed. Glenn Gordinier (Mystic, CT: Mystic Seaport Museum, 2008): 3–21; Sowande M. Mustakeem, *Slavery at Sea: Terror, Sex, and Sickness in the Middle Passage* (Urbana: University of Illinois Press, 2016); Deborah Gray White, *Ar'n't I a Woman?: Female Slaves in the Plantation South* (New York: Norton, 1999).

79 Nella Larsen, *Passing* (New York: Knopf, 1929); Fannie Hurst, *Imitation of Life* (New York: P.F. Collier, 1933); Harper Lee, *To Kill a Mockingbird* (New York: J. B. Lippincott & Co., 1960).

80 See Nina Simone, *The Complete RCA Albums Collection* (RCA/Legacy, 88697938902, 2011, CD). See also Nina Simone, *Forever Young, Gifted & Black: Songs of Freedom and Spirit* (RCA/Legacy, 82876 74413 2, 2006, CD); Nina Simone, *Just Like a Woman: Sings Classic Songs of the 1960s* (RCA/Legacy, 82876 85174 2, 2007, CD).

81 Garland, *The Sound of Soul*, 169–80; Kernodle, "'I Wish I Knew How It Would Feel to Be Free,'" 310–15.

82 For further discussion of Donny Hathaway's life and music, see Joachim Bertrand, "Someday We'll All Be Free: Liner Notes," liner notes for Donny Hathaway, *Someday We'll All Be Free* (Atlantic, 8122798076, 2010, CD), 2–10; Emily J. Lordi, *Donny Hathaway's Donny Hathaway Live* (New York: Bloomsbury Academic, 2016); Charles Waring, "Never My Love: Liner Notes," liner notes for Donny Hathaway, *Never My Love: The Anthology* (ATCO Records/Rhino Records, 8122796543, 2013, CD), 1–22.

83 Garland, *The Sound of Soul*, 1–97; Nelson George, *The Death of Rhythm & Blues* (New York: Pantheon Books, 1988), 59–120; Guralnick, *Sweet Soul Music*, 1–15; Ward, *Just My Soul Responding*, 173–288.

84 Jack Hamilton, *Just Around Midnight: Rock & Roll and the Racial Imagination* (Cambridge: Harvard University Press, 2016), 169–212; Hayes, *Songs in Black and Lavender*; Hayes and Williams, *Black Women and Music*; Timothy Laurie, "Crossover Fatigue: The Persistence of Gender at Motown Records," *Feminist Media Studies* 14, no. 1 (2014): 90–105; Emily J. Lordi, *Black Resonance: Iconic Women Singers and African American Literature* (New Brunswick: Rutgers University Press, 2013); Maureen Mahon, *Black Diamond Queens: African American Women and Rock & Roll* (Durham: Duke University Press, 2020).

5

FUNK, MUSICAL MILITANCY, AND THE BLACK POWER MOVEMENT

Introduction: funk music, funk aesthetics, funk politics, and funk culture

Similar to classic soul, classic funk is frequently disassociated from the politics, aesthetics, and culture of the Black Power Movement, the Black Arts Movement, and the Black Women's Liberation Movement. However, even though it is primarily known as "dance music" and "party music," musically and lyrically classic funk was as wide-ranging and wide-reaching as classic soul. For instance, recurring themes in classic funk include "partying" and "hanging loose," as well as spirituality, sexuality, love, lust, cultural celebration, social commentary, and political critique. Many have hailed funk as the "rawest, most primal form of R&B, surpassing even Southern soul in terms of earthiness." It has been asserted that funk was the "least structured" of the various forms of Black popular music of the 1960s and 1970s, frequently "stretching out into extended jams," and it was undoubtedly the "most Africanized," incessantly building on "dynamic, highly syncopated polyrhythms."[1]

Musically, classic funk borrowed frenzy-filled African American church-influenced vocalizations from gospel; full-throated tales of broken-hearts and busted dreams from the blues; jaw-dropping improvisations and a reinvented, off-kilter sense of swing from jazz; bustling basslines and blaring Stax-styled horn arrangements from rhythm & blues; extended explorations of Black sexuality and Black spirituality, as well as a kind of tongue-in-cheek political critique and social commentary, from soul; flamboyant guitar solos from psychedelic rock; outrageous costumes, hairstyles, make-up, platform-soled boots, and over-the-top theatrics from glam rock; polyrhythmic drum patterns and other "exotic" sounds from African music; and auxiliary percussion instrumentation and drum patterns from Latin music. Funk's highly hybrid musical aesthetic "defied categorization, prompting

DOI: 10.4324/9781003254492-6

music critics and others to label the early funk bands as 'soul groups,' 'dance bands,' 'Black rock,' and 'jazz funk.'"[2] During the Black Power Movement era, soul and funk had similar paths of sonic evolution, incessantly overlapped, and undeniably influenced each other. Initially popularized by jazz, rhythm & blues, and soul musicians, funk can be further contrasted with rhythm & blues and soul in that it was primarily a band-based music, where rhythm & blues and soul eventually came to be dominated by charismatic solo artists and vocal groups, for the most part.[3]

Generally speaking, funk bands composed, produced, and sang their own songs and, similar to jazz bands, worked hard to create a distinct band sound. In fact, as with jazz, funk emphasized improvisation, favoring extended "jams," which ultimately made it one of the first forms of Black popular music to almost completely sidestep the 45-rpm single (three minute and thirty seconds) format. In the midst of the extended jams the messages in classic funk most often revolved around a series of jarring juxtapositions: love *and* lust, comedy *and* tragedy, optimism *and* pessimism; and Martin Luther King-styled integrationism *and* Malcolm X-styled Black nationalism. Consequently, when classic funk is resituated within the milieu in which it emerged it can be viewed as more than merely a rhythmically harder form of rhythm & blues and a psychedelic brand of soul preoccupied with romancing, dancing, and partying. Quite the contrary, funk served as a second soundtrack for the much-misunderstood Black Power Movement and simultaneously converged with, and diverged from, both classic rhythm & blues and classic soul.[4]

Similar to classic soul, classic funk registered the shift from the moderatism of the Civil Rights Movement to the militantism of the Black Power Movement. The unhinged happiness that is easily detected in most classic funk is largely a consequence of African Americans' optimism in light of what were initially perceived as the successes of the Civil Rights Movement (e.g., the Civil Rights Act of 1964, the Voting Rights Act of 1965, the Fair Housing Act of 1968, and other Great Society legislation). Indeed, with the establishment of affirmative action programs in the early 1970s it appeared as though American apartheid would finally be put to rest, and funk, in a sense, would provide the long overdue epitaph.[5]

However, African American optimism quickly turned to pessimism and African American happiness to sadness as scores of Black skilled laborers were either laid off or lost their relatively "good-paying" jobs in the 1970s as a consequence of America's transition from an industrial economy to a technological and service-oriented economy. The once-booming factories that employed working-class and working-poor African Americans eventually shut down or moved their operations elsewhere. At the same time, the government's fiscal conservatism in the 1970s slashed funding for education, job training, social programs, and creative art initiatives aimed at improving the conditions of working-class and working-poor African Americans who had borne the brunt of more than a century of Jim Crow laws and other manifestations of modern American apartheid.[6]

In essence, affirmative action programs were met with anti-affirmative action programs almost immediately. And no matter how long and how loudly conservative and liberal legislators and citizens wrangled over the merits or demerits of affirmative action, from the mid-1970s onward the "subaltern" souls, the folk at the low end of the social ladder, continued to suffer and endure unspeakable social misery. As a matter of fact, by the mid-1970s there was such a strong backlash against the Civil Rights legislation of the 1960s that conservative and liberal Whites alike regularly claimed that they were victims of "reverse discrimination" and, in essence, were being held hostage to the "radical" Civil Rights social policies of the 1960s. In light of this backlash, the high hopes that African Americans entered into the 1970s with eventually turned into resentment and undisguised displays of Black radicalism. Funk, similar to classic soul, registered both the regressivism and progressivism, the resentment and new forms of Black radicalism that came to characterize African American life in the 1970s.[7]

Classic funk continued the hard and heavy, driving rhythms that characterized classic soul at its inception but, by the mid-1970s, were regularly being reduced to the soft-sounding middle-of-the-road (MOR) music primed for the commercial radio format. Funk was a deeper and darker "underground" sound that initially found few White fans in its "pure" and "uncut" form (to paraphrase funkmaster George Clinton in "P-Funk [Wants to Get Funked Up]"). With its references to pimps, players, prostitutes, drugs, drinking, other worlds, extraterrestrials, spaceships, parties, poverty, and Black cultural politics, at its inception funk captured the experiences of economically impoverished African Americans in ways that few other forms of Black popular music have. Reflecting African American optimism, pessimism, and hedonism between the late 1960s and the late 1970s, lyrically and musically classic funk built on the foundation laid by classic rhythm & blues, rock & roll, and soul.[8]

Funk not only continued to explore many of the lyrical themes introduced by soul, but it often did so utilizing a modified *soul aesthetic*. Funk, to reiterate, drew from almost every major form of Black popular music that preceded it: from the spirituals and the blues through to rock & roll and soul. Funk's synthesis of earlier forms of Black popular music not only links it to the soul aesthetic, but also to an often overlooked – albeit extremely important – aspect of the overarching African American aesthetic and its preoccupation with originality, authenticity, and hybridity. In "Characteristics of Negro Expression," which was originally published in 1934, revered Harlem Renaissance writer Zore Neale Hurston observed that "[w]hat we really mean by originality is the modification of ideas." For example, she continued, even "[t]he most ardent admirer of the great Shakespeare cannot claim first source even for him. It is his treatment of the borrowed material" – old myths, legends, folk tales, and other stories – that has garnered him a high place in human history.[9]

Hurston helps us reconceive of both soul and funk as *Black popular music based on "borrowed material."* Here originality has more to do with what one does with the "borrowed material" rather than the "first source[s]" or origins of the material. Acknowledging that much of African American culture was forged from "borrowed material[s]" from either Africa or "White civilization," she furthered shared:

> So if we look at it squarely, the Negro is a very original being. While he lives and moves in the midst of a White civilization, everything that he touches is reinterpreted for his own use. He has modified language, mode of food preparation, practice of medicine, and most certainly the religion of his new country. . . . Everyone is familiar with the Negro's modification of the Whites' musical instruments, so that his interpretation has been adopted by the White man himself and then reinterpreted. . . . Thus has arisen a new art in the civilized world, and thus has our so-called civilization come.[10]

Foreshadowing both the soul and funk aesthetics, Hurston hinted at the ways in which proto-soul and proto-funk Black musicians recycled and remixed the accoutrements of White America to such an innovative, sophisticated, and intriguing extent that their "interpretation has been adopted by the White man himself and then reinterpreted. . . . Thus has arisen a new art in the civilized world, and thus has our so-called civilization come." Instead of conceiving of Black popular music as "nigger noise" (what she mockingly termed "niggerism"), Hurston understood African American music to be part of the reinterpretation and reinvention process that African Americans have been involved in since the dark days of their enslavement. Classic funk is emblematic of African Americans' reinterpretation and reinvention process in the post-Civil Rights Movement 1960s and Black Power Movement 1970s.[11]

Building on, and going beyond, the reinterpretation and reinvention process of the 1920s and 1930s Jazz Age and Harlem Renaissance, funk brought together a spellbinding tangle of the musical *and* radical political impulses between the late 1960s and the late 1970s. Similar to rhythm & blues and soul before it, funk was not merely a reaction to White music, culture, and politics – although, truth be told, it did have its fair share of reactionary and regressive elements. On the contrary, it existed on its own contradictory and often off-kilter terms, for the most part, free from the trappings of Eurocentrism and the cross-over craze to which soul was slowly succumbing in the mid-to-late 1970s.[12]

Funk was audacious in its affirmation of post-Civil Rights Movement African American issues and ills, and unapologetically aimed at working-class and poor Black folk who were in desperate need of its expressions of both reality *and* fantasy. One of the major foundations of every form of Black popular music to rise in its wake (especially rap music), funk handed down more than most folk may realize. Moreover, it may not be going too far to suggest that rap music and hip hop culture cannot be adequately understood without a working knowledge of not only funk's major figures (e.g., James Brown, Sly Stone, and George Clinton) and classic funk beats, but also the spiritual, sexual, cultural, social, and political messages that collectively permeate their music and that uniquely reflect the wider spiritual, sexual, cultural, social, and political world of Black America in the 1970s. Consequently, this chapter will examine the origins and evolution of funk, as well as its meaning, function, and significance for Black America during the Black Power Movement era.

Hard bop: the radical political and musical roots of funk

In *Flash of the Spirit: African & Afro-American Art & Philosophy*, Robert Farris Thompson suggested that the etymology of the word "funk" may be traced back to a Kikongo word, "*lu-fuki*," which essentially means "bad body odor." Noting the inversion of the term within the African American colloquial context of the 1950s and 1960s, he furthered stated:

> The slang term "funky" in Black communities originally referred to strong body odor, and not to "funk," meaning fear or panic. The Black nuance seems to derive from the Kikongo *lu-fuki*, "bad body odor," and is perhaps reinforced by contact with *fumet*, "aroma of food and wine," in French Louisiana. But the Kikongo word is closer to the jazz word "funky" in form and meaning, as both jazzmen and Bakongo use "funky" and *lu-fuki* to praise persons for the integrity of their art, for having "worked out" to achieve their aims. In Kongo today it is possible to hear an elder lauded in this way: "like, there is a really funky person! – my soul advances toward him to receive his blessing" (*yati, nkwa lu-fuki! Ve miela miami ikwenda baki*). Fu-Kiau Bunseki, a leading native authority on Kongo culture, explains: "Someone who is very old, I go to sit with him in order to feel his *lu-fuki*, meaning, I would like to be blessed by him." For in Kongo the smell of a hardworking elder carries luck. This Kongo sign of exertion is identified with the positive energy of a person. Hence "funk" in Black American jazz parlance can mean earthiness, a return to fundamentals.[13]

In other words, similar to *lu-fuki* in Africa, in Black America "funk" signifies the "positive energy of a person." As a result, "funk" in Black popular music parlance most often signifies "soulfulness," "earthiness," and "a return to fundamentals." Additionally, because the word "funk" can mean both "bad body odor" *and* the "positive energy of a person," within African American vernacular culture it can also be connected to the Ifa/Yoruba spiritual concept *asé*. In Yoruba *asé* essentially means "divine energy" or "positive energy," "life-force" in English or "force-vitale" in French, and it is reportedly strongest in body fluids, especially tears, sweat, saliva, semen, breast milk, blood, and urine.[14] Bearing in mind that almost every funk band of repute had some kind of connection to jazz, Thompson's conception of *lu-fuki*/funk and my emphasis on its conceptual connections to *asé* accent not only the African origins of funk – etymologically, spiritually, culturally, philosophically, and musically speaking – but also, and equally important here, the ways in which funk was part of an African American musical and cultural continuum that reached back to the heyday of hard bop between 1955 and 1965.[15]

Although several jazz historians have suggested that hard bop emerged as a reaction to the whitened and lightened, softer sounds of cool jazz in the early-to-mid 1950s, it was actually part of the internal evolution of bebop and a heartfelt response to Charlie Parker's untimely death in March of 1955. Coming of age in the post-World War II period between 1945 and 1955 in which both bebop and rhythm & blues rose to unprecedented popularity, hard bop was essentially a synthesis of these two musics with enough snatches of gospel and blues to lead noted jazz historian James Lincoln Collier in *The Making of Jazz: A Comprehensive History* to suggest that hard bop was an attempt to reclaim jazz and "return [it] to [its] fundamentals."[16] In an interview with Dean Schaffer, renowned jazz producer and historian Michael Cuscuna spoke about the transition from bebop to hard bop, stating:

> Both Art [Blakey] and Horace [Silver] were very, very aware of what they wanted to do. They wanted to get away from the jazz scene of the early '50s, which was the Birdland scene – you hire Phil Woods or Charlie Parker or J.J. Johnson, they come and sit in with the house rhythm section, and they only play blues and standards that everybody knows. There's no rehearsal, there's no thought given to the audience. Both Horace and Art knew that the only way to get the jazz audience back and make it bigger than ever was to really make music that was memorable and planned, where you consider the audience and keep everything short. They really liked digging into blues and gospel, things with universal appeal. So they put together what was to be called the Jazz Messengers.[17]

Because it sought to "get the jazz audience back and make it bigger than ever," hard bop generously drew from jump blues and rhythm & blues, the preeminent Black popular musics between 1945 and 1965. Moving beyond the "blues and standards" bebop style of the mid-to-late 1940s and early 1950s, hard bop musicians such as Horace Silver, Art Blakey, Charles Mingus, Miles Davis, Sonny Rollins, Max Roach, Clifford Brown, Sonny Clark, Lou Donaldson, Hank Mobley, Jackie McLean, Benny Golson, Lee Morgan, and Cannonball Adderley created a new, earthier, and more accessible form of bebop that generally featured melodies that were "simpler" and frequently more "soulful" sounding. The hard bop rhythm section was "usually looser, with the bassist not as tightly confined to playing four-beats-to-the-bar," as was the case with bebop.[18] The endlessly improvising hard bop bassist would eventually morph into the non-stop grooving, slapping, and thumping funk bassist in the 1970s, which included iconic bass players such as Larry Graham (of Sly & the Family Stone and Graham Central Station), William "Bootsy" Collins (of James Brown's original J.B.'s band, Parliament, Funkadelic, and Bootsy's Rubber Band), Marvin Isley (of the Isley Brothers), Verdine White (of Earth, Wind & Fire), Marshall "Rock" Jones (of the Ohio Players), Robin Duhe (of Maze), Louis Johnson (of the Brothers Johnson), Mark "Mr. Mark" Adams (of Slave), and Nate Phillips (of Pleasure).[19]

Hard bop also displayed a strong gospel influence and incorporated "amen chords" (i.e., the plagal cadence) and triadic harmonies into its sound. As I discussed in *Civil Rights Music*, the gospel sound increasingly crept its way into rhythm & blues, and ultimately the synthesis of rhythm & blues and gospel, among other musics, gave way to the emergence of soul.[20] This is to say it was hard bop that first turned to gospel and helped to popularize the gospel sound in Black popular music. And lastly, along with mixing gospel elements with bebop, hard bop horn players and pianists also demonstrated their nuanced familiarity with early rhythm & blues. Writing of the interplay between jazz and rhythm & blues in the 1950s that laid the foundation for both soul and funk, in *Hard Bop: Jazz & Black Music, 1955–1965*, David Rosenthal observed:

> For a while, it was hard to see what the future of Black jazz might be. The early fifties saw an extremely dynamic rhythm & blues scene take shape, including a succession of brilliant doo-wop combos like the Ravens, the Clovers, and the Orioles; a New Orleans school centering on Fats Domino, Professor Longhair, Shirley & Lee, and others; the urban blues of the Muddy Waters and Bobby Bland-type; and much else besides. This music, and not cool jazz, was what chronologically separated bebop and hard bop in ghettos. Young jazz musicians, of course, enjoyed and listened to these R&B sounds which, among other things, begun the amalgam of blues and gospel that would later be dubbed "soul music." And it is in this vigorously creative Black pop music, at a time when bebop seemed to have lost both its direction and its audience, that some of hard bop's roots may be found.[21]

While many music critics have noted the influence of gospel and soul on funk, their work has frequently overlooked the ways in which jazz, and particularly hard bop, contributed to the origins and evolution of funk. Going back to the etymology of the word "funk" in Black vernacular culture, it is interesting to observe that it was hard bop musicians who popularized the term. As Paul Tanner, David Megill, and Maurice Gerow noted in *Jazz*, initially hard bop was called "funky hard bop."[22] As a matter of fact, several classic hard bop songs featured the word "funk" or "funky" in their titles, most famously Horace Silver's "Opus de Funk" (1952), Cannonball Adderley's "Blue Funk" (1958), Kenny Drew's "Funk-Cosity" (1960), Hank Mobley's "Funk in the Deep Freeze" (1957) and "Barrel of Funk" (1956), Donald Byrd's "Pure D. Funk" (1960) and "Sudwest Funk" (1958), Patti Bown's "Waltz de Funk" (1960), the Jazz Crusaders' "Big Hunk of Funk" (1962), Rahsaan Roland Kirk's "Funk Underneath" (1961), and, finally, Grant Green's "Hip Funk" (1962).[23]

Similar to the funk musicians of the 1970s, the hard bop funk musicians of the 1950s and 1960s drew from the panorama of Black popular music between 1945 and 1965 to create their new form of jazz. In this sense, bebop – with its fast tempos, complex harmonies, intricate melodies, and airtight rhythm sections that maintained steady beats based on four-beats-to-the-bar bass playing and the drummer's ride cymbal – was merely one of many forms of music on hard bop-pers' much-broadened musical palette. Hard bop funksters broke with what they perceived to be the "old school" formulas of bebop and the softness and symphonic sounds of cool jazz. Hence, hard bop funk can be viewed as both a funnel and a forum where blues, jazz, gospel, and rhythm & blues came together in creative dialogue. And indeed, it was this dynamic dialogue and synthesis that re-emerged as what is now known as "funk" roughly between 1969 and 1979.[24]

Over fifty years later we might look back at the years between 1955 and 1965 as the last period in which jazz effortlessly attracted the hippest young African American musicians – which is to say, the most musically advanced, those with the most solid technical and improvisational skills, and those with the strongest cultural sense of themselves, not only as entertainers but as distinctly *African American* artists. As David Rosenthal emphasized in "Jazz in the Ghetto: 1950–1970," it was during the turbulent decade between 1955 and 1965 that hard bop was the dominant jazz style in the poverty-stricken neighborhoods where the majority of these young-sters lived. To them, hard bop was hip and expressed the inexpressible feelings of what it meant to be "young, gifted, and Black" in the midst of the Civil Rights Movement.[25]

At times hard bop was bluesy, bleak, and sorrow-filled, but – like gospel, blues, bebop, rhythm & blues, and soul – it transformed and transfigured those pent-up feelings by both exorcising them and reinterpreting them through a Civil Rights Movement-centered worldview, undaunted verve, and history-making musical acumen.[26] In a way, then, *hard bop was the 1960s funk of the Civil Rights Movement, where the James Brown/Sly Stone/George Clinton-styled funk was the 1970s funk of the Black Power Movement.* In keeping with the inversions that are so common within African American colloquial communities, hard bop was "bad" music. Mean-ing "bad" in the sense that James Brown was a "baaad-mother-*you-betta-shut-yo-mouth!*," hard bop was simultaneously cathartic to Blacks and seemingly threatening to Whites. Similar to 1970s funk, hard bop funk refused to fit into nice and neat little categories created by Eurocentric music critics and their minions, and herein lies part of the reason it was so threatening to Whites.[27]

The word "hard" in hard bop suggests that the music offered an outlet for hard feelings, hard thoughts, and hard political points of view that might have been oth-erwise suppressed in light of the soft sounds and crossover craze that preoccupied Motown and the Brill Building in the 1960s. Hard bop classics such as Art Blakey's "Message from Kenya" (1957), "The Freedom Rider" (1961), and "Freedom Mon-day" (1965); Horace Silver's "Safari" (1953), "The Preacher" (1955), "Pyramid" (1958), "The Baghdad Blues" (1959), "The Tokyo Blues" (1962), "The Cape Ver-dean Blues" (1965), "The African Queen" (1965), "Mexican Hip Dance" (1966), "Rain Dance" (1968), and "Serenade to a Soul Sister" (1968); Wayne Shorter's "The Back Sliders" (1961), "Tell It Like it Is" (1961), and "Those Who Sit and Wait" (1961); Lee Morgan's "The Witch Doctor" (1961), "Search for the New Land" (1964), "Mr. Kenyatta" (1964), "Cornbread" (1965), "The Rajah" (1966), and "Zambia" (1966); Cedar Walton's "The Promised Land" (1962) and "Afreaka"

(1967); Curtis Fuller's "Arabia" (1961), "The High Priest" (1963), and "The Egyptian" (1965); Jackie McLean's "116th and Lenox" (1959), "Appointment in Ghana" (1960), "Medina" (1960), "Street Singer" (1960), and "Let Freedom Ring" (1962); and, finally, John Coltrane's "Dakar" (1957), "Bahia" (1958), "Black Pearls" (1958), "Dial Africa" (1958), "Gold Coast" (1958), "Tanganyika Strut" (1958), "Liberia" (1960), "Africa" (1961), "Dahomey Dance" (1961), "Tunji" (1962), "Spiritual" (1962), "India" (1963), and "Alabama" (1963) all in one way or another speak to hard bop's broadened political palette and cultural identification, not only with the Civil Rights Movement but also with the struggles of other oppressed people around the world. Obviously, hard boppers connected African Americans' culture and struggles for freedom with continental African cultures and struggles for freedom.[28]

As if picking up where some of Billie Holiday's protest songs, Bud Powell's tortured piano playing, and Charles Mingus' thunderous bass plucking left off in the 1950s, between the early-to-mid 1960s hard bop audaciously expressed deeper thoughts and darker feelings – thoughts and feelings that frequently and unrepentantly conveyed moral outrage and malicious irony, as well as political depression and social despair that often mirrored the suffering and setbacks of the Civil Rights Movement. However, as Ingrid Monson argued in *Freedom Sounds: Civil Rights Call Out to Jazz and Africa*, jazz in general, and the hard bop of the 1950s and 1960s in particular, sonically registered more than the politics of the Civil Rights Movement – it was also aurally indicative of more than a century of struggle against American apartheid:

> Any account of the politics of race in jazz during the 1950s and 1960s must surely begin with a recognition of the structural significance of Jim Crow policies for the music world. To begin with, the history of this music called jazz, from its origins through the golden age, is coextensive with the history of Jim Crow segregation. In this sense, Jim Crow functioned as a structural condition over which the emergence of the genre took place, and its effects were not limited to the South. Shortly after *Plessy vs. Ferguson* (1896) – the Supreme Court decision that established the doctrine of "separate but equal" – Buddy Bolden's band dazzled New Orleans with a distinctive sound that heralded the synthesis of ragtime, blues, spirituals, classical music, marches, and popular songs that became jazz. At the other end of the period under study, the passage of the Civil Rights Act of 1964 and the Voting Rights Act of 1965 (which dismantled the legal basis for racial segregation) saw the recording of John Coltrane's *A Love Supreme*, the flourishing of Miles Davis's second great quintet, and the experimentalism of Sun Ra's *Heliocentric World*. This is not to suggest that Jim Crow *caused* jazz but to recognize that, throughout the establishment and flourishing of the genre, discriminatory practices in the music industry and society indelibly shaped everyday life for musicians and their audiences. Segregation also concentrated a great deal of African American musical talent in the "racially expected" genres of jazz, blues, and gospel since the opportunities in other genres, such as classical music, were limited.[29]

Hard bop funk, as with the Black Power funk of the 1970s that would follow in its wake, was a form of both *sonic contestation* and *social contestation*. Similar to the emergence of jazz, which was in part a response to *Plessy vs. Ferguson*, hard bop funk arose in the midst of the social and political upheavals that led to, and fueled, the Civil Rights Movement. It was able to convey social messages and make political statements that both rhythm & blues and early rock & roll had to skirt around precisely because it was, for the most part, a non-verbal or lyric-less form of music that was open to multiple interpretations. Connected to the contention that hard bop frequently expressed deeper thoughts and darker feelings is the notion that its non-verbal communication, and often its song titles, actually spoke loudly and quite clearly about how hard boppers felt about "discriminatory practices in the music industry and society."[30]

Hard bop's deeper thoughts and darker feelings were frequently expressed in its preference for slower tempos, extensive use of the minor mode, gospel chords, and blues-based phrasing. Hence, if the popular image of beboppers (wearing berets and horn-rimmed glasses, as well as sporting meerschaum pipes) suggested the aloof intellectual and political dissident, the brash image of hard boppers reached all the way back to the roots of Black popular music, specifically gospel and blues, while simultaneously synthesizing those hallowed roots with rhythm & blues musicians' and Civil Rights workers' African American modernist ethos between 1955 and 1965. This new synthesized gospel, blues, and rhythm & blues-based jazz prompted a new relationship with those aspects of African American culture that were looked down on and dismissed by White America and the Black bourgeoisie. As a result, even though "funk" initially meant an unpleasant odor, within the vibrant vernacular world of hard bop it was transfigured into a musical *and* cultural metaphor that ultimately came to convey African American history, culture, and struggle-centered originality, authenticity, and hybridity. Just as the Civil Rights Movement sought to upset the established social and political order, the first wave of funk between 1955 and 1965 sought to upset the established musical and cultural order by emphasizing aspects of African American history and culture that hard bop funksters believed should be shared and utilized in the ongoing struggle to achieve Civil Rights, social justice, and artistic innovation.[31]

Foreshadowing 1970s funk in relationship to the Black Power Movement, hard bop – again, the funk of the 1950s and 1960s – was more than merely music, and it frequently reflected the major breakthroughs and setbacks of the Civil Rights Movement.[32] Describing hard bop as "music of cultural burial and cultural awakening" in *Freedom Is, Freedom Ain't: Jazz & the Making of the Sixties*, Scott Saul effectively argued that hard bop channeled the artistic, political, and spiritual impulses of the Civil Rights Movement:

> Hard bop was the music of a generation, born in the 1920s and early 1930s, who imaginatively tried to recapture the roots of jazz in gospel and the blues while extending its ambition in the realm of art, politics, and spirituality (and often some combination of the three). Flowing in the post-war period out of cities like Chicago, Indianapolis, Pittsburgh, Detroit, and New York, it

was unabashedly urban music, music that had a gem-like toughness and brilliance, a balance of glamour and grit. Jazz before had been "hot" or "cool," but hard bop was intense, soulful, unfussy, insistent – too agitated to be simply hot, too moody to be simply cool. The music crystallized in tandem with the Civil Rights Movement and was in many ways its sonic alter ego. Like the movement, it grounded new appeals for freedom in older idioms of Black spirituality, challenging the nation's public account of itself and testifying to the Black community's cultural power. And, like the movement again, it worked through a kind of orchestrated disruption – a musical version of what Civil Rights workers called "direct action," which jazz musicians experienced as a rhythmic assertiveness and a newly taut relation between the demands of composition and the possibilities of improvisation.[33]

The funk of the Black Power Movement could be said to sonically capture not only African Americans' artistic, political, and spiritual impulses in the 1970s, but also African Americans' intellectual (in light of the Black Studies Movement), cultural (in light of Black nationalism), and sexual (in light of the Sexual Liberation Movement) impulses in the 1970s. This is not to say that hard bop did not express African Americans' intellectual, cultural, and sexual impulses in the 1950s and early-to-mid 1960s, but that by the late 1960s and throughout the 1970s these collective urges were more pronounced as a result of the radical rhetoric, politics, and aesthetics that characterized the Black Power Movement. Consequently, right alongside rhythm & blues, rock & roll, and soul, hard bop provided a major musical *and* political model for 1970s funk. And when Saul suggested that hard bop was in many senses the "sonic alter ego" of the Civil Rights Movement, his work seems to hint at the ways in which hard bop, by speaking a special truth that was not conveyed by rhythm & blues, rock & roll, soul, or prominent Civil Rights leaders, also harbored some of the tension and turbulence of the times.

As a matter of fact, when we seriously consider the assertion that hard bop was in essence the "sonic alter ego" of the Civil Rights Movement, we are able to reinterpret the decidedly deeper thoughts and darker feelings of the hard bop funksters as, however culturally coded, corollaries of the rhetoric, political values, and desegregationist social visions of Martin Luther King, Ella Baker, Malcolm X, Fannie Lou Hamer, Bayard Rustin, Septima Clark, the National Association for the Advancement of Colored People (NAACP), the National Urban League (NUL), the Congress of Racial Equality (CORE), the Southern Christian Leadership Conference (SCLC), the Student Non-Violent Coordinating Committee (SNCC), and the National Council of Negro Women (NCNW), among others. As with the work of each of these individuals and organizations during the Civil Rights Movement, hard bop harbored the hurt and articulated the excruciating angst African Americans experienced during the decade-long struggle against American apartheid that began with the 1955 Montgomery Bus Boycott and ended with the passage of the Voting Rights Act of 1965.[34]

Truth be told, tension and turbulence are actually at the heart of hard bop, and it can be easily heard *and* heartfelt in Art Blakey's earth-shaking kick drum and clamoring press-rolls; in the pioneering funky piano grooves put down by Horace Silver; in the mercurial and trenchant muted trumpet of Miles Davis; in the roaring and seemingly always over-the-top saxophonic brilliance of Sonny Rollins; in the take-no-prisoners protest songs that Nina Simone never tired of singing; in the alluring "ugly beauty" of Thelonious Monk's rhythmically complex and dissonance-filled piano playing; in the gutbucket blues-influenced simultaneously "Negro spiritual" and "Eastern" spirituality sound John Coltrane seemed to effortlessly coax from his saxophone; in the endless squeaking and slightly sharp notes Jackie McLean seemed to slip into each and every one of his alto saxophone solos; in the volcanic drumming that drove Max Roach's great quintet with Clifford Brown to play like their lives depended on it night after night; in the hair-curling screams and improvisational genius that made it appear as though Charles Mingus was preaching while plucking and often pounding his bass; and, finally, in the histrionic and frequently harsh singing of Abbey Lincoln that seemed to eerily invoke the protest songs of Ma Rainey, Bessie Smith, and Billie Holiday.

The main point of convergence for the hard boppers was, on the one hand, their utilization of their music to express the hard lives and harsh conditions under which most African Americans lived from day to day during the Civil Rights Movement. On the other hand, and part of what made the music more accessible than bebop, by imaginatively synthesizing jazz with gospel and openly borrowing from rhythm & blues, hard bop explored the highs and lows of African American life in the 1950s and 1960s. It could convey some of the sanctity of the spirituals and gospel on Sunday morning while simultaneously alluding to the latest rhythm & blues hit that had everyone bumping and grinding in the juke joint on Saturday night. This same sonic range, from Black spirituality to Black sexuality, can be found in 1970s funk. And whether one turns to the sensuous sounds of the Ohio Players on albums such as *Pain* (1971), *Pleasure* (1972), *Ecstasy* (1973), *Climax* (1974), *Skin Tight* (1974), *Fire* (1975), and *Honey* (1975), or the musical mysticism of Earth, Wind & Fire on albums such as *Last Days and Time* (1972), *Head to the Sky* (1973), *Open Your Eyes* (1974), *That's the Way of the World* (1975), *Gratitude* (1975), *Spirit* (1976), and *All & All* (1977), themes of both Black spirituality and Black sexuality continued to characterize funk in the 1970s.[35]

As it continued to evolve in the 1960s, hard bop was increasingly influenced by soul, and a new "soul jazz" genre emerged. Similar to its incorporation of aspects of rhythm & blues into its sound in the 1950s, hard bop became more "soulful" in the 1960s, and hit songs such as Herbie Hancock's "Watermelon Man" (1962), Lee Morgan's "The Sidewinder" (1963), Donald Byrd's "Cristo Redentor" (1963), Horace Silver's "Song for My Father" (1964), Duke Pearson's "Wahoo!" (1964), and Cannonball Adderley's "Mercy, Mercy, Mercy" (1966) often sound like jazz versions of popular soul songs. In fact, Saul went so far as to say hard bop "was always tying together aesthetics and ethics, the style of soul and the mandate of soul." However, with its unmediated Civil Rights Movement-centered social messages and political statements, at its heart hard bop "hoped to evoke a new mobilization of Black energy." Moreover, through this "new mobilization of Black energy," it aspired to "galvanize a larger 'Freedom Movement' that extended from the early stirrings of the Civil Rights Movement through the late-sixties' mobilizations of the Black community under the signs of 'Black Power' and 'Soul Power.'"[36]

All of this is to say that along with being "music of cultural burial and cultural awakening" (*burying* the setbacks of the Civil Rights Movement and the pop music pretensions of the 1960s and *birthing* a harder and rhythmically heavier sound to coincide with the radical politics of the Black Power Movement), 1970s funk amazingly carried over and captured elements of both the moderatism and the militantism, the integrationism and the suppressed cultural nationalism of the Civil Rights Movement.[37] Perhaps no figure at the core of classic funk's pantheon registers the shift from soul to funk better than "Soul Brother Number One," the acclaimed "Godfather of Soul," James Brown. Part pop star and part cultural icon in the 1960s, Brown provided the soundtrack for the tumultuous coming of age of an entire generation. The mastermind behind a well-oiled soul orchestra, the relentlessly touring and incessantly groundbreaking rhythm & blues machine the James Brown Revue, Brown was raised up and revered as an undeniable symbol of Black working-class success by both the artists and the activists of the Black Power Movement. Uncompromising and unapologetically proud to be "Black" (as opposed to "Negro"), Brown ingeniously made the Black aesthetic accessible to the Black masses. Where the Black radical artists of the Black Arts Movement spent a considerable amount of time debating how best to create Black art that would raise Black consciousness, Brown created Black pride-themed protest songs that won Black hearts and Blacks minds and also moved Black bodies.

"Black and proud!": James Brown and the foundations of funk

Similar to the hard boppers of the 1950s and early 1960s, by the mid-1960s soul artists' work began to show the influence of the burgeoning Black Power Movement. One of the first major soul artists to get "funky" and open their music to the rhetoric and politics of the Black Power Movement was undoubtedly James Brown. He was arguably the most prominent 1960s pop star to openly embrace and celebrate Black pride. More than half a century after he consecutively revolutionized rhythm & blues, soul, and funk (much like Miles Davis did in the jazz genre with key contributions to cool, hard bop, post-bop, electric, and fusion jazz), in the 1960s and 1970s Brown did not mindlessly follow musical trends. On the contrary, he consistently created them. During his most creative period (circa 1965–1977), Brown did not just make music, he offered up what were understood at the time to be anthems. And his anthems consistently captured and conveyed the increasing Black consciousness and the cascade of cultural, social, and political transformations taking place in Black America during the Black Power Movement years. As Rickey Vincent importantly asserted in "James Brown: Icon of Black Power":

> Brown's music captured the popular spirit of defiance, of indignation, of anticipation, and of dignity that had emerged during the Civil Rights Movement. In the early 1960s, a new Negro mood had entered a popular space and Brown's music was a sharp reminder of those aspirations. Yet as "The Movement" became more militarized and assertive, the rhythms of Brown's music captured much of the essence of that aggression. In a symbolic fashion, in much the same way that the direct talk of Malcolm X served to bring about a direct dialogue about race and equality in society, Brown's music pushed against the traditional modes of music-making to become something explicit, articulate, and assertive in ways never before heard in popular music. With phrases like "get it together" and "don't give me integration – give me true communication," Brown's music did not "turn the other cheek." Rather, Brown's music reflected the harsh, unvarnished truths of Black American life. Yet he was capable of utilizing the Black performance tradition to generate transcendent moments of triumph and celebration above all of the trails.[38]

With songs such as "Papa's Got a Brand New Bag," "It's a Man's Man's Man's World," "Money Won't Change You," "Don't Be a Drop-Out," "Cold Sweat," "Get It Together," "Say It Loud – I'm Black and I'm Proud," "Give It Up or Turn It a Loose," "Soul Pride," "I Don't Want Nobody to Give Me Nothing (Open Up the Door, I'll Get It Myself)," "It's a New Day," "Get Up, Get into It, Get Involved," and "Soul Power," from the mid-to-late 1960s Brown's musical and cultural influence provided one of the most prominent unifying forces within the Black popular culture of the Black Power Movement. With his characteristic straight-talk, no-nonsense, quasi-proverbial raps over layers and layers of polyrhythms, the messages in his music seemed to be aimed at the streets, not the pop charts. This lent his music a kind of credibility amongst the Black masses who came to conceive of Brown as a cultural leader. Much like his music, his biography seemed to resonate as a "rags to riches" story with working-class and underclass Black folk in the 1960s and 1970s. In this sense, Brown and his pioneering funk can be re-interpreted as the ultimate bridge between the Black Power Movement and its message music, because he was simultaneously a musical *and* a cultural leader. Brown's blurring of the lines between the musical and the cultural is incredibly emblematic of the ways in which Black politics were inextricable from Black aesthetics during the Black Power Movement. But to really comprehend Brown as both a musical and a cultural leader during the Black Power Movement, it is necessary for us to go back to his humble beginnings in South Carolina.[39]

Born on May 3, 1933, in Barnwell, South Carolina, to Susie Brown and Joseph Gardner, Brown grew up in abject poverty. When he was two years old, his parents separated and eventually divorced after his mother reportedly left his father for another man. His mother subsequently abandoned the family, and until the age of six he lived with his father and his father's live-in girlfriends. By the age of seven he was abandoned by his father and sent to live with his aunt, Hansone "Handsome Honey" Washington, who ran a notorious whorehouse. Dropping out of school in the seventh grade, like many Motown artists, Brown learned his lessons in the streets, hanging out, hustling, shining shoes, sweeping store floors, washing cars and dishes, and, most importantly, singing and dancing.[40]

In 1949, at the age of sixteen, Brown was convicted of armed robbery and sent to a juvenile detention center in Toccoa, which is in upstate Georgia. In jail, he focused on singing and dancing, and he also learned to play guitar, piano, and drums. His passion for music was a turning point. It consumed him and helped him rehabilitate himself. His musical education in prison provided him with a vision of a future filled with music, and he was particularly excited about the possibility of performing and developing a dynamic stage show. Eventually he wrote to the prison parole board explaining his change of heart and how he now wanted to devote his time and energy to performing gospel music. Brown's plea obviously struck a chord with the parole board, and he was granted an early release, only serving six years of his eight-year prison sentence.[41]

By 1955 Brown was out of jail and the lead singer of a gospel group called the Gospel Starlighters, which eventually morphed into a rhythm & blues group called the Flames. Deeply influenced by Louis Jordan, Ray Charles, Roy Brown, Little Willie John, Wynonie Harris, Clyde McPhatter, Jackie Wilson, Hank Ballard, and Little Richard, Brown obsessively soaked up as much of the 1950s rhythm & blues scene as he possibly could, studying the lyrics, music, dance moves, and show-manship of his idols. It was not long before Brown began to produce hit songs, including "Please, Please, Please" (1956), "Try Me" (1958), "I'll Go Crazy" (1960), "Think" (1960), "Lost Someone" (1961), "Night Train" (1961), and "Prisoner of Love" (1963).[42]

By 1964 Brown had grown restless. Constantly touring during the Civil Rights Movement, he saw first-hand how African Americans were being mistreated and the harsh conditions under which they lived and worked – conditions very similar to the ones he grew up in, which is to say he and his band were not immune to American apartheid. They experienced segregation and racial discrimination just like working-class and underclass African Americans. Enough was enough. He made up his mind: More than sweaty, swooning love songs were needed. Brown ingeniously sought to sonically capture the new rhymes and new rhythms of Black America. Almost as if responding to the March on Washington (which took place on August 28, 1963) and the Civil Rights Act of 1964 (which was enacted on July 2, 1964), in July of 1964 Brown released a twelve-bar blues entitled "Out of Sight."[43]

Seeming to sonically replicate the marching, cheering, and call-and-response singing of the March on Washington, "Out of Sight" featured stuttering, lockstep staccato dance rhythms and blaring horn blasts that were, in essence, the poly-rhythmic alter ego of the increasingly pop-oriented and soft-sounding songs that were beginning to pass for rhythm & blues by the mid-1960s. With "Out of Sight," Brown virtually single-handedly re-rooted rhythm & blues in the African rhythms and the blues that had always distinguished Black popular music from mainstream popular music. Reflecting on his breakthrough in his autobiography, *James Brown: The Godfather of Soul*, he wrote:

> "Out of Sight" was another beginning, musically and professionally. My music – and most music – changed with "Papa's Got a Brand New Bag," but it really started on "Out of Sight," just like the change from R&B to soul started with "Think" and "I'll Go Crazy." You can hear the band and me start to move in a whole other direction rhythmically. The horns, the guitar, the vocals, everything was starting to be used to establish all kinds of rhythms at once. On that record you can hear my voice alternate with the horns to create various rhythmic accents. I was trying to get every aspect of the production to contribute to the rhythmic patterns. What most people don't realize is that I had been doing the multiple rhythm patterns for years on stage, but . . . I had agreed to make the rhythms on the records a lot simpler.[44]

By refusing to rhythmically dumb down his music any longer, Brown's game-changing rhythmic experiments were, in essence, the polyrhythmic equivalent to Curtis Mayfield's Civil Rights Movement-centered lyrical experiments on songs such as "It's All Right" (1963), "Keep on Pushing" (1964), "Amen" (1965), and "People Get Ready" (1965).[45] Recorded in February of 1965, Brown's "Papa's Got a Brand New Bag" was in many ways a musical response to Malcolm X's assassination on February 21, 1965, and a sonic harbinger of the five days of fury that have come to be called the "Watts Riots," which rocked Los Angeles between August 11–15, 1965, and resulted in 34 deaths, 1,032 injuries, 3,438 arrests, and over $40 million in property damage. Released on July 17, 1965, "Papa's Got a Brand New Bag" reached *Billboard*'s Hot R&B Singles top slot on August 14, 1965, in the midst of the Watts Riots and held that position for an astonishing eight weeks. It was also Brown's first song to make it into the Top Ten of *Billboard*'s Hot 100, peaking at number eight.[46]

"Papa's Got a Brand New Bag" was, indeed, a "new bag," a different musical direction for Brown. Building on the polyrhythmic experiments initiated with "Out of Sight," "Papa's Got a Brand New Bag" had all of the hallmarks of what would soon be recognized as "funk," with its propulsive percussiveness extending to Brown's gravelly voice and every instrument. Waves of rhythms hit the listeners, hinting at funk's roots in earlier forms of Black popular music. It was gospel and blues, jazz and rhythm & blues, rock & roll and soul all rolled into one, and it had enough moxie to make even the most stoic and stiff-necked listeners get up and dance. Utilizing a series of incredibly talented post-bop jazz and rhythm & blues-cum-soul musicians, Brown's funk stripped down the harmonic and melodic aspects of his music, which consequently exposed the complex rhythmic core of

Black popular music. His band had always been tight and filled with topnotch musicians, but few can deny how Brown's soulful sound changed when several future funk legends joined his band in the mid-1960s.[47]

Part of what made "Out of Sight" such a huge hit obviously had to do with the spirited playing of new band members: alto saxophonist Maceo Parker and his brother drummer Melvin Parker. Bassist Bernard Odum, also a new addition, brought a thunderous thumping and bumping to the lower depths of Brown's sound that was immediately recognizable. When Jimmy Nolen brought his "chicken scratch" rhythm guitar style into the mix, music history was destined to be made. Brown's musical genius, again much like Miles Davis', was not simply his ability to consistently reinvent his music, but also to surround himself with like-minded and forward-thinking musicians who understood that musical innovation is integral to the Black musical tradition.[48] In short, Brown was the maestro, and he conducted his soul-cum-funk orchestra in much the same manner that Duke Ellington or Count Basie conducted their jazz orchestras. In *I Feel Good: A Memoir of a Life of Soul*, Brown insightfully explained:

> I had discovered the power of the percussive upbeat, using the rhythm in an untraditional way, rather than with the horns, or the pianos, or the guitars or the stand-up bass, the standard instruments of R&B. I didn't use them to open the song because I didn't need them anymore! I didn't need "melody" to make music. That was, to me, old-fashioned and out of step. I now real-ized that I could compose and sing a song that used one chord or at the most two. Although "Papa's Got A Brand New Bag" has just two chords, and a melody sung over what is really a single note, it is just as musical as any-thing Pavarotti has ever sung. More important, it stood for everything I was about – pride, leadership, strength, intensity. . . . To me, the song represented so many things at once – the sound of my people, the beat underneath their social contribution, the rise of Black music into the mainstream, the con-tinuing struggles and victories of the Civil Rights Movement, and just about every aspect of the culture that was happening at the time. And all that had come before.[49]

With "Out of Sight," and undoubtedly by the time he recorded and released "Papa's Got a Brand New Bag," James Brown had developed a new method for making *Black consciousness-raising dance music*. By reducing the emphasis on the melodic and harmonic elements of his music Brown ingeniously tapped into the complex rhythmic core of Black popular music. "It was like opening the floodgates to a rhythm-based extension of soul," he asserted, "a physically performed, roots-derived configuration of music that comes straight from the heart. In a sense," he went further, "soul became the perfect marching music for the Civil Rights era, a way to choreograph the burgeoning pride that could be found everywhere."[50] Brown's music increasingly reflected African Americans' aspirations and frustra-tions, and he thought of it as contributing to the soundtrack of the social revolution taking place as the Civil Rights Movement morphed into the Black Power Movement. In his own weighted words:

> What was missing for me and my people was the rhythm of our own revolution – a soundtrack strong enough to bring us to the outside rather than to keep us on the inside. What had always bothered me most about the early days of the Civil Rights Movement was that there was still no organized, external way for Black people to get together and express their anger and frustration as a unit after four centuries of being the White man's punching bag. Saying "stop hitting me" was the most difficult thing to get Black people to do. . . . That was one of the things I most wanted to do through my music – to teach Black people how to very nicely say, "I'm sorry but you're not going to do that to me anymore. I'm too strong, I'm too young, I'm too tough, and most of all, I'm too proud."[51]

It is important to emphasize that Brown conceived of his music as contributing to "a soundtrack strong enough to bring us to the outside rather than to keep us on the inside." Consequently, his music was about breaking down barriers, some musical and some social. Expressing feelings pent up "after four centuries of being the White man's punching bag," Brown's music was striking and stood in stark contrast to virtually all other Black popular music at the time. Some Black music critics have argued that James Brown was the leader of a musical movement in the 1960s and 1970s that drove Black popular music in a more political direction, first via soul and then ultimately through the creation of funk.[52] As Brown put it, soul and funk were the "perfect marching music," the quintessential sound of Black people on the move – physically, spiritually, intellectually, culturally, socially, and politically. And the lyrics and polyrhythms of funk, of the "rhythm-based extension of soul," spoke volumes about African Americans' more militant mood, their more unapologetically *Black* (or, rather, *African*) consciousness.[53]

Brown's brand of funk remixed the rhythms of various forms of Black popular music and placed them together, simultaneously jumping and bumping, swinging and sweating to one overarching – albeit most often polyrhythmic – beat. *Where other pioneers in rhythm & blues and soul built on the lyrical, harmonic, and melodic breakthroughs of previous forms of Black popular music, Brown's music was arguably the first to focus on the rhythmic contributions of previous forms of Black popular music and synthesize them into a completely new form of Black popular music*: funk. In a sense, Brown's emphasis on the distinct rhythms of Black popular music means that at the exact moment when African Americans were seeking to *re-Africanize* themselves by reconnecting with their African heritage during the Black Power Movement, he contributed to *the re-Africanization process* by highlighting the importance of reconnecting with the distinctly African musical elements of African Americans' African heritage. Rhythm has always been associated with the African aspects of African American music, and Brown *re-Africanized* Black popular music in the 1960s and 1970s by "establish[ing] all kinds of rhythms at once" and by "get[ting] every aspect of the production to contribute to the rhythmic patterns." His new rhythm-based approach to making music was, logically, centered around the "rhythm section" – the drums, bass, and guitars – and seemed to incessantly summon Africa with each beat.[54]

By emphasizing rhythm over melody, proto-rap-styled chanting over Motown Black pop-styled singing, Brown and his band literally laid the foundation for funk.[55] After the phenomenal success of "Papa's Got a Brand New Bag," Brown went on to release a series of socially relevant songs that were in clear contrast to the dance ditties and yearning ballads of his early rhythm & blues years.[56] Songs such as "Money Won't Change You" (1966), "Don't Be a Dropout" (1966), "Get It Together" (1967), "Give It Up or Turn It a Loose" (1968), "I Don't Want Nobody to Give Me Nothing (Open Up the Door and I'll Get It Myself)" (1969), "Talkin' Loud & Sayin' Nothing" (1970), "Get Up, Get Into It, and Get Involved" (1970), "Soul Power" (1971), "King Heroin" (1972), "Public Enemy #1" (1972), "Get on the Good Foot" (1972), "I Got a Bag of My Own" (1972), "The Payback" (1974), "Papa Don't Take No Mess" (1974), and "Funky President (People It's Bad)" (1974) unambiguously reflect the radical rhetoric, aesthetics, and politics of the Black Power Movement.[57]

Brown's funk formula ultimately featured a panoply of heavy polyrhythms, choppy guitar riffs, bustling basslines, Stax-styled horn blasts, and hard bop-inspired improvisations that were offset by his gritty, gravel-voiced *gospelisms* and frenzy-filled screeches, which seemed to simultaneously reach back to jazz and jump blues and push forward to rap and hip hop soul. His lyrics and vocal acrobatics were also deeply informed by his regular "rap sessions" with clergy, politicians, local leaders, community activists, community members, and entertainers he met with in almost every city and town the James Brown Revue performed in. In his autobiography Brown recalled that afterhours his dressing room or tour bus was often transformed into a meeting place for local militants, who frequently attached political meanings to his music that he himself had not fully fathomed. Black moderates often went back and forth with Black militants during these rap sessions, and Brown soaked it all up. Ultimately, he developed a distinct, often contradictory political perspective that owed as much to the moderates as it did the militants. He sat in on, and contributed to, heated debates about "Blackness," Black radicalism, Black nationalism, Black capitalism, decolonization, self-defensive violence, war, peace, and Africa, among other topics. Increasingly, members of the Black Panther Party began to turn up at these rap sessions. He noted that they too made a special contribution to his social, political, and cultural education during the movement years.[58]

Brown's music was the heartbeat of Black America during the Black Power Movement, and arguably none of his songs drives this point home better than his immortal Black Power anthem "Say It Loud – I'm Black and I'm Proud." Recorded and released in the aftermath of Martin Luther King's assassination on April 4, 1968, "Black and Proud" was preceded by the sentimental-sounding "America Is My Home" in June of 1968. Disillusioned, morally outraged, and still reeling after King's assassination, Black America would have none of Brown's "America Is My Home" schmaltz. The song flopped, and he caught a lot of flak from the swelling ranks of Black radicals. By July of 1968 Brown wanted to demonstrate that he was still committed to *Black empowerment* and deeply outraged by what seemed to be an all-out assault on Black America.[59]

"Black and Proud" was a career-defining moment for Brown and a major turning point in Black popular music. Prior to "Black and Proud," Black popular music had only hinted at the seething bitterness Black America held toward White America. Returning to the main thesis of *Civil Rights Music*, before "Black and Proud," Black America "implicitly sang what could not be explicitly said."[60] "Black and Proud" changed everything. Undoubtedly, it was the culmination of a protest song and message music tradition that reached back to Billie Holiday's 1939 classic "Strange Fruit." Unlike Nina Simone's 1964 classic "Mississippi Goddamm," which is frequently interpreted as a showtune parody, "Black and Proud" did not have the slightest hint of humor. It was defiant and unapologetically proud to be Black. There was none of the subtle symbolism that characterized the other upbeat Civil Rights anthems of the era, such as Curtis Mayfield's "People Get Ready" and "Keep on Pushing," or Martha Reeves & the Vandellas' "Dancing in the Street," or even Aretha Franklin's "Respect."[61]

Sonically capturing and conveying the ethos of the era, "Black and Proud" fueled the flames of Black nationalism and Black pride at the exact moment when the dream of integration seemed to die with the assassination of Martin Luther King. For many African Americans "Black and Proud" was more than music, and part of its undeniable extra-musical impact centered on its affirmative use and popularization of the term "Black." Indeed, "Black and Proud" almost single-handedly made "Black" the desired nomenclature for African Americans from coast to coast in the late 1960s and, in time, across successive generations. In essence, it was a musical epitaph for the term "Negro," which by the mid-1960s was increasingly being called into question by the young militants of the Civil Rights Movement, who eventually grew into the leaders of the Black Power Movement. Instead of "Black" being interpreted from a Eurocentric, essentially White American point of view, "Black and Proud" helped African Americans radically reinterpret "Black" as something beautiful, as something meaningful and powerful. Instead of the shame previously associated with Blackness, "Black and Proud" made Blackness something to be proud of.[62]

For many in the movement, "Black and Proud" was emblematic of the best of the Black aesthetic.[63] It was as though James Brown fused his frustrations and brimming consciousness with that of all of Black America in the aftermath of Martin Luther King's assassination. The conversations with Black clergy, the rap sessions with Black radicals, the back-and-forth about Black nationalism and Black capitalism all seemed to come together in a synoptic song. Whether consciously or unconsciously, Brown was building on the "we can implicitly sing what we cannot explicitly say" maxim of the Civil Rights Movement. But with "Black and Proud," he was explicit. He said what hundreds, what thousands, what arguably millions of Black folk have wanted to say for centuries. And in saying what others had never dared to say, Brown demonstrated loudly and clearly that Black art and Black entertainment can, in fact, be used to raise Black consciousness. Even more, because his "Black and Proud" message was delivered over rhythms that echoed Africa, his song was interpreted as an extension, as the latest articulation of a longstanding Black musical tradition that at its core involved moralizing through music.[64] It is in this sense that Brown's music was also connected with gospel and freedom songs – two genres of Black sacred music through which Civil Rights Movement members literally moralized via music.[65]

As if channeling Martin Luther King and Malcolm X's high-sounding and hyperbole-filled rhetoric, Brown's "Black and Proud" was a mixture of socially relevant lyrics and super-funky rhythms. Moreover, the song's call-and-response could be said to signify that both Martin and Malcolm were African American preachers who consistently utilized antiphony in both their sermons and their political speeches. More specifically, "Black and Proud" invoked Malcolm with its straight talk and emphasis on Black pride and Black self-determination. Many believe that Malcolm X's influence on: and invocation in: "Black and Proud" is easily detected in the line where Brown sings that Black folk would rather die on their feet than live on their knees.[66] The song seemed to conjure up the spirit of King and the social vision of the Civil Rights Movement with its clever reference to the spiritual "I've Been 'Buked" – paraphrasing the song to emphasize how African Americans have been "'buked" and "scorned" and how they have "been treated bad" and "talked about as sure as you're born."[67]

Like the funksters and political rappers who would follow in his footsteps, Brown sought to make his music speak to the special needs of African Americans, especially the African American underclass. As a consequence, many in White America denounced him for making such a bold statement concerning Black pride. Indeed, for all intents and purposes, White America labeled Brown a rabble-rouser and, from his point of view, "blacklisted" him and banned his records from the pop charts. Writing candidly of this difficult period in his autobiography, Brown sternly stated:

> You shouldn't have to tell people what race you are, and you shouldn't have to teach people they should be proud. But it was necessary to teach pride then, and I think the song did a lot of good for a lot of people. That song scared people, too. Many White people didn't understand it any better than many Afro-Americans understood "America Is My Home." People called "Black and Proud" militant and angry – maybe because of the line about dying on your feet instead of living on your knees. . . . The song cost me a lot of my crossover audience. The racial makeup at my concerts was mostly Black after that. I don't regret recording it, though, even if it was misunderstood. It was badly needed at the time. It helped Afro-Americans in general and the dark-skinned man in particular. I'm proud of that.[68]

In the musical aftermath of "Black and Proud" direct references to race, racism, the ghetto, and poverty became much more prevalent in Black popular music. That is to say, Brown's message music was incredibly influential. In fact, his impact on the popular music and popular culture of the 1960s and 1970s is almost immeasurable. From gospel and jazz to rock and obviously soul, Brown's brand of funk moved bodies *and* minds. From poets, such as the Last Poets and the Watts Prophets, to marquee Motown artists, such as the Temptations, Marvin Gaye, and Stevie Wonder, Brown's songs seem to have made their mark both lyrically and musically. Hence, along with being an innovator in terms of expanding the polyrhythmic palette of rhythm & blues and soul, Brown is also a lyrical innovator – unrepentantly expressing the raw emotions and long-repressed radicalism of Black America as it transitioned from the Civil Rights Movement to the Black Power Movement, from rhythm & blues and rock & roll to soul and funk. Both lyrically and musically, most soul artists followed Brown's lead and began to produce funkier, more militant and socially relevant songs, for example Curtis Mayfield's "Mighty Mighty (Spade and Whitey)" (1969); Sly & the Family Stone's "Don't Call Me Nigger, Whitey" (1969); the Staple Singers' "When Will We Be Paid?" (1969); the Temptations' "Message from a Black Man" (1969); Donny Hathaway's "The Ghetto" (1970); Marvin Gaye's "Inner-City Blues (Makes Me Wanna Holler)" (1971); Funkadelic's "America Eats Its Young" (1972); Eddie Kendricks' "My People . . . Hold On" (1972); Stevie Wonder's "Living for the City" (1973); Smokey Robinson's "Just My Soul Responding" (1973); and Willie Hutch's "Brother's Gonna Work It Out" (1973).[69]

Brown continued to evolve his pioneering funk in the 1970s with classic albums such as *Ain't It Funky* (1970), *Sho' Is Funky Down Here* (1971), *Get on the Good Foot* (1972), *Black Caesar* (1973), *Slaughter's Big Rip-Off* (1973), *The Payback* (1974), *Hell* (1975), and *Reality* (1975). However, by 1976 he seemed to have lost steam, as his music became quite formulaic, almost as if he retreated from the funky polyrhythms he pioneered in favor of softer, simpler, disco-friendly beats. Influencing everyone from Motown to Miles Davis, the Isley Brothers to the Ohio Players, and Parliament/Funkadelic to Earth, Wind & Fire, as the 1970s and disco came to an end and the 1980s and the funk-based rap phenomenon began, Brown's influence appeared even more ubiquitous.[70]

By not only placing a greater emphasis on rhythm but also by proto-rapping about the ongoing harsh realities African Americans faced in the post-Civil Rights Movement period, Brown and his pioneering funk became one of the core models for rappers and rap music. But long before rappers raised him up and revered his music and uncompromising messages in the 1980s and 1990s, Brown's contemporaries recognized his musical and less-is-more lyrical genius. It could be said that Brown's soulful funk helped to update the Black popular music aesthetic and turn it away from the crossover craze and pop pretentions that many believe Black popular music was being held hostage to in the mid-to-late 1960s.[71]

As Brown's music grew lyrically and rhythmically heavier in the late 1960s, Whites who had been moved by the funky sounds of "Out of Sight" and "Papa's Got a Brand New Bag" continued to crave the new music, but since Brown had alienated his White audience with "Black and Proud" there was an opening for one of his, at this point, legions of aural acolytes. Finding his way into the fray, Sylvester Stewart, who is better known by his stage name, Sly Stone, was certainly not a musically reincarnated James Brown. However, by the time Sly & the Family Stone released their more-soul-than-funk debut, *A Whole New Thing*, in July of 1967, he had absorbed enough of Brown's funk, Motown's uptown soul, Stax's Southern soul, and psychedelic rock to jump-start a more White folk-friendly form of funk that would popularize funk in ways that Brown probably never imagined.[72]

"Africa Talks to You": Sly & the Family Stone's psychedelic rock, psychedelic soul, and invention of psychedelic funk

Born in Denton, Texas, on March 15, 1943, Sylvester Stewart moved with his family to San Francisco, California, when he was nine years old. A musical prodigy, by the time he was seven he had mastered the piano. At eleven his musical prowess had progressed considerably and, along with his adroit keyboard work, he was also an accomplished guitarist, bassist, and drummer. Prior to his high school years, he put his musical talent to use in his family's gospel group, The Stewart Four, an experience that profoundly shaped his musical vision and throaty gospel-influenced vocals for the rest of his life. After high school he played in several unsuccessful local bands.[73]

Frustrated and in need of a consistent paycheck to make ends meet, Stewart went to radio school and eventually became one of the first DJs on the new Black radio station KSOL in 1966. That same year he formed a new group, The Stoners, a name which hinted at his increasing fascination with drugs. From the beginning, the Stoners were different. The core of the band featured two Black women (Cynthia Robinson on trumpet and Sly's sister Rose Stone on piano), two Whites (Jerry Martini on saxophone and Gregg Errico on drums), and three Black men (Sly Stone on piano, organ, guitar, bass, harmonica, etc.; Larry Graham on bass; and Sly's brother Freddie Stone on guitar). As they morphed from Sly & the Stoners into Sly & the Family Stone, Sly recruited his younger sister's gospel group, the Heavenly Tones, which featured Vaetta Stewart (a.k.a. Vet Stone), Mary McCreary, and Elva Mouton, and affectionately rechristened them "Little Sister" to handle background vocals.[74]

After the disappointing sales of their debut album, *A Whole New Thing*, in 1967, Sly & the Family Stone went back into the studio determined to make an album that would reach across the chasms of race and class, as well as the increasingly rigid musical categories that racialized rock as "White music" and soul as "Black music." *A Whole New Thing* was, indeed, "a whole new thing," with its rousing mix of psychedelic rock on "I Cannot Make It," soul on "Let Me Hear It from You," and brassy, Stax-styled horn arrangements on "Underdog." A little too eclectic for the times, Sly & the Family Stone made up their minds to make music that would move hearts, minds, and bodies (à la Brown's music from "Out of Sight" in 1964 through "It's Too Funky in Here" in 1979).[75] Sly & the Family Stone had an undeniable funk formula in the making. In essence, playing the part of the more conciliatory and integrationist-oriented Martin Luther King-styled musical genius to James Brown's more militant and Black nationalist-oriented Malcolm X-styled musical genius, Sly & the Family Stone's second album, *Dance to the Music* (1968), was filled with inventiveness and youthful exuberance. With *Dance to the Music* the world got its first glimpse of Sly Stone's genius, as he articulated his Civil Rights Movement-centered vision of peace, brotherly love, and anti-racism over a mind-boggling blend of psychedelic rock, soul, and funk that was every bit as moving as Brown's more jazz, rhythm & blues, and soul-based funk.[76]

By smoothing out the rough edges of both psychedelic rock and soul and simultaneously synthesizing it with a more polished and pop-sounding version of Brown's pioneering funk, *Dance to the Music*, especially the title track, helped to establish a new subgenre within soul: *psychedelic soul*. Drawing on Jimi Hendrix's psychedelic rock, Brown's funk, and his own eclectic gospel-soul genius, Stone's new psychedelic soul sound emphasized Motown-like pop-soul songwriting; Stax-styled blaring horns; heavily distorted organ; fuzz, wah-wah, phaser, and reverb guitar effects; pulsing, popping, slapping, and speaker-rattling basslines; funky backbeat drumming; African and other "exotic" percussion, especially congas, bongos, and chimes; and "trippy" recording studio sound effects and production techniques.[77]

A *Billboard* Pop Singles Top 10 hit, "Dance to the Music" almost immediately influenced and indelibly altered the sound of soul. As a matter of fact, the influence of Sly & the Family Stone's psychedelic soul sound can be easily detected on the Temptations' "Cloud Nine" (1968), "Runaway Child, Running Wild" (1969), "Psychedelic Shack" (1969), "Ball of Confusion (That's What the World Is Today)" (1970), "You Make Your Own Heaven and Hell Right Here on Earth" (1970), "Ungena Za Ulimwengu (Unite the World)" (1971), "Papa Was a Rollin' Stone" (1972), and "Masterpiece" (1973); Curtis Mayfield's "(Don't Worry) If There's a Hell Below, We're All Going to Go" (1970), "Move on Up" (1970), "Get Down" (1971), "Beautiful Brother of Mine" (1971), "Superfly" (1972), "Pusherman" (1972), "Freddie's Dead" (1972), and "Future Shock" (1973); the Supremes' "Love Child" (1968) and "Stoned Love" (1970); Edwin Starr's "War" (1970); the 5th Dimension's *Stoned Soul Picnic* (1968), *The Age of Aquarius* (1969), and *Portrait* (1970); and the Undisputed Truth's "What It Is?" (1971), "Smiling Faces Sometimes (Tell Lies)" (1971), "Mama I Got a Brand New Thing" (1972), "Law of the Land" (1973), "Help Yourself" (1974), "I'm a Fool for You" (1974), "Spaced Out" (1975), "U.F.O.'s" (1975), and "Higher Than Higher" (1975).[78]

Continuing in the psychedelic soul and pop-funk vein, Sly & the Family Stone released *Life* in September of 1968. Somewhere between the explosive tentativeness of *A Whole New Thing* and the commercial inventiveness of *Dance to the Music*, *Life* was not a commercial success, but it was a much more cohesive slice of psychedelic soul and pop-funk than its predecessors. According to music critic Stephen Thomas Erlewine, *Life* "leapfrogged" over *Dance to the Music* "in terms of accomplishment and achievement." The most striking difference was *Life*'s "heavier reliance on psychedelics and fuzz guitars, plus a sharpening of songcraft."[79] Indeed, the album did feature better songwriting, tighter and funkier grooves, and an even heavier dose of sonic psychedelics. To state it outright, Sly & the Family Stone sounded like a band (albeit a genre-jumping psychedelic rock-soul-funk band), and their singing and playing on *Life* reflected the unity they passionately sang about on songs like "Fun," "Harmony," "Life," and "Love City." Boldly building on *Life*, Sly & the Family Stone's fourth album, *Stand!* (1969), focused almost exclusively on the themes of unity, brotherly love, and integration, but it also importantly added hate, racism, sex, and the resilience of the human spirit in the aftermath of the Civil Rights Movement to the mix.[80]

Stand! was a turning point for Sly & the Family Stone. To begin, it had a different lyrical and musical feel than the previous Sly & the Family Stone albums. On *Life*, Stone balanced the heavier political or message tracks "Fun," "Harmony," "Life," and "Love City" with lighter, almost innocuous tracks like "Dynamite!," "Chicken," and "M'Lady." On *Stand!* every track, except for "Sex Machine," revealed a more militant-minded Sly Stone with progressive and often extremely provocative thoughts about serious social and political issues.[81] With even better songwriting on *Stand!*, Stone's lyrical wit was infectious, and with each song displaying a rare funk-based rhythmic brilliance, the grooves were relentless. Erlewine insightfully wrote in his review of the album:

> *Stand!* is the pinnacle of Sly & the Family Stone's early work, a record that represents a culmination of the group's musical vision and accomplishment. *Life* hinted at this record's boundless enthusiasm and blurred stylistic boundaries, yet everything simply gels here, resulting in no separation between the astounding funk, effervescent irresistible melodies, psychedelicized guitars, and deep rhythms. Add to this a sharpened sense of pop songcraft, elastic band interplay, and a flowering of Sly's social consciousness, and the result is utterly stunning.[82]

It was virtually impossible to play the album and not both think deeply *and* dance with abandon. As a matter of fact, it seemed that *Stand!* had something for everyone: blistering Black pride anthems ("Stand!" and "Don't Call Me Nigger, Whitey!"); an uplifting Motown-like pop-soul melody ("Everyday People"); dirty dance floor funk ("Sing a Simple Song"); much-needed optimism ("You Can Make It If You Try"); a commentary on the escalating COINTELPRO-induced paranoia within the Black Power Movement ("Somebody's Watching You"); and an epic thirteen-minute rhythm & blues-based bump and grind track where Sly's fuzz-filled harmonica playing sounds like Little Walter on PCP or LSD ("Sex Machine").[83]

Instead of the joyousness and playfulness that characterized most of their previous music, each song on *Stand!* was conceptually linked by its seriousness and social relevance. Hence, following in the footsteps of Jimi Hendrix's groundbreaking theme-oriented psychedelic rock albums *Are You Experienced?* (1967), *Axis: Bold as Love* (1967), and *Electric Ladyland* (1968), it could be argued that Stone helped to steer funk (and to a certain extent soul as well) toward the concept album format.[84]

Essentially commenting on the entire social, political, and cultural landscape of Black America in the late 1960s, *Stand!* was universal, yet centered on distinctly African American social and political issues. It was broad but narrow enough to appeal to Black nationalist sentiments. It was celebratory and simultaneously solemn. It was frequently lighthearted yet somehow consistently heavy-hearted. It was too Black and too funky to be psychedelic rock, too optimistic and dance-inducing to be the blues, and too psychedelic and anarchic to be soul. By running a Black life-based theme through each track and by finally developing his songwriting to the point where his lyrics perfectly matched the soaring heights and dirty, deep funk depths of his innovative amalgam of psychedelic rock, soul, and funk, Sly Stone garnered a place right alongside Jimi Hendrix and James Brown as a quintessential influence on the evolution of funk in the 1970s.[85]

However, even as he increasingly became the popular face of funk after Brown was blacklisted as a consequence of "Black and Proud," Stone was equally influential on the evolution of soul in the 1970s. As a matter of fact, the move toward concept albums in soul can be directly attributed to the impact of Stone's *Stand!* For example, soul concept albums such as Isaac Hayes' *To Be Continued* (1970), *The Isaac Hayes Movement* (1970), and *Black Moses* (1971); Marvin Gaye's *What's Going On?* (1971), *Let's Get It On* (1973), *I Want You* (1976), and *Here, My Dear* (1978); Stevie Wonder's *Where I'm Coming From* (1971), *Music of My Mind* (1972), *Talking Book* (1972), *Innervisions* (1973), *Fulfillingness' First Finale* (1974), and *Songs in the Key of Life* (1976); Bill Withers' *Just As I Am* (1971), *Still Bill* (1972), and *+'Justments* (1974); the O'Jay's *Back Stabbers* (1972), *Ship Ahoy* (1973), *Family Reunion* (1975), *Survival* (1975), and *Message in the Music* (1976); and Smokey Robinson's *Smokey* (1973), *Pure Smokey* (1974), and *A Quiet Storm* (1975) all bear traces of Stone's influence by threading Black love, Black life, and Black struggle-based recurring themes throughout the course of their albums.[86]

As the 1960s ended and the 1970s began, Black America seems to have reached a crossroad. The high hopes of the Civil Rights Movement no longer seemed realistic in the aftermath of the setbacks of the late 1960s, especially Martin Luther King's assassination and most of White America's apparent indifference to ongoing Black suffering and political struggles. Widespread disenchantment and disarray worked its way through the Black Power Movement: King's assassination; Black Panther Party leader Huey Newton's September 1968 conviction for fatally shooting Oakland police officer John Frey; Black Panther Party leader Bobby Seale's March 1969 indictment and conviction for conspiracy, inciting a riot, and other charges related to his participation in the protests outside of the 1968 Democratic National Convention in Chicago; and Angela Davis' October 1970 through June 1972 jail time for her suspected involvement in the Soledad Brothers' August 1970 abduction. All of the foregoing in many ways foreshadowed that the 1970s would be *a decade of disintegration, as opposed to the long-hoped-for decade of integration and cultural pluralism.*

With most African Americans continuing to be socially segregated and economically exploited, the 1970s was a decade of deep disappointment, and Black popular music, especially funk, registered this desperation and frustration. As if retreating to survey the social and political scene, Sly Stone did not release a follow-up album to *Stand!* in 1970; instead he produced three game-changing psychedelic funk singles in August and December of 1969 that raced up the charts and helped to hold his fervent fan-base. The first single was a dazzling psychedelic soul-styled doo-wop-based ballad called "Hot Fun in the Summertime." With its dreamy lyrics and gently swinging, almost breezy syncopated beat, "Hot Fun" not only captured much of Black America's lingering optimism like only chocolate-covered flower child Sly Stone could, but it also stood in stark contrast to a lot of the lyrical heaviness of *Stand!* Almost as if reassuring his White fan-base that he could still be lyrically lighthearted, the flipside of the "Hot Fun" single featured "Fun" from the Family Stone's third album *Life*.[87]

Sly & the Family Stone's last release of the 1960s was "Thank You (Falettinme Be Mice Elf Agin)," with "Everybody Is a Star" on the flipside. Many critics consider "Thank You" the first sonic salvo announcing the beginning of the Family Stone's second era, during which their music grew more militant and began to privilege heavy funk over psychedelic rock, creating a darker and deeper funk sound. Lyrically the song packed a punch, with every word harboring multiple meanings, and the meanings become even more meaningful when Sly's tortured lead vocals merged with the gospel choir background vocals of Rose Stone, Freddie Stone, Larry Graham, and Little Sister.[88]

Musically the song churned and chugged along like a runaway train metaphorically heading away from White America and back to the heart of Black America. With its darker and deeper funk sound, "Thank You" could be read as Sly Stone saying thank you to Black America for supporting him and accepting him on his own psychedelic rock-soul-funk terms. The song can also be interpreted as Stone's aural assertion that *there quite simply is no single and definitive way to be Black.* Indeed, he was Black but had a serious relationship with psychedelic rock, the Hippie Movement, and other elements of White counterculture. The self-assertiveness of "Thank You" ingeniously gave way to the joyous celebration of difference on its flipside, the aptly titled "Everybody Is a Star."[89]

Sharing the lead vocals with Rose Stone, Freddie Stone, and Larry Graham, on "Everybody Is a Star," Sly Stone synthesized Motownesque pop-soul with gritty Stax-styled Southern soul and produced a secular gospel sound that was at once exuberant and edifying. Seeming to tap into the ethos of both moderate and militant Black America at the dawn of the 1970s, lyrically and vocally Stone remixed his psychedelic soul concept and incorporated more *gospelisms* into his overall sound. With its emphasis on the uniqueness and humble dignity of each person, in a way with "Everybody Is a Star" Stone demonstrated that whether his listeners were a part of moderate Black America, militant Black America, or White America in general, he still loved "everyday people" and deeply believed that all people needed to be empowered and freed from repressive racial, cultural, social, and political restrictions. It was a message that re-emerged as the central motif of Sly & the Family Stone's fifth album, the provocatively titled *There's a Riot Goin' On* (1971).[90]

Sly re-titled the album from its original *Africa Talks to You* in response to Marvin
Gaye's *What's Going On?*, which was released to critical acclaim six months before
There's a Riot Goin' On. According to Miles Marshall Lewis in his book-length
commentary on the album, *Sly & the Family Stone's There's a Riot Goin' On*, "Sly's
title was meant to answer Marvin Gaye's rhetorical question." Hence, Marvin rhetorically asked, "What's going on?," and Sly rhetorically answered, "There's a riot
goin' on."[91]

Whatever vestiges of optimism that continued to linger in Stone's music on
Stand! and the three late 1969 singles had all but disappeared by the time *Riot* was
released. The pop-funk sound had been replaced by an eerie, foreboding deep
funk sound. The beloved band sound of Sly & the Family Stone had been replaced
by the heavily overdubbed, multi-tracked, brooding, and often moody sounds of
Sly Stone, the psychedelic drug-taking and lyric-slurring erratic solo artist. The
Family Stone contributed here and there, but overall, as Lewis noted, most critics
"consider *There's A Riot Goin' On* Sly's first solo album."[92] Echoing Lewis, Erlewine
asserted, "It's easy to write off *There's a Riot Goin' On* as one of two things – Sly
Stone's disgusted social commentary or the beginning of his slow descent into
addiction. It's both of these things, of course, but pigeonholing it as either winds
up dismissing the album as a whole, since it is so bloody hard to categorize."[93] A bit
baffled, he continued,

> What's certain is that *Riot* is unlike any of Sly & the Family Stone's other
> albums, stripped of the effervescence that flowed through even such politi-
> cally aware records as *Stand!* This is idealism soured, as hope is slowly replaced
> by cynicism, joy by skepticism, enthusiasm by weariness, sex by pornogra-
> phy, thrills by narcotics. Joy isn't entirely gone – it creeps through the cracks
> every once and awhile and, more disturbing, Sly revels in his stoned deca-
> dence. What makes *Riot* so remarkable is that it's hard not to get drawn in
> with him, as you're seduced by the narcotic grooves, seductive vocal slurs,
> leering electric pianos, and crawling guitars.[94]

Sly's heavy drug use, the pressures of superstardom, and the unprecedented tidal
wave of Black pride, Black nationalism, and Pan-Africanism sweeping across Black
America in the early 1970s all collided and contributed to his new, even funkier
sound, lyrical outlook, and social vision – as well as, unfortunately, to the Family
Stone's disbanding. As a consequence of Sly missing countless concerts or showing
up too high to perform when he did drag himself out of his drug-induced stupor,
as well as repeatedly missing recording dates to work on their new album, the Family Stone began to painfully drift apart. Embracing both the post-hippie hedonism
and Black radicalism of the early 1970s, Sly's one-man *Riot*, similar to its predeces-
sor *Stand!*, was lyrically and musically sprawling, but there was one big difference,
according to Lewis: "[n]ever before on a Sly & the Family Stone album were songs
open to so much interpretation and, even more so, dripping with cynicism. On the
other hand, you can hardly hear what he's saying for most of the album."[95]

When placed within the historical and musical context in which it emerged, it is conceivable that the bulk of *Riot*'s lyrics are intentionally indecipherable because – as Sly seemed to be saying at the time – "there's a riot goin' on," and riots are nothing if not full of sights and sounds that are difficult to discern. Riots are not rational and do not recognize the rules and regulations of civil society, and perhaps that was precisely the point of Sly's cryptic lyrics. In essence, he produced an album that mirrored the tension and turmoil, the contradictions and confusion ominously engulfing America in the early 1970s, and his muddy vocals and the sweat-drenched, mysterious, almost menacing sound of his solo funk were as intriguing as they were unsettling, as innovative as they were eerie, as esoteric as they were obviously anarchic. Lewis importantly explained:

> Like Radiohead's *Kid A* or even the Rolling Stones' *Exile on Main St.* more recent to the time, a murkiness in the mix of the record inhibits complete comprehension of the words. Sly reportedly "auditioned" random women in the studio to sing on *Riot*, then erased their vocals from the master recordings the morning after they, shall we say, danced to the music. This constant over-dubbing and erasure eventually created a muddy sound on the reel-to-reel tapes that left many of his vocals practically inaudible. Which means people looking for simple platitudes like *everybody is a star* of the past were left straining to decipher what Sly was now saying, what he meant by what he was saying, or what they thought they heard him saying. Again, fans of *Exile on Main St.* had the same problem. But it was much more rare, really totally unheard of, for a Black artist to consciously create such a dilemma for his listeners.[96]

Similar to the funksters and rappers who would soon follow his lead, Sly's message-oriented music placed him at the heart of both American popular culture and American political culture. He was now seen as an *artist* and an *activist*. And as a consequence, his new darker and, for the most part, deeper lyrics and music altered his longstanding image among his White fan base as the sagacious, uplifting, peaceful, and fun-loving "freaky" Black bohemian. Moreover, at the exact tension-filled moment when the "public still believed that music could save and/or change the world – with evidence to the contrary only just surfacing – Sly Stone, if anyone, was expected to bring his universal optimism and acerbic social observations to the table and help everyone make heads or tails of what was happening to the country," Lewis lamented.[97]

Stripped of the buoyancy that was so integral to the success of *Stand!*, *Riot* was the sound of youthful idealism embittered and often enraged. It was the sound of Black America's disillusionment with how little things had really and truly changed for the Black masses in the aftermath of the Civil Rights Movement. It was also Sly Stone's personal rejection of the "Black hippie" stereotype – a rejection that actually reached back to "Thank You (Falettinme Be Mice Elf Agin)" – that seemed to place him, along with his contemporaries Jimi Hendrix, Betty Davis, Shuggie Otis, Funkadelic, Labelle, Mother's Finest, Nona Hendryx, and Mandré, in the new, post-Civil Rights Movement "colored section" reserved for "freaky" Black rock artists.[98]

Writing about Sly's refusal to be a psychedelic Uncle Tom and his evolving relationship with his White audience, Greil Marcus observed: "With *Riot*, Sly gave his audience – particularly his White audience – exactly what they didn't want. What they wanted was an upper, not a portrait of what lay behind the big freaky Black superstar grin that decorated the cover of the album."[99] Consequently, *Riot* revealed that part of Sly's increasing reclusiveness was not merely eccentric behavior on the part of a "Black hippie" superstar, but a reaction to the unrealistic and often anti-Black racist, Blackface minstrelesque demands of his White audience. Sly's response to post-Civil Rights Movement anti-Black racism virtually traveled along the same path as that of the rest of Black America at the time, and – again, like the rest of Black America – it was soul and funk as opposed to psychedelic rock and pop-oriented rhythm & blues that spoke to him in a special way, soothed him, and helped him get in touch with what was happening internally and externally.[100]

As revealed in Joel Selvin's *Sly & the Family Stone: An Oral History*, Sly became quite close with the Black Panther Party in the late 1960s, and his, however subtle, embrace of Panther ideology led him to produce Blacker, funkier, more militant music that in many ways reflected the rhetoric and politics of the Black Power Movement in particular and Black America at the dawn of the 1970s in general.[101] Consequently, in tune with his loose interpretation of Panther ideology, as well as the general sentiment in Black America in the early 1970s, *Riot* reflected the decline of the Civil Rights Movement and the rise of the social disillusionment and political disarray of the Black Power Movement. Recurring references to police brutality and political assassinations on *Riot* obviously pointed to his association with the Panthers. For instance, the FBI's infamous Counter-Intelligence Program (COINTELPRO) was primarily aimed at disrupting and spreading dissension within the Black Panther Party in the late 1960s and early 1970s, as well as disinformation between the Black Panthers and other Black nationalist organizations.[102]

With regard to assassinations, Panthers Bobby Hutton, Arthur Glen Morris, Anthony Coltrale, Robert Lawrence, Steve Bartholomew, Tommy Lewis, Sidney Miller, and Frank Diggs, among others, were assassinated in 1968. And Panthers Nathaniel Clark, Walter "Toure" Pope, Mark Clark, and Fred Hampton, among others, were assassinated in 1969. However, *Riot's* references to police brutality and political assassinations were also indicative of Sly's long-pent-up feelings concerning the assassinations of Malcolm X, Medgar Evers, Martin Luther King, John Kennedy, and Bobby Kennedy, among many others.

Where his music prior to *Riot* was the epitome of optimistic pop radio-friendly funk, on *Riot* optimism was replaced with cynicism, joy with misery, and enthusiasm with unambiguous apathy. Seeming not particularly interested in Black popular music if it didn't have that familiar pop or crossover sound and make them wanna dance with abandon or have ferocious (and "freaky") sex, most of White America at the time closed their ears to Sly's new music *and* new message. Similar to James Brown, soon Sly, too, was blacklisted and abruptly returned to the post-Civil Rights Movement "colored section" reserved for Black musicians who articulated their moral outrage and deep despair regarding African Americans' ongoing social segregation and economic exploitation in the aftermath of the Civil Rights Movement.[103]

Despite the fact that *Riot* produced three hit singles ("Family Affair," "Runnin' Away," and "[You Caught Me] Smilin'"), ultimately it alienated many of the White fans who had lionized Sly and fondly thought of him as a "freaky," funky, and fun-loving Black apostle of psychedelic soul. However, these same White fans who had previously held Sly in such high regard, Dave Marsh maintained, in most instances were not "prepared for such a harsh, direct look at the Black experience."[104] Truth be told, this eventually became the fundamental problematic at the heart of White reactions to Black popular music: In essence, Whites were uncomfortable with unbridled, raw Black popular music, which is what funk at its best represented prior to its descent into disco. Indeed, White reactions to funk could be extremely intense and passion-filled. However, White comprehension and sincere consideration of the diverse and dire post-Civil Rights Movement realities of African Americans captured in, and conveyed through, Black popular music were, for the most part, quite trite.[105]

Black popular music in the 1970s continued to be ardently revered when it satisfied romanticized White presumptions concerning Black over-indulgence in, and Black effortlessness with respect to, pleasure, leisure, singing, dancing, partying, drinking, eating, and, of course, sex. But these romanticized White presumptions did not require any genuine respect for, heartfelt empathy with, authentic historical knowledge of, or sincere commitment to ending the quite often unromantic conditions, nightmarish situations, and de-humanizing circumstances in which these supposedly distinctly "Black characteristics" developed. Consequently, when Sly passionately shared some of the angst, disarray, and resentment that perplexed Black America's collective consciousness in the midst of the Black Power Movement's accelerating disintegration on *Riot*, most of his former White fans seemed absolutely apathetic.[106]

Lyrically and thematically building on the bold *soul music as social commentary* model innovatively explored by Marvin Gaye on *What's Going On?*, with *Riot* Sly offered *soulful deep funk music as social commentary*, in turn helping to establish a trend in 1970s Black popular music where soulsters and funksters explored, commented on, and often acerbically critiqued the underbelly and ongoing struggles of Black America. *Riot's* Black life-centered and Black Power Movement-influenced deep funk tracks, such as "Luv N' Haight," "Africa Talks to You (The Asphalt Jungle)," "Brave & Strong," and "Thank You for Talkin' to Me Africa," stood in stark contrast to the trippy and hippie psychedelic soul that Sly & the Family Stone pioneered on their previous albums. Although White America may have, for the most part, closed its ears to Sly's new *riotous funk*, most of Black America's ears were wide open and deeply moved by the soulful sounds and heartfelt funk they heard on *Riot*. In one of the best discussions of Stone's *Riot* ever published, Greil

Marcus wrote of its enormous and game-changing impact on Black popular music in the 1970s:

> Some months after *Riot* was released – from the middle of 1972 through early 1973 – the impulses of its music emerged on other records, and they took over the radio. I don't know if I will be able to convey the impact of punching buttons day after day and night after night to be met by records as clear and strong as Curtis Mayfield's "Superfly" and "Freddie's Dead," the Staple Singers' "Respect Yourself" and the utopian "I'll Take You There," the O'Jay's "Back Stabbers," War's astonishing "Slipping Into Darkness" and "The World Is A Ghetto," the Temptations' "Papa Was A Rolling Stone," Johnny Nash's "I Can See Clearly Now," Stevie Wonder's "Superstition," for that matter the Stones' *Exile on Main St.* (the White *Riot*) – records that were surrounded, in memory and still on the air as recent hits, by Marvin Gaye's deadly "Inner-City Blues," by Undisputed Truth's "Smiling Faces Sometimes (Tell Lies)," by the Chi-Lites' falsetto melancholy, by *Riot* itself. Only a year before such discs would have been curiosities; now, they were all of a piece: one enormous answer record. Each song added something to the others, and as in a pop explosion, the country found itself listening to a new voice.[107]

The new voice of "heavy" or "deep" funk, as it was called, morphed and moved in many different directions as the 1970s wore on.[108] By rejecting the crossover pop-soul sound Motown perfected in the 1960s; by reconnecting with the roots of Black popular music in gospel, blues, and jazz; and by making music that was in tune with, and an expression of African Americans' post-Civil Rights Movement struggles, James Brown, Sly Stone, and Jimi Hendrix – yes, even Jimi Hendrix when we seriously consider his *Electric Ladyland* (1968), *Band of Gypsys* (1970), and *The Rainbow Bridge Concert* (1971) albums – laid the foundation for what we now know as funk. However, unlike Brown or Hendrix, Stone arguably went the furthest in articulating the aspirations and frustrations of African Americans at the dawn of the 1970s because he expressed those aspirations and frustrations over the course of an entire album, as opposed to a random track or two here and there (à la Brown and Hendrix). Sly's next album, *Fresh* (1973), was even more of a masterpiece than *Riot*, featuring more explicit social commentary and slightly tighter and brighter deep funk grooves. Songs such as "If You Want Me to Stay" and "Frisky" demonstrated that Sly was still a master pop-funk songwriter. However, other tracks such as "In Time," "Let Me Have It All," "Thankful N' Thoughtful," "Skin I'm In," "If It Were Left Up to Me," and "Babies Makin' Babies" also indicated that the *soulful deep funk music as social commentary* motif of *Riot* was more than a mere psychedelic drug-induced fluke.[109]

Fresh is arguably better than *Riot* because of its close-to-the-chest cynicism, more explicit social commentary, beautiful gospel-soul-soaked ballads, and slightly more accessible deep funk rhythms. But because his music was no longer considered optimistic and, therefore, not pop-radio friendly, for all intents and purposes,

Sly began a long drug-induced decline that he has yet to musically recover from. Even though his post-*Fresh* albums, such as *Small Talk* (1974), *High on You* (1975), *Heard Ya Missed Me, Well I'm Back* (1976), and *Back on the Right Track* (1979), all featured a track or two of solid social commentary and beautifully sung soul-funk ballads, Sly Stone's legacy primarily rests on his work between 1967 and 1973 – which is to say, between *A Whole New Thing* and *Fresh*.[110]

By incorporating aspects of James Brown's funk and Jimi Hendrix's psychedelic rock into his own distinct brand of *psychedelic funk*, Sly Stone began a sonic synthesis that, much like fusion jazz in the 1970s, opened funk to the innovations of other, more recent music.[111] Just as Sly began his descent into hedonism and drugs in the mid-1970s, one of his many musical followers rose to prominence with one of the most storied and bizarre funk collectives in music history: George Clinton and Parliament/Funkadelic. Perhaps more than any other funksters Parliament/Funkadelic (or "P-Funk" colloquially) wrote lyrics, created a "cosmic" sound, dressed, and performed in a way that reflected the loves, lusts, lives, and ongoing struggles of working-class and underclass African Americans in the 1970s. Parliament/Funkadelic's music and messages reveal a great deal about Black America in the 1970s and, even though often off-kilter, their musical, cultural, and sexual politics frequently reflected the political idealism *and* social realism, the optimism *and* pessimism, the comedy *and* tragedy swirling through Black America during the Black Power Movement and its immediate aftermath.

P-Funk: George Clinton, Parliament/Funkadelic, psychedelic rock, psychedelic soul, and psychedelic funk

Born in an outhouse in Kannapolis, North Carolina, on July 22, 1941, George Clinton grew up extremely poor, the oldest of nine. His mother, Julious Clinton, struggled to raise her children without a father. Consequently, looking after his many siblings, young George developed several of the organizational skills that would help to make him the mastermind behind three of the greatest funk bands of the 1970s: Parliament, Funkadelic, and Bootsy's Rubber Band. The Clinton family's financial difficulties led them to seek better opportunities up North in Plainfield, New Jersey, where a fifteen-year-old George formed a doo-wop group called the Parliaments in 1956. Working as a hairdresser in one of the most popular barbershops in Plainfield, he came into contact with talented local vocalists and musicians and began rehearsing in the back room of the barbershop. The original Parliaments doo-wop group featured Clinton, Calvin Simon, Grady Thomas, Clarence "Fuzzy" Haskins, and Raymond Davis.[112]

By the early 1960s Clinton was more interested in making music than cutting, coloring, and straightening hair. As the Parliaments evolved from a doo-wop group into a rhythm & blues group, he became fascinated with the Motown sound and believed that the Motor City hit record company was the perfect place for his burgeoning group. After moving to Detroit, he had a less than stellar audition at Motown and, as a result, instead of recording for Motown, the Parliaments only managed a few moderate singles on the fledgling Detroit-based Revilot Records. However, their hard work seemed to have paid off by 1967 when their single "I Wanna Testify" became a top three R&B hit. Unfortunately, their success was short-lived, as Revilot Records went bankrupt (many believe due to Motown's instigation), and Clinton temporally lost his group's name in the first of many legal snafus that would plague him throughout his storied career.[113]

Although Motown was not interested in the Parliaments, it was interested in Clinton's quirky and frequently flippant songwriting – a unique style of songwriting that would provide Parliament, Funkadelic, Bootsy's Rubber Band, Parlet, and the Brides of Funkenstein with an impressive string of hits from the mid-to-late 1970s. Serving as a staff songwriter for Motown, Clinton managed to land his "Can't Shake It Loose" (1968) with Diana Ross & the Supremes and "I'll Bet You" (1970) with the Jackson 5. But he didn't want to spend the rest of his life writing hits for others. He wanted his own band so that he could explore new lyrical and musical directions, many of which were inspired by his time in Detroit and especially his experiences at Motown.[114]

After initially forming a backing band with Detroiters Frankie Boyce, Richard Boyce, and Langston Booth, eventually Clinton recruited New Jerseyites Bernie Worrell on keyboards and synthesizers, Eddie Hazel on lead guitar, Lucius "Tawl" Ross on rhythm guitar, Billy "Bass" Nelson on bass, and Ramon "Tiki" Fulwood on drums to accompanying the Parliaments. This is to say, his late 1960s group consisted of five vocalists and five instrumentalists. It was this new self-contained band that signed with Westbound Records in 1968 and synthesized James Brown's funk, Jimi Hendrix's psychedelic rock, and Sly Stone's psychedelic soul into what they famously dubbed "Funkadelic." Because the Parliaments, at least in name, were still signed to the defunct Revilot Records, Clinton and his new band began to record under the intriguing Funkadelic tag.[115]

As Matt Rogers discussed in *Funkadelic's Maggot Brain*, Funkadelic's first three albums – *Funkadelic* (1970), *Free Your Mind . . . And Your Ass Will Follow* (1970), and *Maggot Brain* (1971) – were a combination of guitar-driven psychedelic rock and bass-heavy psychedelic funk. By the time they recorded the *America Eats Its Young* (1972) double album, only Clinton and Worrell remained of the original line-up. Tawl Ross left the band after he overdosed on LSD and needed rehabilitation. Eddie Hazel and Billy Nelson quit the band because of money disputes – another issue that would consistently plague both Parliament and Funkadelic until their acrimonious disbanding in the early 1980s.[116]

Clinton and Worrell recorded *America Eats Its Young* with two separate bands, the House Guests and United Soul (U.S.), and it was this aggregate of new musicians and bohemians that would ultimately combine and become the core of Parliament/Funkadelic (abbreviated as "P-Funk"). The Cincinnati, Ohio-based House Guests brought bassist William "Bootsy" Collins, guitarist Phelps "Catfish" Collins, drummer Frank "Kash" Waddy, trumpeter Clayton "Chicken" Gunnells, and saxophonist Robert McCullough into the Parliament/Funkadelic fold, while the United Souls placed guitarist Garry Shider and bassist Cordell Mosson in the

P-Funk ranks. With its slightly more soulful and funkier sound, as opposed to the psychedelic funk rock sound featured on their first three albums, *America Eats Its Young* touched on a wide range of political topics, but it did so from Funkadelic's unique point of view: For instance, the title track, "America Eats Its Young," commented on the ways in which war, political corruption, and miseducation demoralized the youth; "Biological Speculation" and "Balance" stressed nature's ability to right wrongs and bring order; and "Wake Up" was about being politically aware.[117]

Along with releasing the first Funkadelic album in 1970, Clinton managed to release the first "Parliament" (as opposed to the "Parliaments") album, *Osmium*, on former Motown songwriting and production team Holland-Dozier-Holland's Invictus Records. According to Ned Raggett in his review of *Osmium*, the "overall sound is much more Funkadelic than later Parliament, if with a somewhat more accessible feel." *Osmium* was, indeed, a musically raw and lyrically sprawling affair, as Raggett observed: "After a stripped-down start, things explode into a full-on funk strut with heavy-duty guitar and slamming drums setting the way, while the singers sound like they're tripping without losing the soul – sudden music dropouts, vocal cut-ins, volume level tweaks, and more add to the off-kilter feeling." He continued, "*Osmium*'s sound progresses from there – it's funk's fire combined with a studio freedom that feels like a blueprint for the future."[118] From the lunatic lyrics on songs like "Moonshine Heather" and "My Automobile" to the subtle social commentary on songs like "Oh Lord, Why Lord/Prayer" and "Livin' the Life," *Osmium* demonstrated the distinct duality of Clinton's musical vision.[119]

In 1973 Clinton signed Parliament to a new recording contract with Casablanca Records. Utilizing the same cast of characters recording under the Funkadelic name, including the newly added "Horny Horns" (which featured former James Brown band trombonist Fred Wesley and saxophonist Maceo Parker, as well as trumpeters Larry Hatcher and Richard "Kush" Griffith, among others), Clinton brilliantly recreated his defunct Parliament psychedelic soul-funk concept. Fred Wesley and the Horny Horns, however, added a hard bop funk and Sun Ra "Arkestra" psychedelic jazz dimension to the mushrooming Parliament/Funkadelic sound and, as a result, mid-to-late 1970s Parliament albums took on some of the spacey, astrological, and intergalactic rhetoric that Sun Ra and his avant-garde jazz "Arkestra" popularized on classic albums such as *The Nubians of Plutonia* (1959), *The Futuristic Sounds of Sun Ra* (1961), *Cosmic Tones for Mental Therapy* (1963), *Other Planes of There* (1964), *The Heliocentric World of Sun Ra* (1965), *Outer Spaceways Incorporated* (1968), *Atlantis* (1969), *Astro-Black* (1972), *Space Is the Place* (1972), *Cosmo-Earth Fantasy* (1974), *Pathways to Unknown Worlds* (1975), *Cosmos* (1976), *A Quiet Place in the Universe* (1977), *Lanquidity* (1978), *Space Probe* (1978), and *On Jupiter* (1979), among many others.[120]

Instead of basing it out of doo-wop and rhythm & blues, the new Parliament would essentially be a jazz horn-driven, gospel soul-influenced funk group. Hence, ultimately Clinton (and his outrageous alter egos "Starchild" and "Dr. Funkenstein") envisioned Funkadelic as his psychedelic rock funk band and Parliament as his psychedelic soul funk band. Solidifying both bands' sounds on Funkadelic's

Cosmic Slop (1973) and *Standing on the Verge of Getting It On* (1974) and Parliament's *Up for the Down Stroke* (1974) and *Chocolate City* (1975), by the mid-1970s Clinton and Parliament/Funkadelic were quickly moving from the musical margins to the musical center. When Parliament's *Mothership Connection* (1976) was certified platinum for selling more than one million albums, Clinton and Parliament/Funkadelic quickly became a major force within the American music industry. By developing a radio-friendly funk group (i.e., Parliament) and continuing to record and release his more avant-garde, psychedelic rock funk group (i.e., Funkadelic), Clinton not only became one of the towering figures of Black popular music in the 1970s, but he also demonstrated the wide range and reach of Black popular music in the 1970s.[121]

During the extraordinarily creative period between 1975 and 1980, Parliament and Funkadelic released a series of albums and hit singles that revolutionized Black popular music in the 1970s and helped to lay the foundation for Black popular music in the 1980s. Parliament/Funkadelic's proto-hip hop aesthetic enabled them to absorb, honor, play with, and frequently parody an extraordinary range of musical styles, flinging them back at the musical universe with a frightening freakiness and flamboyance that usually resulted in some of the most deranged yet danceable psychedelic rock-soul-funk songs of the mid-to-late 1970s. However, it was not simply their musical range that distinguished Parliament/Funkadelic, but also the remarkable social, political, and cultural range of their often parody- and satire-filled lyrics that made them stand out amongst the crowd of critically acclaimed funk bands in the 1970s.[122]

For instance, Parliament's *Chocolate City* was in many ways a response to the rise of Black majorities in several U.S. cities, as well as the election of a number of Black mayors in both large and small cities across the nation in the early 1970s. A short-list of the most noted among the African American mayors elected in "chocolate cities" between 1970 and 1975 – 1975 being the year *Chocolate City* was released – includes Kenneth Gibson in Newark, New Jersey; James McGee in Dayton, Ohio; A. Price Woodard in Wichita, Kansas; Robert Caldwell in Salina, Kansas; Lyman Parks in Grand Rapids, Michigan; James Ford in Tallahassee, Florida; Coleman Young in Detroit, Michigan; Clarence Lightner in Raleigh, North Carolina; Maynard Jackson in Atlanta, Georgia; Thomas Bradley in Los Angeles, California; Doris Davis in Compton, California; and Walter Washington in Washington, D.C. Therefore, celebrating the changing socio-political landscape in the early-to-mid-1970s, Clinton literally *rapped* about "chocolate cities" *and* their "vanilla suburbs," the latter an obvious reference to "White flight" in the 1970s.

Taking all manner of artistic license, instead of rapping about "Washington, D.C.," Clinton traded "D.C." for "C.C." – meaning "chocolate city," of course. The album cover featured a chocolate Lincoln Memorial, Washington Monument, and Capitol Hill melting, presumably (and metaphorically), from the new Black social, political, and cultural fire burning during the Black Power Movement. "Chocolate City's" lyrics re-imagined an entirely African American U.S. federal government, where famous African American musical and cultural icons led the nation in a new social, political, and cultural direction: Muhammad Ali was designated as the president; Aretha Franklin was the first lady; Ike Turner would serve as the secretary of the treasury; Stevie Wonder would be the secretary of fine arts; and Richard Pryor the minister of education.[123]

Between lively chants of "gainin' on ya!," Clinton referenced "forty acres and a mule," and then he stated, "you don't need the bullet when you got the ballot," which was a not-so-obscure reference to Malcolm X's famous 1964 "The Ballot or the Bullet" speech.[124] After mentioning marches and protests, Clinton advised his listeners to make sure they had their "James Brown pass," perhaps referencing Brown's ability to quell some of the urban unrest in the aftermath of Martin Luther King's assassination,[125] or, possibly, referencing Brown's "Black and Proud," which may have meant only Black folk who were "Black" and "proud" were welcomed in Parliament/Funkadelic's musical and cultural world. Consequently, all of this points to the fact that Parliament/Funkadelic's political universe was as broad and offbeat as their musical universe, and after *Chocolate City* – especially on their classic concept albums *Mothership Connection* (1976), *The Clones of Dr. Funkenstein* (1976), *Funkentelechy vs. The Placebo Syndrome* (1977), *Motor Booty Affair* (1978), *Gloryhallastoopid* (1979), and *Trombipulation* (1980) – Clinton used parody and satire to offer his social commentary and political critique. As Amy Wright importantly observed in "A Philosophy of Funk: The Politics and Pleasure of a Parliafunkadelicment Thang!," "[r]ather than openly critiquing political leaders, Clinton used humor to propose a Black counter-hegemony" – meaning a new, essentially post-Civil Rights Movement *and* post-Black Power Movement form of Black radical politics and Black social organization that would provide an accessible alternative to the dominant middle-class White world African Americans were then suffering through and barely surviving in.[126]

With regard to the song "Chocolate City" in particular, Wright asserted, "[i]nstead of replacing White officials with Black leaders of the Civil Rights Movement and Black Power Movement, he [i.e., Clinton] placed Black artists in charge of this new imagined nation, recognizing the significance of popular culture in an increasingly conservative political climate. With a void in leadership that many would argue has persisted until today, Clinton recognized that the Black population held popular culture figures in higher regard and had more faith in their abilities to lead than Black elected officials or Black activists."[127] In light of Black America's disillusionment with Civil Rights leaders and other Black politicians in the 1970s, Parliament/Funkadelic's music could be said to serve as the sound of Black freakiness and Black radicalness in dialogue with U.S. politics and society, as well as the popular culture and popular music of the time. Parliament/Funkadelic gave voice to working-class and underclass African Americans' thoughts and feelings, their frustrations and aspirations that had been ignored by the mostly middle-class leaders of the Civil Rights Movement, the Women's Liberation Movement, the Anti-War Movement, and the New Left Movement.[128]

Undeniably one of the groups hit the hardest by the devastating economic effects of the Vietnam War and de-industrialization, the Black working-class identified with the off-beat alternatives P-Funk offered. In fact, Clinton composed several explicit social commentaries on Black popular culture, poverty, and post-Civil Rights Movement racism. For example, almost the entire *America Eats Its Young* double album, "Cosmic Slop," "Chocolate City," "Funky Dollar Bill," and "You and Your Folks, Me and My Folks" provided stinging social commentary and political critique. Strange as it may seem, Parliament/Funkadelic emphasized and seemed to sincerely believe in music's redemptive, rejuvenating, and transcendent powers, which appeared to only underscore the Sun Ra-inspired outlandish Africanesque extraterrestrials, weird worlds, surreal universes, and alternative realities Clinton invented and incessantly explored in his work between 1976 and 1981. "Through their progressive lyrics, their wild stage show, their crazy appearance, their innovative sound, and their philosophy of funk," Wright wrote, Parliament/Funkadelic "confronted and collapsed Whites' stereotypes of Blacks while producing an alternative sound and style."[129]

In other words, when viewed from the standpoint of the African American working-class and underclass of the 1970s, Parliament/Funkadelic was much more than gobbledygook or insane Black outer-space blather. For all intents and purposes, they were much-needed post-Black Power Movement Black superheroes valiantly fighting both musically and in many other ways metaphorically on behalf of everyday average Black folk in the streets, clubs, churches, and mom-and-pop shops that continued to be the backbone of Black America. "The band's message of Black working-class pride challenged government officials and social scientists who deemed poor Blacks a 'pathological' 'underclass' trapped in a 'cycle of poverty' that resulted from this population's values and behaviors."[130]

In myriad ways, Parliament/Funkadelic offered the Black working-class and underclass both earthly and unearthly – literally, *otherworldly* – alternatives, and there is a sense in which *Mothership Connection* can be interpreted as their critique of what they understood to be the weakening and Whitening of funk and the interloping emergence of disco, as well as their effort to provide African Americans with African alternatives to the ongoing segregation, oppression, exploitation, and depression they contended with day after day on Earth. *Mothership Connection* represents the work of a musical mastermind evolving his philosophy of funk and musical mythology, and it is in bearing this in mind that Wright noted that George Clinton "created a philosophy that promoted freedom through musical, physical, spiritual, sexual, and now intergalactic release," which "appealed to a broad audience, but the music and philosophy remained rooted in African traditions and the working-class Black experience in the United States."[131] It is interesting to observe that at the same time that P-Funk was developing their musical intergalactic tales, an emerging form of African American fiction that combined elements of science fiction, fantasy, and horror began taking shape in the 1970s: Afro-futurism.[132]

Arguably one of the most influential writers within African American science fiction was Octavia Butler, whose first novel, *Patternmaster* (1976), was published the same year as *Mothership Connection*. Detailing a secret history that spanned ancient Egypt to a period far into the future, *Patternmaster* imaginatively dealt with telepathic mind control as well as an extraterrestrial plague. Her other novels, such as *Mind of My Mind* (1977), *Survivor* (1978), *Wild Seed* (1980), and *Clay's Ark* (1984), collectively mirrored many of the themes being explored by Clinton and Parliament/Funkadelic in the late 1970s and early 1980s.[133] Because most of the works in African American science fiction involve fantasy, science, technology, and time-travel, as in Butler's *Kindred* (1979), in the 1990s this literary movement was dubbed "Afro-futurism."[134] Other writers identified with either African American science fiction or "Afro-futurism" include Samuel Delany, Nalo Hopkinson, Nnedi Okorafor, N.K. Jemisin, Andrea Hairston, Nisi Shawl, and Ken Sibanda, among others.

Musically, however, Clinton and Parliament/Funkadelic were not alone in looking to and exploring ancient Egypt, outer space, and other worlds for funky inspiration. Other funk musicians also tapped into the "Afro-futurism" and other-worldliness circulating throughout Black America in the 1970s, especially as the Black Power Movement, for all intents and purposes, came to an end in 1975 as the Black Panther Party buckled under COINTELPRO repression, incarceration, disorganization, and increased drug addiction.[135] Funksters like LaBelle; Earth, Wind & Fire; Betty Davis; the Sylvers; the Isley Brothers; the Commodores; and, late in the decade, Rick James all donned Afro-futuristic-looking sparkling space suits with oversized shoulder pads, super-high glittering platform boots, and over-the-top exotic hairstyles that smacked of a special spacey topsy-turvy Black pride that hinted at a "brand new funk" (à la James Brown) from some other, more Black folk-friendly planet or universe. As a matter of fact, Earth, Wind & Fire went so far as to solicit the services of high-profile magicians David Copperfield and Doug Henning to help them develop a spectacle-filled concert that could rival P-Funk's 1976 "Earth Tour," which featured colorful futuristic space suits and a jaw-dropping oversized spaceship (i.e., the "mothership") landing onstage each night.[136]

Where Parliament/Funkadelic toyed with psychedelia, interplanetary travel, and "Afronauts" (as opposed to astronauts) descending to the Earth, the super group Earth, Wind & Fire's stage show combined Egyptology, African spirituality, and interplanetary travel in their efforts to demonstrate that their extremely successful and incredibly distinctive brand of jazz horn-driven gospel-soul-funk did not recognize borders or boundaries of any sort, whether temporal, spatial, spiritual, musical, cultural, or racial.[137] Hence, although often overlooked, there are a series of themes revolving around *escapism, utopianism, and futurism* that run through most 1970s funk that could be more or less interpreted as a musical and cultural response to the various crises confronting the Black Power Movement in particular, and 1970s Black America in general.[138] Culturally and historically, the escapism, utopianism, and futurism in 1970s funk is important in light of the fact that apparently life for Black folk had become so unlivable that it was only in outer space or in some other world "conjured up," to use Ward's apt words, by psychedelic drugs, mysticism, magic, or through some quasi-Black nationalist vision of a lost Atlantis-like African paradise that it seemed possible for African Americans to finally live in peace and be respected by other people.[139] Socially and politically, the escapism, utopianism, and futurism in mid-to-late 1970s funk symbolized African Americans' retreat, even if only temporarily, from the political radicalism and social vision of the Black Power Movement, and their turn inward, to each other, to their churches and mosques, and to those aspects of African and other non-European cultures that might enable them to once again weather the conservative storm and anti-Black racist onslaught that characterized the late 1970s and the 1980s.

Notes

1 Portia K. Maultsby, "Funk," in *African American Music: An Introduction*, eds. Mellonee V. Burnim and Portia K. Maultsby (New York: Routledge, 2006), 293; "Funk," *All Music Guide*, accessed June 19, 2018, www.allmusic.com/subgenre/funk-ma0000002606/artists. For further discussion of funk music, the funk aesthetic, and the politics of funk, see Tony Bolden, ed., *The Funk Era and Beyond: New Perspectives on Black Popular Culture* (New York: Palgrave Macmillan, 2008); Tony Bolden, *Groove Theory: The Blues Foundation of Funk* (Jackson: University Press of Mississippi, 2020); Matthew P. Brown, "Funk Music as Genre: Black Aesthetic, Apocalyptic Thinking and Urban Protest in Post-1965 African American Pop," *Cultural Studies* 8, no. 3 (1994): 484–508; Kesha M. Morant, "Language in Action: Funk Music as the Critical Voice of a Post-Civil Rights Movement Counterculture," *Journal of Black Studies* 42, no. 1 (2011): 71–82; Dave Thompson, *Funk* (San Francisco: Backbeat Books, 2001); Rickey Vincent, *Funk: The Music, the People, and the Rhythm of the One* (New York: St. Martin's Griffin, 1996).
2 Maultsby, "Funk," 293.
3 Bolden, *Groove Theory*, 11–36; Tony Bolden, "Theorizing the Funk: An Introduction," in *The Funk Era and Beyond: New Perspectives on Black Popular Culture*, ed. Tony Bolden (New York: Palgrave Macmillan, 2008), 13–29; Maultsby, "Funk," 293–95; Vincent, *Funk*, 13–22.
4 Kevin Le Gendre, *Soul Unsung: Reflections on the Band in Black Popular Music* (Bristol, CT: Equinox, 2012), 58–74; Maultsby, "Funk," 293–95; Richard J. Ripani, *The New Blue Music: Changes in Rhythm & Blues, 1950–1999* (Jackson: University Press of Mississippi, 2006), 102–24; Vincent, *Funk*, 13–22; Brian Ward, *Just My Soul Responding: Rhythm & Blues, Black Consciousness, and Race Relations* (Berkeley: University of California Press, 1998), 350–53.
5 Maultsby, "Funk," 293–94; Vincent, *Funk*, 47–59; Ward, *Just My Soul Responding*, 350–69.
6 Maultsby, "Funk," 293–94.
7 Ibid., 294.
8 Vincent, *Funk*, 31–59.
9 Zora Neale Hurston, "Characteristics of Negro Expression," in *Folklore, Memoirs, and Other Writings*, ed. Cheryl A. Wall (New York: Library of America, 1995), 838.
10 Ibid.
11 Ibid., 839.
12 For further discussion of the "softening" of soul music in the mid-to-late 1970s, and for the most noteworthy works that informed my analysis here, see Martha Bayles, *Hole in Our Soul: The Loss of Beauty and Meaning in American Popular Music* (New York: Free Press, 1994), 263–86; Nelson George, *The Death of Rhythm & Blues* (New York: Pantheon Books, 1988), 121–69; Gerri Hirshey, *Nowhere to Run: The Story of Soul Music* (New York: Times Books, 1984), 348–70; Arthur Kempton, *Boogaloo: The Quintessence of American Popular Music* (Ann Arbor: University of Michigan Press, 2005), 301–34; Mark Anthony Neal, *What the Music Said: Black Popular Music and Black Public Culture* (New York: Routledge, 1998), 85–99; Kevin Phinney, *Souled American: How Black Music Transformed White Culture* (New York: Billboard Books, 2005), 238–67; Ward, *Just My Soul Responding*, 417–50.

13 Robert Farris Thompson, *Flash of the Spirit: African & Afro-American Art & Philosophy* (New York: Random House, 1983), 104–5.

14 My interpretation of Yoruba/Ifa religion, and specifically the concept of *aṣẹ*, has been informed by William R. Bascom, *The Yoruba of Southwestern Nigeria* (New York: Holt, Rinehart & Winston, 1969); Roland Hallgren, *The Vital Force: A Study of Àṣẹ in the Traditional and Neo-Traditional Culture of the Yoruba People* (Lund: University of Lund, 1995); Ifa Karade, *The Handbook of Yoruba Religious Concepts* (York Beach: Weiser, 1995).

15 For further discussion of hard bop and post-bop, and for the most noteworthy works that informed my analysis, see Kenny Mathieson, *Cookin': Hard Bop and Soul Jazz, 1954–1965* (Edinburgh: Canongate, 2002); Eric Porter, *What Is This Thing Called Jazz?: African American Musicians as Artists, Critics, and Activists* (Berkeley: University of California Press, 2002), 54–190; David H. Rosenthal, *Hard Bop: Jazz and Black Music, 1955–1965* (New York: Oxford University Press, 1992); Grover Sales, *Jazz: America's Classical Music* (New York: Da Capo, 1984), 47–204; Scott Saul, *Freedom Is, Freedom Ain't: Jazz and the Making of the Sixties* (Cambridge: Harvard University Press, 2003).

16 James Lincoln Collier, *The Making of Jazz: A Comprehensive History* (Boston: Houghton Mifflin, 1978), 435–53.

17 Michael Cuscuna quoted in Dean Schaffer, "Secrets of the Blue Note Vault: Michael Cuscuna on Monk, Blakey, and Hancock," *Collector's Weekly*, August 20, 2010, 1. See also Alan Goldsher, *Hard Bop Academy: The Sidemen of Art Blakey and the Jazz Messengers* (Milwaukee: Hal Leonard, 2002).

18 "Hard Bop," in *All Music Guide*, accessed June 21, 2018, www.allmusic.com/style/hard-bop-ma0000002634; Rosenthal, *Hard Bop*, 10–61.

19 Maultsby, "Funk," 302–6; Vincent, *Funk*, 72–201.

20 Reiland Rabaka, *Civil Rights Music: The Soundtracks of the Civil Rights Movement* (Lanham: Rowman & Littlefield, 2016), 103–58.

21 Rosenthal, *Hard Bop*, 24. See also David H. Rosenthal, "Jazz in the Ghetto: 1950–1970," *Popular Music* 7, no. 1 (1988): 51–56.

22 Paul Tanner, David W. Megill, and Maurice Gerow, *Jazz* (Dubuque, IA: William C. Brown Publishers, 1992), 112–21.

23 Vincent, *Funk*, 42–44.

24 Ibid., 321–22. For further discussion of bebop and cool jazz, see Scott DeVeaux, *The Birth of Bebop: A Social and Musical History* (Berkeley: University of California Press, 1999); Scott DeVeaux and Gary Giddins, *Jazz* (New York: Norton, 2015), 274–342; Ted Gioia, *The Birth (and Death) of the Cool* (Golden: Speck Press, 2009); Eddie S. Meadows, *Bebop to Cool: Context, Ideology, and Musical Identity* (Westport: Greenwood Press, 2003); Thomas Owens, *Bebop: The Music and Its Players* (New York: Oxford University Press, 1995); Porter, *What Is This Thing Called Jazz?*, 54–100.

25 Rosenthal, "Jazz in the Ghetto," 51–56.

26 Ingrid Monson, *Freedom Sounds: Civil Rights Call Out to Jazz and Africa* (New York: Oxford University Press, 2007), 3–106.

27 Robert K. McMichael, "'We Insist-Freedom Now!': Black Moral Authority, Jazz, and the Changeable Shape of Whiteness," *American Music* 16, no. 4 (1998): 375–416; Monson, *Freedom Sounds*, 238–82; Jon Panish, *The Color of Jazz: Race and Representation in Postwar American Culture* (Jackson: University Press of Mississippi, 1997), 3–41; Pat Thomas, *Listen, Whitey!: The Sights and Sounds of Black Power, 1965–1975* (New York: Norton, 2012), 149–74.

28 For more detailed discussion of hard boppers' politics and the politics of hard bop, and for the most noteworthy works that informed my analysis here, see Lisa E. Davenport, *Jazz Diplomacy: Promoting America in the Cold War Era* (Jackson: University Press of Mississippi, 2009), 38–113; Charles Hersch, "'Let Freedom Ring!': Free Jazz and African American Politics," *Cultural Critique* 32 (1995): 97–123; Robin D.G. Kelley, *Africa Speaks, America Answers: Modern Jazz in Revolutionary Times* (Cambridge: Harvard University Press, 2012); Alan Lewis, "The Social Interpretation of Modern Jazz," *Sociological*

Review 34, no. S1 (1986): 33–55; Anthony Macías, "'Detroit Was Heavy': Modern Jazz, BeBop, and African American Expressive Culture," *Journal of African American History* 95, no. 1 (2010): 44–70; Monson, *Freedom Sounds*; Porter, *What Is This Thing Called Jazz?*, 191–239; Rosenthal, *Hard Bop*; Saul, *Freedom Is, Freedom Ain't*; Thomas, *Listen, Whitey!*, 149–74; Penny M. Von Eschen, *Satchmo Blows Up the World: Jazz Ambassadors Play the Cold War* (Cambridge: Harvard University Press, 2006).

29 Monson, *Freedom Sounds*, 6–7, emphasis in original.
30 Davenport, *Jazz Diplomacy*, 38–113.
31 Davenport, *Jazz Diplomacy*, 62–88; Hersch, "'Let Freedom Ring!'"; Macías, "'Detroit Was Heavy'"; Monson, *Freedom Sounds*, 29–237; Thomas, *Listen, Whitey!*, 149–74.
32 Monson, *Freedom Sounds*, 199–237.
33 Saul, *Freedom Is, Freedom Ain't*, 2–3.
34 Davenport, *Jazz Diplomacy*, 62–113; Hersch, "'Let Freedom Ring!'"; Lewis, "The Social Interpretation of Modern Jazz"; Monson, *Freedom Sounds*; Thomas, *Listen, Whitey!*, 149–74.
35 Richard Ashley, "Expressiveness in Funk," in *Expressiveness in Music Performance: Empirical Approaches Across Styles and Cultures*, eds. Dorottya Fabian, Renee Timmers, and Emery Schubert (Oxford: Oxford University Press, 2014), 154–69; Bolden, *The Funk Era and Beyond*; Maultsby, "Funk," 298–306; LaMonda Horton-Stallings, *Funk the Erotic: Transaesthetics and Black Sexual Cultures* (Chicago: University of Illinois Press, 2015), 176–204; Vincent, *Funk*, 178–201.
36 Saul, *Freedom Is, Freedom Ain't*, 3.
37 Ibid., 2.
38 Rickey Vincent, "James Brown: Icon of Black Power," in *The Funk Era and Beyond: New Perspectives on Black Popular Culture*, ed. Tony Bolden (New York: Palgrave Macmillan, 2008), 52–53.
39 For further discussion of James Brown as a simultaneously musical *and* cultural leader, see Xavier Fauthoux, *James Brown: Black and Proud* (San Diego: IDW Publishing, 2018); George, *The Death of Rhythm & Blues*, 98–104; Nelson George and Alan Leeds, eds., *The James Brown Reader: Fifty Years of Writing About the Godfather of Soul* (New York: Plume Book/Penguin Group, 2008); Michael Hanson, "Suppose James Brown Read Fanon: The Black Arts Movement, Cultural Nationalism, and the Failure of Popular Musical Praxis," *Popular Music* 27, no. 3 (2008): 341–65; Waldo E. Martin, *No Coward Soldiers: Black Cultural Politics in Postwar America* (Cambridge: Harvard University Press, 2005), 67–72; James McBride, *Kill 'Em and Leave: Searching for James Brown and the American Soul* (New York: Spiegel & Grau, 2016), 3–11; Martin Munro, "James Brown, Rhythm, and Black Power," in Martin Munro, *Different Drummers: Rhythm and Race in the Americas* (Berkeley: University of California Press, 2010), 182–213; Amy Abugo Ongiri, *Spectacular Blackness: The Cultural Politics of the Black Power Movement and the Search for a Black Aesthetic* (Charlottesville: University of Virginia Press, 2009), 130–36; Anna Scott, "It's All in the Timing: The Latest Moves, James Brown's Grooves, and the Seventies Race-Consciousness Movement in Salvador, Bahia-Brazil," in *Soul: Black Power, Politics, and Pleasure*, eds. Monique Guillory and Richard C. Green (New York: New York University Press, 1998), 9–22; William L. Van Deburg, *New Day in Babylon: The Black Power Movement and American Culture, 1965–1975* (Chicago: University of Chicago Press, 1992), 204–16; William L. Van Deburg, *Black Camelot: African American Culture Heroes in Their Times, 1960–1980* (Chicago: University of Chicago Press, 1997), 197–242; Vincent, "James Brown," 51–72; Ward, *Just My Soul Responding*, 388–93.
40 For further discussion of James Brown's life and music, see Geoff Brown, *The Life of James Brown: A Biography* (London: Omnibus, 2008); James Brown, *James Brown: The Godfather of Soul*, with Bruce Tucker (New York: Macmillan, 1986); James Brown, *I Feel Good: A Memoir of a Life of Soul*, with Marc Eliot (New York: New American Library, 2005); Anne Danielsen, *Presence and Pleasure: The Funk Grooves of James Brown and Parliament* (Middletown: Wesleyan University Press, 2006); Alice Echols, "The

Land of Somewhere Else: Refiguring James Brown in Seventies Disco," *Criticism* 50, no. 1 (2008): 19–41; Peter Guralnick, *Sweet Soul Music: Rhythm & Blues and the Southern Dream of Freedom* (New York: Harper & Row, 1986), 220–45; McBride, *Kill 'Em and Leave*; Cynthia Rose, *Living in America: The Soul Saga of James Brown* (London: Serpent's Tail, 1990); John Scannell, *James Brown* (Montreal: McGill-Queen's University Press, 2012); Chuck Silverman and Allan Slutsky, *The Funkmasters: The Great James Brown Rhythm Sections, 1960–1973* (Miami: Manhattan Music/Warner Brothers Publications, 1997); R. J. Smith, *The One: The Life and Music of James Brown* (New York: Gotham Books, 2012); James Sullivan, *The Hardest Working Man: How James Brown Saved the Soul of America* (New York: Gotham Books, 2008); Vincent, *Funk*, 72–88; Vincent, "James Brown," 51–72; Cliff White and Harry Weinger, "Are You Ready for Star Time!?," liner notes for James Brown, *Star Time* (Polydor, 849 108-2, 1992, CD), 14–45; Douglas Wolk, *James Brown's Live at the Apollo* (New York: Continuum, 2004).

41 Brown, *James Brown: The Godfather of Soul*, 1–53; Smith, *The One*, 7–61; White and Weinger, "Are You Ready for Star Time!?," 15–16.

42 Brown, *James Brown: The Godfather of Soul*, 49–61; Alan Leeds, "A Federal Offense," liner notes for James Brown, *The Singles, Volume 1: The Federal Years, 1956–1960* (Hip-O Select/Polydor, B0007029–02, 2006, CD), 3–21; Alan Leeds, "A King's Ransom," liner notes for James Brown, *The Singles, Volume 2, 1960–1963* (Hip-O Select/Polydor, B0008510–02, 2007, CD), 1–17; Smith, *The One*, 44–76; Cliff White, "Roots of a Revolution: Liner Notes," liner notes for James Brown, *Roots of a Revolution, 1956–1964* (Polydor, 817 304–2, 1989, CD), 3–25; White and Weinger, "Are You Ready for Star Time!?," 16–22; Cliff White and Harry Weinger, "Messing with the Blues: Liner Notes," liner notes for James Brown, *Messing with the Blues, 1957–1975* (Polydor, 847 258–2, 1990, CD), 9–15.

43 Alan Leeds, "Smash Hits," liner notes for James Brown, *The Singles, Volume 3, 1964–1965* (Hip-O Select/Polydor, B0008804–02, 2007, CD), 1–17; Munro, "James Brown, Rhythm, and Black Power," 188–90; White and Weinger, "Are You Ready for Star Time!?," 22–27.

44 Brown, *James Brown: The Godfather of Soul*, 149. For further discussion of the Africanisms in James Brown's music, see Munro, "James Brown, Rhythm, and Black Power," 185–88; Vincent, *Funk*, 31–36; Olly Wilson, "The Significance of the Relationship Between Afro-American Music and West African Music," *The Black Perspective in Music* 2, no. 1 (1974): 3–22.

45 Peter Burns, *Curtis Mayfield: People Never Give Up* (London: Sanctuary, 2003), 21–100; Aaron Cohen, *Move On Up: Chicago Soul Music and Black Cultural Power* (Chicago: University of Chicago Press, 2019), 42–109; Craig Werner, *Higher Ground: Stevie Wonder, Aretha Franklin, Curtis Mayfield, and the Rise and Fall of American Soul* (New York: Crown Publishers, 2004), 63–125.

46 Brown, *James Brown: The Godfather of Soul*, 137–58; Danielsen, *Presence and Pleasure*, 39–41; Leeds, "Smash Hits," 13–17; Harry Weinger and Alan Leeds, "It's a New Day," liner notes for James Brown, *Foundations of Funk: A Brand New Bag, 1964–1969* (Polydor, 531 165–2, 1996, CD), 3–12.

47 Danielsen, *Presence and Pleasure*, 39–42, 73–94; Alan Leeds, "These Are the J.B.'s – Damn Right!," liner notes for The J.B.'s, *The J.B.'s, Funky Good Time: The Anthology, 1970–1976* (Polydor, 314 527 094–2, 1995, CD), 3–10; Maultsby, "Funk," 295–300; Munro, "James Brown, Rhythm, and Black Power," 188–91; Silverman and Slutsky, *The Funkmasters*; Alexander Stewart, "'Funky Drummer': New Orleans, James Brown and the Rhythmic Transformation of American Popular Music," *Popular Music* 19, no 3 (2000): 293–318; Vincent, *Funk*, 73–77; Vincent, "James Brown," 51–57; Weinger and Leeds, "It's a New Day," 3–12; White and Weinger, "Are You Ready for Star Time!?," 27–30.

48 Danielsen, *Presence and Pleasure*, 39–42; Guralnick, *Sweet Soul Music*, 240–45; Leeds, "These Are the J.B.'s – Damn Right!"; Alan Leeds and Harry Weinger, "Soul Pride!: Liner Notes," liner notes for James Brown, *Soul Pride!: The Instrumentals, 1960–1969* (Polydor, 314 517 845–2, 1993, CD), 4–13; Munro, "James Brown, Rhythm, and Black

Power," 191–94; Dean Rudland, "The Godfather's R&B: Liner Notes," liner notes for Various Artists, *The Godfather's R&B: James Brown Productions, 1962–1967* (BGP Records, CDBGPD 194, 2008, CD), 4–12; Smith, *The One*, 108–84; Stewart, "'Funky Drummer,'" 309–12; Vincent, "James Brown," 55–57; Weinger and Alan Leeds, "It's A New Day"; White and Weinger, "Are You Ready for Star Time!?," 22–30.

49 Brown, *I Feel Good*, 80–81.

50 Ibid., 81.

51 Ibid., 81–82.

52 Bolden, *Groove Theory*, 12–21, 34–38; Guralnick, *Sweet Soul Music*, 220–45; Vincent, *Funk*, 72–88; Vincent, "James Brown," 51–72; Ward, *Just My Soul Responding*, 388–93; Weinger and Leeds, "It's A New Day," 3–12; White and Weinger, "Are You Ready for Star Time!?," 27–40.

53 Guralnick, *Sweet Soul Music*, 239–45; Munro, "James Brown, Rhythm, and Black Power," 188–94; Ripani, *The New Blue Music*, 81–124; Scott, "It's All in the Timing," 9–22; Vincent, "James Brown," 57–72; Rickey Vincent, "Pan-Africanism in Funk," in *The Routledge Handbook of Pan-Africanism*, ed. Reiland Rabaka (London: Routledge, 2020), 476–88.

54 Bolden, *Groove Theory*, 12–21; Danielsen, *Presence and Pleasure*, 62–69; Guralnick, *Sweet Soul Music*, 220–45; Munro, "James Brown, Rhythm, and Black Power," 185–94; Ripani, *The New Blue Music*, 81–124; Scott, "It's All in the Timing," 9–22; Stewart, "'Funky Drummer,'" 299–310; Vincent, "James Brown," 57–72; Ward, *Just My Soul Responding*, 388–93. For further discussion of Africanisms in African American music, see Ashenafi Kebede, *Roots of Black Music: The Vocal, Instrumental, and Dance Heritage of Africa and Black America* (Trenton: Africa World Press, 1995); Portia K. Maultsby, "West African Influences and Retentions in U.S. Black Music: A Sociocultural Study," in *More Than Dancing: Essays on Afro-American Music and Musicians*, ed. Irene V. Jackson (Westport: Greenwood, 1985), 25–57; Portia K. Maultsby, "Africanisms in African American Music," in *Africanisms in American Culture*, ed. Joseph E. Holloway (Indianapolis: Indiana University Press, 2005), 326–55; Doug Miller, "The Moan Within the Tone: African Retentions in Rhythm & Blues Saxophone Style in Afro-American Popular Music," *Popular Music* 14, no. 2 (1995): 155–74; J.H. Kwabena Nketia, "African Roots of Music in the Americas: An African View," *Jamaica Journal* 43, no. 16 (1979): 12–17; Richard Alan Waterman, "African Influence on the Music of the Americas," in *Write Me a Few of Your Lines: A Blues Reader*, ed. Steven C. Tracy (Amherst: University of Massachusetts Press, 1999), 17–27; Wilson, "The Significance of the Relationship Between Afro-American Music and West African Music"; Olly Wilson, "'It Don't Mean a Thing if It Ain't Got That Swing': The Relationship Between African and African American Music," in *African Roots/American Cultures: Africa in the Creation of the Americas*, ed. Sheila S. Walker (Lanham: Rowman & Littlefield, 2001), 153–68.

55 Danielsen, *Presence and Pleasure*, 39–42; Alan Leeds, "Take it to the Bridge," liner notes for James Brown, *Funk Power 1970: A Brand New Thang* (Polydor, 531 684–2, 1996, CD), 2–9; Alan Leeds, "Turn on the Heat," liner notes for James Brown, *Make It Funky!: The Big Payback, 1971–1975* (Polydor, 31453 3052–2, 1996, CD), 3–16; Vincent, *Funk*, 72–88; Weinger and Leeds, "It's a New Day," 3–12; White and Weinger, "Are You Ready for Star Time!?," 22–30.

56 See Alan Leeds, "Getting It Together," liner notes for James Brown, *The Singles, Volume 4, 1966–1967* (Hip-O Select/Polydor, B0009472–02, 2007, CD), 1–17; White, "Roots of a Revolution," 3–25.

57 Vincent, *Funk*, 72–88; Vincent, "James Brown," 55–72; Ward, *Just My Soul Responding*, 388–93. See also Leeds, "Take it to the Bridge," 2–9; Leeds, "Turn on the Heat," 3–16; Weinger and Leeds, "It's a New Day," 3–12; White and Weinger, "Are You Ready for Star Time!?," 27–42.

58 Danielsen, *Presence and Pleasure*, 39–108; Hanson, "Suppose James Brown Read Fanon"; Rickey Vincent, *Party Music: The Inside Story of the Black Panthers' Band and How Black*

Power Transformed Soul Music (Chicago: Lawrence Hill Books, 2013), 87–124; Ward, *Just My Soul Responding*, 388–93.

59 Brown, *James Brown: The Godfather of Soul*, 152–207; Alan Leeds, "Say It Loud," liner notes for James Brown, *The Singles, Volume 5, 1967–1969* (Hip-O Select/Polydor, B0010411–02, 2008, CD), 1–18; Alan Leeds, "Say It Live & Loud: Liner Notes," liner notes for James Brown, *Say It Live & Loud: Live in Dallas – August 26, 1968* (Polydor, 31455 7668–2, 1998, CD), 6–12; Smith, *The One*, 185–228; Vincent, "James Brown"; Vincent, *Party Music*, 87–124.

60 Rabaka, *Civil Rights Music*, 71–98.

61 Mary Ellison, *Lyrical Protest: Black Music's Struggle Against Discrimination* (New York: Praeger, 1989); Burton W. Peretti, "Signifying Freedom: Protest in Nineteenth Century African American Music," in *The Routledge History of Social Protest in Popular Music*, ed. Jonathan C. Friedman (New York: Routledge, 2013), 3–18; Rabaka, *Civil Rights Music*; Bernice Johnson Reagon, "Civil Rights and Black Protest Music," in *Civil Rights Since 1787: A Reader on the Black Struggle*, eds. Jonathon Birnbaum and Clarence Taylor (New York: New York University Press, 2000), 24–28; James Smethurst, "A Soul Message: R&B, Soul, and the Black Freedom Struggle," in *The Routledge History of Social Protest in Popular Music*, ed. Jonathan C. Friedman (New York: Routledge, 2013), 108–20; Vincent, *Funk*, 77–80; Vincent, "James Brown," 57–61; Vincent, *Party Music*, 104–13; Ward, *Just My Soul Responding*, 388–93; White and Weinger, "Are You Ready for Star Time!?," 31–37.

62 Brown, *James Brown: The Godfather of Soul*, 196–200; Leeds, "Say It Loud," 11–13; Munro, "James Brown, Rhythm, and Black Power," 190–98; Van Deburg, *New Day in Babylon*, 207–12; Vincent, *Funk*, 55–56; Vincent, *Party Music*, 104–13; Ward, *Just My Soul Responding*, 388–93.

63 Munro, "James Brown, Rhythm, and Black Power," 194–200.

64 Werner, *Change Is Gonna Come*, 137–39.

65 Rabaka, *Civil Rights Music*, 53–102; Van Deburg, *New Day in Babylon*, 207–12; Vincent, *Funk*, 77–165; Vincent, *Party Music*, 104–13; Ward, *Just My Soul Responding*, 388–93.

66 Kevern Verney, "Malcom X and Black Power, 1960–1980," in Kevern Verney, *The Debate on Black Civil Rights in America* (Manchester: Manchester University Press, 2006), 115–33.

67 Taylor Branch, *At Canaan's Edge: America in the King Years, 1965–1968* (New York: Simon & Schuster, 2006); Peniel E. Joseph, *The Sword and the Shield: The Revolutionary Lives of Malcolm X and Martin Luther King, Jr.* (New York: Basic Books, 2020).

68 Brown, *James Brown: The Godfather of Soul*, 200.

69 Alan Leeds, "Ain't It Funky Now," liner notes for James Brown, *The Singles, Volume 6, 1969–1970* (Hip-O Select/Polydor, B0012204–02, 2008, CD), 1–16; Alan Leeds, "New Breed Soul Power," liner notes for James Brown, *The Singles, Volume 7, 1970– 1972* (Hip-O Select/Polydor, B0012728–02, 2009, CD), 1–18; Alan Leeds, "The God-father of Soul," liner notes for James Brown, *The Singles, Volume 8, 1972–1973* (Hip-O Select/Polydor, B0013349–02, 2009, CD), 1–18; Alan Leeds, "The Big Payback," liner notes for James Brown, *The Singles, Volume 9, 1973–1975* (Hip-O Select/Polydor, B0014259–02, 2010, CD), 1–18; Leeds, "Say It Loud," 1–18; Leeds, "Take it to the Bridge," 2–9; Leeds, "Turn on the Heat," 3–16; Van Deburg, *Black Camelot*, 197–242; Van Deburg, *New Day in Babylon*, 204–15; Vincent, *Funk*, 77–165; Vincent, *Party Music*, 104–13; Ward, *Just My Soul Responding*, 388–93; Weinger and Leeds, "It's a New Day," 3–12.

70 Steve Bloom, "I Refuse to Lose," liner notes for James Brown, *Dead on the Heavy Funk!, 1975–1983* (Polydor, 31453 7901–2, 1998, CD), 6–10; Echols, "The Land of Some-where Else"; Alan Leeds, "Refusing to Lose," liner notes for James Brown, *The Singles, Volume 10, 1975–1979* (Hip-O Select/Polydor, B0015279–02, 2011, CD), 1–18; Alan Leeds, "Long Live the King," liner notes for James Brown, *The Singles, Volume 11, 1979–1981* (Hip-O Select/Polydor, B0016037–02, 2011, CD), 1–18; Leeds, "Take it

to the Bridge," 2–9; Leeds, "Turn on the Heat," 3–16; Rickey Vincent, "For Goodness Sakes!," liner notes for James Brown, *Dead on the Heavy Funk!, 1975–1983* (Polydor, 31453 7901–2, 1998, CD), 4–5; White and Weinger, "Are You Ready for Star Time!?:" 41–44.

71 Reiland Rabaka, *Hip Hop's Inheritance: From the Harlem Renaissance to the Hip Hop Feminist Movement* (Lanham: Rowman & Littlefield, 2011), 83–128.

72 Werner, *Change Is Gonna Come*, 103–6.

73 Dalton Anthony, "A.K.A. Sly Stone: The Rise and Fall of Sylvester Stewart," in *Rip It Up: The Black Experience in Rock & Roll*, ed. Kandia Crazy Horse (New York: Palgrave Macmillan, 2004), 39–52; Andrew Darlington, *"Don't Call Me Nigger, Whitey": Sly Stone & Black Power* (New York: Leaky Boot Press, 2014); Jeff Kaliss, *I Want to Take You Higher: The Life and Times of Sly & The Family Stone* (New York: Hal Leonard/ Backbeat Books, 2008), 1–16. For further discussion of Sly Stone's life and music, see Jason Ankeny, "Sylvester 'Sly Stone' Stewart," *All Music Guide*, accessed July 5, 2018, www.allmusic.com/artist/sylvester-sly-stone-stewart-mn0000751663/biography; Mark Reynolds, "On Wanting Sly Stone to Take Us Higher Yet Again," *PopMatters*, accessed May 3, 2017, www.popmatters.com/on-wanting-sly-stone-to-take-us-higher-yet-again-2495394101.html?rebelltitem=1#rebelltitem1; Eddie Santiago, *Sly: The Lives of Sylvester Stewart and Sly Stone* (New York: Lulu.com, 2008); Thompson, *Funk*, 47–53.

74 Ankeny, "Sylvester 'Sly Stone' Stewart"; Stephen Thomas Erlewine, "Sly & The Family Stone," *All Music Guide*, accessed July 5, 2018, www.allmusic.com/artist/sly-the-family-stone-mn0000033161/biography; Darlington, *"Don't Call Me Nigger, Whitey,"* 1–50; Kaliss, *I Want to Take You Higher*, 17–62; Joseph McCombs, "Little Sister," *All Music Guide*, accessed July 5, 2018, www.allmusic.com/artist/little-sister-mn0000266349. For further discussion of Sly & The Family Stone, see Patricia Spears Jones, "Sly & The Family Stone under the Big Tit: Atlanta, 1973," *Kenyon Review* 15, no. 4 (1993): 66–68; Kaliss, *I Want to Take You Higher*; Arno Konings and Edwin Konings, *Sly & The Family Stone* (Amersfoort, Netherlands: BBNC, 2013); Miles Marshall Lewis, *Sly & The Family Stone's There's a Riot Goin' On* (New York: Continuum, 2006); Dave Marsh, "Sly & The Family Stone," in Dave Marsh, *Fortunate Son: Criticism and Journalism by America's Best-Known Rock Writer* (New York: Random House, 1985), 55–60; Alec Palao, "Precious Stone: Liner Notes," liner notes for Sly Stone, *Precious Stone: In the Studio with Sly Stone, 1963–1965* (Ace, CDCHD 539, 1994, CD), 3–6; Alec Palao, "Listen to the Voices: Liner Notes," liner notes for Sly Stone, *Listen to the Voices: Sly Stone in the Studio, 1965–1970* (Ace, CDCHD 1255, 2010, CD), 3–23; Alec Palao, "I'm Just Like You: Liner Notes," liner notes for Sly Stone, *I'm Just Like You: Sly's Stone Flower, 1969–1970* (Light In The Attic, LITA 121, 2014, CD), 1–50; Alec Palao, Arno Konings, Edwin Konings, and Jeff Kaliss, "Higher!: Liner Notes," liner notes for Sly & The Family Stone, *Higher!, 1964–1975* (Epic, 8883746572/Legacy, 88697536652, 2013, CD); Ripani, *The New Blue Music*, 102–24; Santiago, *Sly*; Joel Selvin, *Sly & The Family Stone: An Oral History*, ed. Dave Marsh (New York: Avon Books, 1998); Tom Sinclair, "The Essential Sly & The Family Stone: Liner Notes," liner notes for Sly & The Family Stone, *The Essential Sly & The Family Stone* (Epic/Legacy, E2K 86867, 2003, CD), 8–10; Thompson, *Funk*, 47–53.

75 Bloom, "I Refuse to Lose," 6–10; Vincent, "For Goodness Sakes!," 4–5; Weinger and Leeds, "It's a New Day," 3–12.

76 Kaliss, *I Want to Take You Higher*, 35–62; Palao, Konings, Konings, and Kaliss, "Higher!," 5–7; Reynolds, "On Wanting Sly Stone to Take Us Higher Yet Again"; Santiago, *Sly*, 53–127; Selvin, *Sly & The Family Stone*, 46–91.

77 Darlington, *"Don't Call Me Nigger, Whitey,"* 31–102; Kaliss, *I Want to Take You Higher*, 35–62; Konings and Konings, *Sly & The Family Stone*, 3–27; Palao, Konings, Konings, and Kaliss, "Higher!," 5–7; Santiago, *Sly*, 23–97.

78 Kaliss, *I Want to Take You Higher*, 35–82.

79 Stephen Thomas Erlewine, "Review of *Life*, by Sly & the Family Stone," *All Music Guide*, accessed July 5, 2018, www.allmusic.com/album/life-mw0000651996.

80 Darlington, *"Don't Call Me Nigger, Whitey,"* 60–187; Kaliss, *I Want to Take You Higher*, 35–62; Vincent, *Party Music*, 49–55.

81 Vincent, *Party Music*, 54–55.

82 Stephen Thomas Erlewine, "Review of *Stand!*, by Sly & The Family Stone," *All Music Guide*, accessed July 5, 2018, www.allmusic.com/album/stand%21-mw0000195756.

83 Kaliss, *I Want to Take You Higher*, 63–82; Vincent, *Funk*, 89–99; Vincent, *Party Music*, 54–55.

84 It is extremely important not to overlook Jimi Hendrix's enormous influence on funk, especially the mind-boggling music of major funkmasters Sly Stone, George Clinton and Parliament/Funkadelic, the Isley Brothers, War, Betty Davis, and Rick James. For further discussion of Hendrix and his pioneering guitar-centered *funk rock*, see Aaron Lefkovitz, *Jimi Hendrix and the Cultural Politics of Popular Music* (New York: Palgrave Macmillan, 2018); Charles Shaar Murray, *Crosstown Traffic: Jimi Hendrix and the Post-War Rock & Roll Revolution* (New York: St. Martin's Press, 1989); John Perry, *Jimi Hendrix's Electric Ladyland* (New York: Continuum, 2004).

85 Kaliss, *I Want to Take You Higher*, 63–82; Vincent, *Funk*, 89–119; Vincent, *Party Music*, 54–55.

86 George, *The Death of Rhythm & Blues*, 108–11; Neal, *What the Music Said*, 61–72; Ward, *Just My Soul Responding*, 353–80.

87 Darlington, *"Don't Call Me Nigger, Whitey,"* 54–137; Kaliss, *I Want to Take You Higher*, 63–106; Vincent, *Funk*, 94–95.

88 Darlington, *"Don't Call Me Nigger, Whitey,"* 54–137; Kaliss, *I Want to Take You Higher*, 63–82; Palao, Konings, Konings, and Kaliss, "Higher!," 50–51; Vincent, *Funk*, 94–95; Ward, *Just My Soul Responding*, 358–59.

89 Anthony, "A.K.A. Sly Stone," 46–52; Kaliss, *I Want to Take You Higher*, 63–82; Palao, Konings, Konings, and Kaliss, "Higher!," 50–51; Santiago, *Sly*, 54–163; Vincent, *Party Music*, 55–61; Ward, *Just My Soul Responding*, 358–59.

90 Kaliss, *I Want to Take You Higher*, 71–82; Palao, Konings, Konings, and Kaliss, "Higher!," 50–51; Selvin, *Sly & The Family Stone*, 42–119.

91 Lewis, *Sly & The Family Stone's There's a Riot Goin' On*, 69–118. See also Palao, Konings, Konings, and Kaliss, "Higher!" 8–9; Vincent, *Funk*, 96–97.

92 Lewis, *Sly & The Family Stone's There's a Riot Goin' On*, 97.

93 Stephen Thomas Erlewine, "Review of *There's a Riot Goin' On*, by Sly & The Family Stone," *All Music Guide*, accessed July 5, 2018, www.allmusic.com/album/theres-a-riot-goin-on-mw0000197579.

94 Ibid.

95 Lewis, *Sly & The Family Stone's There's a Riot Goin' On*, 72. See also Kaliss, *I Want to Take You Higher*, 83–106.

96 Lewis, *Sly & The Family Stone's There's a Riot Goin' On*, 73, emphasis in original.

97 Lewis, *Sly & The Family Stone's There's a Riot Goin' On*, 72.

98 Anthony, "A.K.A. Sly Stone," 46–52; Darlington, *"Don't Call Me Nigger, Whitey,"* 151–267; Lewis, *Sly & The Family Stone's There's a Riot Goin' On*, 17–68.

99 Greil Marcus, *Mystery Train: Images of America in Rock & Roll Music* (New York: E.P. Dutton, 1975), 89.

100 Darlington, *"Don't Call Me Nigger, Whitey,"* 146–290; Kaliss, *I Want to Take You Higher*, 83–106; Lewis, *Sly & The Family Stone's There's a Riot Goin' On*, 69–118.

101 Selvin, *Sly & The Family Stone*, 94–98. See also Darlington, *"Don't Call Me Nigger, Whitey,"* 146–290.

102 See Joshua Bloom and Waldo E. Martin, *Black Against Empire: The History and Politics of the Black Panther Party* (Berkeley: University of California Press, 2016), 199–215; Ward Churchill, *To Disrupt, Discredit and Destroy: The FBI's Secret War Against the Black Panther Party* (New York: Routledge, 2009); Ward Churchill and Jim V. Wall, *Agents of Repression: The FBI's Secret Wars Against the Black Panther Party and the American Indian Movement* (Boston: South End, 1988).

103   Darlington, *"Don't Call Me Nigger, Whitey,"* 177–290; Kaliss, *I Want to Take You Higher,* 83–126.

104   Marsh, "Sly & The Family Stone," 59.

105   George, *The Death of Rhythm & Blues,* 121–70; Neal, *What the Music Said,* 85–99; Vincent, *Party Music,* 55–66; Ward, *Just My Soul Responding,* 357–60, 408–15.

106   Darlington, *"Don't Call Me Nigger, Whitey,"* 157–289; Kaliss, *I Want to Take You Higher,* 83–126; Ward, *Just My Soul Responding,* 357–60.

107   Marcus, *Mystery Train,* 79–80.

108   The "deep funk" designation is typically used to describe "obscure funk recordings that appeal mostly to zealous collectors and groove fanatics. Like deep soul, the term deep funk can evoke the strongly African American essence of the music, but deep funk also carries the connotation of a collector digging through crates of old records, looking for that special rare, underground find. It can be vocal or instrumental, but in most cases, it's about rhythm, groove, and musicianship, not songwriting. Deep funk rarely innovates within the form, generally taking its cues from the hard, lean brand of funk epitomized by James Brown and the Meters, or – depending on the level of musicianship – moving into jazzier, more improvisational territory. Some of it was recorded for major labels and lost in the shuffle, and some was cut for small independent labels with poor distribution. Whatever the specifics, deep funk represents the sound of funk on its most elemental, grass-roots level." "Deep Funk," *All Music Guide,* accessed July 5, 2018, www.allmusic.com/style/deep-funk-ma0000011931.

109   Stephen Thomas Erlewine, "Review of *Fresh,* by Sly & The Family Stone," *All Music Guide,* accessed July 5, 2018, www.allmusic.com/album/fresh-mw0000193344; Vincent, *Funk,* 96–97.

110   Anthony, "A.K.A. Sly Stone," 50–52; Darlington, *"Don't Call Me Nigger, Whitey,"* 178–289; Kaliss, *I Want to Take You Higher,* 107–44; Thompson, *Funk,* 49–50; Vincent, *Funk,* 97–99.

111   For further discussion of fusion jazz (aka jazz rock or rock jazz) and its relationship to funk, especially funk jazz, see Julie Coryell and Laura Friedman, *Jazz-Rock Fusion: The People, The Music* (Milwaukee: Hal Leonard, 2000); Kevin Fellezs, *Birds of Fire: Jazz, Rock, Funk, and the Creation of Fusion* (Durham: Duke University Press, 2011); Stuart Nicholson, *Jazz-Rock: A History* (London: Omnibus, 2001); Kenneth R. Trethewey, *Jazz-Fusion: Blue Notes and Purple Haze* (Torpoint: Jazz-Fusion Books, 2016).

112   Lloyd Bradley, *George Clinton: The Authorized Biography of George Clinton* (Edinburgh: Canongate, 2006), 1–28; George Clinton, *Brothas Be, Yo Like George, Ain't That Funkin' Kinda Hard on You?: A Memoir,* with Ben Greenman (New York: Atria/Simon & Schuster, 2014), 5–31; Diem Jones, *#1 Bimini Road: Authentic P-Funk Insights* (Oakland, CA: Sufi Warrior Publishing, 1996); David Mills, Larry Alexander, Thomas Stanley, and Aris Wilson, *George Clinton & P-Funk: An Oral History,* ed. Dave Marsh (New York: Avon, 1998), 1–22; Kris Needs, *George Clinton & The Cosmic Odyssey of the P-Funk Empire* (New York: Omnibus Press, 2014), 7–76; Thompson, *Funk,* 84–102; Vincent, *Funk,* 231–33; Marcel Visser and Arno Konings, *George Clinton and P-Funk: A Pictorial Career Overview* (Amersfoort: BBNC, 2013); Sabrina-Marie Wilson, *Multifarious Funk: The Evolution and Biography of George Clinton and the Parliament/Funkadelic Empire,* ed. Tony Rose (Phoenix: Retro Books, 2017), 1–32.

113   Bradley, *George Clinton,* 21–64; Clinton, *Brothas Be, Yo Like George,* 32–71; Needs, *George Clinton,* 77–96.

114   Clinton, *Brothas Be, Yo Like George,* 32–71; Needs, *George Clinton,* 77–96.

115   Clinton, *Brothas Be, Yo Like George,* 32–71; Needs, *George Clinton,* 77–121. For further discussion of Parliament/Funkadelic (abbreviated as P-Funk), see Robert M. J. Bowman, "Music for Your Mother," liner notes for Funkadelic, *Music for Your Mother: Funkadelic 45s, 1969–1976* (Westbound Records, 2WB-CD-1111, 1992, CD), 2–22; Danielsen, *Presence and Pleasure;* Lewis Dene, "The Very Best of Funkadelic: Liner Notes," liner notes for Funkadelic, *The Very Best of Funkadelic, 1976–1981* (Charly

Records, CPCD 8306–2, 1998, CD), 2–7; Derrick Drisdel, *George Clinton, Double O.G.* (New York: Icon Books, 2011); Horace Maxile, "Extensions on a Black Musical Tropology: From Trains to the Mothership (and Beyond)," *Journal of Black Studies* 42, no. 4 (2011): 593–608; Mills, Alexander, Stanley, and Wilson, *George Clinton & P-Funk*; David Mills, "The 12 Collection," liner notes for Parliament, *The 12" Collection and More* (Casablanca, 314 546 109–2, 1999, CD), 3–4; Matt Rogers, *Funkadelic's Maggot Brain* (New York: Continuum, 2013); Dean Rudland, "Motor City Madness: Liner Notes," liner notes for Funkadelic, *Motor City Madness: The Ultimate Funkadelic Westbound Compilation* (Westbound Records, 2WBCD-1119, 2005, CD), 4–15; Greg Tate, "Doin' It in Your Earhole," liner notes for Parliament, *Tear the Roof Off, 1974–1980* (Casablanca/Chronicles, 314 514 417–2, 1993, CD), 3–10; Marc Taylor, *A Touch of Classic Soul, Vol. 2: Soul Singers of the Late 1970s* (New York: Aloiv Publishing, 2001), 207–22; Rickey Vincent, "Glory B Da Funk's on Me! Liner Notes," liner notes for Bootsy Collins, *Glory B Da Funk's on Me! The Bootsy Collins Anthology* (Warner Archives/Rhino Records, R2 74276, 2001, CD), 5–32; Amy Wright, "A Philosophy of Funk: The Politics and Pleasure of a Parliafunkadelicment Thang!," in *The Funk Era and Beyond: New Perspectives on Black Popular Culture*, ed. Tony Bolden (New York: Palgrave Macmillan, 2008), 33–50.

116 Rogers, *Funkadelic's Maggot Brain*, 1–73. See also Bowman, "Music for Your Mother," 7–15; Mills, Alexander, Stanley, and Wilson, *George Clinton & P-Funk*, 23–89; Rudland, "Motor City Madness," 8–11.

117 Bowman, "Music for Your Mother," 14–17; Clinton, *Brothas Be, Yo Like George*, 72–107; Needs, *George Clinton*, 97–162; Rudland, "Motor City Madness," 10–13.

118 Ned Raggett, "Review of *Osmium*, by Parliament," *All Music Guide* accessed July 7, 2018, www.allmusic.com/album/osmium-mw0000139848.

119 Bowman, "Music for Your Mother," 7–15; Needs, *George Clinton*, 97–121; Tate, "Doin' It in Your Earhole," 3–10.

120 For further discussion of the incomparable Sun Ra and his avant-garde jazz "Arkestra," including his enormous influence on Black popular music beyond the jazz genre as well as 1960s and 1970s Black aesthetic and Black political culture more generally, see Daniel Kreiss, "Appropriating the Master's Tools: Sun Ra, the Black Panthers, and Black Consciousness, 1952–1973," *Black Music Research Journal* 28, no. 1 (2008): 57–82; Graham Lock, *Blutopia: Visions of the Future and Revisions of the Past in the Work of Sun Ra, Duke Ellington, and Anthony Braxton* (Durham: Duke University Press, 1999), 13–76; John F. Szwed, *Space Is the Place: The Lives and Times of Sun Ra* (New York: Pantheon Books, 1997); Paul Youngquist, *A Pure Solar World: Sun Ra and the Birth of Afrofuturism* (Austin: University of Texas Press, 2016).

121 Bowman, "Music for Your Mother," 16–22; Lloyd Bradley, *Where'd You Get That Funk From?: George Clinton, Black Power, and the Story of P-Funk* (New York: Grove/Atlantic, 2008), 77–219; Clinton, *Brothas Be, Yo Like George*, 108–38; Needs, *George Clinton*, 142–87; Rudland, "Motor City Madness," 11–15; Tate, "Doin' It in Your Earhole," 3–10; Vincent, *Funk*, 238–43; Ward, *Just My Soul Responding*, 353–57.

122 Bradley, *Where'd You Get That Funk From?*; Needs, *George Clinton*, 122–66; Tate, "Doin' It in Your Earhole," 3–10; Ward, *Just My Soul Responding*, 353–57; Wright, "A Philosophy of Funk," 36–43.

123 Bradley, *Where'd You Get That Funk From?* 122–219; Danielsen, *Presence and Pleasure*, 125–32; Clinton, *Brothas Be, Yo Like George*, 139–54; Needs, *George Clinton*, 163–212; Wright, "A Philosophy of Funk," 41–43.

124 Malcolm X, "The Ballot or the Bullet," in Malcolm X, *Malcolm X Speaks: Selected Speeches and Statements* (New York: Grove-Weidenfeld, 1990), 23–44.

125 James Brown, *The Night James Brown Saved Boston*, directed by David Leaf (Los Angeles: Shout! Factory, 2009, DVD); Sullivan, *The Hardest Working Man*, 85–88, 131–39.

126 Wright, "A Philosophy of Funk," 42.

127 Ibid., 42–43.

128 Bradley, *Where'd You Get That Funk From?* 158–231; Needs, *George Clinton*, 142–266; Vincent, *Funk*, 239–49; Wright, "A Philosophy of Funk," 38–41.

129 Wright, "A Philosophy of Funk," 38. See also Maxile, "Extensions on a Black Musical Tropology," 593–608.

130 Maultsby, "Funk," 298–300, 305–6; Ward, *Just My Soul Responding*, 353–57; Wright, "A Philosophy of Funk," 38–41.

131 Wright, "A Philosophy of Funk," 44. See also Vincent, "Pan-Africanism in Funk," 483–86.

132 Needs, *George Clinton*, 188–233.

133 Octavia E. Butler, *Patternmaster* (Garden City, NY: Doubleday, 1976); Octavia E. Butler, *Mind of My Mind* (Garden City, NY: Doubleday, 1977); Octavia E. Butler, *Survivor* (Garden City, NY: Doubleday, 1978); Octavia E. Butler, *Wild Seed* (Garden City, NY: Doubleday, 1980); Octavia E. Butler, *Clay's Ark* (New York: St. Martin's Press, 1984).

134 Octavia E. Butler, *Kindred* (Garden City, NY: Doubleday, 1979).

135 Bloom and Martin, *Black against Empire*, 339–89; Churchill, *To Disrupt, Discredit and Destroy*; Churchill and Wall, *Agents of Repression*; Vincent, *Party Music*, 263–338.

136 Danielsen, *Presence and Pleasure*, 113–218; Maultsby, "Funk," 301–2; Vincent, *Funk*, 166–266; Ward, *Just My Soul Responding*, 356–58; Wright, "A Philosophy of Funk," 43–47.

137 Philip Bailey, *Shining Star: Braving the Elements of Earth, Wind & Fire*, with Keith Zimmerman and Kent Zimmerman (New York: Viking, 2014); Earth, Wind & Fire, *Shining Stars: The Official Story of Earth, Wind & Fire*, directed by Kathryn Arnold (New York: Eagle Vision/RED Distribution, 2001, DVD); Taylor, *A Touch of Classic Soul, Vol. 2*, 106–28; Vincent, *Funk*, 186–88; Vincent, "Pan-Africanism in Funk," 482–83; Maurice White, *My Life with Earth, Wind & Fire*, with Herb Powell (New York: Amistad, 2016), 147–215.

138 Maultsby, "Funk," 298–300; Erik Steinskog, *Afrofuturism and Black Sound Studies: Culture, Technology, and Things to Come* (New York: Palgrave Macmillan, 2017), 75–174; Gayle Wald, "Soul Vibrations: Black Music and Black Freedom in Sound and Space," *American Quarterly* 63, no. 3 (2011): 673–96; Ward, *Just My Soul Responding*, 357–58.

139 Ward, *Just My Soul Responding*, 357.

CONCLUSION

Blackness. Power. Music. — *ad infinitum*

When the cultural and musical expressions of the Black Power Movement are critically examined, they reveal how incredibly inextricable politics and aesthetics were in Black America between roughly 1965 and 1975. Addressing a wide range of issues, such as post-Civil Rights Movement racism, police brutality, economic exploitation, and underemployment, the advances of the Black Power Movement typically take a back seat to those of the Civil Rights Movement.[1] In fact, as Dan Berger observed in "Rescuing Civil Rights from Black Power," in the twenty-first century a kind of deep dichotomous thought has emerged where most often the Civil Rights Movement is primarily presented as "noble and nonviolent" and the Black Power Movement as "vicious and violent."[2] Berger continued:

> The Civil Rights Movement is presented as noble, nonviolent, and limited to the South, where its greatest enemy was vigilante White violence rather than an entrenched state system of White supremacy. Individual White terror, protected by backward southern sheriffs, is presented as the main enemy of African Americans and the movement in general. Such a paradigm . . . implicates Black Power as the antithesis of Civil Rights — a violent and unnecessary overreaction.[3]

Echoing Berger's contention that in contemporary scholarship and in the contemporary social imagination the Black Power Movement is most often conceived of as "vicious and violent," in her seminal article "Black Freedom Studies," Jeanne Theoharis also noted the Black Power Movement's reductive characterization as "violent and dangerous."[4] Building on the pivotal scholarship of William Chafe, John Dittmer, Barbara Ransby, Charles Payne, Jacquelyn Dowd Hall, and Peniel Joseph, among others, Theoharis argued that it is important to reconceive of the Civil Rights Movement and the Black Power Movement as a continuum, a

DOI: 10.4324/9781003254492-7

combined "Black Freedom Movement."[5] When we reconceive of the Civil Rights Movement and the Black Power Movement as one long Black Freedom Movement, she continued, we move "our understandings of the movement beyond a dichotomy between Civil Rights and Black Power both ideologically and chronologically." In fact, these "strict distinctions have rendered issues like self-defense, internationalism, Black history, and police brutality outside of Civil Rights, while keeping desegregation, civil disobedience, and engagement in the political process separate from Black Power."[6] Further critiquing historically inaccurate and one-dimensional characterizations of the Black Power Movement as "violent and dangerous" and nicely and neatly commencing in 1965 in the aftermath of Malcolm X's assassination in February and the Watts Rebellion in August, Theoharis stated in a striking passage:

> This rethinking moves Black Power out of the riots and rebels narrative that it often occupies and shows it instead as a series of organized local, national, and international movements that have their roots in the 1940s and 1950s. Black Power did not appear after the 1965 Watts riot, or after the media heard Stokely Carmichael and Willie Ricks proclaim it in 1966, but represented, as Peniel Joseph explains, "a powerful, political movement that redefined and deepened American democracy." It had early roots in A. Phillip Randolph's all-Black March on Washington Movement that organized against discrimination in the army, defense industries and federal government; in Black women's organizing against the "legal lynching" of Rosa Lee Ingram who was given a death sentence after defending herself against an aggressive White sharecropper in 1947; in Robert Williams' rebuilding of the Monroe NAACP chapter in the 1950s; and in many militant youth chapters of the NAACP in the 1950s and 1960s. It was an indigenously developed set of tactics which can be seen in Black parents creating their own schools in Boston and Milwaukee, in Black sharecroppers forming their own political party in Lowndes County, Alabama, in Brooklyn CORE members planning a stall-in to disrupt the first day of the World's Fair. It developed within a series of groups like the Black Panther Party, the CORE, the Young Lords Party, the Congress of African Peoples, the National Welfare Rights Organization (NWRO) and the US Organization, which pushed city and state governments to provide equitable public services to communities of color, promoted the election of Blacks to city government, and cultivated the profound interest in African and African American history, literature, and culture within the Black community. Ideologically, theologically, and strategically rooted, nationalism was not just born out of anger and was often continuous with struggles in the 1930s, 1940s, and 1950s.[7]

Decidedly moving beyond the dichotomous thinking that sees the Black Power Movement as the antithesis of the Civil Rights Movement and the mainstream "riots and rebels narrative" of the Black Power Movement, throughout this book

I have followed Black Freedom Studies scholars' lead and explored the roots of Black Power music in the "long Civil Rights Movement" and, most especially, in Civil Rights music.[8] Soul and funk did not develop in a historical vacuum or simply fall from the sky like light rain in the springtime. On the contrary, and much like the Civil Rights music that directly preceded them, soul and funk have deep extra-musical, Black Power Movement-based meanings that are frequently either lost or grossly misunderstood by people who did not actively participate in the movement or were not in some significant way associated with the movement. Just as the Civil Rights Movement evolved into the Black Power Movement, Civil Rights music metamorphosized into Black Power music. Many of the major themes of Civil Rights music were carried over into Black Power music. In fact, key Black Power music compilations such as *Change Is Gonna Come: The Voice of Black America, 1963–1973*; *Black Power: Music of a Revolution*; *Listen, Whitey!: The Sounds of Black Power, 1967–1974*; *Power to the Motown People!: Civil Rights Anthems and Political Soul, 1968–1975*; *Freedom, Rhythm & Sound: Revolutionary Jazz & The Civil Rights Movement, 1963–1982*; *Liberation Music: Spiritual Jazz & The Art of Protest on Flying Dutchman Records, 1969–1974*; *Black Fire!, New Spirits!: Radical and Revolutionary Jazz in the U.S.A., 1957–1982*; *Celestial Blues: Cosmic, Political, and Spiritual Jazz, 1970–1974*; *Soul of a Nation, Vol. 1: Afrocentric Visions in the Age of Black Power – Underground Jazz, Street Funk, and the Roots of Rap, 1968–1979*; and *Soul of a Nation, Vol. 2: Jazz Is the Teacher, Funk Is the Preacher – Afrocentric Jazz, Street Funk, and the Roots of Rap in the Black Power Era, 1969–1975* all illustrate that Civil Rights Movement themes like "desegregation, civil disobedience, and engagement in the political process" were lyrically and sonically situated right alongside conventionally conceived Black Power Movement themes such as "self-defense, internationalism, Black history, and police brutality."[9]

As was witnessed in the preceding chapters, the Black Power Movement was more than the radical rhetoric-spewing angry Black men and angry Black women caricatures it is frequently reduced to in many quarters in the twenty-first century. Moreover, the Black Power Movement and the Black aesthetic continue to influence contemporary Black political culture and Black popular culture. Just as I argued that soul and funk can be conceived of as the culmination of postwar Black popular music between 1945 and 1975, the politics and aesthetics of the Black Power Movement can also be conceived of as the climatic synthesis of postwar Black politics and Black aesthetics. Moving from the moderatism that characterized the Civil Rights Movement to the militantism that distinguished the Black Power Movement, the evolution of Black popular culture between 1965 and 1975 often mirrored the evolution of Black political culture during the same time period. Frequently the lines between Black political culture and Black popular culture were blurred during the Black Power Movement, and many musical leaders became cultural icons, if not outright quasi-political leaders.[10]

Even though the Civil Rights Movement utilized Black popular music as a form of cultural, social, and political expression, it is important to emphasize how cultural awareness, and Black cultural consciousness in particular, made a huge difference between the messages in Civil Rights music when compared with those contained in Black Power music.[11] Black Power music obviously illustrates a greater awareness of Black cultural consciousness. This means that qualitatively different conceptual tools are needed when and where we come to an examination of the Black Power Movement and the ways in which its ideology was expressed through its protest songs and message music. If, indeed, many members of the Black Power Movement understood it to be fundamentally a *Black empowerment movement*, then critical engagements of Black culture, the emergence of Black cultural consciousness, and the politics of Blackness are crucial for understanding the cultural meaning and legacy of the movement. However, something similar could be said, indeed should be said, concerning the emergence of the discourse on the Black aesthetic during the Black Power Movement. Critical histories of the Black Power Movement should take into consideration the ways in which the Black popular culture and Black popular music of the movement captured and conveyed aspects of the movement that may not have been chronicled, critiqued, or celebrated elsewhere in movement documents and artifacts.[12] This brings to mind a key point Amy Abugo Ongiri made in *Spectacular Blackness: The Cultural Politics of the Black Power Movement and the Search for the Black Aesthetic*, where she wrote:

> If the Civil Rights Movement successfully made racism into a moral failing, the Black Power Movement successfully recast the relationship between urban culture, modernity, and African American identity, thereby establishing African American authenticity as defining hip, urban authenticity and cool. . . . By defining African American identity outside its traditional boundaries and limitations, imagining it as empowered with both opportunity and possibility, the Black Power Movement both highlighted the critique of postindustrial culture inherent in the celebration of urban vernacular culture by Black Arts Movement poets such as Haki Madhubuti, Larry Neal, and Amiri Baraka, and also created an astounding array of aesthetic and cultural innovations.[13]

A lot of the soul and funk that emerged during the Black Power Movement assisted in the movement's successful recasting of the "relationship between urban culture, modernity, and African American identity." Where Ongiri turned to several of the key poets of the Black Arts Movement as especially ripe examples of the ways in which movement members critiqued "postindustrial culture" via their "celebration of urban vernacular culture," throughout this book I have turned to many of the soul and funk musicians of the Black Power Movement and explored the unique ways their compositions and performances incessantly embodied and expressed a new kind of "hip[ness], urban authenticity and cool." Soul and funk musicians' expressions of "hip[ness], urban authenticity and cool" influenced the ways African American identity evolved from the Civil Rights Movement/Black church-based "Negro" identity prevalent between 1945 and 1965 into the unapologetically empowered "Black" identity touted by the Black Power Movement (and its many offshoot micro-movements) between roughly 1965 and 1975. As Judson Jeffries noted in *Black Power in the Belly of the Beast*, "Negroes began to refer to themselves as *Black*. And being Black was not just about one's skin color or race, but more important one's state of mind. Advocates of Black Power called on *Black* people to think Black."[14]

As with the music of the Civil Rights Movement, the music of the Black Power Movement demonstrates that the movement created its own distinct culture and that it was often the movement music emerging out of the movement culture that was used to politicize and mobilize the Black masses.[15] As the previous chapters have illustrated, much of the music of the Black Power Movement was in one way or another created in response to the rhetoric, politics, and aesthetics of the movement. As a consequence, a lot of this music was eventually utilized as sources of inspiration or ways to vent frustrations. Whether we turn to soul or funk, both of these musical forms seemed to incorporate aspects of the Black aesthetic and, in their own unique ways, called into question the dominant White aesthetic of the 1960s and 1970s. In calling the dominant White aesthetic standards into question, soul and funk musicians, whether consciously or unconsciously, ideologically aligned themselves with the Black Arts Movement and its promotion of the Black aesthetic. Hence, here we have come back to Ongiri's contention that the Black Power Movement defined African American identity "outside its traditional boundaries and limitations, imagining it as empowered with both opportunity and possibility." Soul and funk musicians made major contributions to the Black Power Movement's definition of Blackness, of what it meant to be "Black" as opposed to "Negro." In other words, again whether consciously or unconsciously, 1960s and 1970s soul and funk musicians frequently blurred the lines between commercial Black popular music and critical Black consciousness-raising popular music.[16]

The leaders of the Black Arts Movement obviously advocated for critical Black consciousness-raising art. Undoubtedly, that was the core concern of the Black aesthetic and one of the most distinctive features of Black Arts Movement discourse. However, it is important to acknowledge that the influence of the Black Arts Movement and its advocation of the Black aesthetic was not limited to highbrow or elite Black artists, including avant-garde jazz musicians such as Sun Ra, Ornette Coleman, John Coltrane, Archie Shepp, Albert Ayler, Pharoah Sanders, Alice Coltrane, Cecil Taylor, Jeanne Lee, Muhal Richard Abrams, Amina Claudine Myers, and the Art Ensemble of Chicago, among others.[17]

Ideologically working in unison with the Black Power Movement, the Black Arts Movement helped Black artists who were members of the movement, as well as those who were not active members of the movement, *Blackenize/African Americanize* the "Negro aesthetic" and evolve it into the Black aesthetic.[18] Historically rooted and culturally grounded in the African American experience and the broader African diasporan experience, the Black aesthetic enabled a wide range of Black artists to confront and critique the Eurocentrism and anti-Black racism seemingly inherent in most Western European and European American aesthetic standards. In short, as a conceptual tool and artistic instrument, the Black aesthetic allowed countless Black artists to literally *decolonize* and *Blackenize/African American-ize* their respective artistic creations.[19]

With regard to Black popular music in particular, the Black aesthetic inspired many African American musicians to offer up alternatives to European American music, art, and culture. To reiterate, it was not merely avant-garde jazz musicians who were either directly or indirectly influenced by the Black aesthetic, but soul and funk musicians as well. And it was these musicians who collectively deconstructed Western European and European American musical borders and boundaries and reconstructed African American and African diasporan history, culture, and politics-based music theories, methods, and performance styles. Moreover, it was this *dialectical musical deconstruction and reconstruction* that not only ideologically connected most Black popular music produced between 1965 and 1975 with the broader Black Power Movement, but it was also this *dialectical musical deconstruction and reconstruction* that made this music extremely meaningful for members of the movement.[20]

As Gregory Freeland noted, the music of the Black Power Movement consistently "created metaphorical and emotional meanings as well as ideological meanings through lyrics and rhythms that helped to frame the BPM [i.e., the Black Power Movement] as more than an image of Black urban unrest and anti-White rhetoric, as it is sometimes characterized."[21] When we acknowledge that the lines between commercial and critical consciousness-raising Black popular music were regularly blurred during the Black Power Movement, then and there we also need to acknowledge that when the various Black popular musics prevalent during the movement are taken together they represent a stream of Black music that was inspired by the Black experience and intended to raise awareness about Black history, Black culture, Black politics, Black economics, and ongoing post-Civil Rights Movement struggles.[22] Freeland importantly asserted that "much of the music of the BPM [i.e., the Black Power Movement] was written in response to BPM ideology and in turn ended up being further inspiration for the BPM."[23] Similarly, Waldo Martin stated that "Black music has both influenced and been deeply influenced by the Black Freedom Struggle."[24]

With the weakening or Whitening and lightening of soul between the mid-to-late 1970s, some genres of jazz and funk filled the void and offered edifying messages for listeners who remained interested in: and committed to: Black consciousness-raising.[25] For instance, Nina Simone, Oscar Brown, Jr., Gil Scott-Heron, Marlena Shaw, Roy Ayers, Leon Thomas, Gary Bartz, Lonnie Liston Smith, James Mtume, Cymande, Bayeté (Todd Cochran), the Last Poets, and the Watts Prophets all contributed often uncategorizable, genre-jumping, and boundary-blurring Black protest songs and message music from the early-to-mid 1970s. Furthermore, Freeland enters the fray again by importantly reminding us that even during the declining years of the Black Power Movement "several commercial musicians inconsistently continued to produce music that contained aspects of racial pride and political rights."[26] Indeed, up to the very last days of the Black Power Movement and throughout its aftermath, iconic soul artists continued to release protest songs and message music, albeit more jazz- and funk-influenced protest songs and message music. Whether we turn to Donny Hathaway's *Everything Is Everything* (1970), *Donny Hathaway* (1971), and *Extension of a Man* (1973); Curtis Mayfield's *Back to the World* (1973), *Sweet Exorcist* (1974), and *There's No Place Like America Today* (1975); Stevie Wonder's *Innervisions* (1973), *Fulfillingness' First Finale* (1974), and *Songs in the Key of Life* (1976); the O'Jays' *Ship Ahoy* (1973) and *Survival* (1975); or songs such as Parliament's "Chocolate City" (1975) and the Isley Brothers' "Fight the Power" (1975), Black cultural and political themes continued to free-float through Black popular music through the mid-1970s. Again, even as the Black Power Movement went into decline in the mid-1970s, musicians continued to compose, perform, and release protest songs and message music that inspired beleaguered movement members and the Black masses more generally.[27]

The Black Power Movement, when it is all said and done, was *simultaneously a cultural, social, political, and artistic macro-movement composed of several micro-movements, such as the Black Arts Movement, the Black Women's Liberation Movement, and the Black Studies Movement.* In its own sometimes warped and sometimes wicked ways, it embodied both what might be considered the "best" and the "worst" of Black cultural, social, and political movements. With that being said, it is important here to bear in mind something that Robin D.G. Kelley perceptively wrote in *Freedom Dreams: The Black Radical Imagination*, where he asserted that the "desires, hopes, and intentions of the people who fought for change cannot be easily categorized, contained, or explained."[28]

Furthermore, for those who would quickly and flippantly label the Black Power Movement a full-out flop, it is important to caution them to keep in mind Kelley's caveat when he warned us against judging whether a movement was a "success" or a "failure" based on whether or not it was able to achieve *all* of its goals. To speak candidly here, serious social and political movements, as well as insurgent cultural aesthetic movements, are often not so much about eradicating each and every ill on their respective agendas as they are about critical consciousness-raising, decolonizing and radicalizing the wretched of the earth, and inspiring them to begin their processes of self-transformation *and* social transformation. Kelley insightfully contended:

> Unfortunately, too often our standards for evaluating social movements pivot around whether or not they "succeeded" in realizing their vision rather than on the merits or power of the visions themselves. By such a measure, virtually every radical movement failed because the basic power relations they sought to change remain pretty much intact. And yet it is precisely these alternative visions and dreams that inspire new generations to continue to struggle for change.[29]

In hindsight, it is relatively easy for us to point to the "failures" of the Black Power Movement. But even as we observe what movement members did not do, what they failed to do, it is extremely important to point to what they did – and, even more, to the ways their social, political, and cultural work continues to inspire and provide *paradigms for praxis*.[30] The cultural meaning of the Black Power Movement extends far beyond its rhetoric and sloganeering, and the music emerging from the movement was a special medium through which the values of the movement were propagated. Values such as having a strong sense of self, cultural pride, and a belief in Black political representation and Black economic empowerment were conveyed through the music of the movement just as much as through speeches, books, poems, plays, and paintings.[31] In fact, a case could be made that of all of the arts advocated by the Black Arts Movement, Black popular music was arguably the art form most accessible to the Black masses. Or, at the least, Black popular music was the form of Black art that seemed to regularly capture the hearts and minds of the masses and help them raise their awareness of the ongoing post-Civil Rights Movement struggle between 1965 and 1975.[32]

Part social and political movement and part cultural aesthetic movement, the Black Power Movement undoubtedly represented many things to many different people. This study has examined its meaning for soul and funk musicians and the ways in which the ideology of the movement inspired and altered the composition and performance of Black popular music between 1965 and 1975. Just as there is no quick and easy way to "homogenize and sanitize" the Black Power Movement, it is equally true that there is no way to quickly and easily reduce it to a bunch of anti-White rabble-rousing and violence.[33] Truth be told, the Black Power Movement and its music were not about hating White people but actually about loving and empowering Black people and teaching them the long-overdue lesson of learning to love themselves. This, in all honesty, is one of the greatest lessons and lingering legacies of the Black Power Movement and Black Power music. Blackness. Power. Music. – *ad infinitum*.

Notes

1 See Devin Fergus, *Liberalism, Black Power, and the Making of American Politics, 1965–1980* (Athens: University of Georgia Press, 2009); Kevin Gaines, "The Historiography of the Struggle for Black Equality Since 1945," in *A Companion to Post-1945 America*, eds. Jean-Christophe Agnew and Roy Rosenzweig (Malden: Blackwell, 2006), 229–31; Hasan Kwame Jeffries, "Searching for a New Freedom," in *A Companion to African American History*, ed. Alton Hornsby (Malden: Blackwell, 2005), 499–511; Peniel E. Joseph, ed., *The Black Power Movement: Rethinking the Civil Rights-Black Power Era* (New York: Routledge, 2006), 3–4.

2 Dan Berger, "Rescuing Civil Rights from Black Power: Collective Memory and Saving the State in Twenty-First-Century Prosecutions of 1960s-Era Cases," *Journal for the Study of Radicalism* 3, no. 1 (2009): 1.

3 Ibid., 3–4.

4 Jeanne Theoharis, "Black Freedom Studies: Re-imagining and Redefining the Fundamentals," *History Compass* 4, no. 2 (2006): 353.

5 Ibid., 347–54. See William H. Chafe, *Civilities and Civil Rights: Greensboro, North Carolina, and the Black Struggle for Freedom* (New York: Oxford University Press, 1980); Daniel E. Crowe, *Prophets of Rage: The Black Freedom Struggle in San Francisco, 1945–1969* (New York: Routledge, 2000); John Dittmer, *Local People: The Struggle for Civil Rights*

in Mississippi (Urbana: University of Illinois Press, 1995); Jacquelyn Dowd Hall, "The Long Civil Rights Movement and the Political Uses of the Past," *Journal of American History* 91, no. 4 (2005): 1235–263; Joseph, *The Black Power Movement*; Charles M. Payne, *I've Got the Light of Freedom: The Organizing Tradition and the Mississippi Freedom Struggle* (Berkeley: University of California Press, 2007); Charles M. Payne and Adam Green, eds., *Time Longer Than Rope: A Century of African American Activism, 1850–1950* (New York: New York University Press, 2003); Barbara Ransby, *Ella Baker and the Black Freedom Movement: A Radical Democratic Vision* (Chapel Hill: University of North Carolina Press, 2003).

6 Theoharis, "Black Freedom Studies," 352.

7 Ibid., 353. See also Peniel Joseph, ed., "Black Power Studies: A New Scholarship," *The Black Scholar* 31, no. 3/4 (2001): 1.

8 Hall, "The Long Civil Rights Movement"; Reiland Rabaka, *Civil Rights Music: The Soundtracks of the Civil Rights Movement* (Lanham: Rowman & Littlefield, 2016).

9 Theoharis, "Black Freedom Studies," 353.

10 Gregory Freeland, "Music and the Civil Rights Movement, 1954–1968," in *Teaching the American Civil Rights Movement: Freedom's Bittersweet Song*, ed. Julie Buckner Armstrong (New York: Routledge, 2012), 125–46; Gregory Freeland, "'We're a Winner': Popular Music and the Black Power Movement," *Social Movement Studies* 8, no. 3 (2009): 261–88; Waldo E. Martin, *No Coward Soldiers: Black Cultural Politics in Postwar America* (Cambridge: Harvard University Press, 2005), 44–81; Mark Anthony Neal, *What the Music Said: Black Popular Music and Black Public Culture* (New York: Routledge, 1998), 55–84; Amy Abugo Ongiri, *Spectacular Blackness: The Cultural Politics of the Black Power Movement and the Search for a Black Aesthetic* (Charlottesville: University of Virginia Press, 2009), 124–58; Shana L. Redmond, *Anthem: Social Movements and the Sound of Solidarity in the African Diaspora* (New York: New York University Press, 2014), 141–220; James Edward Smethurst, *The Black Arts Movement: Literary Nationalism in the 1960s and 1970s* (Chapel Hill: University of North Carolina Press, 2005), 57–99; Chris Stone, "'My Beliefs Are in My Song': Engaging Black Politics through Popular Music," *OAH Magazine of History* 20, no. 5 (2006): 28–32; William L. Van Deburg, *New Day in Babylon: The Black Power Movement and American Culture, 1965–1975* (Chicago: University of Chicago Press, 1992), 204–16; William L. Van Deburg, *Black Camelot: African American Culture Heroes in Their Times, 1960–1980* (Chicago: University of Chicago Press, 1997), 197–242; Brian Ward, *Just My Soul Responding: Rhythm & Blues, Black Consciousness, and Race Relations* (Berkeley: University of California Press, 1998), 388–416.

11 Rabaka, *Civil Rights Music*, 53–202.

12 Freeland, "'We're a Winner,'" 271–81; Martin, *No Coward Soldiers*, 44–81; Neal, *What the Music Said*, 55–84; Jeffrey Ogbar, *Black Power: Radical Politics and African American Identity* (Baltimore: Johns Hopkins University Press, 2004), 110–16; Ongiri, *Spectacular Blackness*, 88–158; Smethurst, *The Black Arts Movement*, 57–99; Stone, "'My Beliefs Are in My Song,'" 28–32; Van Deburg, *New Day in Babylon*, 204–16; Van Deburg, *Black Camelot*, 197–242; Ward, *Just My Soul Responding*, 388–416.

13 Ongiri, *Spectacular Blackness*, 189–90. See also Smethurst, *The Black Arts Movement*, 100–246.

14 Judson L. Jeffries, ed., *Black Power in the Belly of the Beast* (Urbana: University of Illinois, 2006), 5, emphasis in original.

15 Martin, *No Coward Soldiers*, 44–81; Rabaka, *Civil Rights Music*, 1–52; Sterling Stuckey, "Going through the Storm: The Great Singing Movements of the Sixties," in Sterling Stuckey, *Going through the Storm: The Influence of African American Art in History* (New York: Oxford University Press, 1994), 265–82; Ward, *Just My Soul Responding*, 173–336, 388–416.

16 Freeland, "'We're a Winner'"; Martin, *No Coward Soldiers*, 44–131; Neal, *What the Music Said*, 25–124; Stone, "'My Beliefs Are in My Song'"; Pat Thomas, *Listen, Whitey!: The Sights and Sounds of Black Power, 1965–1975* (New York: Norton, 2012); Van Deburg, *Black Camelot*, 197–242; Rickey Vincent, *Party Music: The Inside Story of*

the Black Panther' Band and How Black Power Transformed Soul Music (Chicago: Lawrence Hill Books, 2013), 87–166; Ward, *Just My Soul Responding*, 388–450.

17 John D. Baskerville, *The Impact of Black Nationalist Ideology on American Jazz Music of the 1960s and 1970s* (Lewiston, NY: Mellen Press, 2003); Philippe Carles and Jean-Louis Comolli, *Free Jazz/Black Power* (Jackson: University Press of Mississippi, 2016); Frank Kofsky, *Black Nationalism and the Revolution in Music* (New York: Pathfinder, 1991); George Lewis, *A Power Stronger Than Itself: The AACM and American Experimental Music* (Chicago: University of Chicago Press, 2008); Martin, *No Coward Soldiers*, 56–66, 73–77; Scott Saul, *Freedom Is, Freedom Ain't: Jazz and the Making of the Sixties* (Cambridge: Harvard University Press, 2003), 209–38; Smethurst, *The Black Arts Movement*, 57–84; Thomas, *Listen, Whitey!*, 149–74; Valerie Wilmer, *As Serious As Your Life: Black Music and the Free Jazz Revolution, 1957–1977* (London: Serpent's Tail, 2018).

18 For more on the *Blackenization/African Americanization* of the "Negro aesthetic" and its evolution into the Black aesthetic, see Van Deburg, *New Day in Babylon*, 181–247.

19 On the *decolonization* and *Blackenization/African Americanization* of Black art during the Black Power Movement, see Lisa Gail Collins and Margo Natalie Crawford, eds., *New Thoughts on the Black Arts Movement* (New Brunswick: Rutgers University Press, 2006); Monique Guillory and Richard C. Green, eds., *Soul: Black Power, Politics, and Pleasure* (New York: New York University Press, 1998); Howard Rambsy, *The Black Arts Enterprise and the Production of African American Poetry* (Ann Arbor: University of Michigan Press, 2011), 125–60; Smethurst, *The Black Arts Movement*, 1–99; Van Deburg, *New Day in Babylon*, 112–247; Van Deburg, *Black Camelot*, 62–83.

20 Ongiri, *Spectacular Blackness*, 124–58; Thomas, *Listen, Whitey!*; Vincent, *Party Music*, 263–308.

21 Freeland, "'We're a Winner,'" 272.

22 Ibid., 262–63; Martin, *No Coward Soldiers*, 44–81; Thomas, *Listen, Whitey!*; Van Deburg, *Black Camelot*, 197–242; Vincent, *Party Music*, 87–166; Ward, *Just My Soul Responding*, 388–450.

23 Freeland, "'We're a Winner,'" 281.

24 Martin, *No Coward Soldiers*, 48.

25 For further discussion of the weakening or Whitening and lightening of soul between the mid-to-late 1970s, see Nelson George, *The Death of Rhythm & Blues* (New York: Pantheon Books, 1988), 121–69; Neal, *What the Music Said*, 101–24; Ward, *Just My Soul Responding*, 417–50.

26 Freeland, "'We're a Winner,'" 282.

27 Ibid., 271–81; Martin, *No Coward Soldiers*, 44–81; Neal, *What the Music Said*, 101–24; Ongiri, *Spectacular Blackness*, 124–58; Thomas, *Listen, Whitey!*; Van Deburg, *Black Camelot*, 197–242.

28 Robin D.G. Kelley, *Freedom Dreams: The Black Radical Imagination* (Boston: Beacon, 2002), ix.

29 Kelley, *Freedom Dreams*, ix.

30 Joseph, *The Black Power Movement*, 21–25; Judson L. Jeffries, "The Fall and Legacy of the Black Power Movement," in *Black Power in the Belly of the Beast*, ed. Judson L. Jeffries (Urbana: University of Illinois, 2006), 297–308; Ogbar, *Black Power*, 191–98.

31 Martin, *No Coward Soldiers*, 44–81; Van Deburg, *New Day in Babylon*, 9–28.

32 Freeland, "'We're a Winner,'" 261–88; Martin, *No Coward Soldiers*, 44–81; Neal, *What the Music Said*, 55–124; Ogbar, *Black Power*, 110–16; Ongiri, *Spectacular Blackness*, 124–58; Smethurst, *The Black Arts Movement*, 57–99; Stone, "'My Beliefs Are in My Song,'" 28–32; Van Deburg, *New Day in Babylon*, 204–16; Van Deburg, *Black Camelot*, 197–242; Ward, *Just My Soul Responding*, 388–416.

33 Freeland, "'We're a Winner,'" 284–85.

INDEX

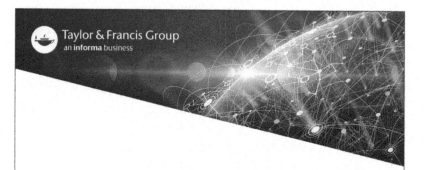